Paul and Gender

Reclaiming the Apostle's Vision for Men and Women in Christ

CYNTHIA LONG WESTFALL

Baker Academic

a division of Baker Publishing Group
Grand Rapids, Michigan

Published by Baker Academic
a division of Baker Publishing Group
P.O. Box 6287, Grand Rapids, MI 49516-6287
www.bakeracademic.com

Printed in the United States of America

Library of Congress Cataloging-in-Publication Data
Names: Westfall, Cynthia Long, author.
Title: Paul and gender : reclaiming the apostle's vision for men and women in Christ / Cynthia Long Westfall.
Description: Grand Rapids : Baker Academic, 2016. | Includes bibliographical references and index.
Identifiers: LCCN 2016027537 | ISBN 9780801097942 (pbk.)
Subjects: LCSH: Sex—Biblical teaching. | Gender identity—Biblical teaching. | Bible. Epistles of Paul—Criticism, interpretation, etc.
Classification: LCC BS2655.S49 W47 2016 | DDC 227/.06—dc23
LC record available at https://lccn.loc.gov/2016027537

21 22 23 24 25   9 8 7 6 5

In keeping with biblical principles of creation stewardship, Baker Publishing Group advocates the responsible use of our natural resources. As a member of the Green Press Initiative, our company uses recycled paper when possible. The text paper of this book is composed in part of post-consumer waste.

To those who are ready to accept
a paradigm shift from God:

May you find a reason to believe.

Contents

Preface

This book is an attempt to explain the Pauline passages that concern gender and to move toward a canon-based Pauline theology of gender. The passages concerning gender that are in the Pauline canon will be taken into account and interpreted according to the texts' terms and claims—that is, biblical texts that claim to be written by Paul demand that they should interpret, and be interpreted by, the other writings that claim to be by Paul. These texts also place themselves within certain contexts, including the narrative of Paul's life, so that they may be read in those contexts. There are five priorities that guide the interpretation and canonical theology:

1. The results will attempt to be faithful to the texts and contexts in the Pauline corpus.
2. The interpretations will seek to be intelligible within a reconstruction of the narrative of Paul's life.
3. The specific interpretations will attempt to be understandable within the context of language, culture, and situation in which the texts place themselves.
4. The interpretations will strive to be coherent within the general context of Pauline theology if possible, given the text, context, language, and culture.
5. Contemporary theological constructs and applications should strive to be consistent and coherent with an interpreter's contemporary (biblical) worldview.

While it is acknowledged that dissonance, incoherence, inconsistency, and changes in thought are possible within any writer or speaker's collected work (contested or uncontested), if there is a coherent and relevant interpretive choice available that effectively lies within these five guidelines, that choice is preferable. In the case of the Pauline corpus, coherence and consistency with Paul's teaching and other apostolic teaching were transparent criteria for selection and inclusion in the canon.

Most studies that claim to be about Paul and gender or about gender and the Bible are really about the role of women in the church, home, and society. While women's issues are of central interest and clearly render this study timely and relevant, I take the position that the Pauline passages on women cannot be adequately understood or applied apart from a corresponding understanding of the Pauline passages on men. Furthermore (as stated above), passages on men and women must be understood and coherent within Pauline theology as a whole, and particularly in the passages and letters in which the texts are embedded. Finally, as I contend in this study, the Pauline texts address men's issues in the church, home, and society that are also of grave importance and relevance.

I wrote this book for four reasons. First, gender issues were important for Paul, and they continue to be important in the life of faith and the academy, particularly within the context of Western culture in the twenty-first century. Diligent work on a biblical and a systematic theology of gender needs to continue as a priority in the academy. Applications in denominations, local churches, and the home need to be placed under an informed biblical scrutiny and accountability. This discussion should not be cut short or settled by authoritative statements, political strategies, or the popular influence of conferences, charismatic speakers, or internet blogging. We have barely begun to scratch the surface of issues that concern humanity as male and female, issues that may well be as complex as the theology of the Trinity or the theology of the relationship between the human and divine in the person of Christ. Its complexity demands commensurate effort.

Second, I had acquired a new set of perspectives and methodological lenses with which to study the issues, not the least of which was modern linguistics. I predicted that I would be able to make a unique contribution to the discussion if I reexamined the texts within the contexts in which language is understood, particularly by studying the effect of context, genre, and register on meaning. I combined these new perspectives with an ongoing interest and specialization in history.

Third, a clear understanding of the issues and a conviction about how these passages may be interpreted and applied is essential for me to function with integrity in the classroom, the academy, and the church. A woman in biblical studies who teaches in a seminary context, participates in a variety of forums in the academy, and functions in a local church cannot easily dodge the issue of Paul and gender; that issue is always the elephant in the room, and it is imperative to understand the dynamics at play and to serve with necessary conviction.

Fourth, I would like to make the way forward easier for others and particularly the next generation. This has been a controversial topic, with serious implications and consequences: social, political, and religious structures and use of power are at play; men have lost their positions and/or their reputation, whatever their view; and it is relevant for addressing the misogyny, abuse, discrimination, and pressure at various levels that are practiced against women globally and sometimes in faith contexts. At my stage of life and with my circumstances, I judge that I am in a position to take risks and pay whatever price is demanded to clear obstacles and make the paths hopefully straighter for those who come after me.

With this study, I hope to have something of value to offer various target groups. I intend to make a contribution to the academic discussion on gender that stands apart from considerations of faith and practice. I aim to help biblical interpreters distinguish between the text and what inferences and presuppositions have been assumed for interpreting the text. I want to demonstrate the relationship between context and the meaning of a text. I expect to advance understanding of the complex practice of gender in the social contexts of the first century. Finally, I hope to legitimize a place for reading the Pastoral Epistles in the discussion of a Pauline theology of gender, regardless of one's views about the origin of the text.

For the communities that hold the Bible to be authoritative in faith and practice, I intend to establish that an interpreter of the Bible can hold a high view of the text and its authority and at the same time interpret Paul in a way that departs from the more traditional or conservative interpretations and positions on the theology of gender.

Perhaps my most central target is the large number of people in the faith community who occupy a gray or middle area in this discussion, including those in denominations, churches, parachurches, and the academy. This study will demonstrate a way forward for many people in the faith community who have been uncomfortable with the more traditional teaching and practice in the church concerning gender but have not been convinced by alternate interpretations of some of the texts that have been central in the discussion (particularly 1 Tim. 2:12). I get the impression that some people are looking for a reason to believe differently, and I hope to offer some viable alternatives.

Finally, I hope that this study supports and equips Christians to serve boldly in the area of their gifting, regardless of their social status, race, or gender. I particularly want women to be fully free to follow Jesus and imitate Paul with prophetic conviction, sacrifice, and service whether they are supported by their faith community or not. After all, Jesus and Paul were never supported by the traditional religious authorities; they did not wait for permission, yet we all need to remember that their path was not the safe or easy way.

There are many people who have contributed to this study whom I cannot mention by name. I want to thank my mentors Dr. Craig Blomberg and Dr. Stanley Porter. Thanks particularly to the steering committees and participants in the ETS Evangelicals and Gender session, and to my students who contributed to the dialogue. Thanks to the group who conducted the survey on women who choose to veil, particularly my daughter Dr. Aubrey Westfall. Thanks to all my teaching assistants and particularly Dr. Jonathan Numada, who edited this manuscript. I offer a final thank-you to James Ernest for bringing all the protracted research and writing to completion.

Abbreviations

Bible Texts and Versions

CEB	Common English Bible	NET	New English Translation (Bible)
ESV	English Standard Version		
ET	English translation (and its versification)	NIV	New International Version (2011)
KJV	King James Version	NJB	New Jerusalem Bible
LXX	Septuagint	NKJV	New King James Version
MT	Masoretic Text	NLT	New Living Translation
NAU	New American Standard Bible (Updated, 1995)	NRSV	New Revised Standard Version
		TNIV	Today's New International Version
NEB	New English Bible		

Primary Sources: Ancient Texts

Hebrew Bible/Old Testament

Gen.	Genesis	Neh.	Nehemiah
Exod.	Exodus	Esther	Esther
Lev.	Leviticus	Job	Job
Num.	Numbers	Ps(s).	Psalm(s)
Deut.	Deuteronomy	Prov.	Proverbs
Josh.	Joshua	Eccles.	Ecclesiastes
Judg.	Judges	Song	Song of Songs
Ruth	Ruth	Isa.	Isaiah
1–2 Sam.	1–2 Samuel	Jer.	Jeremiah
1–2 Kings	1–2 Kings	Lam.	Lamentations
1–2 Chron.	1–2 Chronicles	Ezek.	Ezekiel
Ezra	Ezra	Dan.	Daniel

Hosea	Hosea		Col.	Colossians
Joel	Joel		1–2 Thess.	1–2 Thessalonians
Amos	Amos		1–2 Tim.	1–2 Timothy
Obad.	Obadiah		Titus	Titus
Jon.	Jonah		Philem.	Philemon
Mic.	Micah		Heb.	Hebrews
Nah.	Nahum		James	James
Hab.	Habakkuk		1–2 Pet.	1–2 Peter
Zeph.	Zephaniah		1–3 John	1–3 John
Hag.	Haggai		Jude	Jude
Zech.	Zechariah		Rev.	Revelation
Mal.	Malachi			

New Testament

Matt.	Matthew
Mark	Mark
Luke	Luke
John	John
Acts	Acts
Rom.	Romans
1–2 Cor.	1–2 Corinthians
Gal.	Galatians
Eph.	Ephesians
Phil.	Philippians

Apocrypha and Septuagint

1 Esd.	1 Esdras
1–4 Macc.	1–4 Maccabees
Sir.	Sirach
Tob.	Tobit
Wis.	Wisdom of Solomon

Old Testament Pseudepigrapha

2 Bar.	2 Baruch (Syriac Apocalypse)
1 En.	1 Enoch (Ethiopic Apocalypse)
4 Ezra	4 Ezra

Ancient Nonbiblical Christian and Jewish Sources

Ancient Manuscripts
P. Oxy.   Oxyrhynchus Papyri

Apostolic Fathers
Mart. Pol.   Martyrdom of Polycarp

Josephus
J.W.   Jewish War

Philo
Abr.   De Abrahamo (On the Life of Abraham)

Congr.   De congressu eruditionis gratia (On the Preliminary Studies)

Flacc.   In Flaccum (Against Flaccus)

Ios.   De Iosepho (On the Life of Joseph)

Spec.   De specialibus legibus (On the Special Laws)

Qumran Scrolls
1QHᵃ   1QHodayotᵃ
1QS   Rule of the Community

Rabbinic Literature

b. Giṭ. Babylonian Talmud, trac-
        tate *Giṭṭin*

b. Menaḥ. Babylonian Talmud, trac-
        tate *Menaḥot*

b. Soṭ. Babylonian Talmud, trac-
        tate *Soṭah*

b. Yoma Babylonian Talmud,
        tractate *Yoma* (=
        Kippurim)

Pesiq. Rab Kah. Pesiqta de Rab
        Kahana

Greek and Latin Works

Achilles Tatius

Leuc. Clit. *Leucippe et Clitophon
        (The Adventures of Leu-
        cippe and Cleitophon)*

Apuleius

Metam. *Metamorphoses (The
        Golden Ass)*

Aristotle

Eth. nic. *Ethica nicomachea (Nico-
        machean Ethics)*

Gen. an. *De generatione animalium
        (Generation of Animals)*

Physiogn. *Physiognomonica
        (Physiognomonics)*

Artemidorus Daldianus

Onir. *Onirocritica*

Athanasius

Syn. *De synodis (On the Councils of
        Ariminum and Seleucia)*

Callimachus

Hymn. Dian. *Hymnus in Dianam
        (Hymn to Diana or
        Artemis)*

Cicero

Att. *Epistulae ad Atticum*

Mur. *Pro Murena*

Cyril of Alexandria

Pulch. *De Recta Fide ad Pulcheriam
        et Eudociam*

Dio Cassius

Hist. rom. *Historia romana (Roman
        History)*

Epictetus

Diatr. *Diatribai (Dissertationes)*

Eusebius

Hist. eccl. *Historia ecclesiastica (Ec-
        clesiastical History)*

Vit. Const. *Vita Constantini (Life of
        Constantine)*

John Chrysostom

Hom. Col. *Homiliae in epistulam ad
        Colossenses*

Plato

Leg. *Leges (Laws)*

Resp. *Respublica (Republic)*

Plutarch

Pel.   *Pelopidas*

Pseudo-Hippolytus

Consum.   *De consummation
              mundi*

Quintilian

Inst.   *Institutio oratoria (Institutes
           of Oratory)*

Seneca

Ben.   *De beneficiis*

Ep.   *Epistulae morales*

Stobaeus

Flor.   *Florilegium*

Strabo

Geogr.   *Geographica (Geography)*

Tacitus

Ann.   *Annales*

Thucydides

Hist.   *History of the Peloponnesian
           War*

Ulpian

Dig.   *Digesta (The Digest)*

Secondary Sources: Journals, Periodicals, Major Reference Works, and Series

AB	Anchor Bible
ABS	T&T Clark Approaches to Biblical Studies
AGJU	Arbeiten zur Geschichte des antiken Judentums und des Urchristentums
AHR	*American Historical Review*
ANRW	*Aufstieg und Niedergang der römischen Welt: Geschichte und Kultur Roms im Spiegel der neueren Forschung*
ATJ	*Ashland Theological Journal*
BBB	Bonner biblische Beiträge
BBR	*Bulletin for Biblical Research*
BCBC	Believers Church Bible Commentary
BDAG	W. Bauer, F. W. Danker, W. F. Arndt, and F. W. Gingrich. *Greek-English Lexicon of the New Testament and Other Early Christian Literature*. 3rd ed. Chicago: University of Chicago Press, 1999.
BECNT	Baker Exegetical Commentary on the New Testament
BHL	Blackwell Handbooks in Linguistics
BIS	Biblical Interpretation Series
BLG	Biblical Languages: Greek
BSac	*Bibliotheca Sacra*
BTB	*Biblical Theology Bulletin*
BWANT	Beiträge zur Wissenschaft vom Alten und Neuen Testament

BZ	*Biblische Zeitschrift*
BZNW	Beihefte zur Zeitschrift für die neutestamentliche Wissenschaft und die Kunde der älteren Kirche
CamBC	Cambridge Bible Commentary
CBQ	*Catholic Biblical Quarterly*
ChrTo	*Christianity Today*
Colloq	*Colloquium*
CTL	Cambridge Textbooks in Linguistics
DEL	Describing English Language
DNTB	*Dictionary of New Testament Background*. Edited by Craig A. Evans and Stanley E. Porter. Downers Grove, IL: InterVarsity, 2000.
DPL	*Dictionary of Paul and His Letters*. Edited by Gerald F. Hawthorne, Ralph P. Martin, and Daniel G. Reid. Downers Grove, IL: InterVarsity, 1993.
DSar	*Daughters of Sarah*
ECHC	Early Christianity in Its Hellenistic Context
EKKNT	Evangelisch-katholischer Kommentar zum Neuen Testament
EvQ	*Evangelical Quarterly*
FCNTECW	Feminist Companion to the New Testament and Early Christian Writings
FT	*Feminist Theology*
FZPhTh	*Freiburger Zeitschrift für Philosophie und Theologie*
GNS	Good News Studies
GPBS	Global Perspectives on Biblical Scholarship
Hist	*Historia*
HTR	*Harvard Theological Review*
IBC	Interpretation: A Bible Commentary for Teaching and Preaching
ICC	International Critical Commentary
Int	*Interpretation*
IRM	*International Review of Mission*
IVPNTC	IVP New Testament Commentary Series
JAAR	*Journal of the American Academy of Religion*
JBL	*Journal of Biblical Literature*
JETS	*Journal of the Evangelical Theological Society*
JGRChJ	*Journal of Greco-Roman Christianity and Judaism*
JRS	*Journal of Religion and Society*
JSNT	*Journal for the Study of the New Testament*
JSNTSup	Journal for the Study of the New Testament: Supplement Series
JSOTSup	Journal for the Study of the Old Testament: Supplement Series
JSSR	*Journal for the Scientific Study of Religion*

JTS	*Journal of Theological Studies*
LCL	Loeb Classical Library
LNTS	Library of New Testament Studies
LSJ	H. G. Liddell, R. Scott, and H. S. Jones. *A Greek-English Lexicon*. 9th ed. with supplement. Oxford: Clarendon, 1996.
MNTC	Moffat New Testament Commentary
MNTSS	McMaster New Testament Studies Series
MSBBES	Monographic Series of "Benedictina": Biblical-Ecumenical Section
MTSS	McMaster Theological Studies Series
NCCS	New Covenant Commentary Series
NEchtB	Neue Echter Bibel
Neot	*Neotestamentica*
NIBC	New International Biblical Commentary
NICNT	New International Commentary on the New Testament
NIDNTT	*New International Dictionary of New Testament Theology*. Edited by C. Brown. 4 vols. Grand Rapids: Zondervan, 1975–85
NIGTC	New International Greek Testament Commentary
NIVAC	New International Version Application Commentary
NovT	*Novum Testamentum*
NPNF[1]	*Nicene and Post-Nicene Fathers*, Series 1
NTG	New Testament Guides
NTM	New Testament Monographs
NTS	*New Testament Studies*
OELE	Oxford English Language Education
PastPres	*Past and Present*
PriscPap	*Priscilla Papers*
PSt	Pauline Studies
PTh	Pauline Theology
RBS	Resources for Biblical Study
RefJ	*Reformed Journal*
ResQ	*Restoration Quarterly*
RHC	Romans through History and Culture
SBG	Studies in Biblical Greek
SBJT	*Southern Baptist Journal of Theology*
SBLDS	Society of Biblical Literature Dissertation Series
SBLMS	Society of Biblical Literature Monograph Series
SCJ	*Stone-Campbell Journal*
SemeiaSt	Semeia Studies
SNTSMS	Society for New Testament Studies Monograph Series
SR	*Studies in Religion*

STS   Studies in Theology and Sexuality
Them   *Themelios*
ThTo   *Theology Today*
TJ   *Trinity Journal*
TNTC   Tyndale New Testament Commentary
TR   Theology and Religion
TynBul   *Tyndale Bulletin*
VE   *Vox Evangelica*
WBC   Word Biblical Commentary
WLQ   *Wisconsin Lutheran Quarterly*
WUNT   Wissenschaftliche Untersuchungen zum Neuen Testament
WW   *Word and World*
ZNW   *Zeitschrift für die neutestamentliche Wissenschaft und die Kunde der*
           älteren Kirche

Introduction

"Gender" refers to the characteristics that define, describe, and differentiate male and female. Paul's theology, teaching, and practice concerning gender are currently central issues in biblical studies and areas that concern biblical studies. Some scholars are polarized on various issues, some scholars want to agree to disagree, many scholars have nuanced views that lie between the extremes of the various positions, some scholars are waiting to be convinced, and some wish to sidestep the issues and ignore them. Meanwhile, public opinion is being mobilized for battle in certain places such as the churches, denominational and interdenominational leadership organizations, higher education, and secular forums in such a way that makes any middle ground in the various views concerning gender difficult to occupy. This book reframes gender issues in the light of coherence within Pauline theology, consistency in interpretation, and a fresh application of methodology that will promote discussion and carry it to new ground. It also suggests some fresh readings that could resolve some of the notorious interpretive problems in certain passages. In order to address the issues effectively, this study includes the entire Pauline canon and reads the texts in light of their own claims of authorship, recipient(s), and circumstances.[1] This book is a call for all who study Paul and

---

1. For a summary of the discussion on the canonicity of Paul's Letters, see A. G. Patzia, "Canon," *DPL*, 85–92. This study is not precisely the same as canonical criticism, but it has some resemblance to that and to narrative criticism, which assumes the world that the author creates in order to understand and interpret the literature. For a canonical approach, see Brevard S. Childs, *Old Testament Theology in a Canonical Context* (Philadelphia: Fortress, 1989). Alan Padgett argues for "the canonical sense of Scripture" in understanding the ethics of submission, gender roles, and servant leadership in the New Testament (*As Christ Submits to the Church: A Biblical Understanding of Leadership and Mutual Submission* [Grand Rapids: Baker Academic, 2011], 21–30). For an example of narrative criticism, see R. Alan Culpepper, *Anatomy of the Fourth Gospel: A Study in Literary Design* (Philadelphia: Fortress, 1983). For those who

1

gender to learn to distinguish between the assumptions and presuppositions that they use to make sense of the texts.

Biblical scholars often assume that Paul's theology about gender directly corresponds with Greek philosophical thought (Aristotelian) and Greco-Roman social practices. There is no question that this is the assumption lying behind the traditional interpretations of the Pauline passages on gender. However, this study will suggest that the traditional readings on gender reflect Greek thought and categories that were not accepted by either Paul or Jesus. Rather, the presuppositions of Greek philosophical thought were imposed on the texts quite early in the history of the church and reinforced throughout the history of interpretation. Therefore, the traditional interpretation is a primary dialogue partner for this study.

While the power relationships between male and female are not by any means the only gender issue, the traditional interpretation of 1 Timothy 2:12 is often treated as a citadel that dominates biblical interpretation, church policy, and praxis on gender, which can be overturned (hypothetically) only with incontrovertible proof or a rejection of the canonical status of 1 Timothy and ultimately a rejection of the Bible as an authority for life and practice. This study will try to show that the traditional interpretations of 1 Timothy 2:12 and other passages on gender are based on information, assumptions, and inferences that are imposed on the text, part of the interpreter's embedded theology, and/or the direct and inevitable outcome of how the understanding of the passage has been taught, preached, and discussed in various venues by teachers, preachers, parents, and companions. Consequently, the traditional assumptions and inferences are often unacknowledged and even conferred with an inspired status of being "what God says." These assumptions have been combined with atomistic readings that are removed from the biblical situation, time, and culture.[2]

These traditional interpretations fail to recognize that Paul does not adopt the dominant culture but rather critiques it.[3] Paul equates the Greco-Roman

---

dispute the Pauline authorship of any given epistle or set of epistles, this study of Paul can be compared to David Clines's study of the masculine Jesus in the canonical Gospels, which he distinguishes from the historical Jesus or the portraits of Jesus in the individual Gospels. See D. J. A. Clines, "*Ecce Vir*; or, Gendering the Son of Man," in *Biblical Studies/Cultural Studies: The Third Sheffield Colloquium*, ed. J. Cheryl Exum and Stephen D. Moore, JSOTSup 266 (Sheffield: Sheffield Academic, 1998), 352–75.

2. Studies of the biblical time and culture are represented by Wayne A. Meeks, *The First Urban Christians: The Social World of the Apostle Paul* (New Haven: Yale University Press, 1983); Jerome H. Neyrey and Eric C. Stewart, eds. *The Social World of the New Testament: Insights and Models* (Peabody, MA: Hendrickson, 2008).

3. For Paul's ability to move within various cultures in the Greco-Roman world and address them, see Clarence E. Glad, "Paul and Adaptability," in *Paul in the Greco-Roman World: A Handbook*, ed. J. Paul Sampley (Harrisburg, PA: Trinity Press International, 2003), 17–41.

culture with the "world." He urges the church not to conform to the "world," and he calls the church out of the "world." Paul particularly critiques and subverts the dominant culture's construction of gender, sexuality, and power. Yet the first-century mission to the gentiles needed strategies to survive within the Greco-Roman culture and its values. This study suggests that traditional readings confuse Paul's theology with his missional adaptation to the cultural gender practices; those strategies allowed the church to reach the Greco-Roman culture and to survive within that culture and even to thrive.

There has been a major problem with a lack of consistent methodology in the interpretation of the texts. Traditional readings of texts on gender are not based on hermeneutics that are consistently applied to passages addressing or concerning gender, nor are they consistent with hermeneutics that we generally apply to other texts to determine what a text originally meant. Within the tradition of interpretation, the passages that concern gender have not been understood in the contexts of the discourses in which they occur, the biblical theology of the Pauline corpus as a whole, the narrative of Paul's life, a linguistic understanding/analysis of the Greek language, or an understanding of the culture that is sociologically informed.[4] The support of the traditional readings assumes the strength of their position, and the analyses of the texts are therefore argumentative and assume the conclusions.

Beyond unacknowledged or unexamined assumptions and presuppositions and problematic methodologies, there are significant indications that the traditional readings of the text are problematic on other levels. First and foremost, the traditional readings of texts on gender have not resulted in making sense of Paul's Letters. For example, the traditional readings of 1 Timothy 2:12 and 1 Corinthians 14:34–35 do not satisfactorily resolve the interpretive problems and superficial textual incoherence of the passages in their context, but rather increase them.[5] Correct "guesses" or hypotheses about the information, assumptions, and inferences ought to make better sense of the text

---

4. Judith Gundry-Volf points out the importance of the narrative for a coherent reading: "Paul's teachings on sexuality and gender are especially appropriate for conducting a test case of 'narrative coherence,' in that Paul's discourse on gender is, arguably, one of the most glaring examples of dissonance in the NT" ("Putting the Moral Vision of the New Testament into Focus: A Review," *BBR* 9 [1999]: 278). For an explanation of Paul's theology in the context of the wider story of Paul's life, see F. F. Bruce, *Paul, Apostle of the Heart Set Free* (Grand Rapids: Eerdmans, 1977). For the narrative world of an epistle, see Norman R. Petersen, *Rediscovering Paul: Philemon and the Sociology of Paul's Narrative World* (Philadelphia: Fortress, 1985). For reading Paul in the context of the larger story of Israel, see J. R. Daniel Kirk, *Jesus Have I Loved, but Paul? A Narrative Approach to the Problem of Pauline Christianity* (Grand Rapids: Baker Academic, 2011).

5. See E. E. Ellis, "Pastoral Letters," *DPL*, 658–66. It is difficult to accept that an early blatant attempt to hijack Pauline theology would be successful. Each interpreter comes to the text

by uncovering what the intended reader(s) would have to know, assume, and infer to make the passages coherent.

Second, traditional readings of the texts have been used and are being used overtly in a social construction of a theology of power and control that privileges one group over another (males over females), and those readings are controlled by the privileged group (males). Many representatives of the traditional readings are transparently invested in maintaining the power and control of men over the church, academy, and home. Students of linguistics have been sensitized about the use of language and interpretation to create and maintain power. Using power language and justifying it in the history of interpretation typically has gone beyond the Pauline texts while claiming that the traditional interpretation is what the text says, and anyone who rejects that interpretation is accused of rejecting Paul's teaching. However, the traditional interpretation of Paul's gender passages flies directly in the face of Paul's and Jesus's teachings on power and authority within the Christian community.

Third, until very recently (ca. 1980s), traditional readings have assumed the ontological inferiority of women through the entire history of interpretation, and it is implausible to think that an interpreter can effectively shed the foundational assumptions of the traditional view and still coherently maintain the remainder of interpretations and applications virtually intact. Unless a scholar or interpreter assumes the superiority of men and inferiority of women as a presupposition for understanding the texts on gender, they cannot legitimately claim that his or her interpretation is in line with the traditions of Christianity. Conversely, those who promote traditional practices concerning gender must recognize the trajectory that they occupy in church tradition. Can they legitimately use traditional support for their interpretations and applications while they try to dissociate themselves from charges that they promote the ontological inferiority of women and superiority of men?

Fourth, we understand now more than ever before how the individual impacts interpretation and how shared knowledge and culture of groups affect interpretation. Paul's passage on incorporating the diversity of the spiritual gifts of everyone in the body of Christ in 1 Corinthians 12–14 presumably would prevent one group or individual from privileging their own role over the church. However, though gender will clearly be one of the primary things that will reflect diversity in one's interpretation of passages on gender, the traditional male-dominated readings of passages about men and women have been effectively executed and maintained unilaterally. Women have been explicitly

with certain assumptions and tends to select the interpretive options that are consistent and coherent with their own presuppositions about Paul, the text, and the context that frames it.

excluded from explaining the texts to men or in many cases from even sharing or verbalizing their understanding of the texts, even though texts such as
1 Timothy 2:12 and 1 Corinthians 11:3–16 and 14:34–35 primarily address
women's culture, concerns, and practices. In other words, women have not
been fully included in the interpretation of their own mail. On the other hand,
passages that address men's culture are not often recognized or interpreted
as gender passages. The result is confusion between what is addressed to all
believers, what is addressed to women, and what is addressed to men.

Therefore, there are several reasons why the traditional interpretations of
the Pauline passages on gender should be carefully examined and should not
be privileged by the serious scholar or any interpreter who is dedicated to
understanding the meaning of the biblical texts. This study will show that the
first problem in understanding these texts is not primarily that the traditional
readings are unfair or unjust, but that on several counts they are implausible
readings in a first-century Greco-Roman context. On the other hand, this
investigation will not necessarily support or privilege previous nontraditional
interpretations or attempts to reconstruct the context in a way that changes
the reading, but will apply the same critical standards to all interpretations.

This study will address some of the lacunae in the hermeneutics and methodologies that have been applied to the analysis of the Pauline passages traditionally understood as addressing gender.[6] This introduction has explained
the approach of the study. Chapter 1 discusses the impact of information
about the Greco-Roman culture on the meaning of the texts, particularly in
understanding the significant cultural practice of veiling and the part that men
as well as women played in the practice. Chapter 2 explores Paul's teachings
on gender roles in the context of culture and concludes that Paul did not
support traditional Greco-Roman gender roles for the church, even though
he maintained the appearance of traditional gender relationships in order to
protect the church's reputation and enable its outreach, much like the practice
of Western missionaries in Islamic cultures. Chapters 3, 4, and 5 construct
a Pauline theology of gender from the Pauline teachings of creation, the
fall, and eschatology. This places the discussions about central issues such as

---

6. In research that supports this study, I applied systemic functional linguistics (SFL) to the
Greek language. One of the foundational theories of SFL is that in using language, members of
a culture "construct the social semiotic, whereby social reality is shaped, constrained and modified" (M. A. K. Halliday, *Language as Social Semiotic: The Social Interpretation of Language
and Meaning* [London: Edward Arnold, 1978], 126). In addition, the study of the passages in
their literary context has been informed by discourse analysis. Discourse analysis cannot be
reduced to a single methodology or approach. However, for an overview with an explanation
of key concepts, see Cynthia Long Westfall, *A Discourse Analysis of the Letter to the Hebrews:
The Relationship between Form and Meaning*, LNTS 297 (London: T&T Clark, 2005), 22–87.

1 Timothy 2:12 and headship in the broader context of Pauline thought and other texts on these topics, and views gender practices in the light of Paul's eschatological goals (as Paul consistently does). Chapter 6 contrasts Paul's theology on gender and the body with the church's traditional theology and practice about gender and sex; it urgently calls for a concentrated development of a coherent biblical theology on that part of the professing academy and the church that addresses crucial issues for the contemporary church. Chapter 7 argues specifically for consistent hermeneutics on how biblical passages should be interpreted by both genders and applied to both genders: women should interpret and apply instructions to all believers concerning the function of each believer in the church and the call to ministry with exactly the same hermeneutics as used by men. Chapter 8 examines the central relationship of Paul and gender to his theology of authority; it finds that the traditional interpretations assume a theology of authority in ministry and Christian relationships that both Paul and Jesus opposed. Pauline theology of ministry was based on metaphors of slavery and service so that any believer (gentile, slave, or female) could assume any function in the house church without violating the hierarchy of the Greco-Roman culture. Finally, chapter 9 provides a reinterpretation of 1 Timothy 2:11–15, drawing together the insights from the previous chapters. Crucial assumptions that affect exegesis are identified and evaluated, and then a plausible and coherent understanding of the text is suggested in light of the text's contexts and content. The conclusion summarizes the argument of this study and suggests applications in various contexts for the church and the individual who accept the Pauline teaching as authoritative for life and practice.

one

Culture

Our understanding of the language and culture of the first-century Greco-Roman world is vital to interpreting the Pauline Letters. This chapter shows how the context of culture helps to explain Paul's language when he addresses gender and gender concerns.[1] It is necessary to understand what Paul was trying to do with words in the light of the culture. The context of culture includes behavior that "is typical, recurrent, general."[2] These patterns of behavior are the way a culture works. It consists of typical social relationships and roles that apply across many situations, yet it also includes typical behavior within specific situations in that culture.[3] Cultural and linguistic information about gender is demonstrated through the culture and specifically through the structure of the language, as well as the vocabulary, symbols, and metaphors. However, a culture's language structure, symbols, and metaphors that involve gender should not be equated with the message of a speaker who utilizes that

1. This approach can be compared to Norman Petersen's approach in *Rediscovering Paul: Philemon and the Sociology of Paul's Narrative World* (Philadelphia: Fortress, 1985); see the chapter "Social Structures and Social Relations in the Story of Philemon" (89–199).
2. Gerd Theissen, *The Social Setting of Pauline Christianity: Essays on Corinth*, ed. and trans. John H. Schütz (Philadelphia: Fortress, 1982), 176–77. See the introduction to Theissen's book by John Schütz. Instead of *culture*, Schütz refers to the "social matrix" or the "social world" of early Christianity (1–2).
3. This description combines a description of society from social science with linguistic descriptions of register. See, e.g., T. O. Beidelman, *The Kaguru: A Matrilineal People of East Africa* (New York: Holt, Rinehart & Winston, 1971), 30; M. A. K. Halliday, *Language as Social Semiotic: The Social Interpretation of Language and Meaning* (London: Edward Arnold, 1978), 31–32.

language. When Paul employs the structure and vocabulary of the Greek language or refers to cultural symbols, metaphors, or practices about gender, we need to be alert as to how much of Greco-Roman cultural practices and worldview are part of Paul's message, and what cultural assumptions are truly adopted by him. For example, in the patterns that merely express grammatical gender, there is no choice, so there is no meaning. On the other hand, does Paul utilize "filter mechanisms" that select some features of the culture and language as relevant to his message, while he excludes other features as irrelevant?[4] Does Paul utilize and redefine common metaphors and practices in such a way that their meanings are transformed? The answer to this question in this study will be yes: Paul exploits Hellenistic literature, philosophy, symbols, and language to take every thought captive to Christ (2 Cor. 10:5). We will see this, for example, in his discussion about the veil and his use of the metaphor of "head." Paul used the Koine Greek language within a specific historical context; he was writing to specific recipients in specific historical situations. However, it does not follow that Paul accepted all historical-cultural and linguistic conventions that he utilized in communication as theologically normative for his Christian worldview. Precisely what was accepted as normative and what was rejected or altered must be determined.

1.1 Paul's Hellenism and Palestinian Judaism

Paul lived in and moved back and forth between the broader hellenized culture and Palestinian Judaism. How is Paul to be understood in his relationship to Greco-Roman culture? By definition, since he was a Jew born in Tarsus, Paul was a Hellenistic Jew. However, according to both Paul and Luke, Paul identified himself as a Pharisee descended from a Pharisaic line with impeccable Jewish credentials (Phil. 3:4–6; Acts 23:6). Paul's claim that he was "a Hebrew born of Hebrews" (Phil. 3:5) may have meant that he spoke Aramaic or Hebrew in the home.[5] According to Luke's account, Paul most likely first received an elementary Hellenistic education in Tarsus,[6] and then later received a formal

---

4. This is informed by linguistic theory regarding frames of discourse or scenarios that involve shared information between participants. One word, such as *restaurant*, can evoke a bundle of information. However, there is a limit on how much of the frame is incorporated. See Gillian Brown and George Yule, *Discourse Analysis*, CTL (Cambridge: Cambridge University Press, 1983), 236–56.

5. See Richard N. Longenecker, *Paul, Apostle of Liberty* (Grand Rapids: Baker, 1976), 22; W. R. Stegner, "Paul the Jew," *DPL*, 503–11, esp. 504.

6. Andrew Pitts's analysis of Acts 22:3 is persuasive, where he takes Tarsus as the referent of ἐν τῇ πόλει ταύτῃ, therefore indicating that Paul was brought up in Tarsus and came to Jerusalem after receiving a basic Hellenistic education in Tarsus as well. We would not assume

education in Judaism in Jerusalem, where he was thoroughly trained in the law under Gamaliel (Acts 22:2–3). What does this say about his orientation to the Greco-Roman and Palestinian Jewish cultures of his day? In the first half of the twentieth century, it was argued that Paul's primary orientation was to a syncretistic hellenized Judaism, in which popular Greco-Roman philosophy provided the background of his thought.[7] In the second half of the twentieth century, the consensus of scholarship experienced a profound shift and began to argue that Paul's primary orientation in life and thought was to Palestinian Judaism.[8] However, Palestinian Judaism was clearly embedded in Hellenism,[9] and first-century Jewish culture included complex sets of beliefs that were not uniform. Nevertheless, Judaism as a whole differentiated itself from the dominant Greco-Roman worldview and consciously resisted assimilation while continuing to exist as a subculture.

One area in which Palestinian Judaism differentiated itself was sexual ethics. It has been convincingly argued that there is continuity between Paul's ethical teachings about sexuality and the Jewish legal traditions.[10] Most importantly, Peter Tomson demonstrated that Paul affirmed the law in his view on sexual relationships and sexuality.[11] In the Greco-Roman world wide-ranging sexual license was practiced, though a clear double standard existed

---

that he received formal classical rhetorical training, but rather continued with rabbinic training at the point that a Hellenist would study rhetoric. See Andrew Pitts, "Paul and Hellenistic Education: Assessing Early Literary and Rhetorical Education" (MA thesis, McMaster Divinity College, 2007), 26–69.

7. The traditional post-Reformation understanding is that Paul's opponents were Jews who were legalists and therefore did not regard Paul as having a Jewish worldview. F. C. Baur set the course for interpreting Paul within the Greco-Roman philosophical and religious world of his day in, e.g., *Paul, the Apostle of Jesus Christ: His Life and Work, His Epistles and Doctrine*, trans. Eduard Zeller (London: Williams & Norgate, 1873).

8. The turning point was the introduction of "the new perspective on Paul." E. P. Sanders's contribution was to rethink the nature of Paul's "Judaizing" opponents. See E. P. Sanders, *Paul and Palestinian Judaism: A Comparison of Patterns of Religion* (Philadelphia: Fortress, 1977). James D. G. Dunn is one of the scholars best known for working out the implications of Paul's thought in, e.g., *The New Perspective on Paul: Collected Essays*, WUNT 185 (Tübingen: Mohr Siebeck, 2005). "For the vast majority of scholars, Paul's world had suddenly changed," with Sanders's work as the tipping point (S. J. Hafemann, "Paul and His Interpreters," *DPL*, 673). Scholarship is moving toward the view that Judaism was diverse.

9. See Martin Hengel, *Judaism and Hellenism: Studies in Their Encounter in Palestine during the Early Hellenistic Period* (London: SCM, 1974), 103–6; Lee I. Levine, *Judaism and Hellenism in Antiquity: Conflict or Confluence?* (Peabody, MA: Hendrickson, 1998).

10. However, see David G. Horrell's overview of approaches to Pauline ethics (*Solidarity and Difference: A Contemporary Reading of Paul's Ethics* [London: T&T Clark, 2005], 7–46), and note his conclusion, in agreement with V. P. Furnish, that "neither Paul's 'Jewishness' nor his 'Hellenism' should be 'one-sidedly' emphasized" (45).

11. Peter J. Tomson, *Paul and the Jewish Law: Halakha in the Letters of the Apostle to the Gentiles* (Minneapolis: Fortress, 1990); Tomson, "Paul's Jewish Background in View of His Law

in the sexual expectations for men and women that reflected the culture's beliefs about gender, hierarchy, and privilege.[12] Paul's fundamental teaching on Christian behavior directly confronted prevalent Greco-Roman sexual practices and expectations:

> Finally, brothers and sisters, we ask and urge you in the Lord Jesus that, as you learned from us how you ought to live and to please God (as, in fact, you are doing), you should do so more and more. For you know what instructions we gave you through the Lord Jesus. For this is the will of God, your sanctification: that you abstain from fornication; that each one of you know how to control your own body in holiness and honor, not with lustful passion, like the Gentiles who do not know God; that no one wrong or exploit a brother or sister in this matter, because the Lord is an avenger in all these things, just as we have already told you beforehand and solemnly warned you. (1 Thess. 4:1–6 NRSV)

Paul not only confronted the sexual licentiousness of Hellenistic culture, but also, what is much more revolutionary, he continued the Christian and Jewish practice of not maintaining a double standard of sexual ethics.[13] Although sexuality is only part of the gender issues, if Paul's sexual ethics have any logical coherence, then it is a significant indicator that Paul's theology of gender is going to be distinct from that of the dominant Greco-Roman culture. The claim that Paul would uncritically adopt a Greco-Roman model in the construction of his ethics or theology, particularly for his theology of gender, should be carefully reexamined.[14]

On the other hand, Paul was a part of the Greco-Roman culture and displayed familiarity with the formal and material characteristics of ethical

---

Teaching in 1 Corinthians 7," in *Paul and the Mosaic Law*, ed. James D. G. Dunn, WUNT 89 (Tübingen: Mohr Siebeck, 1996), 251–70.

12. Rodney Stark summarizes, "Although virginity was demanded of brides, and chastity of wives, men tended to be quite promiscuous and female prostitutes abounded in Greco-Roman cities—from the two-penny *diobolariae* who worked the streets to high-priced, well-bred courtesans. . . . Greco-Roman cities also sustained substantial numbers of male prostitutes, as bisexuality and homosexuality were common" (*The Rise of Christianity: How the Obscure, Marginal Jesus Movement Became the Dominant Religious Force in the Western World in a Few Centuries* [San Francisco: HarperSanFrancisco, 1997], 117).

13. For Paul's confrontation with the sexual ethics of the Greco-Roman culture, see 1 Cor. 6:18; Gal. 5:19–21; Col. 3:5; 1 Thess. 4:3–5. See also Matt. 5:28; Heb. 13:4.

14. The view that Paul adopted Greco-Roman household codes that are based on Aristotle's teaching is prevalent among Pauline scholars. However, this assumption needs to be critically reexamined and challenged in the light of more recent perspectives on Paul, even more so in the light of the contexts of the codes themselves and the differences between the Pauline teachings and that of broader Greco-Roman literature. See below in chap. 2.

Hellenistic literature. Granted, he did not hesitate to "employ current forms, concepts, and standards, even secular ones, already familiar to his readers."[15] Paul was a first-century Hellenistic Jew who chose a Palestinian Jewish worldview as his primary orientation, and who also undertook a Christian mission to the Greco-Roman culture. In conducting this gentile mission, Paul lived within Greco-Roman culture as one who understood it and thus was well positioned to explain spiritual realities foreign to his recipients by using concepts that were familiar and easily understood. Paul stood at the intersection of Christianity, Judaism, and the broader Hellenistic world. From that position he reread the law in relationship to his encounter with Christ on the road to Damascus and to his ministry experiences in the gentile revivals in Antioch and his gentile mission. As a result, he critiqued not only aspects of Greco-Roman culture but also aspects of Jewish culture and elements in the developing institutional culture of the early church. Paul's utilization of Greco-Roman linguistic forms, cultural concepts, and ethical standards concerning gender needs to be carefully read and examined in light of the discourses and contexts in which these occur—in order to distinguish between what he critiques, what he transforms, and what he adopts.

1.2 The Pauline Relationship with the Church and Greco-Roman Society

Paul attempted to establish gentile churches within the context of the mainstream of Greco-Roman culture. His general purpose in writing his letters was to further his mission to the gentiles by spiritually forming, guiding, and correcting the gentile churches that had been founded by his mission team (with the exception of the church in Rome, which presumably did not have an apostolic foundation and was a unique mixture of Jew and gentile).[16] Paul was very successful at contextualization for the purposes of communication and evangelism, which largely accounts for the success of his mission. One of the tricky aspects of Pauline studies involves accounting for the fact that in order to communicate spiritual realities, Paul would seek to use Greek language and metaphors that were meaningful to his Greco-Roman recipients (Rom. 6:19

15. Victor Paul Furnish, *Theology and Ethics in Paul* (Nashville: Abingdon, 1968), 65. According to Furnish, this indicates that Paul approves the Hellenistic traditions he utilizes. However, this should no more be assumed than it should be assumed that I agree with Furnish's argument because I quote him.

16. For the Jewish-gentile nature of the Roman church, see Robert Jewett's discussion on the history of Christianity in Rome, in *Romans: A Commentary*, ed. Eldon J. Epp, Hermeneia (Minneapolis: Fortress, 2007), 59–61.

NRSV: "I am speaking in human terms because of your natural limitations").[17] However, though he used Greek language embedded in the Hellenistic world-view, he intended for the church to be distinct from "the world," which for him was a term that corresponded roughly to Greco-Roman society and culture.[18] In other words, in order for his message to be communicated meaningfully, he deliberately employed commonly understood metaphors, conventions, and cultural institutions to transform the churches into a movement that was spiritually and ethically countercultural. To achieve this, Paul utilized common figures of speech, but did so in a manner so that such expressions frequently diverged from their normal meaning. Understanding Paul's beliefs about gender cannot simply be a matter of studying the meaning of words, understanding facts about the culture, and then imposing Greco-Roman notions of gender onto Paul.

Instances of language and particularly figures of speech are to be correctly understood in the context of the communicator's thought: the message of any communication must be understood in terms of its intended pragmatic effect on its recipients. When a speaker/writer is trying to motivate listeners/recipients to perform a given action, different rhetorical strategies may be used other than simply issuing direct commands for people to take a certain course of action. Although this latter practice may be effective in some cases, it will not be effective in all cases; sometimes the literal meaning is too provocative and may easily cause the listener/recipient to reject the message as unwelcome, inappropriate, or incomprehensible. A well-known example is found in Shakespeare's *Julius Caesar*, where the dramatist re-creates Marc Antony's eulogy for Caesar, which turned public opinion against Caesar's assassins. Shakespeare's speech features the repeated phrase "Brutus is an honorable man," which is the opposite of what the eulogist really wished to communicate. Yet if Marc Antony had started his speech with "Kill Brutus," the crowd would have turned on him. Instead, Marc Antony uses verbal irony (in a trope), whereby his words convey the opposite of their usual meaning. By doing so, Marc Antony slips under the hearers' guard, and the speech has the intended pragmatic effect. Such speech practices that

17. See Eckhard J. Schnabel, *Paul the Missionary: Realities, Strategies and Methods* (Downers Grove, IL: InterVarsity, 2008), 155–74; also, for one clear example among many others presented by scholars in the same volume, see Hans Dieter Betz, "Transferring a Ritual: Paul's Interpretation of Baptism in Romans 6," in *Paul in His Hellenistic Context*, ed. Troels Engberg-Pedersen (Minneapolis: Fortress, 1995), 84–118.

18. As Norman Petersen puts it, "Behind Paul's superficially homogeneous language there lies an intricate network of social roles and relationships that spans two different institutional domains. To decode Paul's role language, we need a sociological cipher as well as a dictionary of everyday language" (*Rediscovering Paul*, 24).

invert meanings were recognized as one of the four fundamental opera-
tions of figures of speech by classic rhetoricians.[19] This chapter provides
some cultural background in key areas that inform our interpretation of
gender in Paul. It will show that Paul's intended pragmatic effects for some
of his teachings on gender subvert and transform what was familiar to his
recipients, even effecting the opposite of what is frequently held to be the
literal interpretation.

1.3 Contrast between Rhetoric and Practice in the First Century

When we look at the first-century context of opinions toward gender, we are
not dealing merely with actual recorded practices regarding gender, but also
with first-century prejudices and rhetoric about what proper practices should
be—that is, what the projected ideal man or woman should be.[20] In Greco-
Roman society, legislating and enforcing the "proper" behavior of women
was a major concern for authorities because they believed that disorder in the
household had seditious ramifications for the welfare of the empire. Therefore,
cults and sects were often attacked because of the wild behavior of the women
participants.[21] In order for Paul's gentile mission to succeed, the behavior of
Christian women would need to be consistent with what was practiced by
women in the broader first-century Greco-Roman world. Therefore, Paul's
gender concerns were often missional when he addressed gender roles in the
church and the home, and his intention was for believers to fit into the culture
while remaining ethically pure. Fitting into the first-century culture was a
different proposition than fitting into the culture of the twenty-first century.
Modern Western preconceptions of how the genders normally behave and
interact with one another are markedly different from the preconceptions of
Greco-Roman culture.

19. See, e.g., Quintilian, *Inst.* 9.1.4 for a definition of "trope."

20. Margaret MacDonald writes about the importance of the interplay between the image
of the ideal or stereotypical male or female and reality: "Image *shapes* reality. It is not only the
case that image shapes reality in the sense that all communication about historical happenings
is affected by the priorities, beliefs, and norms embedded in the systems of particular cultures;
rather, we must also be aware that image shapes reality in the sense that during any given historical moment the *actors themselves* will experience and react to a reality that is profoundly
shaped by such symbol systems" (*Early Christian Women and Pagan Opinion: The Power of
the Hysterical Woman* [Cambridge: Cambridge University Press, 1996], 120, emphasis original).

21. For discussion of how there were certain stereotyped criticisms of the Dionysus cult,
the Egyptian Isis cult, and Judaism, which were attacked for their immoral effect on women,
see David L. Balch, *Let Wives Be Submissive: The Domestic Code in 1 Peter*, SBLMS 26 (Chico,
CA: Scholars Press, 1981), 65–80.

1.3.1 The Influence of Aristotle on the Rhetoric

One of the factors that contribute to the disparity between practice and rhetoric is the continued influence of Aristotle on Greco-Roman society and culture. Wherever Hellenism went, it brought Athenian philosophy. With Athenian philosophy came rhetoric about the nature of male and female from the Athenian classical period that continued to be influential as early and medieval church philosophy developed.

Aristotle advised his male readers on how to govern their wives because of women's essential inferiority. Greeks believed that a gender-based hierarchy is based on the ontological nature of women and men rather than the standards or conventions of culture. According to Aristotle and Greek thought, the cosmic hierarchy is expressed in two genders that have mutually exclusive qualities. The perfect body is male/man, whose natural state is physical and political strength, rationality, spirituality, superiority, activity, dryness, and penetration. Meanwhile, female/woman embodies humanity's negative qualities, which are physical and political weakness, irrationality, fleshliness, inferiority, passivity, wetness, and being penetrated. Male and female represent the hierarchy (superior/inferior), societal status (more/less), and sex role (penetrator/penetrated).[22] Platonic-Aristotelian ideas about the ontological nature of men and women and the relationship of the household to the general society had a direct influence on Roman Stoics and Hellenistic Jews such as Philo and Josephus, who appear to carry forward the same arguments and assumptions.[23] In classical Athenian society, women were restricted to the seclusion of the domestic sphere (cloistered) as a measure of control, and they could leave the house only for religious ceremonies and in the company of their guardian. Philo's ideal for women in first-century Alexandria was little different, if not even more restrictive:

> A woman, then, should not be a busybody, meddling with matters outside her household concerns, but should seek a life of seclusion. She should not show herself off like a vagrant in the streets before the eyes of other men, except when she has to go to the temple, and even then she should take pains to go, not when the market is full, but when most people have gone home, and so like a free-born lady worthy of the name, with everything quiet around her, make her oblations and offer her prayers to avert the evil and gain the good. (*Spec.* 3.171)[24]

22. Aristotle, *Gen. an.* 728a.18–20; 737a.25–35; 775a.15.
23. See, e.g., Philo, *Ios.* 8.38–39; 11.54.
24. Francis H. Colson, G. H. Whitaker, Ralph Marcus, eds. and trans., *Philo*, LCL (Cambridge, MA: Harvard University Press, 1929–62), 7:583.

Philo, like Josephus and Paul, was writing for a hellenized Jewish or a Hellenistic-Roman audience, and there are a broad variety of views on women in early Jewish sources.[25]

The Greek/Athenian model for gender was easily combined with the rhetoric of Octavian's strict moral laws (18 and 9 BCE) for at least the Roman upper class, which ostensibly were part of an effort to restore the traditional values of the Roman Republic in culture and religion.[26] Octavian's laws targeted promiscuity as well as a low-population crisis among the Roman elite. He promoted the marriage of women, discouraged women from committing adultery, rewarded motherhood, and established dress codes for women that signaled a woman's legal status and class.[27] Men's elite male rank was reinforced, and Octavian said that fathers were "worthy to be called by this name [father] in the same way as I am."[28] Octavian became the paterfamilias of the empire, and the empire was run by his "imperial household." His power over the Roman Empire was explicitly supported by a traditional view of the elite male, where the paterfamilias had absolute power over the family. Penalties and rewards pressured single men to marry and have children, and they were discouraged from having affairs with matrons.[29]

Therefore, the rhetoric of Hellenistic culture and the language of empire gave a powerful message of inferiority, control, restriction, and even the seclusion of women. On the other hand, men were not free from pressures and punishments urging them to assume their prescribed gender roles. Men were seen in every part of the public sector, but they were restricted and constrained by the rhetoric about gender in ways that women were not. More was expected in terms of specific character traits if not actual labor, and a harsher measure was applied to them. A man who displayed emotions, behavior, or characteristics labeled as feminine was shamed and despised for assuming

25. See C. S. Keener, "Marriage," *DNTB*, 690.

26. Bruce Winter argues that Roman women appear to be traditionally less restricted to the private sphere than Greek women. But then, at the end of the Roman Republic, a "new" type of woman emerged in certain circles in Rome among the upper class who claimed the same sexual liberties as men, and Octavian's laws reacted against this development among the women (*Roman Wives, Roman Widows: The Appearance of New Women and the Pauline Communities* [Grand Rapids: Eerdmans, 2003], 17–38). But see Lynn Cohick's critique of Winter (Cohick, *Women in the World of the Earliest Christians: Illuminating Ancient Ways of Life* [Grand Rapids: Baker Academic, 2009], 72–75), arguing convincingly that the "new woman" was "more a poetic fiction and a political smear than a historical reality" (75).

27. As per the Lex Julia de adulteriis coercendis and Lex Julia maritandis ordinibus, enacted in the year 18 BCE (further emended in 9 BCE by the Lex Papia Poppaea). See Winter, *Roman Wives*, 39–58; Diana E. E. Kleiner, *Cleopatra and Rome* (Cambridge, MA: Belknap, 2009), 32.

28. Dio Cassius, *Hist. rom.* 56.3.6, 3.8, my translation.

29. Winter, *Roman Wives*, 49.

a categorical low-status role. For example, certain emotional expressions and displays of grief in mourning the death of a loved one were considered feminine. Men who lived in certain regions of the Roman Empire, or even Hellenists, could be disrespected and ridiculed by Romans as effeminate. This is because some areas, such as Egypt, were known for women/wives who exercised more freedom or authority than was allowed in the Roman ideal.[30] Although there was a real potential of upward mobility and increased economic prosperity in the Roman Empire, honor came from knowing and keeping one's place.[31] The future of a man was more rigidly determined by his father's occupation, status, and entangling patron-client alliances, not to mention the fact that arguably the majority of adult males at any given time were not firstborn sons, who were heirs, but were still under the authority of a master or their own paterfamilias. All but Caesar were theoretically answerable to at least one patron, and patrons and male heirs had their own serious obligations to their clients.[32]

1.3.2 Greco-Roman Gender Behavior

We need to recognize a distinct difference between the actual evidence concerning the behavior of men and women and the literary rhetoric about gender. In the Greco-Roman world there was a greater variety of gender behavior for women than is generally acknowledged in the literature, but it is revealed in inscriptions, the papyri (court cases and letters), and historical accounts. There were significant variations in functions for women in different locations in the Roman Empire. Athens, Jerusalem, Rome, and Alexandria represent a rough continuum, from the most restrictive roles for women in Athens to the most unrestricted roles in Alexandria.[33] Yet to some degree throughout the Roman

30. Marc Antony's infatuation with Hellenism (as opposed to the Latin culture here) and his relationship to Cleopatra as her consort, given her authority and her function in the Isis cult, gave Octavian the opportunity to characterize Antony as effeminate and extravagant.

31. The social stratification of the empire was concerned with the exercise of power: "Who gets what and why?" The system is intentionally set up so the upper strata control the power, wealth (land, slave labor, rents, taxes), and status.

32. As discussed below, "The patron-client relationship is the basic building block of the Greco-Roman society" (D. A. deSilva, "Patronage," *DNTB*, 766). The system was an infrastructure of networks of favor and loyalty between socially unequal persons.

33. For the conditions in Egypt, see Sarah B. Pomeroy, "Women in Roman Egypt: A Preliminary Study Based on Papyri," in *Reflections of Women in Antiquity*, ed. Helene P. Foley (New York: Gordon and Breach Science, 1981), 303–22. Yet in Alexandria, as mentioned above, Philo suggested that married and unmarried women be confined to the house in a way consistent with women's confinement in Athens during the classical period. See the breakdown of diversity of women's behavior in the first-century Roman Empire as given in Ben Witherington III, *Women and the Genesis of Christianity* (Cambridge: Cambridge University Press, 1990), 10–26.

Empire, women were involved in a range of nontraditional activities, including functioning as patrons, business owners, and cultic and public officials. A woman who exhibited what were considered manly virtues and strengths might be given some positive recognition or honor, particularly if she were upper class and donated a large sum of money or performed a necessary service.

Thus during the first century there was social ferment and some fluidity for the actual behavior of women, but very traditional concepts of gender roles were alive and well for both men and women. While some inscriptions and papyri tell us the story of an increasing range of women's activities that are roads to some forms of economic and social power and honor, the funerary inscriptions and epithets do not praise women for things that would be considered accomplishments and sources of honor for men, but rather for their conformity to traditional female stereotypes and Roman ideals.[34] Behavior that might gain recognition and honor for upper-class women could gain criticism and condemnation for other women in different circumstances. Consequently, when a cult was considered dangerous, the activities of women and the authority of their husbands came under public scrutiny, and what might be acceptable behavior in their first-century context could be represented as dishonorable deviations from the rhetoric of the Greco-Roman ideal. In this way, the feminine and masculine Greek stereotypes and Roman ideals were used as primary weapons to attempt to control, discredit, or disable a dangerous cult or sect.

1.4 Gender and Greco-Roman Values

Several Greco-Roman values inform our understanding of gender in the Pauline corpus. The complementary values of honor and shame are clearly part of Paul's rhetoric when he addresses gender issues, and the context for his comments must be understood. In addition, the patron-client relationship and reciprocity that form the building blocks of the culture also inform the relationships between husbands and wives.

34. As Riet van Bremen states,
> These "traditional" ideas about women are . . . not just the hobbyhorses of a few moralists, out of touch with reality. They are, to a great extent, mirrored in the language used in the inscriptions. In seeming contradiction to the public activities and independent behavior of these women, the most frequent epithets used for women are to be found in exactly the traditional feminine area of modesty, loving dedication to husband and family, piety, decency, etc., an ideology which also pervaded the numerous funerary inscriptions from all over the Greek world, set up by "ordinary" Greeks. ("Women and Wealth," in *Images of Women in Antiquity*, ed. Averil Cameron and Amélie Kuhrt [London: Routledge, 1993], 234)

Thus there is a noted discrepancy between the ideology and the archaeological evidence regarding women's freedoms and activities.

1.4.1 Honor and Shame

Honor refers to a person's worth in the court of public opinion, which makes a verdict based on how well that person embodies the qualities and behaviors of the group values.[35] The Greco-Roman ideal appeared to support a binary model that Zeba Crook describes but challenges as having "honor on one end and shame on the other, with men on one end and women on the other, with elite on one end and non-elite on the other."[36]

Honor for men came in knowing one's place or identity (birth, social class and status, wealth, and patronage), conforming to society's expectations and essential values consistent with one's place, and competing for honor with one's social peers. Each man contributes to the orderly life of the city, involving agreement and unity on the one hand, and courage in battle on the other.

The female version of so-called honor was the primary female "virtue" of shame, which was comprised of deferential behavior, modesty, and chastity that enhanced the honor of the male head of the household (see Sir. 26:10–16; 42:9–12; 4 Macc. 18:6–8; Thucydides, *Hist.* 2.45.2).[37] Crook challenges this binary model of honor and shame, particularly the suggestion that women did not have honor. He points out that women were, in fact, given honor in practice for "being witty, brave, aggressive, and loyal to the state."[38] He concludes, "There appears to have been an ideal world and a lived world, and in the lived world women *did* participate in public life, *did* compete for honor, *could* have greater honor than their husbands, *did* act as benefactors, and *were* given crowns, statues, and seats of honor."[39]

Certainly it is wrong to assume that Paul would not speak of women having honor in 1 Corinthians 11:2–16 because of prevalent cultural ideals, since clear references to the honor of particular women may be found in various sources. However, as Margaret MacDonald insists, "image shapes reality," and women apparently had little worth as a group.[40] Crook's observations illustrate the difference between rhetoric and practice in the Greco-Roman culture (described above). The low value of the female in the society was also reflected in the widespread practices of infanticide and abandonment of

---

35. See David A. deSilva, "Honor and Shame," *DNTB*, 518.

36. Crook, "Honor, Shame, and Social Status Revisited," *JBL* 128 (2009): 610.

37. See S. C. Barton, "Social Values and Structures," *DNTB*, 1129, 1130. Some have claimed that shame indicated women's value, but this argument falls short of the reality: women were valued so little that widespread infanticide practiced on female infants led to a shortage of females in the Roman Empire.

38. Crook, "Honor, Shame," 605.

39. Ibid., 609, emphasis original.

40. MacDonald, *Early Christian Women*, 121.

female babies.[41] It was very common to raise only one daughter per family, which, together with maternal mortality, contributed to a shortage of women during the Roman Empire that created a population crisis. Therefore, when Paul gives honor and recognition to so many female members of the Roman church in Romans 16, it stands out as a significant deviation from the cultural practice and ideal.

A woman's violation of the virtues of modesty and chastity brought great shame on her family and diminished its status. In areas of the world where similar standards and views of family honor still exist, honor is sometimes restored to the family by "honor killing," as it was in the first century.[42] It occurs when a woman or girl is killed for bringing shame on her family. Honor killing is described in a newspaper article in the *Hamilton Spectator*, which covered the executions of four Muslim women by their family in Ontario: "A dominant member of the family, usually male, decrees a woman's actions or relationships diminish the status of the family in the eyes of their peers. So for the wrong choice of a boyfriend, for committing adultery, and even for acts of harmless rebellion such as wearing Western clothes or makeup, women are sometimes executed."[43]

In Middle Eastern cultures, as well as other cultures with similar elements to the Greco-Roman society, the dishonor to the family may in practice boil down to simple defiance of male authority in the details. The male authority may then determine whether a given detail brings shame or not.

When it is a matter of cultural norms or ideals in an honor culture, both the husband and wife are subject to the authoritative expectations of that culture. No one in Greco-Roman culture defended a husband's right to exercise his authority over his wife by allowing or endorsing behavior that was considered shameful. The Babylonian Talmud includes a second-century report in which

41. Stark, *Rise of Christianity*, 118.

42. Moyer Hubbard describes "demographic borrowing" as a well-established practice among social historians, which is "drawing meaningful analogies between societies that appear to be similar in salient respects, but where one is well documented and the other is not" ("Kept Safe through Childbearing: Maternal Mortality, Justification by Faith, and the Social Setting of 1 Timothy 2:15," *JETS* 55 [2012]: 753). See also Kenneth E. Bailey, "Informal Controlled Oral Tradition and the Synoptic Gospels," *Them* 20, no. 2 (1995): 4–11. Bailey states his methodology as applied to oral tradition: "We intend to present the concrete reality of our own experience of more than three decades of life and study in the Middle East among communities of great antiquity that still preserve in oral form much of what is important to them" (4). See also Bailey, *Jesus through Middle Eastern Eyes: Cultural Studies in the Gospels* (Downers Grove, IL: InterVarsity, 2008); Bailey, *Paul through Mediterranean Eyes: Cultural Studies in 1 Corinthians* (Downers Grove, IL: InterVarsity, 2011).

43. Howard Elliott, "Honour Killing a Brutal Import," *Hamilton Spectator*, July 30, 2009, A16.

Rabbi Meir calls a certain man a "bad man" because he does not divorce his wife for a list of offenses that includes unbound hair. He concludes, "Such a one it is a religious duty to divorce."[44] Significantly, he was not exhorted to take authority over his wife or control her as a required course of action, as if the wife's behavior were a case of disobedience. He is not blamed for her behavior; he is blamed for not having the appropriate response.

1.4.2 The Patron-Client Relationship

All social classes participated in the patronage system in some way by forming relationships of reciprocity, considered to be the basic building block of Greco-Roman society. The patron-client relationship is "marked by the mutual exchange of desired goods and services."[45] The relationship between a husband and wife was placed in the broader context of the patronage system. Though it may occur between people of equal social status as "friendships," the default paradigm of the relationship is between people of unequal social status (a benefactor and a recipient).[46] A person who receives a gift also receives an obligation to respond appropriately to one's benefactors with gratitude and loyalty. As Seneca says, "He who intends to be grateful, let him think how he shall repay a kindness while he is receiving it" (*Ben.* 2.25.3).[47] David deSilva summarizes, "Goods and opportunities were channeled down from above, and respect, public praise and loyal service were returned from below, again within the context of mutual commitment."[48]

The husband and wife were usually unequal partners in the patronage system in the Greco-Roman world. The husband functioned as the benefactor, and the woman functioned as the inferior party in the marital relationship, unless she brought a large dowry into the marriage.[49] Patronage between unequal pairs often consisted of both authority and reciprocity, which were

44. See *b. Giṭ.* 90a–b.

45. David deSilva, "Patronage and Reciprocity: The Context of Grace in the New Testament," *ATJ* 31 (1999): 33. As deSilva describes, "Someone of lesser power, honor and wealth seeks out the aid of a person of superior power, honor and wealth. The kinds of benefits exchanged between such people will be different in kind and quality, the patron providing material gifts or opportunities for advancement, the client contributing to the patron's reputation and power base" (*Honor, Patronage, Kinship & Purity: Unlocking New Testament Culture* [Downers Grove, IL: InterVarsity, 2006], 97).

46. deSilva, *Honor, Patronage*, 99.

47. Seneca, *On Benefits Addressed to Aebutius Liberalis*, trans. Aubrey Stewart (London: George Bell and Sons, 1887), 42.

48. deSilva, *Honor, Patronage*, 118.

49. Russ Dudrey concludes that in such an arrangement, "The patriarchs of ancient households were likely to feel that they *owned* their wives, their children, and their slaves" ("'Submit Yourselves to One Another': A Socio-Historical Look at the Household Code of Ephesians

reflected in the household.[50] The wife received her identity, social position, and a share in the property from her husband and her husband's family (with the exception of the Roman practice of marrying without *manus*).[51] The husband received authority and honor in the household, his house was managed, and he obtained his legal heirs from the marital relationship, heirs who would make their contributions to the family economy.

The two had equivalent and reciprocal obligations toward each other. Many of the ancient writers stressed the "duty," "responsibility," and "care" that went with the husband's authority.[52] In return, the wives were to strive to be "worthy women." Piety, chastity, domesticity, and submissiveness were virtues that defined the "worthy woman."[53] A Neo-Pythagorean text of the third or second century BCE asserted, "A woman's greatest virtue is chastity. Because of this quality she is able to honor and to cherish her own particular husband."[54] Providing the husband with unquestioned legitimate offspring was one of the primary ways that a woman could honor her husband.[55] So the basic patronage relationship is reflected in the marital relationship, where the benefactor or patron is the superior in power, wealth, status, honor, and value, and the wife, who is the recipient of his

5:15–6:9," *ResQ* 41 [1999]: 39, emphasis original). However, the assumed ownership of women as a cultural ideal is disputed.

50. Craig Evans associates benefaction with authority and power: "Luke's readers would readily interpret the reference to 'benefactors' in the context of rulers and the mighty, the very people who lord it over others, defining their tyrannical rule with the euphemism 'benefaction.' Luke's readers knew that the epithet 'benefactor' (εὐεργέτης) was commonly bestowed on gods, kings, and wealthy and powerful men who contribute to society" ("King Jesus and His Ambassadors: Empire and Luke-Acts," in *Empire in the New Testament*, ed. Stanley E. Porter and Cynthia Long Westfall, MNTSS 10 [Eugene, OR: Pickwick, 2010]: 125–26).

51. In the late Roman Republic, marriage without *manus* (*sine manu*) was common, whereby the wife remained under the authority of her father or guardian and retained her property from her family lineage. It also meant that she had no rights over her husband's property (see Sarah B. Pomeroy, *Goddesses, Whores, Wives, and Slaves: Women in Classical Antiquity* [New York: Schocken, 1975], 155). It was beneficial to wealthy women and altered the reciprocity of the marital relationship. Consequently, it tended to destabilize marriages.

52. See deSilva, *Honor, Patronage*, 179.

53. Piety, chastity, modesty, and other traits of "worthy women" were often simply given as abbreviations on Roman tombstones, which shows they were understood as common or stereotypical (Richmond Lattimore, *Themes in Greek and Latin Epitaphs* [Urbana: University of Illinois Press, 1942], 290–99). Dudrey rightly argues that though we must beware of drawing conclusions through anecdotal sources and diachronic literature rather than synchronic literature, the diachronic picture of the social reality for wives is evident in the literary and nonliterary evidence spanning Proverbs and Homer to Egyptian papyri and Roman legal material and tomb inscriptions ("'Submit Yourselves,'" 32). Dudrey describes these character traits as ubiquitous or "supercultural" (ibid., 38–39).

54. Text from a Pythagorean sect in Italy, cited in Mary R. Lefkowitz and Maureen B. Fant, *Women's Life in Greece and Rome* (Baltimore: Johns Hopkins University Press, 1982), 104.

55. Dudrey, "'Submit Yourselves,'" 29.

care, returns respect, public praise, and loyal service, honoring him particularly through her obedience and chastity. This is why in Ephesians 5:22–27, although Paul does not affirm the ontological superiority and priority of men, he is able to draw a comparison between the benefits that the church receives from Christ and the tangible benefits that a wife receives from her husband and build on it, in terms both of reciprocity for the wife and of an increased obligation of benefaction/service for the husband.[56] His "filter mechanism" is apparent in the syntactic link between the woman's submission and mutual submission in Ephesians 5:21[57] and in the instructions to the husband, where the wife is given the same status and treatment as a male, since she is his "body."

1.5 Gender and Public and Domestic Spheres

Men and women were expected to belong to two different systems in the Greco-Roman world: the public sphere and the domestic sphere.[58] The activities within these spheres perpetuated traditional roles for men and women that were common in the Hellenistic world and were related to the traditional values of the Greek classical period. The Stoic Hierocles summarized the traditional Greek gender roles aptly: "These therefore are to be divided after the accustomed manner; rural, forensic, and political works are to be attributed to the husband; but to the wife, such works as pertain to spinning wool, making of bread, cooking, and, in short, everything of a domestic nature."[59]

The husband's "rural" work included providing the raw materials for the wife's labor from farming, and the public function of any economic transactions was considered to be a man's role and part of the public domain. Women's work and responsibilities in the domestic sphere had a lower value and status

56. Therefore, the Greco-Roman cultural values convincingly explain how the husband is the source of life (head) of the wife, not only in the creation account, but also because of the very real dependence of women on their husbands, thus answering one of Thomas Schreiner's primary objections to the meaning of "head" as "source," when he asks, "In what meaningful sense can one say that a husband is the source of his wife?" ("Head Coverings, Prophecies, and the Trinity: 1 Corinthians 11:2–16," in *Recovering Biblical Manhood and Womanhood: A Response to Evangelical Feminism*, ed. John Piper and Wayne Grudem [Wheaton: Crossway, 1991], 127).

57. Ephesians 5:18–23 forms one sentence in the Greek, and the instructions to wives in v. 22 are grammatically dependent on the mutual submission in v. 21 because of the ellipsis (omission) of the verb "submit" in v. 22.

58. Notice avoidance of the "public/private" polarity. Different cultures have different concepts of personal space and privacy; this reality clouds the very real distinctions and social separation that the Greek and Greco-Roman culture delineated.

59. Hierocles, *Household Management*, in Stobaeus, *Flor.* 4.85.21, in *Ethical Fragments of Hierocles, Preserved by Strobaeus*, trans. Thomas Taylor (1822, repr., Mobile, AL: Evergreen Books, 2011), digital edition.

in Greco-Roman culture: making clothing (spinning and weaving), laundering (washing and ironing), bathing children and men, providing and serving food, and, last but not least, bearing and nurturing children. Most of the tasks were comparable to slave's work, and in fact they were delegated to slaves whenever possible, with the possible exception of spinning, which was considered the quintessential feminine occupation for all classes. Therefore, references to these domestic functions should be understood as effeminate or "women's work." The nature of Christ's actions toward the church and the husband's actions toward the wife in Ephesians 5:25–33 would have been understood as "women's work." The representation of the church as the bride would have been effeminate, according to Greco-Roman values. Consequently, Paul is subverting male privilege in the home and church. He promotes a model of servanthood and low status, consistent with the humility of Christ's incarnation, precisely for men, who have power and position in the Greco-Roman social system.[60]

The fact that women were secluded or restricted to the home during some time periods and in some locations did not mean that they held no authority; rather, it was recognized that the domain of women's authority was in the domestic sphere, while the man's authority was in the public sphere. A husband conceivably could override his wife's authority and control the domestic domain, but that was not the ideal for Plato or the Greco-Roman model. According to Plato, a woman's one task or "social service" was submission.[61] However, he contested that women took the "superior part" and filled the slot of ruler in some relationships: "Is not the right of father and mother one of [those relationships]? And in general would not the claim to rule offspring be a claim universally just? Certainly."[62] He expanded the list of relationships to include noble-ignoble, older-younger, and masters-slaves. In each of these relationships women could fill the slot of ruler.[63] Hierocles is well known for saying that the husband is the ruler and the wife is the ruled, but he also considered it best if men governed men's work and women governed women's work, where the woman is a "ruler" who has authority over the house and servants.[64] The exercise of women's legitimate authority

60. For how these domestic functions and the inclusion of men in the metaphor of the church as the bride of Christ involved effeminate behavior, dress, and role-play that would be considered shameful for men, see §1.1; §3.2.

61. Plato, *Resp.* 4.433a, c–d.

62. Plato, *Laws*, ed. and trans. R. G. Bury, LCL (Cambridge, MA: Harvard University Press, 1967), 1:211–12.

63. Plato, *Leg.* 3.690a–d.

64. As manager of the house, see Hierocles, *On Marriage*, in Stobaeus, *Flor.* 4.67.24; concerning the equitable division of labor and interchangeability of roles, see Hierocles, *Household Management*, in Stobaeus, *Flor.* 4.85.21.

over children, servants, and slaves in the home and various aspects of the domestic sphere is indisputable, whether they were widows who functioned as the heads of their households or whether they were wives who managed the homes.

From the start of the Hellenistic period, some of the lines between the public and domestic spheres were blurred in that women were entering the public sphere in various capacities (as noted above). However, regardless of inconsistency with the actual behavior of women in the Hellenistic and Greco-Roman period, traditional values were still in place and were strengthened through positive rhetoric and polemic. They were held up as standards by which individuals and fringe religious sects were judged.[65] However, the opposite did not hold true. There was not a detectable complementary movement for "stay-at-home fathers" who took responsibility for domestic tasks, as there is now in some Western cultures. Some of the domestic tasks were done by men in the public domain and involved economic transactions, such as laundry or food services. However, the standards for masculinity appear to have remained more stable in practice, consistent with the reluctance of those in a position of privilege to surrender their advantage. Also, the requirement of chastity or sexual fidelity was not typically binding for the man in the Greco-Roman world, in contrast with the expectations for women.

1.6 First Corinthians 11 and the Head Covering

Now we may consider a plausible reading of Paul's teaching on a woman's head covering in 1 Corinthians 11:3–16 that is informed by relevant cultural aspects, accounts for the vocabulary, and reflects the formal features in the passage. Corinth was a Roman colony in a Greek location. Roman paradigms may explain some of the cultural features, particularly in terms of religious customs and dress. The way in which Roman law regulated and informed gender conduct in this Roman colony is relevant to the study of 1–2 Corinthians. However, it is also clear that the Greek philosophical schools (such as the Sophists) and their models of authority and leadership were heavily influential in Corinth, perhaps more so than in Rome.[66]

65. See Balch's extended argument about the Greco-Roman criticism of minority religious communities that focused on precisely how women related to their husbands (*Let Wives Be Submissive*, 63–80).
66. "Roman law, culture and religion were dominant in Corinth, and Latin was the city's official language, but the Greek traditions and philosophies of the area and the mystery cults from Egypt and Asia were also strongly represented" (S. J. Hafemann, "Letters to the Corinthians," *DPL*, 173).

1.6.1 Sexual Behavior and Women in Corinth

Corinth was in a strategic military and commercial location because it controlled a strategic section of overland movement between Italy and Asia, across the Isthmus of Corinth. Consequently, it was known for its wealth, religious temples and rites, and its vice—particularly for its sexual vice. It was a place that offered every kind of sexual experience available to men (so "to act like a Corinthian" was to engage in sexual immorality) and the term "Corinthian girl" was a euphemism for a prostitute.[67] There was no upper class, but instead a class of nouveau riche was created by Corinth's prosperity. However, Paul indicates that the Corinthian church did not draw its membership only from the wealthy elite but rather mostly from those who lacked status or power (1 Cor. 1:26).

It is difficult to confidently re-create what kinds of freedom would be available to or chosen by women in Corinth who were not slaves or prostitutes in this morally volatile context—how do women act and dress when they are going to church on Moulin Rouge or Bourbon Street? Sometimes conservative subcultures and practices for women subsist and persist directly in reaction to more permissible contexts. In such settings it is possible that respectable women would tend to cover up more than normal.[68] In such a context, was it likely that Christian women would knowingly flout "the Roman legal convention that epitomized marriage"[69] in the Corinthian house church? Or rather, would they be more careful and resistant to risking exposure and vulnerability in what some might have argued was a safe domestic context? How would the scenario be further complicated if low-status Corinthian house churches included women slaves or prostitutes? Slaves, prostitutes, and freedwomen were prohibited from veiling.[70] It is assumed by virtually all scholars that

67. At least this was true in Plato's time. See Jerome Murphy-O'Connor, *St. Paul's Corinth: Texts and Archaeology*, GNS 6 (Wilmington, DE: Michael Glazier, 1983).

68. In the Canadian culture and especially in the GTA (Greater Toronto Area—one of the most culturally diverse areas of the world), there are incidents where women of Muslim extraction don Western dress contrary to their family's wishes, but there are also many cases where young Muslim women and girls voluntarily and even militantly don traditional Muslim dress (the burka or a Pashmina head covering with a long skirt and sleeves known as "hijab" [*ḥijab*]). Often they choose traditional dress of their own volition and resist efforts of authorities and family to persuade them to do otherwise.

69. So Winter argues (*Roman Wives*, 96).

70. However, Craig Keener, in common with Winter, proposes a different kind of class conflict than is argued here; on the basis of Greco-Roman statues of women from this period having unveiled heads, he suggests that upper-class women would show off their hairstyles following the imperial court, while lower-class women would follow a more conservative interpretation of modesty (*Paul, Women & Wives: Marriage and Women's Ministry in the Letters of Paul* [Peabody, MA: Hendrickson, 1992], 30–31).

women were flouting the convention of wearing a veil in the house church and were corrected by Paul in 1 Corinthians 11:3–16. The situation in Corinth, together with the dress-code issue and the formal features of the text, suggest that there are other, more plausible contexts than have been typically explored for the context of the passage.

1.6.2 The Practice of Veiling

The issue in 1 Corinthians 11:3–16 is primarily the proper dress code for women and men when they pray or prophesy in the house churches. The directive is far more clear than the theology that supports it: a woman should cover up or veil her head when she prays to God or prophesies in the church, but the expected behavior is the opposite for a man, who should pray and prophesy with his head uncovered. Thus the difference between men and women is not a distinction of roles in church, but rather how they function differently in those roles. Women and men may serve God in the same ministries, but there are different requirements that involve gender-specific apparel. It is not an instance of a double standard whereby men have no restrictions while women are restricted; both are restricted, but the focus of the passage is on women.

As Jennifer Heath states, "The veil is vastly misunderstood."[71] It is important to establish what the head covering meant for women in Greco-Roman culture, and what it meant to have an uncovered head. Michelle Auerback summarizes an argument for veiling: "Icons, statements, have meaning only in a culture that knows what they mean."[72] But in traditional biblical studies, most have assumed that veiling means "submission" in 1 Corinthians 11:3–16 without delving into understanding the meanings that veiling had for women in the ancient Eastern Mediterranean culture or in its continued widespread use in a number of modern cultures. As Kenneth Bailey observes, "In traditional Middle Eastern society, from the days of the Jewish rabbis to the present, a woman was and is obliged to cover her hair in public."[73] In her discussion of the background of veiling in Islam, Leila Ahmed states,

> The rules on veiling—specifying which women must veil and which could not—were carefully detailed in Assyrian law. . . . The veil served not merely to mark

---

71. Heath, introduction to *The Veil: Women Writers on Its History, Lore, and Politics*, ed. Jennifer Heath (Berkeley: University of California Press, 2008), 1.

72. Auerback, "Drawing the Line at Modesty: My Place in the Order of Things," in Heath, *Veil*, 207. Auerback is summarizing Talmud and Torah scholar Haviva Ner-David, *Life on the Fringes: A Feminist Journey toward Traditional Rabbinic Ordination* (Needham, MA: JSL Books, 2000).

73. Bailey, *Jesus*, 248.

the upper classes but, more fundamentally, to differentiate between "respectable" women and those who were publically available. That is, use of the veil classified women according to their sexual activity and signaled to men which women were under male protection and which were fair game.[74]

Assyrian law required aristocratic wives, daughters, and concubines to wear veils, but prostitutes and slaves were forbidden to wear veils.[75] Bruce Winter asserts that during the Roman Empire, "It can be confidently concluded that the veiled head was the symbol of the modesty and chastity expected of a married woman."[76] Octavian tried to legislate modesty in the way elite Roman women dressed their hair in public.[77] However, across cultures, including Roman culture, the veil was also employed as a sacred vehicle or an indication of devotion.[78]

In biblical studies much discussion is devoted to the style of the veil. The fact that styles seem to vary in paintings and statues has led some to suggest that we cannot have confidence in exactly what Paul meant by the words that are usually translated as "on his head" (κατὰ κεφαλῆς ἔχων in v. 4), "with her head unveiled" (ἀκατακάλυπτος in vv. 5, 13), and the verb "veil" (κατακαλύπτο-μαι in vv. 6, 7).[79] However, the practice, assumptions, and rationale behind

74. Ahmed, *Women and Gender in Islam: Historical Roots of a Modern Debate* (New Haven: Yale University Press, 1992), 14–15.

75. The Assyrian law on veils is recorded in a text from the thirteenth century in Middle Assyrian Law 40, in *The Assyrian Laws: Edited with Translation and Commentary*, ed. G. R. Driver and John C. Miles (Oxford: Clarendon, 1935), 407–9. Lloyd Llewellyn-Jones tentatively concludes that similar conventions applied to women in the Hellenistic period. Llewellyn-Jones's book is the definitive work for the practice of veiling in ancient Greece through the Greco-Roman world (from 900 BCE to 200 CE): *Aphrodite's Tortoise: The Veiled Woman of Ancient Greece* (Swansea: Classical Press of Wales, 2003), 121–54; see 140–42, concerning slaves.

76. Winter, *Roman Wives*, 80. See also Preston T. Massey, "Long Hair as a Glory and as a Covering: Removing an Ambiguity from 1 Corinthians 11:15," *NovT* 53 (2011): 52–72. Massey argues for the same conclusion from classical Greek literature and Plutarch.

77. Octavian's legislation gave veiling political overtones that might surprise the Western reader who may unconsciously assume the separation of church and state in matters of dress. However, veiling is currently a political hot potato in Western nations as well as the Middle East.

78. Heath, introduction to *Veil*, 4.

79. Jerome Murphy-O'Connor argues that Paul is referring to hair length ("Sex and Logic in 1 Corinthians 11:2–16," *CBQ* 42 [1980]: 482–500; Murphy-O'Connor, "1 Corinthians 11:2–16 Once Again," *CBQ* 50 [1988]: 265–74). There is also some argument that Paul is referring to a woman's hairstyle of binding her hair up modestly instead of covering her hair. See Philip B. Payne, *Man and Woman, One in Christ: An Exegetical and Theological Study of Paul's Letters* (Grand Rapids: Zondervan, 2009), 204–10. But the reasoning is based primarily on the meaning of 1 Cor. 11:15, which says that a woman's long hair is given to her as a covering. This is not persuasive, given the evidence that the use of a head covering is extensive across religions, history, and regions; examples of forms of veiling are found on statues and paintings throughout the Roman Empire, but particularly in Roman and Palestinian contexts.

the requirements to veil in the Eastern Mediterranean are consistent over a significant stretch of time, so that, while we must allow for a diversity of styles according to regions and time periods, we may draw some observations about the symbol and function of a head covering in the Eastern Mediterranean with considerable confidence, particularly since using some form of head covering was a widespread practice and moral requirement among women in early Christianity, rabbinic Judaism, and Islam in this area.[80] It usually concealed the hair, much like the head covering worn as the hijab.

1.6.3 The Western Worldview and Veiling

A primary problem is that our current consensus on how 1 Corinthians 11:3–16 has been formed and framed has been established by scholars holding a Western worldview, lacking any cultural context with which to interpret the symbol of the veil/head covering in Corinth, and not understanding the function of the veil in Islam today, particularly from the woman's point of view. Lloyd Llewellyn-Jones describes the sociopolitical baggage that veiling has accumulated. It is assumed that the veil is and was understood as an institutional form of oppression and subjugation of women in Islam, and that women of all times would resist submitting to such symbols if they had the opportunity.[81] Yet conceptions of the veiling are also used to highlight female sexuality and the concept of "oriental hedonism" with stories of kidnapping, harems, and scandal. Finally, veiling is associated with the image of terror via Muslim fundamentalism and the Islamic threat to the West.[82]

The interpretation of the text has been influenced by twentieth-century Western women's resistance to the veil and other traditional female apparel. In Iran in the twentieth century, when the culture was Westernized, women were required to remove their veils, but when conservative Islam came into power, they were required to veil again. The resistance of some women against submitting to the veil seemed to be paradigmatic of the resistance of women in Corinth. However, the fact that many Iranian women first vehemently resisted removing their veils is overlooked, partly because their experience was not part of the public discourse until much later. The course of feminism

---

80. Furthermore, Preston Massey argues convincingly that κατακαλύπτω can be understood as referring only to "textile coverings" and not unbound hair ("The Meaning of κατακαλύπτω and κατὰ κεφαλῆς ἔχων in 1 Corinthians 11:2–16," *NTS* 53 [2007]: 502–23).

81. The interpretations of women's behavior in Corinth sound a lot like bra burning in the 1960s. As one man observed to me, "It has always seemed to me that the issue in 1 Corinthians 11 is the same as what I see with parochial school uniforms—the girls are always hiking up their skirts shorter, unbuttoning their blouses lower, and wearing their sweaters tighter."

82. Llewellyn-Jones, *Aphrodite's Tortoise*, 5–6.

in the Western world, and certain practices in the 1960s and 1970s such as burning the bra, seem to have parallels to the apparent rebellion of women against similar restrictions in clothing that have been interpreted as signaling the subordinate status of women as a class. However, now we have access to women's narratives from cultures practicing women's veiling that tell another story. We find that there is a strong current of pious fundamentalist women in Islam and Judaism who choose to veil for reasons that sound quite similar to Paul's rationale in 1 Corinthians 11:3–16. However, we are not completely dependent on later anthropological parallels that run the risk of being anachronistic. The story of women who refuse to remove the veil and the reasons for wearing it may be traced back to Assyrian culture. A fuller understanding of the function of the veil in the Eastern Mediterranean results in the coherent reading of a passage that has confounded interpreters who assume that they know the situational context of the topic, and the purpose of what Paul said, even though they have difficulty in following his argument from point to point.

1.6.4 The Rationale behind Veiling

The probable basis for Paul's argument is the accepted conventions for the respectable dress of Roman matrons, together with the widespread practice of head covering in the eastern areas of the empire (including Palestine). Paul's concern appears to extend to any woman in the congregation who would prophesy and pray, including slaves, freedwomen, the unmarried, and widows.[83] The Roman matron's dress code signified her rank as well as "her status and role as a sexually mature woman in Roman society."[84] On the other hand, an unveiled head signified sexual availability, so that a woman slave or a freedwoman was prohibited from veiling.

Paul's line of reasoning supports this understanding by saying that an uncovered head represents a woman's being disgraced in a manner similar to having her head shaved, which destroys her appearance and therefore diminishes her value (1 Cor. 11:5–6).[85] This meaning of an uncovered head was

83. According to Craig Keener, both Roman women and men covered their heads in worship ("Man and Woman," *DPL*, 585). But this would not be the standard that Paul was appealing to, since he did not want men to cover their heads.

84. Winter, *Roman Wives*, 82. Winter says that a woman involved in promiscuity would not be allowed to wear the honorable clothing of a Roman matron.

85. Some suggest that a shaved head was the punishment for adultery, but that appears to have been a practice in Visigoth law; see Fabrice Virgili, *Shorn Women: Gender and Punishment in Liberation France*, trans. John Flower (London: Berg, 2002), 182. According to Virgili, the practice "reveals the sexual dimension associated with women's hair, something also recognized through the actions of displaying it, hiding it, or cutting it off" (183). However, in the Roman

shared by Roman law, which stated that if a woman was not dressed like a matron (including wearing a veil/binding her hair) and a man tried to seduce her or accost her, he was not liable for prosecution for assault.[86] This is also consistent with the convention that a woman's hair was sexually arousing, and showing one's hair was interpreted as solicitation or availability—a view that was prevalent then and still is now in some areas of the Middle East.[87] This is partly because a woman's hair was considered to be the chief element of her beauty, and men are rendered powerless (and therefore not liable) in the presence of that beauty.[88]

This explains why Paul could write in 1 Corinthians 11:15 that a woman's long hair is her glory and given to her as a natural beauty accessory (περι-βολαίου, a "cloak"),[89] and at the same time argue that she should cover it up. He argues that he wants all women to cover their hair while praying and prophesying, even those who are not allowed to veil in the culture, such as female slaves.[90] The worship service in the house church was not the time or place to signal sexual availability to the men; therefore, across the various cultures of the Roman Empire, women prayed in the churches with their heads covered (1 Cor. 11:16). Paul, in common with other members of his culture, thought that hair was sexy or a means of attraction (11:15). A modest and chaste woman's beauty was not supposed to be on public display but should be shown only to her husband.[91] In summary for that culture, a woman's

Empire the punishments for adultery were most often murder, divorce, and/or the confiscation of a woman's dowry/property.

86. Ulpian, *Dig.* 47.10.15.15.

87. For the connection of hair, beauty, and lust, see Keener, *Paul, Women & Wives*, 28–30. The talmudic tractate *Berakot* states that a woman's leg, voice, and hair cause sexual excitement. The same view about hair persists among the socially conservative in the Middle East today. Rafsanjani, a recent prime minister of Iran, defended his country's practice of requiring women to cover their hair: "It is the obligation of the female to cover her head because women's hair causes vibrations that arouse, mislead and corrupt men" (quoted in Jan Goodwin, *The Price of Honor: Muslim Women Lift the Veil of Silence on the Islamic World* [Boston: Little, Brown, 1994], 107). Troy W. Martin argues from Aristotle, Euripides, and the disciples of Hippocrates that hair was considered part of genitalia ("Paul's Argument from Nature for the Veil in 1 Corinthians 11:13–15: A Testicle Instead of a Head Covering," *JBL* 123 [2004]: 75–84).

88. Achilles Tatius indicates the function of a woman's hair in the case where Leucippe's hair was shaved: she was robbed of τῆς κεφαλῆς τὸ κάλλος ("the beauty of her head") (*Leuc. Clit.* 8.5).

89. To claim that the long hair was actually the covering that Paul had in mind creates more of a contradiction than to see her long hair as an accessory, like a beautiful cape that wraps around her.

90. Llewellyn-Jones, *Aphrodite's Tortoise*, 140–42.

91. The nature of the sexual attraction of women's hair and the fact that an uncovered head was indecent are overplayed by Martin ("Paul's Argument"), who argues that περιβόλαιον is a testicle. For a response, see Mark Goodacre, "Does περιβόλαιον Mean 'Testicle' in 1 Corinthians 11:15?," *JBL* 130 (2011): 391–96.

hair represented her feminine beauty, and the way she dressed her hair represented her honor. Beauty and honor both reflect the range of meaning of δόξα ("glory") and allow for Paul's extensive wordplay in this passage. Covered hair in public represented modesty, honor, status, and protection for a woman, and an uncovered head in public disgraced a woman and put her sexually at risk.[92]

1.6.5 Possible Reasons for Restricting Veiling

The fact that house churches were conducted in the private domain may have created confusion for the Corinthian church and raised certain questions. In the home, a head covering was not required for women because they were in the presence of relatives. Was the house church meeting in the home a public meeting, or was it regarded as a family gathering? After all, Christians used terminology from the language of family and called one another "brother" and "sister."[93] The function of veils as symbols of societal status in the church could have been an issue as well. What about women who have been prostitutes in the past, or female slaves, all of whom are forbidden by Octavian's law and other local customs to wear a veil?

A unisex dress code of an uncovered head for praying and prophesying might have been suggested as a solution by the Corinthian church leadership. The regulation of veiling was the prerogative of men; they would be the ones who would most naturally see the need to set a policy. In Roman practice, both men and women covered their heads to pray. Paul apparently taught men in the churches to pray with an uncovered head as a sign of humility, contra Roman practice (1 Cor. 11:4), so the men may have thought that what is sauce for the gander would be sauce for the goose. However, while a man's uncovered head was a sign of his humility before God, a woman's uncovered head was not a sign of a woman's humility before God; rather, it sent out a signal about her sexual availability that could be tantamount to solicitation.[94]

92. For the woman, covering her head was a sign of piety. In the Talmud, a woman was asked why she was so fortunate, and she replied, "Throughout the days of my life the beams of my house have not seen the plaits of my hair" (b. Yoma 47a in The Soncino Babylonian Talmud, trans. Leo Jung [Teaneck, NJ: Talmudic Books, 2012], digital edition). So the pious woman did not uncover her hair even at home. Rabbi Meir, in the second century, criticized a man for not divorcing his wife for a list of offenses that included unbound (unfastened) hair and bathing with men (b. Giṭ. 90a–b).

93. In anthropology and ethnography these relationships are called "fictive kinship" because they are not based on blood or marriage.

94. Note the ruling, ca. 10–22 CE, by M. Antistius Labeo in Ulpian, Dig. 47.10.15.15: Si quis virgines appellasset, si tamen ancillari veste vestitas, minus peccare videtur: multo minus, si meretricia veste feminae, non matrum familiarum vestitae fuissententiarum si igitur non matronali habitu femina fuerit et quis eam appellavit vel ei comitem abduxit, iniuriarum tenetur ("If someone solicits virgins, if nevertheless they were clothed like slaves, he appears to do less

But cultural ideals about what was proper could be abandoned by someone in favor of priorities that were ostensibly theological.

It is usually assumed without question that Paul was correcting the Corinthian women. However, the passage is more coherent if it is assumed that the Corinthian women were refusing to remove their head coverings or veils, but were being pressured or encouraged to remove their veils by those in authority, men in the house church, or possibly even their own husbands. This is a type of scenario that is being played out repeatedly in cultures that veil. Women of their own volition wear traditional dress because they are uncomfortable displaying their hair (and arms and legs) in public, or refuse to remove it in home gatherings and parties while governments, men, and even some other women family members insist on the removal for various reasons and motivations.[95] A similar scenario is repeated twice in Jewish literature. Queen Vashti refused King Xerxes's order to come out of the harem and "display her beauty" to his banquet of prominent military and political leaders (Esther 1:11). Susanna's veil was removed against her will by two corrupt Jewish elders in Susanna 1:31–33: "Now Susanna was a woman of great refinement and beautiful in appearance. As she was veiled, the scoundrels ordered her to be unveiled, so that they might feast their eyes on her beauty. Those who were with her and all who saw her were weeping" (NRSV).

Both passages demonstrate situations in which a woman's husband or authority wanted her to unveil in a public venue against the woman's will. While the men in these cases had voyeuristic motives, there could be other motivations for restricting women's veiling.

Paul's argument in 1 Corinthians 11:6 could sound corrective and confrontational to women if one presumes Western values and behavior, but the language and grammar do not demand it; it is rather explaining the

---

wrong: much less is he guilty of injury if the woman is clothed like a harlot, not being clothed as a matron, [or] if the woman was not in dress befitting a matron when someone solicits them or abducts them as a companion for himself"). Translation by Robert C. Knapp, *Invisible Romans: Prostitutes, Outlaws, Slaves, Gladiators, Ordinary Men and Women—The Romans That History Forgot* (London: Profile Books, 2011), 260. See also Kelly Olson, *Dress and the Roman Woman: Self-Presentation and Society* (New York: Routledge, 2008), 51. In addition, as Gene Green observes, "The communal gathering of the church around the meal threw men and women into a proximity that would become a source of temptation" (*Jude and 2 Peter*, BECNT [Grand Rapids: Baker Academic, 2008], 15). He based his observation in part on Sir. 9:2–9, which concludes, "Never dine with another man's wife, or revel with her at wine; or your heart may turn aside to her, and in blood you may be plunged into destruction" (NRSV). This danger was not unique to Jewish culture.

95. As Mohja Kahf asserts, "We hear story after story of the poor women forced to veil, and she exists, yet forced *unveiling* has been the experience of the last century for far greater masses of Muslim women" ("From Her Royal Body the Robe Was Removed: The Blessing of the Veil and the Trauma of Forced Unveilings in the Middle East," in Heath, *Veil*, 31).

rationale. Paul is recognizing that if a woman takes off her veil, she might as well have a shaved head, because she has been shamed.[96] Pious women in the culture who were concerned with their reputation would agree with that assessment and resist exposing themselves to shame. In addition, in this culture men were the ones who regulated veiling according to their own interests. They were most likely to object to an unqualified woman such as a slave wearing a veil in church, and would require a more detailed theological justification.[97]

There is an additional dynamic that may well be the most relevant factor in the probability that veiling was restricted. Keeping certain classes of women unveiled was considered to be in the interests of men as a group, and laws were made and enforced that prevented women who were deemed without honor from veiling, which included prostitutes, slaves, freedwomen, and women in the lowest classes. This not only signaled that such women were sexually available, but also maintained the social order and a distinction between classes.[98] There is little doubt that a male slave owner would generally object to his female slave wearing a veil for legal, social, economic, domestic, and, often, personal reasons; it was a symbol that would limit his control over her. Paul's support of *all* women veiling equalized the social relationships

96. In reminiscing about the movements against veiling in the Middle East, Kahf recalls September 28, 1982, in Damascus, where young soldiers under the socialist dictatorship were forcing women to remove their veils at gunpoint: "To try to enter into [the women's] feelings if you do not wear hijab, imagine having your blouse removed while passersby watch, or your underwear. Such a parallel is a realistic translation of a hijabed woman's mortification at being unveiled in public. Several heart attacks from this section of the city are reported in hospitals that day" (ibid., 34).

97. Carolyn Osiek and Margaret MacDonald argue that female slaves occupied a legal and ethical "grey area," where Christian masters and some church leaders may not have necessarily considered sexual activity with their slaves to be sexual sin (*A Woman's Place: House Churches in Earliest Christianity* [Minneapolis: Fortress, 2006], 95–117, esp. 109–16). See also Jennifer A. Glancy, "Obstacles to Slaves' Participation in the Corinthian Church," *JBL* 117 (1998): 481–501. On the other hand, women in Corinth are characterized by Paul as not being theologically astute, and he thinks that they might be dependent on their husbands for explanations of teaching and prophecy (1 Cor. 14:35).

98. This distinction was part of Assyrian law and inherited by subsequent cultures. See Fadwa El Guindi, *Veil: Modesty, Privacy, and Resistance* (Oxford: Berg, 1999), 11, 14; Nikki R. Keddie and Beth Baron, introduction to *Women in Middle Eastern History: Shifting Boundaries in Sex and Gender*, ed. Nikki R. Keddie and Beth Baron (New Haven: Yale University Press, 1991), 3. This was maintained by Muhammad when he ruled on the same issues (though some maintain that he required women to veil their face as well as cover their hair). He required all women in Islam to veil, with one exception: he maintained the most basic class distinction and did not allow slave women to veil, which would symbolize that they were sexually forbidden to their masters and other men. It appears to have been a political concession to his leadership and army (Fatima Mernissi, *The Veil and the Male Elite: A Feminist Interpretation of Women's Rights in Islam*, trans. Mary Jo Lakeland [New York: Basic Books, 1987], 178–88).

in the community; inasmuch as such veiling was in his control, he secured respect, honor, and sexual purity for women in the church who were denied that status in the culture.

1.6.6 Evidence That the Women in Corinth Did Not Want to Remove Their Veils

The lax ethical environment in Corinth, the reputed presence of large numbers of prostitutes, Paul's concerns about male sexual behavior, and possible "broad-minded" sexuality in the congregation indicate a potentially unsafe environment for women. According to 1 Corinthians 1:26, the majority of women in the Corinthian church were not from the elite classes. Lower-class women in such vulnerable situations would be less likely to take risks by sending potentially dangerous signals. I suggest that the kind of gentile woman who was a first-generation convert to Christianity or Judaism would want to be pious according to the culture's standards for women and wear a head covering.[99] She would tend to be more influenced by Roman law's depiction and protection of the high status of a modest woman.[100] In other words, the Corinthian women's behavior and values would reflect the double standard between men and women that was prevalent in the Greco-Roman world. On the other hand, the Corinthian men, who arguably were "broad-minded" about their own sexual behavior in Corinth and in the culture at large, would be more exposed to, and influenced by, popular Roman trends in public. Some of the men might have been quite interested in encouraging women in the congregation who were not their relatives to pray and prophesy without a veil and could easily have found a theological basis for it.

The reading that women could either be refusing to remove their head coverings in the house church or requesting the right to wear a veil not only fits the historical behavior of pious women, but also better accounts for two

99. Contra Antoinette Clark Wire, who assumes that Paul's general purpose and rhetoric are geared toward criticizing women prophets who "do not cover their heads when praying or prophesying, probably are active in speaking in tongues with or without interpretations, and are not asking their own men questions at home" (*The Corinthian Women Prophets: A Reconstruction through Paul's Rhetoric* [Minneapolis: Fortress, 1990], 17). It should not be assumed that women are always the targets of Paul's criticism, particularly given the positive statements about women in 1 Cor. 11:3–16.

100. According to Stark, Christianity's condemnation of divorce, incest, marital infidelity, and polygamy was one of the main attractions of women to Christianity and increased women's status in the church as opposed to the society (*Rise of Christianity*, 104; see the entire chapter on the role of women, 95–128). Contra Winter: "By deliberately removing her veil while playing a significant role by praying or prophesying in the activities of worship, the Christian wife was knowingly flouting the Roman legal convention that epitomized marriage" (*Roman Wives*, 96).

features in the passage. In 1 Corinthians 11:10 Paul writes, "Because of this a woman should have authority over her head [ὀφείλει ἡ γυνὴ ἐξουσίαν ἔχειν] because of the angels." If women's behavior had been the problem, then this sentence poses an interpretive problem. This is why most translations assume that ἐξουσίαν ("authority") is a figure of speech, and paraphrase it liberally as "a symbol of authority on her head" to better fit into their presumed flow of the argument.[101] However, as the subject of the sentence, the nominative "woman" is the subject of the infinitive, the one who has authority (ἡ γυνὴ ἐξουσίαν ἔχειν). If women were trying to remove their head coverings, it would appear to mean that the congregation should allow a woman to do what she wants and take it off.[102]

Therefore, the "literal" meaning of this sentence makes sense in Paul's argument if women wanted to do the correct thing and follow the practice of other churches: either women, some women, or a woman wanted to wear the head covering in the house church, especially while praying and prophesying (1 Cor. 11:16), thereby exercising good judgment in regard to veiling. The phrase "because of the angels" would then form a cohesive tie with 1 Corinthians 6:2–3: "Or do you not know that the saints will judge the world? And if the world is to be judged by you, are you not competent to settle trivial suits? Do you not know that we are to judge angels—to say nothing of ordinary matters?"[103] Women and men were supposed to be learning to exercise good judgment in ordinary matters in preparation for future responsibilities. Therefore, if women were (correctly) refusing to submit to suggestions or

101. The NET assumes that ἐξουσίαν ἔχειν refers to the veil or head covering without allowing the formal equivalent option that women are given authority over their own head (see NET notes for 1 Cor. 11:10). This is because of the parallels of 11:10 (διὰ τοῦτο ὀφείλει ἡ γυνή) with 11:7 (ἀνὴρ μὲν γὰρ οὐκ ὀφείλει). For a list of how translations interpret and add interpretive glosses to this passage so that women are not the ones with authority over their heads, see James D. Miller, "Translating Paul's Words about Women," *SCJ* 12 (2009): 61–71.

102. But see Payne, *Man and Woman*, 183, where he suggests that Paul means to "control" the head by binding the hair. See also Craig S. Keener, "Let the Wife Have Authority over Her Husband (1 Cor. 11:10)," *JGRChJ* 2 (2001–5): 146–52, where he suggests the "head" is the husband, which might reflect the mutuality of the passage and paraphrases the mutuality expressed by the woman's authority over her husband's body in 1 Cor. 7:4.

103. For another possible interpretation, see §3.5.6.1. Many commentators believe that the mention of angels refers to spiritual beings that oversee the cosmic order. These angels would be tempted to fall into lust over human women and sin or would be offended at the presence of impurity within the congregation (Mark Finney, "Honour, Head-Coverings and Headship: 1 Corinthians 11:2–16 in Its Social Context," *JSNT* 33 [2010]: 31–58, esp. 52; Joseph A. Fitzmyer, "A Feature of Qumran Angelology and the Angels of 1 Corinthians 11:10," *NTS* 4 [1957]: 48–58). Other scholars believe the angels to be human messengers from other churches, and not spiritual beings. See Alan G. Padgett, "Paul on Women in Church: The Contradiction of Coiffure in 1 Cor. 11:2–16," *JSNT* 20 (1984): 81; Murphy-O'Connor, "1 Corinthians 11:2–16 Once Again," 271.

directions to not veil or to remove their veils, the Corinthian church needed
to be convinced that women should be allowed to use their own judgment or
follow their own convictions in this matter.[104]

After suggesting that women be allowed to make their own judgment, Paul
tells the male recipients in 11:13 to learn to exercise equally as good judgment
as the women in this matter, "Judge for yourselves" (ἐν ὑμῖν αὐτοῖς κρίνατε),
to determine whether "it is proper" (πρέπον ἐστίν) for women to pray with
their uncovered heads; and the argument is that nature itself should lead
them to agree with the women. What is confusing to the Western reader is
the inference that would be obvious within the audience's culture: it is *proper*
for a woman's glory and beauty to be covered in an act of devotion and when
she is in mixed company.[105]

Therefore the passage makes sense without suggesting a figure of speech for
ἐξουσίαν ("authority," 11:10). But most translators render this as "a woman
ought to have *a symbol of* authority on her head," which actually inverts the
meaning of the grammar and vocabulary to indicate that the women should
be under authority when they pray or prophesy rather than have authority
over their own heads. However, if that were Paul's intention, there would have
been no need to use a euphemistic figure of speech that would be confusing
and unclear. Members of the Greco-Roman culture would have fully agreed
with a literal statement about a woman being under the authority of her
father, husband, or guardian. The justifications for this problematic reading
are several powerful assumptions about the passage that are not consistent
with the culture or the text: that the occasion for the letter is the Corinthian
women's misbehavior; that the head covering symbolizes submission to the
husband that Corinthian women would wish to remove; and that Paul's message is that women must visibly display their submission to their husbands
while praying or prophesying. These assumptions are not consistent with or
based on the meaning of the icon of veiling in the culture.

1.6.7 Evidence That the Corinthian Men Would Have Restricted Veiling

One indication in the text that may suggest that men are the ones who
have a problem with the head covering is a formal feature in 1 Corinthians
11:16. Paul throws down a last challenge to those who are against women
covering their heads: "If anyone [τις] wants to be argumentative [φιλόνεικος]
about this . . ." If Paul had wanted to correct women's behavior, one would

---

104. For this view, see Keener, *Paul, Women & Wives*, 39–42.
105. See, e.g., Alan G. Padgett, *As Christ Submits to the Church: A Biblical Understanding
of Leadership and Mutual Submission* (Grand Rapids: Baker Academic, 2011), 118–21.

expect the τις to be qualified by a feminine noun (γυνή), and the adjective "argumentative" could be expressed with a feminine singular form such as φιλονεικία, rather than a masculine singular adjective.[106] In the idiom of the Greek language, though the masculine may include women as referents, it could not be understood as restricted to women alone. This usage would be grammatically odd had Paul been addressing women as the opponents.

Also, notice how Paul indicates that someone may well try to fight with him over this issue. Most women in the first-century culture would have been extremely reluctant to have conversations with a man who was not her husband, let alone argue with Paul.[107] On the other hand, Paul identifies arguing and anger in the church community in Ephesus as a gender-specific problem for men (1 Tim. 2:8).

In addition, Paul's argument is theologically complex and sophisticated. Yet he indicates in 1 Corinthians 14:35 that the Corinthian women may have had difficulty in following the teaching during meetings. It is far more likely that Paul's theological discussion on veiling was geared toward men and their questions. In summary, since the practice of veiling and its restrictions were regulated by men throughout the Greco-Roman world, it makes far more sense that men would be raising the questions and suggesting restrictions on veiling. When it is understood that Paul's directive for *all* women to veil was against the cultural practice, the likelihood of Paul being in conflict with restrictions imposed by the Corinthian men is even more likely.

1.6.8 The Relationship between "Head" and Veiling

The cultural context that informs this passage illuminates Paul's brief theological answers as to why the woman should cover her head and the man should not. Paul recognizes that the head covering communicates something different for each gender. The man uncovers his head in prayer to God because his uncovered head honors God.[108] However, in Middle Eastern culture a

106. The suggestion that men were restricting veiling is supported by the grammar that can be seen in a comparison of 1 Cor. 11:16 with 1 Tim. 5:16:

If anyone [εἰ δέ τις] is disposed to be contentious . . . (1 Cor. 11:16 NRSV)

If any believing woman [εἴ τις πιστή] has relatives who are really widows . . . (1 Tim. 5:16 NRSV)

If women were the only ones who were contentious, we would expect a feminine pronoun, noun, or another feminine modifier used substantively, as in 1 Tim. 5:16.

107. See Craig S. Keener, "Learning in the Assemblies: 1 Corinthians 14:34–35," in *Discovering Biblical Equality: Complementarity without Hierarchy*, ed. Ronald W. Pierce and Rebecca Merrill Groothuis (Downers Grove, IL: IVP Academic, 2005), 166–67.

108. It is possible that it signals humility as well, in contrast to the practice of the nobility covering their head while they pray. In §3.5.5.1 we will see that an uncovered head means

woman of the proper class covered her head to signal devotion and modesty. Her covered head also directly signaled her own honor, and the honor of her family—particularly her paterfamilias, the source of her identity.[109] Paul draws upon the complex meaning of the symbol to make a theological argument for veiling based on the creation account.

Throughout the passage (1 Cor. 11:3–16), Paul associates the different practices in gender to the creation account by continual allusion, and the whole argument should be understood in that light. The language of the origins of life and creation in the image of God in 11:7–12 forms cohesive ties with 11:3. I will argue that the allusions to Genesis 1–2 in the context constrain the possible variety and range of the metaphorical meanings of "head" in the Greek language to refer to the source of life, so that it could be paraphrased, "But I want you to realize that every man's life comes from Christ, woman's life comes from man, and Christ's life comes from God." Although "head" will be discussed more fully in chapter 3, it is appropriate to discuss here how the context selects the meaning of the word "head" specifically in 1 Corinthians 11:3–16 and how Paul relates it to the cultural practice of veiling.

The English language does not have the same range of metaphorical meanings for "head" that the word κεφαλή had in ancient and Koine Greek, and the assumed connection between "head" and our phrase "head of the household" is a bond that is quickly forged and difficult to break, particularly since we know that the brain is the control center of the body. But neither of these associations is part of the Greek culture or language. Joseph Fitzmyer suggests a range of meaning that is fair as a starting point. He breaks down the semantic range of κεφαλή into four meanings. First, it means "head" in the anatomical sense of the word (the vast majority of occurrences). Second, it is a synecdoche for the whole person in a number of occurrences. Third, it has the metaphoric sense of "source" in seven sources. Fourth, he finds that the word is a metaphor for "leader, ruler, person in authority" in sixteen passages.[110] Fitzmyer concludes,

---

that a man's worship and spiritual transformation are on display, and that vulnerability may have been problematic for men of status in the Greco-Roman culture. A man with high status might want to be more invisible when he is in a posture of supplication. However, there is no conclusive evidence of when men began to remove their head coverings as a sign of humility, and some think that it began in the Middle Ages. Another problem is the practice in Judaism requiring men to wear a yarmulke during prayer, but that is likely to be a post-70 CE practice.

109. However, the recognition of patriarchy is not necessarily women's motivation in veiling, which has been clear when husbands and sons confront the women in their family to stop the practice of veiling. If patriarchy was initially foundational to veiling, women who participate in veiling have attached their own meaning and importance to it in a way that is essential to their identity, piety, honor, and their obedience to their God.

110. The interested reader can become familiar with the discussion through the following sources: Stephen Bedale, "The Meaning of κεφαλή in the Pauline Epistles," *JTS* 5 (1954): 211–15;

These examples show us that *kephalē* could indeed be used in the sense of "source." Though it does not occur in as many instances as *kephalē* in the sense of "ruler, leader," there is no reason to see it as the meaning intended in 1 Corinthians 11:3, as claimed by writers such as Barrett, Bruce, Cervin, Cope, Delobel, the Mickelsens, or Murphy-O'Connor. For the question still remains whether the meaning "source" is any better than the traditional understanding of *kephalē* as "leader, ruler."[111]

The sixteen passages in which he claims that the word is a metaphor for authority could each be reevaluated and challenged,[112] but let us assume Fitzmyer's analysis for the sake of argument and explain why "source," as in "the source of life," is a better understanding of κεφαλή in the context of 1 Corinthians 11:3–16.[113]

On the one hand, there is little "authority" language to constrain the word to mean "ruler" or "authority" so as to indicate that the message is about a husband's authority over his wife when she prays or prophesies. The references to authority in this passage are the authority of a woman over her own head (11:10) and what is considered to be proper within the cultural ideal and nature or custom (φύσις in 11:14). Furthermore, Paul does not tell women to wear whatever their husbands want them to wear. Authority is not the topic. In this passage women's function in praying and prophesying is no more restricted by their marital relationship or the authority of their husbands than men's prayer is restricted by their marital status. On the contrary, there is an explicit statement of mutuality, interdependence, and reciprocity in male-female

Robin Scroggs, "Paul and the Eschatological Woman," *JAAR* 40 (1972): 283–303; Murphy-O'Connor, "Sex and Logic"; Berkeley Mickelsen and Alvera Mickelsen, "Does Male Dominance Tarnish Our Translations?," *ChrTo* 5 (1979): 23–29; Mickelsen and Mickelsen, "The 'Head' of the Epistles," *ChrTo* 20 (1981): 20–23; Wayne Grudem, "Does *Kephalē* ('Head') Mean 'Source' or 'Authority Over' in Greek Literature? A Survey of 2,336 Examples," *TJ* 6 (1985): 38–59, also as an appendix in George W. Knight III, *The Role Relationship of Men and Women: New Testament Teaching*, rev. ed. (Grand Rapids: Baker, 1985); Richard S. Cervin, "Does κεφαλή Mean 'Source' or 'Authority Over' in Greek Literature? A Rebuttal," *TJ* 10 (1985): 85–112; Mickelsen and Mickelsen, "What Does *Kephalē* Mean in the New Testament?," in *Women, Authority & the Bible*, ed. Alvera Mickelsen (Downers Grove, IL: InterVarsity, 1986), 97–110; Philip B. Payne, "What Does *Kephalē* Mean in the New Testament? Response," in Mickelsen, *Women, Authority*, 118–32; Joseph A. Fitzmyer, "Another Look at ΚΕΦΑΛΗ in 1 Corinthians 11:3," *NTS* 35 (1989): 503–11; Fitzmyer, "*Kephalē* in 1 Corinthians 11:3," *Int* 47 (1993): 52–59; Wayne Grudem, "Appendix 1: The Meaning of *Kephalē* ('Head'): A Response to Recent Studies," in Piper and Grudem, *Recovering Biblical Manhood and Womanhood*, 425–68.

111. Fitzmyer, "*Kephalē* in 1 Corinthians 11:3," 54.

112. We will see in §3.5.1 that "head" may refer to a leader or an ancestor, but in most cases it collocates with figures of authority yet is not the equivalent of "authority." Furthermore, the meaning of κεφαλή should be determined from a larger corpus in the Greek language.

113. We will return to a more detailed discussion of the range of meaning of κεφαλή in chap. 3.

relationships: "In any case, in the Lord woman is not independent of man, nor is man independent of woman. For just as woman came from man, so man comes through woman. But all things come from God" (1 Cor. 11:11–12).

On the other hand, the references to the creation account in the passage, and particularly as in 11:7, are used by Paul to resume, explain, and expand his theological statement in 11:3. In the near context, the statement that woman came from man and woman was created for the sake of man suggests that the origin of man's and woman's life is in view in 11:3. Furthermore, this reading is reinforced by the occurrence of "head" in kinship registers, where it will refer to a parent or ancestor/progenitor as the source of a person's life, or to the image of the parent (a metaphor based on family resemblance), or what Thiselton might call a "synecdoche."[114] In this passage Paul explicitly draws a parallel between man being born from woman and woman being created from man (11:12), which indicates that he has drawn the metaphor of the man being woman's head from the language of kinship. This will be discussed in greater depth in chapter 3, in the context of gender and creation.

1.6.9 Glory and the Head

If Paul stresses the mutuality and interdependency between male and female in 1 Corinthians 11:11–12, then the question is what is in view in 11:7: "For a man should not have his head covered, since he is the image and glory of God. But the woman is the glory of the man." Some have taken this to mean that the image of God is in some way different for women and the glory is diminished in women, but this is a problematic reading of Genesis 1–2, and not the only possible reading of Paul. Rather, in Genesis 1:26–27 and 5:1–2, male and female are explicitly created in the image of God, and in Genesis 2:21–22 woman triply bears the image of God by being formed directly by God, by her extraction from man rather than from the dirt, and by being one flesh with the man in marriage. The creation of woman in God's image should be assumed. What can it mean then that man is the glory of God, but woman is the glory of man?

In the context, man shows his humility in appearing before God as the unadorned image of God, and woman shows honor to God, herself, and her family by diminishing her glory/beauty in public and in worship.[115] It appears

---

114. See Anthony C. Thiselton, *The First Epistle to the Corinthians*, NIGTC (Grand Rapids: Eerdmans, 2000), 816–22, esp. 821: "the term also functions as *synecdoche for the whole*" (emphasis original). See, e.g., Philo, *Congr.* 61; Artemidorus Daldianus, *Onir.* 1.2.

115. Keener explains, "It is far more gracious to say that than to state, 'Women are too beautiful and will distract the eyes of undisciplined men during the worship services,' although that may have been part of the problem at Corinth" (*Paul, Women & Wives*, 37).

that because of the way he applies glory to women and their hair, Paul believes that women are visually the glory of the glory—that is, women have the greater glory.[116] The fact that woman was created for man's sake (1 Cor. 11:9) indicates the purpose of her greater beauty and her attraction for men. It also indicates that Adam was the one who needed Eve as a companion, partner, and procreator; he benefited from her creation, not the other way around.[117] It is in this context that he says in 11:10 that, as a result of the circumstances of the creation of woman, all women should have the right to cover their heads during the church service. However, he is quick to say that his pronouncement does not mean he is declaring that woman is independent from man, or vice versa (11:11). This last statement may indicate Paul's awareness that his support for "women's rights" to cover their heads may override the conventional authority of some of the Corinthian men over their wives, sisters, daughters, or slaves, and he is making it clear that he is not empowering women to operate independently without consideration of their family or masters.

In this passage a woman's relationship to "a man" could potentially include a woman's appropriate concern for her family honor (whether father, husband, son, brother, etc.), as the man is biblically and existentially the source of her life and identity. However, that is not the message of the passage. Rather, Paul's argument is that the woman's "head" must be covered in worship, so that glory is directed to God.[118] The metaphor of "head" is essential to the argument. Man is the woman's head (literally), the woman's head is particularly her man's glory, and the hair on her head is her glory and the glory of her husband as well. This was true in the culture both in terms of his reputation/honor and in terms of her beauty/attraction. A woman's beauty both provokes jealousy and enhances her husband's status, which would be in direct competition with God's glory in worship. The concern is with God's honor and glory, not the honor and glory of the males in the house church, nor the glory and beauty of women who pray and prophesy.[119]

Part of the problem of interpreting the passage has been that Paul interprets women's attributes in a positive light: a woman's hair is the glory of her

---

116. For an expanded explanation, see §3.2. Contra Wire, who claims, "Paul is not using 'glory' to mean 'copy' nor even 'splendor' so much as 'honor' in contrast to shame" (*Corinthian Women Prophets*, 120). The culture combined the concepts of splendor/beauty and honor in relationship to the head covering.

117. See §3.6.

118. As Wire states, "Paul argues that an uncovered woman leading in worship disrupts or dishonors the glory of God because she represents man's glory at the time and place where God alone is to be glorified" (*Corinthian Women Prophets*, 121).

119. See §3.6.

head. Her hair is something valuable that needs to be protected and managed appropriately. While Western readers have not be able to understand why a woman would be required to cover her hair if it is her glory, Middle Eastern readers who veil believe that a woman's hair is a danger to all men and to her family's honor.[120] In Middle Eastern culture, from the past to the present, certain actions or behaviors of women are seen as vital in diminishing the status of their family. Some of these actions and relationships are standard in a given culture, such as failing to adhere to an appropriate style of dress or committing adultery. While that is the starting point of Paul's argument, and he appears to endorse the cultural ideals about the relationship of the woman to the paterfamilias, the development of his argument actually equalized the relationship between men and women, established their relative value, and brought out the reciprocity of their origin: although woman came from man, man also came from woman. His focus and concern are not reinforcing or increasing the authority or control of husbands over their wives, but rather ensuring that God is glorified, that the women are not personally disgraced or shamed while they pray and prophesy, and that they not send out an inappropriate message through their dress by displaying their hair while they minister and worship. If women were resisting taking off their head coverings, Paul was supporting them, their judgment, and their honor within the house church and within the community, possibly even against the church leadership.

This chapter has demonstrated that an understanding of the first-century Greco-Roman culture can deeply affect the interpretation of the New Testament. This study disproves the presupposition in biblical studies that the veil symbolized a woman's submission to her husband. Wearing the veil was not a private symbol, but rather a public practice regulated by law and custom, and men as well as women were expected to submit to the custom. Briefly, the veil represented a woman's honor, status, and protection. Once the practice of veiling is understood, five things become apparent:

- Men were the ones in the culture who made the laws for veiling, and they thought it was in their interest to prevent certain classes of women from veiling.

120. As Llewellyn-Jones states, "Many veil societies . . . view female sexuality as acutely dangerous and threatening to men and to the social order as a whole" (*Aphrodite's Tortoise*, 259). See his entire chapter on "Veiling the Polluted Woman" (259–81) to understand the typical pejorative nature of male ideology in cultures where that view stands in contrast with Paul's language.

- It was (and is) common for women to resist removing their veil because it symbolizes honor and protection.
- It is more likely that women who were not allowed to veil in public would want to wear a veil in the community to symbolize that they were made righteous by Christ.
- Paul's direction for all women to veil was countercultural and favorable toward women.
- The practice of all women wearing the veil equalized social relationships in the Christian community.

two

Stereotypes

Many interpreters assume that Paul reinforced gender stereotypes in the Greco-Roman culture because they believe that the household codes found in the Pauline Epistles contain simple reiterations and reinforcements of what is typical for a man's role and a woman's role in the Greco-Roman household (e.g., Col. 3:18–4:1 // Eph. 5:18, 21–6:9). This assumption is a very odd starting point for a theology of gender, given the fact that in Romans 12:1–2 Paul urges nonconformity with the culture. Paul was very cognizant of the pressures of his culture that were attempting to mold him into the stereotypical male roles of leader and orator. Paul was explicit in rejecting those models for himself and for his churches in both his theology and his exhortations.

So, is it true that "Paul never met a stereotype that he didn't like"? Did Paul accept or reinforce the gender roles pervasive in his culture? If he did not, did he at least believe that men and women were created to function in different spheres and to fulfill distinct roles? To answer these questions, I will first explore gender roles and gender theories that were prevalent in first-century Greco-Roman culture, which is the proper context of the recipients of the Pauline Epistles. I will then survey some of Paul's marked use and application of metaphors that reflect gender from the point of view of that cultural context. First I will examine masculine metaphors that are applied to all believers, and then I will look at a passage where Paul applies feminine gender metaphors specifically to men. I suggest that Paul uses and adapts common Hellenistic masculine and feminine metaphors in ways that are formational, but also in ways that are transformational. These metaphors are formational when he takes a familiar image such as a Greek athlete, or some other stereotypical gender role, and gives it a new meaning with a spiritual goal. The metaphors are particularly transformational when masculine imagery is applied to women and feminine imagery is applied to men. As a result, men and women are spiritually equipped to move their imitation of Christ to a new level. Rather than approving or appropriating the gender roles and hierarchical structures common to Hellenistic culture, Paul seeks to purposely create dissonance in the minds of his audience through his use of gender in metaphors in order to construct new identities and relationships for both males and females in Christ.

Stereotypical Greco-Roman beliefs about the nature of men and women were part of Paul's social world in Tarsus, but they are not consistent with the creation account in the Hebrew Bible, which informs Paul's theology when he is addressing gender roles (1 Cor. 11:1–16; 1 Tim. 2:8–15). Nevertheless, many recent studies on Paul assume that he was reflecting a Hellenistic worldview.[1] Some scholars find evidence of Paul's supposed acceptance of the Greco-Roman worldview when he talks about Hellenistic icons such as athletics, and they see it expressed especially when he addresses women. However, other studies, such as Robert Seesengood's analysis of athletic imagery, show that Paul altered Hellenistic metaphors and constructed new identities.[2] When Paul takes certain metaphors that are stereotypical for one gender and applies them to all believers, I suggest that he is employing an important strategy in constructing new identities. The impact of such alterations is intended to be spiritually formative for members of both genders who hear his message.

2.1 Male Metaphors Applied to All Believers

Paul often applied masculine imagery to all believers. This includes characteristics such as strength and ability in war, athletic competition, and gladiatorial

1. However, there is a shift in Pauline studies that is reevaluating Paul's relationship to Judaism and Hellenism, so that strong dichotomies between Judaism and Hellenism are no longer maintained. Rather, Judaism borrowed from and adapted to Hellenism—a strategy employed by Paul in his contextualizing of Christianity for Hellenistic culture. For instance, the collection of essays in Troels Engberg-Pedersen, ed., *Paul in His Hellenistic Context* (Minneapolis: Fortress, 1995) argues that Hellenism was central to Paul's cultural setting, and that he was at ease employing Hellenistic metaphors and argumentative styles. Paul's church-planting activities had parallels to the starting of new local cult-associations, and his interpretation of the rite of baptism reinterpreted John the Baptist's penance ritual as an initiation rite (Hans Dieter Betz, "Transferring a Ritual: Paul's Interpretation of Baptism in Romans 6," in Engberg-Pedersen, *Paul in His Hellenistic Context*, 88–117), and at times he employed rhetoric and Stoic terms in his epistles (Engberg-Pedersen, "Stoicism in Philippians," in Engberg-Pedersen, *Paul in His Hellenistic Context*, 256–90).

2. Seesengood, *Competing Identities: The Athlete and the Gladiator in Early Christian Literature*, LNTS 346 (London: T&T Clark, 2006).

combat. Strength is primarily seen as a masculine characteristic, but for Paul, strength was, above all, divine strength. He was confident in God's power working in him as an apostle (1 Cor. 2:4), and in the strength that God gave him in all circumstances (Phil. 4:13). He sought to extend the fullness of God's power to other believers. For example, he prays that the believers in Colossae would be strengthened with all power according to God's glorious might (Col. 1:11), and he also prays that the Ephesian believers would know God's incomparably great power for those who believe (Eph. 1:19). D. J. A. Clines emphasizes that in traditional societies weakness is not a desirable male trait and is associated with femininity. However, Paul boasts about his personal weakness because God's power is made perfect in weakness (2 Cor. 12:9), which is the only valid strength and power in God's church. Such a paradigm for strength relativizes the advantages of traditional male strength; Paul invites Hellenistic gentile women in Asia Minor, perhaps for the first time in their experience, to potentially share in equal power with men.[3]

2.1.1 All Christians as Spiritual Warriors

Paul uses metaphors from war to describe the role and behavior of both himself and his ministry team (2 Cor. 6:7; 10:3–4; 1 Tim. 1:18), and he uses similar metaphors to describe the Christian life in a more general sense. All believers, male and female, are exhorted to put on the full armor of God, which is the full regalia of the Roman soldier, as a metaphor for resisting evil (Eph. 6:10–17; cf. Rom. 13:12; 1 Thess. 5:8).[4] The belt is truth, the breastplate is righteousness, the footwear is associated with the gospel of peace, the shield is faith, the helmet is salvation, and the sword of the Spirit is the word

---

3. Contra D. J. A. Clines, "Paul, the Invisible Man," in *New Testament Masculinities*, ed. Stephen D. Moore and Janice Capel Anderson, SemeiaSt 45 (Atlanta: Society of Biblical Literature, 2003), 181–92. In his discussion of the concept of strength in Paul, Clines asserts, "For Paul . . . to be a man is to be strong" (182). However, the passages where Paul describes strength as accessible to believers are not limited to men. According to Paul's own admissions of weakness, his description of weak women (γυναικάρια) who are preyed upon by unscrupulous men (2 Tim. 3:6) would not disqualify such women from accessing the power of God's strength if they allow God to perfect his power in their weakness (2 Cor. 12:9).

4. Perhaps because of these Roman militaristic images of war, but even more so because of Paul's speech against his opponents and his focus upon Jesus's crucifixion, John G. Gager and E. Leigh Gibson "see Paul as a violent *personality* in his actions, his language, and in his ideology of Gentiles and their world as a world of violence" ("Violent Acts and Violent Language in the Apostle Paul," in *Violence in the New Testament*, ed. Shelly Matthews and E. Leigh Gibson [London: T&T Clark, 2005], 16, emphasis original). However, the gentile world did prove to be violent toward both Paul and early Christianity. Paul had been a violent persecutor of the church, but after conversion he himself became a target of abuse. If he identified himself with the cross, which was a symbol of violence, he did so from the viewpoint of a victim.

of God. These aspects of spiritual warfare that the armor symbolizes are essential for all Christians, regardless of their gender. By applying masculine warfare imagery to all Christians, Paul invited and encouraged women to identify directly with one of the ultimate virile male icons of their culture.[5]

2.1.2 All Christians as Athletes

Similarly, Paul uses the metaphor of the athletic contest for both himself and his ministry team (2 Tim. 4:7; 1 Tim. 6:12). Metaphorically, Paul urges the Corinthians to join with him in contests drawn from the Greek gymnasia, where Greek boys were physically trained as an essential part of their education and formation into men:

> Do you not know that in a race all the runners run, but only one gets the prize? Run in such a way as to get the prize. Everyone who competes in the games goes into strict training. They do it to get a crown that will not last; but we do it to get a crown that will last forever. Therefore I do not run like a man running aimlessly; I do not fight like a man beating the air. No, I beat my body and make it my slave so that after I have preached to others, I myself will not be disqualified for the prize. (1 Cor. 9:24–27)

Similarly, συναθλέω means "to be an athlete." It is significant that in Philippians, Paul explicitly describes Euodia and Syntyche as women who "fought" or "competed" (συνήθλησάν) alongside him as part of his team of fellow workers (Phil. 4:2–3).[6] Athleticism clearly belonged to the public sphere and was considered part of the masculine Greco-Roman gender role.[7]

In a similar passage in Philippians 3:4–15a, Paul portrays those who might take confidence in their Jewish identity or in their relationship to the law, yet he invites the mature to join him in not depending on identity markers or triumphs in the past, but rather to press on to know Christ and become like

5. Contra Clines, who apparently takes the metaphor literally, claiming Christian soldiers must be "all male, since female soldiers are hardly in view" ("Paul, the Invisible Man," in Moore and Anderson, *New Testament Masculinities*, 185). Perhaps Sandra Hack Polaski has a more serious charge: "Both Paul's culturally constructed masculinity and the structures of the language in which he writes function to marginalize women. . . . [He] writes as if the masculine gender, and indeed, the male body, is normative" (*A Feminist Introduction to Paul* [St. Louis: Chalice, 2005], 17). However, since he utilizes feminine metaphors in the same normative way, this would not be the case.

6. See Adolphus Chinedu Amadi-Azuogu's discussion "Women as 'Fellow Athletes' of Paul," in *Gender and Ministry in Early Christianity and the Church Today* (Lanham, MD: University Press of America, 2007), 11–14.

7. This is comparable to contemporary motivational practices that urge women to achievement and confirm them by calling them "studs" as a compliment.

him in his death. He utilizes the metaphor of racing toward a goal and winning the prize in a competition, yet Paul makes clear that the prize will not be exclusively his, but rather will belong to all who are mature.

> Brothers and sisters, I do not consider myself yet to have taken hold of it. But one thing I do: Forgetting what is behind and straining toward what is ahead, I press on toward the goal to win the prize for which God has called me heavenward in Christ Jesus. All of us who are mature should take such a view of things. (Phil. 3:13–15)

Robert Seesengood is struck by how Paul combines the spiritual "essence" of Hellenism with a Judaic spirit of piety through these choices of athletic metaphors. Paul has transformed the conventional athletic motif and "used a metaphor that celebrates, at its base, intense individual competition and struggle in order to articulate a new communal (non-differentiated) identity."[8] These metaphors are drawn from the masculine sphere and effectively connect images familiar to Hellenist men with the spiritual goals of self-denial, proclamation, and identification with Christ. However, it would have been more transformational for the Hellenist women, particularly for those who had led semi-segregated lives. In his metaphors and writings, Paul applies the masculine experience of competition to women converts in order to connect them with spiritual goals.[9]

The masculine metaphors of athlete, soldier, and gladiator provided women with bravery to face persecution and martyrdom, in acts that astounded people because bravery and courage were thought to be male character traits not possessed by women. Stephanie Cobb states,

> An analysis of the martyrologies reveals that Roman cultural values were at the very core of Christian identity. The stories of the martyrs depict Christians as more masculine—a principal Roman attribute—than non-Christians. The Christian identities that emerge from these martyrologies suggest that the question "Are you a Christian?" was answered by one's actions: to be a Christian was to embody masculinity.[10]

Eusebius brought this out in writing about the martyrdom of Blandina, a slave girl who provided a great example of endurance under torture for her

---

8. Seesengood, *Competing Identities*, 32.

9. It is true that, by the first century, women competed in certain events and competitions, and there were even voluntary women gladiators starting during the reign of Nero. However, they were more of a novelty at the time Scripture was written and were by no means stereotypical.

10. L. Stephanie Cobb, *Dying to Be Men: Gender and Language in Early Christian Martyr Texts* (New York: Columbia University Press, 2008), 2–3.

faith in Lyons: "[Blandina was] a small, weak, despised woman who had put on Christ, the great invincible champion."[11] His interpretation implies that Paul's exhortations to imitate both Christ and himself were understood by Eusebius as positively countering feminine weakness with masculine strength. When the young mother Perpetua was arrested for her faith, she refused to obey her father's repeated command that she sacrifice to the emperor. At the point of being executed, Perpetua had a vision where she was transformed into a gladiator: "I was stripped and changed into a man. And my supporters began to rub me down with oil, And there came forth a man wonderously tall . . . and said: 'this Egyptian if he prevails over her, shall kill her with a sword; and, if she prevail over him, she will receive this bough.'"[12] Perpetua's attitude broke with conventional femininity; the authorities noticed and retaliated with a death in the arena that symbolically humiliated her sexually. The early church noticed and celebrated her resistance for the faith, yet at the same time it toned down her defiance to better fit the expectations for women in the Greco-Roman culture.[13]

2.1.3 All Christians as Brave

Paul's command to the Corinthians to "be manly" or "to become a man" (ἀνδρίζεσθε) in 1 Corinthians 16:13 is an interesting *hapax legomenon* in the New Testament.[14] In a presentation on gender roles, Robert Saucy quoted this word in Greek with the gloss "Act like a man!" without reference to its context to support his view that the Bible taught and affirmed traditional gender roles.[15] In other words, he took it as commanding men to act within their gender role.

11. Eusebius, *Hist. eccl.* 5.1.4, in Eusebius of Caesarea, *The History of the Church from Christ to Constantine*, trans. G. A. Williamson (Baltimore: Penguin Books, 1965), 200.

12. Tertullian, *The Passion of Perpetua* 10.15–24 (3.2.3), in *Some Authentic Acts of the Early Martyrs*, trans. E. C. E. Owen (London: SPCK, 1933), 84–85. "I changed into a man" may sound like an application of Paul's command to "become a man" in 1 Cor. 16:13 (ἀνδρίζεσθε), but Tertullian's Greek text is less similar: ἐγενήθην ἄρρην, in which ἄρρην is the singular masculine nominative form of ἄρσεν.

13. See Seesengood, *Competing Identities*, 92–105; David M. Scholer, "'And I Was a Man': The Power and Problem of Perpetua," *DSar* 15 (1989): 10–14; Brent Shaw, "The Passion of Perpetua," *PastPres* 139 (1993): 5; see also 4.

14. See Johannes P. Louw and Eugene A. Nida, eds., *Greek-English Lexicon of the New Testament: Based on Semantic Domains*, 2nd ed. (New York: United Bible Societies, 1989), 2:307. Ἀνδρίζομαι is placed in semantic domain 25.165 as an attitude or emotion, under N: "Courage, Boldness." See also BDAG, 76. This word is the basis of a series of conferences that promote masculinity and male leadership (Act Like Men conferences, http://actlikemen.com), which implies that this word supports distinct gender roles and responsibilities for men. However, this word is written to the entire church of Corinth, both men and women.

15. Saucy participated in a book review of *Discovering Biblical Equality*, in a study session on "Evangelicals and Gender," Evangelical Theological Society, San Antonio, November 18, 2004.

It is often translated according to this sense in *The Martyrdom of Polycarp*: "Be strong, Polycarp, and act like a man!" (Ἴσχυε, Πολύκαρπε, καὶ ἀνδρίζου),[16] though the metaphorical sense of "Be brave!" would be appropriate for anyone facing lions in the arena. However, in 1 Corinthians 16:13 the command is unambiguously addressed to the recipients in the letter's conclusion and should be understood as a metaphor meaning "to conduct oneself in a courageous way,"[17] or "to exhibit courage in the face of danger—to be brave, to be courageous."[18] The verse reads, "Keep alert, stand firm in your faith, be courageous, be strong." The application of the command to men reiterated the culture's notion of the masculine virtue of bravery. As is indicated by the etymology of the metaphor, bravery was a male virtue and fear was a female virtue. When a woman displayed bravery, which was recognized by the Greco-Roman culture as a virtue, she was often considered to be manly in a positive sense.[19]

It seems likely that Paul's use of masculine metaphors was not understood by his audiences as primarily directed at men, nor were they considered by his recipients as irrelevant to women. Rather, masculine language opened up new possibilities and motivations for constructive spiritual behavior for women. Masculine imagery particularly provided new ways to cope with pressure and persecution. At least some Christian women were significantly changed when Paul put a spiritual sword in their hand.

2.2 Feminine Metaphors Applied to All Believers

Paul referred to himself with feminine imagery in a manner similar to how he took on the identity of a slave. There is definitely a question as to how Paul's gentile recipients would have read and understood his use of female imagery in reference to himself and other males. In the Greco-Roman culture, virtue was manly, and males were stringently cautioned against displaying any kind of effeminate behavior, dress, role-playing, or emotion.[20]

16. *Mart. Pol.* 9.1, my translation. It is a command addressed to Polycarp in the arena by a voice from heaven.
17. BDAG, 76.
18. Louw and Nida, *Greek-English Lexicon*, semantic domain 25.165 in 1:307.
19. Jorun Økland correctly states that in Hellenistic culture, it was thought by many that "women who become more and more virtuous, also become more and more manly" (*Women in Their Place: Paul and the Corinthian Discourse of Gender and Sanctuary Space*, JSNTSup 269 [London: T&T Clark, 2004], 51).
20. Similar to the traditional Greco-Roman view on women, the Hellenistic view of masculinity with polarized gender distinctions can be traced from Aristotle to Seneca. See Aristotle, *Physiogn.* 807Ib; Seneca, *Ep.* 122.7; Quintilian, *Inst.* 11.1.3. Whereas women displaying men's virtues may be admired, men who displayed characteristics considered feminine were severely criticized.

2.2.1 Maternal Imagery

Paul utilized images of childbirth and breast-feeding as metaphors for his own pastoral care. He also applied feminine imagery to the churches he addressed, though they were more often depicted as infants or children.[21] Paul most likely developed his female imagery for leadership from sources in the Hebrew Bible/Septuagint and Jewish literature.[22] For example, Paul's maternal imagery is similar to how Moses characterized God's expectations of him as a leader. Moses asked God what he had done to deserve the burden of caring for and leading the Israelites: "Did I conceive all these people? Did I give them birth? Why do you tell me to carry them in my arms, as a nurse carries an infant to the land you promised on oath to their ancestors?" (Num. 11:12). In the case of Israel, both beneficial and punitive distress is often characterized as childbirth (e.g., Jer. 4:31; 6:24). Finally, the intense responsibility of leadership was directly comparable to the responsibility of mothers and nurses, who were the primary care providers for children. Isaiah uses maternal imagery to illustrate God's compassion on, intimacy with, and commitment to Zion:[23] "Can a woman forget her nursing child, or show no compassion for the child of her womb? Even these may forget, yet I will not forget you. See, I have inscribed you on the palms of my hands; your walls are continually before me" (Isa. 49:15–16 NRSV). In other words, Isaiah infers that a mother's commitment to her child is the ultimate example of human loyalty. In the Qumran literature, the Teacher of Righteousness mixes feminine and masculine imagery:

> You have appointed me as a father to the children of mercy
>   and as a guardian to men of portent.
> They open the mouth wide like a nursing child,
>   and as a child delights in the embrace of its guardian. (1QH^a
>   20:23–25)[24]

Therefore, in light of the Hebrew Bible and Second Temple literature, the use of feminine imagery for men in leadership and even for God was not unknown. However, when Paul applied this imagery to his relationship with

21. See, e.g., 2 Cor. 6:13; 12:14, where Paul refers to the Corinthian church as infants and sees himself in a parental role of providing for them.

22. See Beverly Roberts Gaventa, *Our Mother Saint Paul* (Louisville: Westminster John Knox, 2007), 8–9. For a sample of women's labor representing distress in additional Second Temple literature, see *1 En.* 62.4; *2 Bar.* 56.6; *4 Ezra* 4.42.

23. On feminine imagery for God in the Bible, see Jann Aldredge Clanton, *In Whose Image? God and Gender* (New York: Crossroad, 1990).

24. Michael Owen Wise, Martin G. Abegg, and Edward M. Cook, *The Dead Sea Scrolls: A New Translation*, rev. ed. (San Francisco: HarperSanFrancisco, 2005), 190.

his gentile churches, the effect must have been somewhat stunning and provocative, because in the broader Greco-Roman culture men were specifically discouraged from identifying themselves with the female role.

In Galatians 4:19, Paul uses a metaphor from pregnancy and childbirth: "My little children, I'm going through labor pains again until Christ is formed in you." Paul depicted himself as in labor, yet it was the Galatians themselves who were pregnant: Christ was "being formed" in them like a fetus.[25] In 1 Corinthians 3:1–2, Paul draws upon the imagery of breast-feeding and early child care to describe the pastoral care necessary for new or immature believers: "Brothers and sisters, I could talk to you not like spiritual people but like unspiritual people, like babies in Christ. I gave you milk to drink instead of solid food, because you were not ready for it."[26] While in the Corinthian case the reference to breast-feeding them was somewhat pejorative, it was a primary metaphor for exemplary care in the case of the church plant at Thessalonica: "We did not ask for special treatment from people—not from you or from others, although we could have thrown our weight around as Christ's apostles. Instead, we were gentle with you like a nursing mother[27] caring for her own children" (1 Thess. 2:6–7).[28] It is significant that Paul identified with these biological feminine roles, which most differentiate women from men, and placed intimate feminine roles in contrast with the stereotypical dominance of male leaders.[29] Paul's use of maternal imagery for pastoral care illustrates a compatibility of pastoral care with feminine commitment and the female role of nurture, yet he does not assume that a male is incapable of comparable intimacy, care, and commitment.[30] It thus is odd that Paul

25. For an extended discussion of "The Maternity of Paul," see Gaventa, *Our Mother Saint Paul*, 29–39.

26. For an extended discussion of "Mother's Milk and Ministry," see ibid., 41–50. But also see O. Larry Yarbrough's suggestion that a male nurse was in view, in "Parents and Children in the Letters of Paul," in *The Social World of the First Christians: Essays in Honor of Wayne A. Meeks*, ed. L. Michael White and O. Larry Yarbrough (Minneapolis: Fortress, 1995), 132–33. However, a stereotypical role of a male nurse in providing milk for infants is less convincing in an age before the advent of bottles and formula.

27. It is possible that the reference to τροφός here is to a wet nurse rather than a nursing mother, often a slave who would maintain a nurturing and intimate relationship with the children and the household.

28. For further expansion on "Apostles as Infants and Nurses," see Gaventa, *Our Mother Saint Paul*, 17–28.

29. Cf. Jesus's teaching in Mark 10:41–45 // Matt. 20:24–28, where he similarly rejects the Greco-Roman model of authority in favor of assuming the status and behavior of a servant or slave.

30. In the near context of 1 Thess. 2:11–12, Paul also compares his pastoral care to a father's behavior, yet the behavior he describes is most consistent with a loving relationship that is not provided exclusively by a male parent: "As you also know, we treated each of you like a father

defines pastoral care as maternal nurturing, but historically, women have been excluded from church positions that entail pastoral care on the basis of other Pauline writings. What is even stranger is that sometimes the basis for doing so has been ontological.

2.2.2 The Imagery of Romance and Marriage

When Paul describes different relationships, he often expects men to assume a woman's role in his metaphors, and he does not hesitate to exploit romantic or even sexual roles. Often men in Western cultures find this role reversal difficult to process and may be tempted to ignore or downplay Paul's language. However, when viewed through the lens of Middle Eastern cultures, ancient or modern, Paul's projection of female status and feminine roles onto male believers would be considered far more controversial and offensive than the projection of male roles and status onto women. Paul's application of female metaphors to men would have been interpreted as insulting and galling by his recipients, just as they would be by conservative Muslim men in the Middle East today.

In 2 Corinthians 11:1–3, Paul portrays himself in the role of a father and the Corinthian church as a betrothed virgin. Paul describes himself as jealous for their sexual purity because he has promised them as a church to one husband, Christ, and he has the goal of presenting the church to Christ as a pure virgin. Paul indicates that he is afraid that they are going to lose their virginity through deception. As an illustration of the danger, he draws on the Genesis 3 account of Eve's deception by the serpent, and he is worried that the Corinthians, like Eve, will be deceived by the serpent's cunning. Paul is saying that he thinks the Corinthians are in danger of becoming like dishonored unmarried girls or women. This identifies the Corinthian church with those who are considered to be among the most shamed humans in Middle Eastern culture, because they have brought dishonor on their families and communities.

---

treats his own children. We appealed to you, encouraged you, and pleaded with you to live lives worthy of the God who is calling you into his own kingdom and glory." Appealing, encouraging, and pleading with love are not truly gender-specific behaviors, such as are childbirth and nursing. Therefore, Beverly Gaventa may overstate her claim when she says, "Maternal imagery appears in contexts referring to the ongoing nature of the relationship between Paul and the congregations he founded; paternal imagery, by contrast, regularly refers to the initial stage of Christian preaching and conversion" (*Our Mother Saint Paul*, 6). Paternal imagery that explicitly refers to Paul as a father in the Pauline Epistles is not very common. In two cases the paternal imagery refers to conversion as an event in the past (1 Cor. 4:15; Philem. 1:10), and none of the feminine imagery can be read in that way. However, Paul often refers to his recipients as his children, and he characterizes his relationship with Timothy as a father-son relationship in Phil. 2:22. The image of Paul as a father would be implied in the other references to his recipients as children.

There is a long record of "formal or functional recognition of a family's 'right to kill' promiscuous or unfaithful women" that spans recorded history.[31] Even women who are victims of rape have been killed because a woman is essentially shamed through the sexual act, and it brings shame upon her family, whether she is a willing participant or not. Under Gaddafi's regime during the recent Libyan civil war, teenage girls allegedly were raped and then forced to execute captured rebels, which was intended as the ultimate insult against the men who would dare to defy him. Therefore, Libyan males coined a saying: "Cut my throat but do not get a girl to shoot me in the back."[32] Being executed by a girl who had dishonored her family and country by her sexual impurity was an intentional insult that further shamed the victims. So, in exhorting the Corinthians, Paul is casting himself as a family member responsible for a betrothed virgin. His honor is on the line, and his audience is comparable to a woman whom he sees as capable of committing the gravest error that a woman can commit in the Greco-Roman culture.

2.3 Feminine Metaphors Applied to Men

For scholars who support Pauline authorship for Ephesians, the household codes are often thought to be incontrovertible evidence that Paul adopted Greco-Roman cultural gender roles as the biblical norm for marriage.[33] Therefore, Ephesians 5:21–25 is of particular interest in this study on account of its use of gender metaphors applied to husbands. In the address to wives, the husband's headship is compared to Jesus's own headship of the church.

31. Mohammed I. Khalili, "A Comment on Heat-of-Passion Crimes, Honor Killings, and Islam," *Politics and the Life Sciences* 21, no. 2 (2002): 38. As Matthew Goldstein observes, as early as the Codes of Hammurabi and Assura, a woman's virginity was the property of the family. Honor killings of women were part of the culture of ancient Rome, and if men did not take action against female adulterers in their family, they were actively persecuted ("The Biological Roots of Heat-of-Passion Crimes and Honor Killings," *Politics and Life Sciences* 21, no. 2 [2002]: 28–37).

32. Richard Pendelbury and Vanessa Allen, "Gaddafi's Girl Executioner," *Daily Mail*, August 29, 2011, http://www.dailymail.co.uk/news/article-2031197/Gaddafis-girl-executioner-Nisreen-19-admits-shooting-11-rebel-prisoners.html. This story was broadcast in many other venues for national and international news.

33. Ephesians is part of the Pauline corpus, but together with Colossians, it is categorized as deutero-Pauline due to its alleged unique style and vocabulary, its dependence on Colossians, and its distinctive theology (see, e.g., Werner Georg Kümmel, *Introduction to the New Testament*, trans. Howard Clark Kee [Nashville: Abingdon, 1975], 357–63). The consequence is that they are often omitted from much of the feminist and scholarly discussion about Paul's view of gender, which tends to deal with only the Pauline *Hauptbriefe*, and many scholars do not hesitate to read these *Hauptbriefe* in contradiction to the material found in Colossians, Ephesians, and the so-called Pastoral Epistles.

Jesus's headship is specifically demonstrated in his function as the Savior, who gave his life up for the church and sanctified it. The title "savior" is consistent with the male role of warrior, protector, provider, and patron in Greco-Roman culture.[34] However, gender metaphors shift when the husband is addressed.

The unit about wives and husbands is structurally focused on men's responsibility to love their wives. Their love is illustrated by the explanation of what it means to be the head of their wife, which constrains the range of the meaning of "head" and will be further discussed below with the treatment of household codes.[35] Men's function as a head is constrained and illustrated by specific examples of Jesus's relationship to the church, with the added element that the wife is the husband's body.

The instructions to husbands in Ephesians 5:21–33 are particularly interesting for our study.[36] The focus of the passage is on the husband's responsibilities, teasing out the implications of the analogy between the husband and Jesus Christ, and the metaphor of the husband as the head of the wife. These two roles assigned for the husband are often interpreted to bestow authority on the husband, but in context, Paul turns the analogy and the metaphor on their heads. The passage consists of language play that recasts the man as the bride of Christ and the wife as the man's male body. The responsibilities that Paul assigns to the husband are domestic chores delineated as women's work in the culture.

2.3.1 Husbands' and Women's Work and Roles

When the husbands are addressed, the male role is not described in terms of the expected categories of responsibilities in the public domain of warrior, protector, provider, and patron. Instead, the imagery quickly shifts to household scenes of bathing, clothing (spinning and weaving), laundering, feeding, and nurturing, because Jesus is depicted as providing these services for the church, which is both his bride and his body.[37] Bathing, spinning, weaving, and

34. The household code and its function in its context in Ephesians, as well as women's submission, will be discussed further in chap. 3.

35. See chap. 3.

36. For a more extensive treatment of Ephesians 5:1–6:9, see Cynthia Long Westfall, "'This Is a Great Metaphor!': Reciprocity in the Ephesians Household Code," in *Christian Origins and Greco-Roman Culture: Social and Literary Context for the New Testament*, ed. Stanley E. Porter and Andrew Pitts, ECHC 1 (Leiden: Brill, 2013), 561–98.

37. In view of the formal features of the text, it is strange that Ernest Best states that from 5:25 onward, "Christ's headship over the church and its subordination to him is taken for granted and used as a basis for an argument by analogy for the subordination of wives to husbands" (*Ephesians*, NTG [Sheffield: JSOT Press, 1993], 537). However, the focus of the passage and

laundering were perpetual household needs,[38] but the cleansing with water in 5:26 may include a figurative reference to a bride's prenuptial washing, and the clothing and laundering (including spot removal, washing, and ironing) in 5:27 may refer to obtaining and maintaining a bride's wedding clothes.

This depiction of Jesus's sanctification of the church is often interpreted as being fulfilled in the future culminating marriage of the Lamb,[39] but it is also an allusion to the extended metaphor of Yahweh's past adoption and marital covenant with Israel (Ezek. 16:1–13). At birth and at puberty, neither a midwife nor a mother nor a servant had love, pity, or compassion to care for the newborn Israel or to cleanse and clothe Israel when she reached puberty, so Yahweh performed these services for her.[40]

The force of the metaphor must not be lost or confused: both the Old Testament imagery and Paul are portraying God, Christ, and the husband as performing services for a bride or wife. These services are constrained to the domestic realm through either the nature of the acts themselves or the comparison to the personal care of the husband's own body. The domestic realm is the women's domain and role in ancient Greek, Hellenistic culture, and Judaism. Particularly in Hellenistic culture, these are explicit household functions that women and slaves provide for men and other women. Within the household context of bathing, laundering, and clothing—anticipating the quotation of Genesis 2:24, which speaks of becoming one flesh—Paul's extension of self-maintenance to the wife would similarly sound like a role reversal to a Hellenist. The preparation and serving of food was women's or slaves' work, as was all household care that involved nurturing (θάλπει, Eph. 5:29).[41] Besides childbearing, one of the primary purposes for obtaining a

---

the force of the imperatives are clearly placed on the husband's role and responsibilities, while the references to wives submitting and honoring are almost asides, most likely because they are "given information" for the culture. There is no argument about the wife's submission.

38. See Craig S. Keener, *The IVP Bible Background Commentary: New Testament* (Downers Grove, IL: InterVarsity, 1993), 552.

39. See, e.g., Thomas R. Schreiner, *Paul, Apostle of God's Glory in Christ: A Pauline Theology* (Downers Grove, IL: InterVarsity, 2001), 221.

40. The treatment of a newborn was ordinarily performed by a midwife. See John H. Walton, Victor H. Matthews, and Mark W. Chavalas, *The IVP Bible Background Commentary: Old Testament* (Downers Grove, IL: InterVarsity, 2000), 701.

41. The word θάλπω is used only one other time in the New Testament, in 1 Thess. 2:7, to refer to a nursing mother (or possibly a wet nurse) in a similar context where Paul compares his apostolic ministry among the Thessalonians to maternal care of an infant. Harold Hoehner, favorably quoting Ralph Martin, says that ἐκτρέφει and θάλπει are affectionate words "from the language of the nursery" (Hoehner, *Ephesians: An Exegetical Commentary* [Grand Rapids: Baker Academic, 2002], 766, citing Martin, "Ephesians," in *The Broadman Bible Commentary*, ed. Clifton J. Allen [London: Marshall, Morgan & Scott, 1971], 11:170). They are even used

wife is that she will provide these services or manage the household so that
slaves can provide them.[42]

2.3.2 Men as Christ's Bride

To top it all, we must not lose sight of the fact that in this passage men not
only are the grooms or husbands, but also are included in the figure of the
church, the bride of Christ, which is his church. As members of the church,
men receive the love, nurture, and care from Christ (Eph. 5:29). Together
with other believers, they have been turned into a radiant bride by Christ,
washed, cleaned, and clothed in feminine wedding garments (5:26–27).[43] The
depiction of the church as Christ's bride not only refers to wearing women's
clothes, but also explicitly refers to the sexual union where the two become
one flesh. The positive view of the church's feminine role in the unity of the
sexual union challenges the Greco-Roman view of the sex role of the female
as one who is shamed and dominated through penetration. The culture's
pejorative female sexual role is reversed so that in Christ all believers share in
the same relationship to him not only as his bride, but also as his body and
his siblings, who are equal heirs. If this reading is correct, then a proposed
later authorship of Ephesians as originating in the gentile churches some
fifty years after Paul's death is less plausible because it appears to be rooted
firmly in a Second Temple Jewish worldview that is opposed to and directly
confronting a Greco-Roman worldview of gender.

Therefore, we may conclude that female metaphors were applied to the
men in Pauline gentile churches in a way that was not only spiritually formational, but also countercultural and transformational. It moved them out
of their culturally defined space in the same way that women were able to
stretch beyond their culturally defined limitations when Paul applied masculine metaphors to all believers. In Ephesians 5:22–23, the cultural expectation
of women's submission is reinforced, but in reality the inferiority and low

---

for breast-feeding. While the LXX occurrences are not limited to women's work, they certainly
are in that register when occurring with other household responsibilities.

42. Clinton Arnold cites Best, *Ephesians*, as the source for a papyrus marriage contract that
"delineates the husband's responsibilities for his wife: 'to cherish and nourish and clothe her'"
("Ephesians," in *Zondervan Illustrated Bible Backgrounds Commentary*, ed. Clinton E. Arnold
[Grand Rapids: Zondervan, 2002], 334). However, Best gives no information on the papyrus, but
in turn cites Friedrich Preisigke, *Wörterbuch der griechischen Papyrusurkunden* (Amsterdam:
A. M. Hakkert, 1969), 1:665, and produces this text: θάλπειν καὶ τρέφειν καὶ ἱματίζειν αὐτήν.
However, this is not a marriage contract; it is a widow's petition for justice, taken from Jean
Maspero, *Papyrus grecs d'époque byzantine* (Cairo: Institut Français d'Archéologie Orientale,
1911), vol. 1, no. 67005: 18–33; see 33, line 132.

43. At the same time, women become the man's male body (Eph. 5:28–29).

status of women are subverted when men are commanded to exercise their headship by acting more like women. More specifically, by bathing, clothing, feeding, and nurturing the women, men are treating women as the superior when viewed from within the Greco-Roman cultural paradigm. On the other hand, the function of the entire church as Christ's bride reverses the shame that was directly connected with the female's sexual function in the Greco-Roman culture. Therefore, the passage beautifully illustrates mutual submission within a relationship that is legally hierarchical in the Roman Empire, and recasts the female gender positively, in a way that reflects the evaluation of woman in the creation account (Gen. 1:31).

This chapter shows how Paul utilized and redefined gender stereotypes in the Greco-Roman culture regularly in his epistles. It has done this by showing how he utilized gender-specific masculine behavior to describe all believers, including women, and how he utilized gender-specific feminine behavior for all Christians and unmistakably attributed women's work and roles to husbands also. In addition, he gave a positive evaluation of women that was in stark contrast with the Aristotelian Greco-Roman appraisal of women. Like Jesus, he challenged the presuppositions of the Greco-Roman hierarchy that were based on male priority and preeminence. The question is this: What did Paul mean, intend, and seek to do and accomplish in the way he has used the Greek language? Clearly, he was not committed to defending the Greco-Roman gender roles. Nor was he supporting the Roman imperial theology and the hierarchy upon which Caesar's authority rested. The answer is that he was attempting to equip male and female believers to follow Christ. Women needed to make adjustments to their identity and function in order to exercise power, conduct spiritual warfare like a warrior and gladiator, and pursue spiritual goals like an athlete. They needed to grow up to maturity rather than metaphorically remain in immaturity under a guardian. Men (including Paul) needed to make adjustments to their identity and function in order to recognize vulnerability, nurture other believers, quell aggression, and follow Christ in humility, suffering, and submission. We will see that Paul recognized gender differentiation, but that he continually referred to the creation account for his understanding and argument about how male and female operate in the "already and not yet" eschatological Christian community.

three

Creation

Paul refers to the creation account when he addresses gender issues such as the relationship between a husband and wife. He particularly finds deep theological significance in the creation of woman from man, and he uses the creation passage to support certain practices in the church and household and to shed light on profound theological mysteries.[1] Without question, the purpose for male and female at creation is foundational in any discussion on gender, but in the Pauline corpus it cannot be studied apart from the fall and eschatology. Paul assumes the purposes of creation when he discusses their eschatological fulfillment in the new creation. He is deeply interested in (1) how Jesus Christ fulfilled the purposes God intended for humanity at creation, (2) how Jesus reversed the effects of the fall, and (3) how God has and will complete his purposes for humanity, both male and female, in Jesus Christ. Therefore, Paul's understanding of the purposes behind the creation

---

1. The contexts are often misidentified or unrecognized in two of the most important passages on gender: 1 Cor. 11:3–16 and 1 Tim. 2:8–15. The context of 1 Cor. 11 is order in worship for women and men, but it is more often treated as if it were a household code concerned with submission between husbands and wives. On the other hand, it is usually assumed that the context of 1 Tim. 2:1–15 is order in worship for women, but key factors suggest that 1 Tim. 2:8–15 is a partial household code and 1 Tim. 2:12 addresses the behavior of a wife and husband (see §9.1.5). One primary reason for the confusion is that in Greek γυνή means "woman" and "wife," and ἀνήρ means "man" and "husband" and can also be the default for "person" in the same way that "man" is sometimes used in English. Part of the contribution of this study is to make an argument for these alternate contexts and to demonstrate the impact of these contexts on interpretation.

of humanity is revealed most fully in his discussions of Christ's work as the second Adam, the believer as part of the new creation, and human eschatological destiny.

I have already raised some of the issues that relate to gender and creation, but now we will look at each concern specifically in the context of the creation account. These concerns include how Paul relates the image of God to male and female, how he relates the glory of God to male and female, what Paul believes the creation account reveals about the destiny of humanity, what the order of creation determines for male and female in Paul's writing, and how Paul relates creation to his discussions of headship. Paul's references to the creation of male and female must be carefully examined in terms of what he actually said, what the creation account says, and how it fits into the context of his argument.

Studies on the citation of the Old Testament in the New Testament caution against the uncritical importation of a given citation's context. However, when Paul's use of the creation account in Genesis 1–2 consists of allusions to the narrative or narrative summaries rather than creative wordplay or textual support of an argument that is divorced from the original context, it draws one's attention to the source text. Therefore, when Paul alludes to the creation of male and female in 1 Corinthians 11:3–16, Ephesians 5:21–33, and 1 Timothy 2:11–15, the allusions activate the entire narrative for the reader. Paul interprets Genesis, and Genesis in turn interprets Paul.

It has been claimed that Pauline instructions based on the creation account must be normative.[2] However, there should be no a priori assumption that any Pauline command, prohibition, or instruction supported by the creation account is a "transcendent norm" (or a universal conclusion) as opposed to an occasional or culturally bound application. Confessional traditions agree that all Scripture, including the creation account, is useful for reproof and correction (2 Tim. 3:16), which includes specific applications to problems that are limited to situations and culturally bound issues. Therefore, any assumption that a citation of the creation account must indicate a transcendent norm is a problematic presupposition. Both Jesus and Paul believed that the biblical account of the creation of humanity as male and female conveys transcendent norms about gender, but Paul also cited it to support his argument for veiling in 1 Corinthians 11:3–16, which is a culturally bound application. It is a logical fallacy to suggest that transcendent norms or universal premises can be used only to support normative or universal

2. See, e.g., Thomas R. Schreiner, *Paul, Apostle of God's Glory in Christ: A Pauline Theology* (Downers Grove, IL: InterVarsity, 2001), 408–9.

conclusions.[3] A biblical understanding of creation may be applied to specific situations involving specific individuals, be embedded in a dialogue, address problematic theology or practice in a Pauline church, or critique the Second Temple or Greco-Roman culture. In addition, this erroneous hermeneutical restriction of citations or allusions to the creation account to transcendent norms is inconsistent with the best evangelical hermeneutic and homiletic traditions, which attempt to find relevant, fresh, and specific applications of scriptural norms for their contexts in every sermon.

Some interpreters have suggested that, according to Paul, women do not bear the image of God in the same way as men, and some have supported primogeniture in the order of creation—that is, the order of creation indicates the priority of men. Most have found hierarchical authority in "headship" and, similarly, have considered it a fact that Paul taught that woman was created to serve man as a subordinate assistant. But are these interpretations the best readings of the Pauline texts on creation? Are these suggestions consistent with more general categories of Pauline theology? These assertions can be tested in the light of the Pauline texts.

3.1 Gender and the Image of God

Scripture begins with creation in Genesis 1 and climaxes with the creation of humanity, male and female, in God's image:

> So God created humankind in his image, in the image of God he created them; male and female he created them. God blessed them, and God said to them, "Be fruitful and multiply, and fill the earth and subdue it; and have dominion over the fish of the sea and over the birds of the air and over every living thing that moves upon the earth." (Gen. 1:27–28 NRSV)

Paul alludes to this passage every time he talks about the images of Adam and God in humanity and of the image of God in Jesus Christ. Thus Paul refers to humanity as bearing the image of Adam (the man of "dirt") as a result of the fall, but Jesus Christ as bearing the image of God, so that believers in Christ bear both his image and the image of God (1 Cor. 15:49; 2 Cor. 3:18; 4:4; Col. 1:15; 3:10). According to D. J. A. Clines, in the new creation, as described in Colossians 3:10–11, God creates a "'new human' . . . 'according

---

3. This logical fallacy consists of an incorrect understanding of how syllogisms may involve universal propositions and specific applications. Therefore, the assumption that the creation account would support only "omnitemporal norms" is what D. A. Carson calls an "improperly handled syllogism" (*Exegetical Fallacies*, 2nd ed. [Grand Rapids: Baker, 1996], 94–101).

to the image of its creator,'" an action that "overlooks or dissolves the boundaries between Jew and Greek, slave and free, male and female."[4]

However, in 1 Corinthians 11:7, Paul states that man "is the image and glory of God; but woman is the glory of man" (TNIV). In this verse Paul conflates Genesis 1:27 with the narrative in Genesis 2, which specifies that woman was created out of man. Clines writes,

> In 1 Corinthians 11:7 Paul speaks of males (anēr) generally (not Christian men specifically) as "being" (hyparchōn) the image and glory of God, and implies women are not. Because every male "is" God's image and glory (presumably meaning he is created after God's image and expresses God's glory), every female is subordinated to man and expresses that male's glory.[5]

Clines infers that Paul "implies" that woman was not made in the image of God at creation. He further infers that the phrase "woman is the glory of man" indicates subordination. Nevertheless, under the heading "In Reference to Christians," Clines states that in Colossians 3:10–11 Paul explicitly includes the female believer as being the "'new human'" who is "progressively 'renewed' . . . 'according to the image of its creator.'"[6] Clines's first inference places Paul in flat contradiction to Genesis 1:27 and Genesis 5:1–2, where it is said that woman was created in God's image. He fails to deal with the fact that female believers' "renewal" (τὸν ἀνακαινούμενον) to God's image in Christ (Col. 3:10–11) becomes paradoxical. With Clines's understanding, woman would be renewed to something that she was not created to be and so places Paul in contradiction with himself.[7] Notice that he highlights the woman's subordination but does not refer to the man's subordination in his headship relationship. His belief that being the "glory of man" indicates subordination contradicts the female's share in dominion in Genesis 1:28, and misses the positive association of glory in 1 Corinthians 11:3–16 (discussed below).[8] This is a case where Genesis should interpret Paul, and the Pauline corpus should interpret Paul.

4. Clines, "Image of God," DPL, 427. This view was included without an alternative view in a dictionary that expresses established conclusions and "summarized discussions" (Gerald F. Hawthorne, Ralph P. Martin, and Daniel G. Reid, preface to DPL, ix). Thus, according to this reference work, Paul taught that women are not in God's image, a view taken to be an established conclusion and not particularly controversial in mainline scholarship.
5. Clines, "Image of God," 427.
6. Ibid.
7. Paul makes it clear elsewhere in the corpus that all those in Christ are being changed from glory to glory, into Christ's image, who is the image and glory of God (e.g., Rom. 8:29; 2 Cor. 3:18).
8. Typically, 1 Cor. 11:3–16 is read as a polemic against the Corinthian women and as entitling men to have authority over women, even though the topic is about men and women leading in

In Genesis 1:27 and 5:1–3, it is said that Eve was specifically created by God in his own image. In Genesis 2:21–24, Eve was also in the image of Adam because she was bone of his bones, flesh of his flesh, and one flesh in marriage (cf. Eph. 5:31). Therefore, Eve is threefold in the image of God because Eve was formed directly by God in his image; she was formed from Adam, who bore God's image before the fall (in contrast to Adam, who was formed from dirt); and she became one flesh with Adam in their sexual union. It follows that Paul's specific assertion of the female believer's *renewal* to God's image in Colossians 3:10–11 is consistent with the creation of Eve in Genesis, not a non sequitur. Therefore, the creation of male and female in the image of God is clear from the Genesis narrative, and the renewal of male and female in the image of God is a dominant theme in Paul. The assumption that women were created in the image of God may legitimately be used to interpret 1 Corinthians 11:7.

How, then, can we understand 1 Corinthians 11:7, where Paul asserts that man is in the image and glory of God, but woman (in contrast) is the glory of man? The answer is that Eve, like every descendent of Adam and Eve, had a multiple identity. For example, we may justifiably infer that Paul would say that Seth, the son of Adam and Eve, was in God's image. However, Genesis emphasizes that Seth was in Adam's postfall likeness, "according to his image" (Gen. 5:3). Paul similarly contrasts the image of Adam in humanity with the image of Christ/God in a way that appears to be mutually exclusive: "Just as we have borne the image of the man of dust, we will also bear the image of the man of heaven" (1 Cor. 15:49 NRSV). Therefore, Seth and all men after Adam have a multiple identity in that they retain the image of God but are also in the image of Adam, their fallen progenitor, if they are not in Christ.

This provides a paradigm, or a very close analogy, that helps us to understand what Paul is saying about woman. Similar to Seth, Eve had a multiple identity: she both was made in the image of God and was the glory of Adam because she was created directly from him. She was uniquely in Adam's image and even a part of him, so that they were one flesh in a way that was inseparable and distinguished from the descendants' relationship to the parents (Gen. 2:23–24). If every man is the glory of God in the pattern of Adam, then, as Paul infers from the creation passage, woman in the pattern of Eve is the "glory of the glory," which matches the force of Adam's positive evaluation

---

the same way (by praying and prophesying), and the text states nothing directly about man's authority. However, being "the glory of man" as opposed to being the "glory of God" is taken as a corrective "lesser glory."

in Genesis 2:23–24. It is something more, or something in addition, that is included in her multiple identity rather than something less, secondary, or missing.[9]

3.2 The Glory of God and the Glory of Man

Paul sees a distinction between the glory of men and the glory of women in their appearance.[10] When Paul looked at a man praying and prophesying, he saw the action of uncovering his head as reflecting the image and glory of God, and his appearance was in harmony with the worship of God (1 Cor. 11:4, 7).[11] The man glorified God unless he grew long hair in an effort to appeal and seduce with his appearance.[12] This practice would be disgraceful or degrading for both men and women in the context of worship, since long hair was not considered glorious for a man (1 Cor. 11:14).

In contrast, Paul states that woman is the glory of man, and her hair is her glory. Paul's statements that woman is the glory of man (v. 7), woman was created for man's sake (v. 9), and every man is born from a woman (v. 12) have strong textual ties with 1 Esdras 4:14–17, which clarifies what Paul meant. In other words, there are too many associations between Paul and 1 Esdras 4:14–17 for them to be coincidental. Paul's allusion to "woman is the glory of man" has been confusing to interpreters, but in the light of 1 Esdras, the meaning becomes clear. It is also closely associated with the creation account, so that it provides a narrative framework to understand

9. On the other hand, in the Genesis account, it was "not good" for man to be without woman (Gen. 2:18). The account stresses Adam's need for Eve.

10. This is in agreement with Philip Payne in that the issue is appearance (*Man and Woman, One in Christ: An Exegetical and Theological Study of Paul's Letters* [Grand Rapids: Zondervan, 2009], 204; cf. 204n24).

11. Paul's restriction against men covering their heads corrected a Roman practice of wearing the toga over the head during prayer or sacrifice, as shown in a statue of Augustus in Corinth. For an overview of the practice, see David E. Garland, *1 Corinthians*, BECNT (Grand Rapids: Baker Academic, 2003), 517–18. However, Garland argues that it is not a correction of a problem but only hypothetical. It is not clear why he takes that position, unless he is simply convinced that the argument is directed against women and supports men. He claims that the shame or dishonor of covering the head lies in the association of the headdress with pagan sacrifice (ibid., 518). However, this is not supported by any feature in the text. The practice may have been associated with men of status.

12. See Payne's argument, where men's long hair refers to "effeminate hair" (*Man and Woman*, 200–204), which would correct or hypothetically avert any attempt in the congregation of men seducing men. Since bisexuality was rampant in the culture, it could have been a potential problem in Corinth. At least in principle, a man's use of hair for display and seduction could be distracting and problematic for everyone. Paul's pejorative statement about long hair for men corresponds with similar statements in the Greco-Roman culture.

the passage.[13] In the context, three of King Darius's bodyguards hold a contest in which they must name one thing that is the strongest. The first says "wine," the second says "the king," and the third argues convincingly that women are stronger than either of them, but truth is the strongest of all.

> Gentlemen, is not the king great, and are not men many, and is not wine strong? Who is it, then, that rules them, or has the mastery over them? Is it not women? *Women gave birth to the king and to every people that rules over sea and land. From women they came*; and women brought up the very men who plant the vineyards from which comes wine. Women make men's clothes; *they bring men glory; men cannot exist without women.* (1 Esd. 4:14–17 NRSV, emphasis added)

In 1 Esdras 4:17, the statement that women bring men glory, or rather produce glory for men (ποιοῦσιν δόξαν τοῖς ἀνθρώποις), may be recast in the singular as "woman is the glory of man." This by no means indicates subordination, as Clines assumes,[14] but rather describes the power that women have over men. Understanding this passage as an allusion to 1 Esdras 4:14–17 explains why Paul qualified his statements with the caveat "Nevertheless, in the Lord woman is not independent of man" (1 Cor. 11:11).

Like 1 Corinthians 11:3–16, so also 1 Esdras 4:14–22 forms strong textual ties with Genesis 2, not only with the statements that women produce glory for men, and that men cannot exist without women,[15] but also with the climax of the passage in Genesis 2:24, where a man leaves his father and mother and clings to his wife:

> If men gather gold and silver or any other beautiful thing, and then see a woman lovely in appearance and beauty, they let all those things go, and gape at her, and with open mouths stare at her, and all prefer her to gold or silver or any other beautiful thing. A man leaves his own father, who brought him up, and his own country, and clings to his wife. With his wife he ends his days, with no

---

13. Thus 1 Cor. 11:7–15 demonstrates complex textual relationships with Gen. 2 and 1 Esd. 4:14–22. This is an issue involving the use of the Old Testament in the New Testament. Steve Moyise states that there are three ways to understand these textual allusions: intertextual, narrative, and rhetorical (*Paul and Scripture: Studying the New Testament Use of the Old Testament* [Grand Rapids: Baker Academic, 2010], 111). In this case, the idea is that Paul is evoking narrative frameworks from both Genesis and 1 Esdras.

14. Clines assumes, "Because every male 'is' God's image and glory (presumably meaning he is created after God's image and expresses God's glory), every female is subordinated to man and expresses that glory" ("Image of God," 427).

15. In light of Gen. 2:18–20, "Neither was man created for the sake of woman, but woman for the sake of man" in 1 Cor. 11:9 (NRSV) indicates that man needed woman. See §3.6.

thought of his father or his mother or his country. Therefore you must realize that women rule over you! Do you not labor and toil, and bring everything and give it to women? (1 Esd. 4:18–22 NRSV)

This passage is consistent with enduring beliefs in the Middle East that woman's beauty is dangerous and causes men to lose control.[16] A woman's hair is a primary part of her beauty, which is the rationale behind veiling. If a woman prays or prophesies with an uncovered head, the glorious appearance of her hair competes with the worship of God because it displays the "glory of man" (1 Cor. 11:15).[17] As far as a woman was concerned, her uncovered head was a stigma because it symbolized sexual availability, impurity, and low status in the culture (1 Cor. 11:5–6).[18] If the symbolism of the veil is properly understood and the flow of Paul's argument is carefully followed, one can arrive at the same understanding of 1 Corinthians 11:7–16 without reference to 1 Esdras 4:14–22. However, the identification of these textual ties should be convincing to those who are open to understanding the Pauline corpus in its first-century literary and cultural contexts.

The problem was that a woman's uncovered head both detracted from the glory of God and shamed the woman. A woman's head covering diverts attention away from man's glory to God's glory.[19] Eve was created to power-fully attract Adam, which was the point of the positive climax of creation,

16. Men typically have considered women's beauty to be not only superior to men's, but also extremely dangerous. This seems to be in palpable contrast to the messages that Western women receive. Western women are more likely to pick up messages of inadequacy about their appearance—hence the epidemic of eating disorders. The Platonic influence on Christianity and the growth of asceticism may have nurtured a persistent aberrant reaction or approach-avoidance not only to sex, but also to women, which Paul did not share.

17. On the basis of 1 Cor. 11:15, Payne argues that modest hairstyles are in view instead of shameful head coverings (*Man and Woman*, 204–7); see also Elisabeth Schüssler Fiorenza, *In Memory of Her: A Feminist Theological Reconstruction of Christian Origins* (London: SCM, 1983), 226–30. Payne and others cannot understand why a woman would be required to cover her "glory," or how the hair could be a cloak and still need an additional covering. However, the attraction or glory of a woman's hair is precisely the reason why various cultures wanted it covered, and this is a pervasive practice. "Cloak" should be taken as adornment or a beauty accessory given by nature and reserved for a woman's husband. Nevertheless, Payne's basic understanding of the flow of the argument is consistent with this study. Similarly, the suggestions that "authority on the head" must be a headdress that indicates the woman's authority to use prophetic speech is unlikely not only in view of the idiom, but also given the demonstrably wide practice of women veiling for modesty. Contra Morna D. Hooker, "Authority on Her Head: An Examination of 1 Corinthians 11:10," *NTS* 10 (1964): 410–16.

18. On the rationale of the veil and the culture's view about women's hair, see §1.6.4.

19. Thus Paul's discussion beautifully illustrates the universal approach-avoidance to woman's beauty as the source of pride and shame for herself and her family.

but worship is not the time or place to experience that dynamic.[20] Rather, prohibiting women from wearing veils in the house church was inappropriate, unsafe, and disrespectful to women and their families.[21] On the other hand, if men were trying to prohibit female slaves, freedwomen, and lower-class women from wearing veils, Paul was protecting the most vulnerable members in the church and granting them the dignity and status of a sister in Christ. Whatever the case, by arguing on behalf of all women, Paul subverted several aspects of the Greco-Roman culture with this mandate, including the status and entitlement of men, as well as women of high status, who were the beneficiaries of the cultural regulations and restrictions on veiling.[22]

In conclusion, though woman is man's glory (in contrast with man being only the image and glory of God), it does not follow that Paul is indicating that woman does not bear the image of God, or that she has a lesser glory than the man. The Pauline corpus maintains that all believers, male and female, are on exactly the same footing in terms of the ontological image and glory of God. Female believers are renewed in the image of God in the

20. In the much less segregated worldview of Western culture, the responsibility of women to be modest in appearance needs to be balanced with men's responsibility to resist lust (cf. Matt. 5:28). This is illustrated in Garrison Keillor's description of the author's inappropriate daydreams about "copulation" in church. Here he fixates on a woman in the pew in front of him, attracted by her neck and hair: "Once again your mind drifts from the shore as your eyes settle on the back of Joyce Johnston's neck, the part in her hair and two stout braids, which never interested you before but suddenly your mind slips into dark waters, you and she are by the creek, and she takes off her dress—*just like that*! Says, 'Let's go swimming,' and takes off her dress—no underwear, naturally, and you can't help but look at her, this fine woman, a pillar of the youth program, now naked in bright sunlight, walking into the water and holding your hand, and now you turn and embrace—and right then, Bob snapped his Bible shut and descended from the pulpit" (*Lake Wobegon Days* [New York: Penguin, 1986], 323–24). The avoidance of this dynamic is the justification behind many women choosing to wear a hijab.

21. Garland writes that Paul's "purpose is not to write a theology of gender but to correct an unbefitting practice in worship that will tarnish the church's reputation" (*1 Corinthians*, 514). However, since Paul is suggesting that all women veil, the practice is countercultural because female slaves, courtesans, freedwomen, and lower-class women were not allowed to veil. Rather, the issue appears to be the focus of worship and demonstrating respect to all without prejudice.

22. There is a comparable scenario in the history of Islam that illustrates ways in which men had a vested interest in the practice of veiling. Muhammad ordered that all Muslim women wear veils in order to stop them from being sexually harassed in the streets of Medina: disrespectful treatment of his wives constituted a direct insult. However, the army rebelled against female slaves veiling, and Muhammad reluctantly relented because it was a time when he needed the army's support. The result was that only free women were allowed to veil and were protected from sexual harassment and exploitation in the streets. In other words, the veiling of slave women was contrary to the interests and rights of the slave owners, and contrary to the interests of men in general, who believed that the sexual availability of this group of women was their right. See Fatima Mernissi, *The Veil and the Male Elite: A Feminist Interpretation of Women's Rights in Islam*, trans. Mary Jo Lakeland (New York: Basic Books, 1987), 178–87.

same way as men. However, when it comes to external appearance, there is a difference between the glory of men and the glory of women. In common with the culture, Paul believed that God created women to be more attractive or more glorious, so that she is the glory of man. This becomes a pragmatic problem at the very point when women attempt to manifest the Spirit in prophesying (1 Cor. 11:5; 12:7, 10), or when they lead in prayer in order to worship God. However, the mandate to veil should be understood neither as a polemic against women nor as a subordination of women to men, because veiling was their protection and a sign of whatever status and honor a woman could possess in the Greco-Roman culture.[23] Therefore in cultures that veil, women have often tried to resist the command by husbands or authorities to unveil. It was a privilege and a protection that Paul extended to all women in the congregation in reformation of the cultural practice.

3.3 The Purposes and Destiny for Gender in Creation

As argued above, when Paul alludes to Genesis 1–2, it should lead us to read the two texts together. Paul is interested not only in the image of God being renewed in humanity across the boundaries that include race, status, and gender, but also in creation's mandate in Genesis 1:28: "God blessed them, and God said to them, 'Be fruitful and multiply, and fill the earth and subdue it; and have dominion over the fish of the sea and over the birds of the air and over every living thing that moves upon the earth'" (NRSV).

However, Paul reveals his understanding of the purposes of creation primarily in his description of the fall's effects and his eschatological discussions of restoration and renewal at Jesus's second coming. Briefly, life that was created to multiply was subjected to decay and death (Rom. 5:12–14; 6:23; 1 Cor. 15:21–22),[24] and the good creation that was supposed to be ruled by humanity was subjected to futility (Rom. 8:19–22). Humans, who were created to rule together in unity, became divided in hostility and embedded in patterns of oppression, which, according to the creation account, started with male and female and extended to include groups such as Jews, gentiles, slaves, and free persons (1 Cor. 12:13; Gal. 3:28; Col. 3:11).[25] Through Jesus Christ, God is

---

23. On the meaning of the veil, see §1.6.

24. Anthony Thiselton summarizes, "All humanity is trapped in the corporate and structural consequence of sin" (*The First Epistle to the Corinthians: A Commentary on the Greek Text*, NIGTC [Grand Rapids: Eerdmans, 2000], 1225).

25. Peter O'Brien speaks of the "subdivisions of the human family" (*Colossians, Philemon*, WBC 44 [Waco: Word, 1982], 192), and Richard Longenecker speaks of "old divisions and

reversing the fall, tearing down the dividing walls, and bringing eternal life
by being all in all. However, both humanity and the world wait for the end
of decay, death, futility, and oppression at Jesus's second coming. Dominion
will be restored to both male and female in Christ, which is consistent with
the mandate for dominion at creation.[26]

Paul appeals directly to the creation of male and female in his description
of the unity of the church. He held that the unity, the one-flesh relationship
intended in the creation of man and woman (Gen. 2:24), was still valid for
marriage and a model for Christ and the church (Eph. 5:21–32). When viewed
in the context of Paul's general appeals for unity in making Jews and gentiles
into one humanity (Eph. 2:14), his argument for the unity of one flesh in
marriage extends to a profound understanding of Christ's relationship to the
church (cf. Eph. 5:32). I suggest that Paul interpreted the relationship between
male and female in the creation passage in Genesis 2 with a stock metaphor
in Greek (κεφαλή) and developed an innovative theology of relationships
between God, Jesus Christ, humanity, the church, and male and female that
was meaningful in the context of the Greco-Roman culture. This will be discussed below, in section 3.5. In summary, Paul saw the purpose of unity for
all of humanity in Christ, across the boundaries, as communicated through
the one-flesh unity between Adam and Eve.

3.4 Gender and the Order of Creation

Does Paul suggest that men have some kind of primogeniture relationship
to women because of the order of creation? As mentioned above, Genesis
1:27–28 indicates unambiguously that male and female were created in the
image of God and that both were given authority/dominion. In Genesis 2,
the narrative loops back and focuses in more detail on the creation of male
and female. Paul refers to various aspects in the way Adam and Eve were
created, and he finds theological significance in the details of the account
that inform him about the nature of humanity, male and female, and husbands and wives:

> The first man was from the earth, a man of dust; the second man is from heaven.
> (1 Cor. 15:47 NRSV)

---

inequalities" that "cover in embryonic fashion all the essential relationships of humanity, and
so need to be seen as having racial, cultural, and sexual implications as well" (*Galatians*, WBC
41 [Nashville: Nelson, 1990], 156–57).

26. For more on gender and eschatology, see chap 5.

Indeed, man was not made from woman, but woman from man. (1 Cor. 11:8 NRSV)

For Adam was formed first, then Eve. (1 Tim. 2:13 NRSV)

Each allusion refers to a different aspect of the creation account and supports a different point or argument. The reference in 1 Corinthians 15:47 is a pejorative evaluation of Adam's formation from dirt compared with Christ's origin from heaven.[27] In Paul's theology we can see that he was not impressed with the biological origin of Adam. In contrast, he was impressed with the biological origin of woman from the man. While the woman bore the image of the "man of dirt," she was actually formed from a higher order in creation, since Adam was already formed and alive through a direct act of God, and she was made from him. Therefore, woman is man's glory, or the glory of the glory, but this "something more" is not described as hierarchical either in the Pauline corpus or in the creation account. Hierarchy (human dominion over the earth and its other creatures) is addressed in Genesis 1:27–28, but Genesis 2 addresses other themes.[28]

3.4.1 Who Is First? Mutuality in Origin

There is a paradoxical relationship between male and female running through 1 Corinthians 11:3–16 that is comparable to the discussion of mutual authority between husbands and wives over each other's bodies in 1 Corinthians 7:3–7. Eve was created from Adam, which, Paul argues, is paradigmatic for male and female;[29] but he also states that every man comes from woman in the birth process. Following his statement that woman ought to have authority over her head, he qualifies his support of a woman's authority or rights with a statement of mutual dependence: "Nevertheless, in the Lord woman is not independent of man nor man independent of woman. For just as woman came from man, so man comes through woman; but all things come from God" (1 Cor. 11:11–12 NRSV). This is hardly arguing for the priority of man based on the order of creation, but rather that the creation of woman from man

27. "Humanity as such finds its model in the first Adam, who was created from earth's soil (Gen. 2:7, Hebrew and LXX) and shares the mortality and fragility of what belongs to those whose σῶμα is made from that which disintegrates into dust in the grave" (Thiselton, *Corinthians*, 1286).

28. The issue of authority was addressed in Gen. 1:27–28, but it is not an explicit theme or focus in the account of the creation of woman.

29. I suggest that the creation of woman out of man is paradigmatic for woman's dependence on man and her vulnerability throughout history. In most cultures, women have drawn their identity from men.

evens out the balance, since every man comes from woman, in contrast with 1 Esdras 4:15–16. Consequently, male and female are explicitly interdependent in Paul's theology of origins. In the context of 1 Corinthians 11:3–16, Paul diplomatically mitigates any inappropriate independence of women as a result of his support of their desire to veil.

However, male and female would not be interdependent if the creation order was reversed and if the first man came out of woman. This could be the possible context for Paul's summary of the creation account in 1 Timothy 2:13–14. Given the virgin birth of Christ and the life experience of every human coming out of a woman, a creative reversal might have seemed to be in order for women in Ephesus who would not have a significant commitment to the Old Testament. A reversal of the order of creation would be more coherent, more consistent, more economical, and a logical variation, particularly for a woman who had participated in a goddess religion such as the worship of Artemis in Ephesus, or a fertility cult.[30] A woman may think, "It is clear from the virgin birth that a man's involvement in the birth process is dispensable in divine providence, so why would God need or want to make man first?" And so, an old wives' tale could be born that would begin to circulate in mischievous fun or in earnest as a competitive creation myth around the hearth.

We know that such myths, genealogies, and old wives' tales were circulating in Ephesus and were a big problem for Timothy; all three terms could describe the same problem and refer to the false teaching among the Ephesian women: the genre (myths in 1 Tim. 1:4; 4:7), the content (genealogies in 1 Tim. 1:4), and the source (old wives' tales in 1 Tim. 4:7). We also know of an early recorded myth that (1) reversed the role of male and female in the order of creation and deception in the fall, (2) possibly could be dated as early as the second century CE, and (3) was part of gnostic literature that

---

30. There are modern counterparts to this kind of syncretism. For a year or two after conversion, I believed that reincarnation was consistent with John 3:3, which speaks of being born again. The clairvoyant and psychic Jeane Dixon persuasively taught this reinterpretation of Scripture in her autobiography, and I recall that I tried to convincingly verbalize my beliefs, to the frustration of my Christian friends. I was finally disabused of this belief when I submitted to the teaching of a local church, but it took some time. Such reinterpretations and subversions of the apostolic reading of any text were a danger in the early church, and even more so because the literacy rate was not as high among women, and when access to a semi-segregated culture was limited. Furthermore, we see this kind of lag between orthodox belief and syncretism among men in Ephesus in Acts 19:13–20, where members of the church were actively practicing sorcery—presumably men as well as women. After the dramatic exorcism of demons in a man (in the episode of the sons of Sceva), some of the believers burned their magic scrolls, and their value amounted to 136 years of wages. That is as much of an indication of the syncretism that existed in Ephesus as it is an indication of a faithful response to Paul's exorcism. How many did not burn their magic scrolls?

originated in oral tradition. This is one of the scenarios that Richard and Catherine Kroeger suggested was the background for Paul's restatement of the creation narrative in 1 Timothy 2:13.[31] It could have had a similar textual transmission as the New Testament canon. There was a period of oral transmission of the gospel (the life of Jesus) followed by its conversion into written records; the second-century dating is consistent with the age of early New Testament manuscripts, though we believe that the New Testament, and particularly some of the Pauline Epistles, were first written far earlier. Thus there is sufficient evidence to suggest that there might have been a myth circulating among the women in first-century Ephesus that reversed the accounts of the creation and fall, and perhaps it was antecedent to the gnostic oral tradition.

The fact is, Paul simply states that "man was formed first" to support a prohibition against a woman or a wife teaching and acting like a materfamilias who controls/dominates her husband. This prohibition would not apply to all men because (1) the referent in 1 Timothy 2:12 is singular ("man"), indicating a one-on-one relationship, and (2) women owned slaves and had servants over whom they legitimately taught and acted as a mistress.[32] The prohibition was in some way relevant to the narrative of Adam and Eve, their deception in the fall, and childbirth, so the context best fits the relationship between a husband and wife. How does the fact that man was formed first support the prohibitions? Determining the logical relationship between the prohibitions and Paul's brief summary of the creation and fall involves an inference that the reader must make to understand the meaning of the passage. It may be assumed that the first reader had all the information needed to understand the logical connections.

If an erroneous myth about creation was (already) circulating among the women, Paul would be correcting the myth. On the other hand, since Paul commands a woman to learn in 1 Timothy 2:11, this could be an analogy to

31. See "On the Origin of the World," in *The Nag Hammadi Library*, ed. James M. Robinson, rev. ed. (San Francisco: HarperSanFrancisco, 1988), 170–89 (available at http://gnosis.org/naghamm/origin.html). See also Richard Clark Kroeger and Catherine Clark Kroeger, *I Suffer Not a Woman: Rethinking 1 Timothy 2:11–15 in Light of Ancient Evidence* (Grand Rapids: Baker, 1998), 217–21.

32. For the sake of argument, we may agree with Albert Wolters's conclusions about the meaning of αὐθεντέω in "A Semantic Study of αὐθέντης and Its Derivatives," *JGRChJ* 1 (2000): 145–75. He concludes, "It is clear that all these examples illustrate the verb αὐθεντέω in the sense 'to be an αὐθέντης,' and are semantically dependent on the meaning 'master' (or its variant 'doer')" (160). Without question, in the Greco-Roman culture, if the woman assumed the role of teaching and acting like a master over her husband, it would be considered abusive because it would have been humiliating.

the order of spiritual formation and the transmission of sound teaching described in 2 Timothy 2:2.[33] In that case, a man should receive the sacred trust of instruction directly from Timothy and then take responsibility to teach his wife individually in the home, which would indicate a specific procedure in the practice of discipleship.[34] As in 1 Corinthians 14:35, Paul's solution for a lack of knowledge among the women is individual instruction for women in the home, which accounts for the shift from (plural) "women" (1 Tim. 2:9–10) to (singular) "woman" (2:11–12). The wife should receive instruction with the same humility and quiet demeanor as the men are commanded to have (without anger or argument, as in 2:8). The prohibition would then mean that Paul did not want the order or process of teaching to be reversed in the home. As one of Paul's solutions to the false teaching in Ephesus, he wanted corrective teaching to be transmitted from himself, through Timothy, and to the men, each of whom was to teach his wife. Timothy could not access individual women without violating propriety. He had to work through proper channels within the context of the culture.

Consequently, the prohibition that restricts the way a woman should act toward a man in 1 Timothy 2:12b (αὐθεντεῖν ἀνδρός) does not constitute a reversed mandate or a command for a man to act like a master toward his wife, or for men to act that way toward the women in the church. Here Paul prohibits a woman from subjugating, controlling, or abusing a man, but he never commands a man to subjugate, control, master, or abuse (αὐθεντεῖν) a woman, even though such behavior was acceptable in the Greco-Roman culture. No one has yet found a single text in the documents of the early church where anyone suggests that a man should exercise this sort of authority over his wife,[35] or instructs a church leader to exercise this kind of authority over a member of the church, male or female.[36] No one has found a text where

33. For a fuller exegesis of 1 Tim. 2:8–15, see chap. 9. However, a number of elements in this crucial passage apply to creation and the fall.

34. This is similar to the case of the Jews having the advantage of being trusted with the oracles of God (Rom. 3).

35. On the contrary, John Chrysostom prohibits husbands from doing this to their wives. Chrysostom says that the husband's role is to love, and the wife's role is to obey. He then says, "Therefore, don't be abusive because your wife is submissive to you" (μὴ τοίνυν, ἐπειδὴ ὑποτέτακται ἡ γυνὴ αὐθέντει) (*Hom. Col.* 27–31, my translation). Chrysostom explicitly rules out reversing the prohibition to women.

36. A church leader could rightly seize control or dominate a problem, a situation, or a process (πρᾶγμα) that may concern people, such as the ruling in a court case or the selection of papal representatives. However, a person who is the direct object of the verb αὐθεντέω is being compelled against one's will and often forced, injured, or killed. It is comparable to the difference between eradicating illiteracy and eradicating illiterates. See Cynthia Long Westfall, "The Meaning of αὐθεντέω in 1 Timothy 2:12," *JGRChJ* 10 (2014): 138–73.

a church leader rightly does this to an individual or group of people.[37] In other words, there is no evidence that Paul is prohibiting women from doing something that men are authorized and expected to do.[38] Rather, 1 Timothy 2:12b is a prohibition of inappropriate female priority and improper exercise of power, possibly based on an incorrect or inadequate narrative about creation. It does not follow that αὐθεντεῖν ("acting like a master") corresponds to a correct sort of male power in the church community, such as pastoral care. Jesus's and Paul's teachings consist of examples of servanthood, and the principle to treat others as yourself. Therefore, turning the prohibition on its head and suggesting that αὐθεντεῖν represents male priority on the basis of the order of creation is a non sequitur or logical fallacy that is inconsistent with Pauline theology. Paul never tells men to subjugate (ὑποτάσσω) women or anyone else. Rather, he tells women to submit themselves in the household codes, and in this passage he commands them to learn with a submissive attitude (1 Tim. 2:11: μανθανέτω ἐν πάσῃ ὑποταγῇ). In the same way, elsewhere Paul tells Christians to submit themselves to one another (e.g., Eph. 5:21; Phil. 2:1–5). A command to submit does not constitute a reversed mandate for the other to subjugate.

3.4.2 The Pauline Meaning of "First" and "Last" in Narrative

Thomas Schreiner and many other scholars find a Pauline transcendent norm of God's purposes for gender in creation in 1 Timothy 2:13:[39]

For Adam was formed first, then Eve.

Ἀδὰμ γὰρ πρῶτος ἐπλάσθη, εἶτα Εὕα.

---

37. It is notable that Pope Leo I, the bishop of Rome, was asked by the Eastern Roman emperor and empress to take this action to authorize the Council of Chalcedon (*Concilium universal Chalcedonense anno 451* [2.1.1–2]). At this point the bishop of Rome was starting to assume the role of pope. This term worked well for the supreme spiritual authority and ruler, but even then it was not done to a person. It came to be applied to the members of the Trinity, representing their unrestricted power over creation, and this action was performed on the destruction of Sodom and Gomorrah and the wicked (Eusebius, *Vit. Const.* 2.48.1.8; Athanasius, *Syn.* 27.3.18).

38. Perhaps the KJV gloss "usurp" gives the impression that women are doing what men are authorized to do. Of course, in the first place, believers were never supposed to usurp power. In the second place, the Roman paterfamilias traditionally had the right of life and death over his wife, but Paul consistently and directly confronted the Roman and Greek models of male authority. Therefore, if women were indeed "usurping" the traditional Roman male role of the paterfamilias in an attempt at role reversal, they would be adopting the very model of dominion and power that Jesus and Paul were confronting, correcting, and prohibiting.

39. See Schreiner, *Paul*, 408–9.

From this six-word creation narrative, many scholars infer "the temporal priority" of Adam[40] and conclude, "This indicates that God intended male authority."[41] They take this to be an obvious inference and claim it as what the Bible actually says.[42] But the topic of 1 Timothy 2:9–15 is not men and their authority (they are addressed in 2:8 and corrected for anger and arguing). Furthermore, Paul's words in 1 Timothy 2:13–14 are not propositional statements of transcendent norms, but rather a very brief narrative summary from Genesis 2:5–22. Paul's topic concerns the correction of problems among the women (1 Tim. 2:9–10), and the topic is the spiritual formation of the individual woman in 1 Timothy 2:11, which would most likely be done by the husband at home, as Paul directed in 1 Corinthians 14:34–35. Whatever the case, Paul wants women to be taught the right story. It was common and expected for women elders to take responsibility for the spiritual formation of the younger women (Titus 2:3–4), but the women in Ephesus may have lost Paul's trust as a group. In fact, the older women were the source of the problem (1 Tim. 4:7).[43] It is grammatically possible (or even probable) that in 1 Timothy 2:12 Paul was suspending the Ephesian women from all teaching duties until the false teaching among them was corrected.[44]

40. See, e.g., Wayne Grudem, *Evangelical Feminism and Biblical Truth: An Analysis of More Than One Hundred Disputed Questions* (Sisters, OR: Multnomah, 2004), 30, 30n13. See also George W. Knight III, *The Pastoral Epistles: A Commentary on the Greek Text*, NIGTC (Grand Rapids: Eerdmans, 1992), 142–43; Craig L. Blomberg, *1 Corinthians*, NIVAC (Grand Rapids: Zondervan, 1994), 216; Thomas R. Schreiner, "An Interpretation of 1 Timothy 2:9–15: A Dialogue with Scholarship," in *Women in the Church: An Analysis and Application of 1 Timothy 2:9–15*, ed. Andreas J. Köstenberger and Thomas R. Schreiner, 2nd ed. (Grand Rapids: Baker Academic, 2005), 106–7.

41. William Mounce draws this inference without explanation, simply stating that, for Paul, 1 Tim. 2:13 means that man has authority, citing 1 Cor. 11:8–9 (*Pastoral Epistles*, WBC 46 [Nashville: Nelson, 2000], 130). But 1 Cor. 11:8–9 talks about the interdependence of who comes from whom. However, the meaning of "head" plays a crucial role in 1 Cor. 11:3–16, and if a theology of authority is assumed in the word "head" from the creation account, then the creation context here would seem to support male authority, though that is not the topic.

42. The theological meaning of a biblical narrative must be inferred unless the narrator gives an explanation. Most modern scholars reject using biblical narrative for theology in principle (you can interpret a story to mean many things), so it is interesting that Paul's narrative statement in 1 Tim. 2:13 has been consistently treated as a theological principle. The Yale school (narrative theology), Pentecostals, and postmodern biblical scholars have stressed the theological importance of biblical narrative.

43. Myths or old wives' tales are highlighted by Paul as a dangerous lure for even Timothy (1 Tim. 4:7: γραώδεις μύθους).

44. This could be indicated by the Greek grammar and syntax: διδάσκειν ("to teach") is fronted, with five words between it and αὐθεντεῖν ("to master/dominate"), which takes a genitive, here ἀνδρός ("a man"); διδάσκειν does not take a genitive. Either this is a general ban on teaching, or it is a true hendiadys where αὐθεντεῖν must interpret διδάσκειν in order for διδάσκειν

Throughout the Genesis narrative, it is clear from the beginning that someone who was born or came first did not necessarily have authority. Primogeniture among brothers was continually subverted, so Genesis cannot be used to provide an argument for male authority based on Adam being formed first.[45] Cain was born first, but Abel received God's favor. Esau was born first, but God chose Jacob, and it was determined that Esau would serve Jacob. Reuben was born first, but the line of Christ came through Judah, and Joseph saved the family and assumed authority over them. Manasseh was Joseph's firstborn, but Jacob placed his right hand on Ephraim's head to say that he would become greater.

In the Pauline corpus, for those in Christ, Jesus is the firstborn of all of us (Rom. 8:29; Col. 1:15, 18), which relativizes relationships among his followers. Furthermore, it would be incorrect to extrapolate some general principle of primogeniture or particularly temporal priority in relationships within the church from Jesus's unique role: he is the only firstborn among believers. The contrast between the first human/Adam and Jesus as the "last Adam"/second human (ὁ ἔσχατος Ἀδάμ, 1 Cor. 15:45; ὁ δεύτερος ἄνθρωπος, 15:47) shows that the character of Paul's thought is eschatological and looks to the end rather than the beginning.[46] The Jews were chosen first, but then God grafted in the gentiles (Rom. 11:17). In the Pauline communities, gentiles such as Titus could be in leadership positions over churches that included Jews, but being first indicates a responsibility for the Jews: the Jews were entrusted with the advantage of the oracles of God (Rom. 3:2), and Jewish apostles were the eyewitnesses to Jesus. And in regard to Paul himself, Jesus appeared to him "last of all, as to one untimely born" (1 Cor. 15:8 NRSV). Paul was clear that being last did not mean he was dependent on the apostolic "pillars" for either his gospel or his calling as a leader, and he even confronted Peter (Gal. 2:13–3:14). Paul's theology and understanding of the meaning of "first" and "last" in narrative inform interpretation, and there is no argument for priority for those who are first temporally.

In conclusion, when Paul talks about being "first" temporally in narrative, it does not refer to authority or priority; and when he talks about being temporally "last," it does not refer to subordination, but it can indicate some

---

to take ἀνδρός as its object. Some interpreters want to have their cake and eat it too by treating ἀνδρός as the direct object of διδάσκειν, but insisting that αὐθεντεῖν cannot interpret διδάσκειν.

45. Richard Hess asserts, "The norm among the patriarchs is *not* primogeniture but God's blessing on the second or third born" ("Equality with and without Innocence: Genesis 1–3," in *Discovering Biblical Equality: Complementarity without Hierarchy*, ed. Ronald W. Pierce and Rebecca Merrill Groothuis [Downers Grove, IL: InterVarsity, 2004], 84, emphasis original).

46. Similarly, David came first, then Jesus came as the son of David, but David called him "Lord" (Matt. 22:42).

kind of order. If Paul was not setting a false myth straight, or explaining the reason for maternal mortality, he might have been using typology to indicate a sort of order in spiritual formation in the correction of deception and false teaching. In 1–2 Timothy, Paul was carefully guarding the transmission of that trust; it could make sense that Paul is trusting the men in Ephesus as those who are or would be spiritually formed first to guard the transmission of the trust in their households and correct the problem of deception and false teaching among the women, which was in accordance with cultural propriety.

3.5 Creation and Headship

How you understand the word "head" involves a crucial exegetical choice that will in large part determine your biblical theology of gender. If you want to understand what Paul meant when he used the word κεφαλή ("head"), you will want to be sure that you do not treat the English translation as if it were the Greek text. "Head" is a rich and varied metaphor in English, but in the context of the family ("head of the house") or an organization ("head of the department"), it refers to "hierarchical authority." Therefore, any other attempts to explain how κεφαλή functioned as a metaphor in the Greek language seem ludicrous.[47] You may have been told that "head" means "source, like the source of a river," and probably found it difficult to see any theological significance in a comparison between a wife and her husband and a river and its headwaters. Even though this may have a connection to the creation of Eve from Adam, what does it tell us? As Schreiner writes,

> Paul says that "the husband is the head of the wife as Christ is the head of the Church" in [Eph. 5:23]. In what meaningful sense can one say that a husband is the source of his wife? Wives do not exist by virtue of their husband's existence. Wives do not derive their life from the husbands. The meaning "source" here makes Paul's statement hard to comprehend since it is difficult to see how husbands are the source of their wives.[48]

47. For a detailed breakdown of the "multiple meanings" of "head," see Thiselton, *Corinthians*, 812–22. Thiselton lists (1) authority, supremacy, leadership; (2) source, origin, temporal priority; and (3) synecdoche and preeminence, foremost, topmost. He concludes, "Paul deliberately uses a *polymorphous concept*, through a word that has *multiple meanings*" (811, emphasis original).

48. Thomas R. Schreiner, "Head Coverings, Prophecies, and the Trinity: 1 Corinthians 11:2–16," in *Recovering Biblical Manhood and Womanhood: A Response to Evangelical Feminism*, ed. John Piper and Wayne Grudem (Wheaton: Crossway, 1991), 127.

Schreiner asks a very good question, and his doubts will resonate with any modern reader who is reading the text in English. I suggest that there is a problem with an unhelpful definition, and the significant cultural differences make it difficult to appreciate or even recognize the logic of Paul's theology.[49] Schreiner's question could have actually been directed at the creation account. What is the theological significance of woman being created out of man? I suggest that Paul utilized the metaphor of "head" to answer this very question in 1 Corinthians 11:3–16 and Ephesians 5:21–33.

The first-century Greco-Roman culture and the ancient Near East were vitally interested in a person's origins in terms of place and family. An individual's genealogy was an official identification, and Greeks used the metaphor of "head" to describe these important kinship relationships. Both uses relate "source" to family ties. In the Greco-Roman world, a person's origins defined who that person was and thus were profoundly meaningful; our handicap is that, according to the American dream, we want to transcend our origins. However, Paul uses this metaphor to explain a network of relationships that could be characterized as family ties and identity, a meaning that is foundational for the connection between man and woman in the creation account.

3.5.1 The Meaning of "Head" (κεφαλή)

Κεφαλή is a key word that Paul utilizes in gender passages alluding to or citing the creation account in Genesis 1–2. In ancient and Koine Greek, κεφαλή refers to the head of a body and had a range of meaning that reflects Greek beliefs about the function of the head in relation to the body, including biological functions. Paul's use of κεφαλή in the marriage relationship is applied to the relationship of believers to Christ, Christ to God, and the relationship of all humanity to Adam.

The range of meanings for "head" in English is not the same as the semantic range of κεφαλή.[50] The range of meaning for κεφαλή includes the head of

---

49. See above, §1.4.2, for a description of the patron-client relationship between the husband and wife, in which the husband can be said to be the source of life for his wife because typically she is dependent on him for her identity, social position, and property/shelter, and he is her access to the raw materials from which she prepares food and clothing.

50. In other words, the semantic range of "head" in English is not the same as the semantic range of κεφαλή; that reality needs to be one of the most basic principles in translation. The English for "head" is also a metaphor for hierarchical authority in Hebrew and Latin, all of which has led to confusion as to the New Testament metaphoric meaning of κεφαλή, not only in passages concerning men and women such as 1 Cor. 11:3–16 and Eph. 5:18–33 but also passages in which it is applied to Christ alone (e.g., Eph. 1:2; 4:15; Col. 1:18; 2:10, 19).

a man or beast, which was expanded to metaphors that included identity,[51] source, life, and provision.[52] It did not mean "authority" in idiomatic Greek, which is evident from its entry in Liddell and Scott's *Greek-English Lexicon*. However, "head" was a metaphor for authority in the Hebrew Bible. Out of 171 instances in which "head" means "authority," those who support its meaning as "authority" argue that the Septuagint translators turned it into Greek as κεφαλή only six times (Judg. 11:11; 2 Sam. 22:44; Ps. 18:43 [17:44 LXX]; Isa. 7:8–9 [2×]; Lam. 1:5). None of these passages has intertextual ties with 1 Corinthians 11:3 or the relationships depicted in the household codes.[53] They might be poor translation choices by the Septuagint translators, or (with the exception of Lam. 1:5)[54] they may reflect a foundational and symbiotic relationship between an ancient king and his people (present and future) or territory.[55] We find that κεφαλή often occurs in contexts of authority and preeminence because the function of being the source of identity and life can be the basis of authority or preeminence in the culture. Colossians 2:9–10 is one example of the close association between authority and source: "For in him the whole fullness of deity dwells bodily, and you have come to fullness in him, who is the head of every ruler [ἀρχῆς] and authority [ἐξουσίας]" (NRSV).

This passage is cited by Schreiner as an unambiguous example of "head" as "authority" (cf. Col. 2:15).[56] However, the point of Colossians 2:10 is that

51. The function of the head as a person's identity is demonstrated by busts that represent the whole person in statuary.

52. LSJ has five categories, but the final three are closely related to the metaphoric extensions of the first two: the bust of Homer indicates that the head represents his entire person, and the pièce de résistance is closely related to the head as the "noblest part." The idiom κατὰ κεφαλῆς (1 Cor. 11:4) for a head covering or a wig is related to the literal head of a human. See LSJ, "κεφαλή," 945.

53. Judges 11:11 involves a relationship between Jephthah and the people, and it is interesting that "head" occurs with, but is differentiated from, "commander." In contrast, 2 Sam. 22:44 has intertextual ties with Ps. 18:43 and refers to David as the "head" of "nations" (ἐθνῶν). Isaiah 7:8–9 refers to a relationship between a king, his capital, and his country. Thus, these examples take place in a similar register or semantic domain, which is not the semantic domain of passages that concern gender or the relationship between God and Jesus Christ.

54. Lamentations 1:5 (LXX) merits further study, with its complex wordplay between "oppress," "face," and "head," and the translator's gloss with the preposition εἰς (ἐγένοντο . . . εἰς κεφαλήν; cf. Ps. 118:22 LXX//Matt. 21:42; Mark 12:10; Luke 20:17; Acts 4:11; 1 Pet. 2:7).

55. See Payne, *Man and Woman*, 117–37. See also Richard S. Cervin, "Does κεφαλή Mean 'Source' or 'Authority Over' in Greek Literature: A Rebuttal," *TJ* 10 (1989): 85–112. Contra Wayne Grudem, "The Meaning of κεφαλή ('Head'): An Evaluation of New Evidence, Real and Alleged," *JETS* 44 (2001): 25–65. Grudem's examples are unconvincing: he appears to define "source" too narrowly and tends to label by context rather than using lexical methodology and teasing out the semantic contribution.

56. Schreiner, "Head Coverings," in Piper and Grudem, *Recovering Biblical Manhood and Womanhood*, 128. Therefore, though Schreiner claims that Jesus cannot be the source of the

Christ is the source of the believer's fullness in the same way that he is the head (source and sustainer) of every ruler and authority. This meaning is made clearer because Paul has already emphatically made this point in Colossians 1:15–17, which explicitly includes the powers in 2:10: "He is the image of the invisible God, the firstborn of all creation; for in him all things in heaven and on earth were created, things visible and invisible, whether thrones or dominions or rulers [ἀρχαά] or powers [ἐξουσίαι]—all things have been created through him and for him. He himself is before all things, and in him all things hold together" (NRSV).

Therefore, the reference to Jesus as the head of rulers and authorities may sound like it means the assumption of authority over them, but both the point of the passage and the close context indicate that it actually means that he is their source—that is, their creator.

One way that κεφαλή occurs distinctively is in language used for family, paternity, and ancestry.[57] This includes references to progenitors as "head" because they are the source or origin of a family's life (which is a biological relationship),[58] and their "head" or "face" bears the family identity (which is genetic).[59] Children draw both life and a family resemblance from their ancestors/parents, and even from siblings, as the entire family is the source of one's identity. So both parents and children can be represented by one another's head. This is how Paul uses κεφαλή: to refer to the origin or source of life and identity in the context of family relationships—husband and wife, church community as a family, and God the Father and his Son, Jesus Christ.

The familial metaphor of "head" is closely related to the concepts of patronage, leadership, and honor in the Greco-Roman culture, because the provision of life and identity creates a costly reciprocal obligation. According to David deSilva, "Children are held to have incurred a debt to their parents that they can never repay, so that the virtuous person will honor the parents, and 'return the favors' bestowed by the parents throughout childhood for the remainder of the parents' lives."[60] Paul reflects this sense of obligation when

---

powers in Col. 2:10, because these clearly are the demonic powers that he will disarm in Col. 2:15, these do not exist apart from him independently, nor does anything else.

57. As Thiselton states, "Today's chain of literal and metaphorical associations is so exclusively bound up with institutional authority (witness the use of the term 'headship' in late twentieth-century debates) that this translation and interpretation suggest a narrower focus than Paul probably has in mind" (*Corinthians*, 820).

58. For example, Philo uses "head" for a progenitor: "Like the head of a living creature, Esau is the progenitor of all the clans mentioned so far; [his name] is sometimes interpreted as 'product' and sometimes as 'oak'" (*Congr.* 61).

59. See the discussion below on Artemidorus Daldianus, *Onir.* 1.2.

60. David A. deSilva, *Honor, Patronage, Kinship & Purity: Unlocking New Testament Culture* (Downers Grove, IL: InterVarsity, 2006), 186.

he says, "If a widow has children or grandchildren, they should first learn their religious duty to their own family and make some repayment to their parents; for this is pleasing in God's sight" (1 Tim. 5:4 NRSV). Therefore, Paul indicates that reciprocity is the appropriate response for the gift of life. Paul selects reciprocity as relevant to his message and gospel of grace.

Similar to parents' gift of life to their children, Christ gives believers their lives and identities as children of God; but those two functions are neither synonymous nor interchangeable with his lordship. In other contexts, such as the military, "head" may be associated with a leader, but it is used to describe a certain function of the leader, such as in Plutarch, *Pelopidas* 2.1, where the safety (life) of the troops depends on the survival of the head: the general's life.[61] So, κεφαλή occurs in contexts of leadership, because the metaphoric importance of the head is consistent with the function of authority; but they are not synonymous. There is order implied in the metaphor, but the order is organic rather than hierarchical.

Paul's references to "face" and "image" are directly connected to the definition of κεφαλή ("head") as a metaphor for life, source/origin, and identity, all of which are related to one's heritage. "Seed" or "sperm" (σπέρμα) is also connected, and it conveys a genetic relationship between parent and child or a progenitor and descendants.[62] Aristotle and Pythagoras taught that the head was the source of sperm, which traveled down the spinal cord or filtered through the body to the genitals.[63] This relationship became part of a network

61. "The light-armed troops are like the hands, the cavalry like the feet, the line of men-at-arms itself like chest and breastplate, and the general like the head, then he, in taking undue risks and being overbold, would seem to neglect not himself, but all, inasmuch as their safety depends on him, and their destruction too" (Plutarch, *Pel.* 2.1, in *Plutarch's Lives*, trans. Bernadotte Perrin, LCL (London: Heinemann, 1914), 5:343). This illustrates the belief that the life is in the head, and the head is the source of life for the body, because if the head is removed or injured, the body dies.

62. Note 1 John 3:9: "Those who have been born of God do not sin, because God's seed abides in them; they cannot sin, because they have been born of God" (NRSV). Paul does not include semen (*sperma*, "seed") in his discussions of the identity of Jews through descent as the seed of Abraham (2 Cor. 11:22), and Jesus's royal identity through descent as the seed of David (Rom. 1:3). However, most of Paul's references to "seed" concern the fulfillment of the promises in Abraham's descendants (σπέρμα): Jesus who is the seed of Abraham (Gal. 3:16, 19), those who become the "seed of Abraham" through faith (Rom. 4:13–18; Gal 3:29 which is connected to the idea of adoption in Gal 4:6) and those who are the seed of the promise (Rom. 9:7–8).

63. For example, Aristotle thought that the head was the source of sperm, especially the area around the eyes (σπερματικώτατος), which connects sight to sexual indulgence (*Gen. an.* 747a). For the pervasive influence of Aristotle, see above, §1.3.1. Pythagoras said that "semen is a drop of the brain [τὸ δὲ σπέρμα εἶναι σταγόνα ἐγκεφάλου]" (Diogenes Laertius, *De vitis philosophorum: Libri X* [Leipzig: Sumptibus Ottonis Holtze, 1870], 102). This quotation is referenced by Justin Smith, who summarizes the Pythagorean view: "The male semen is a product of the brain and bone marrow, which were seen in ancient medicine as part of one and the same bodily system. This view is attributed to the Pythagoreans; a succinct aphorism preserved by Diogenes Laertius

of Greek metaphors and idioms that are known as "semantic domains." Some of these associations with "head" are made explicit in Artemidorus Daldianus (second century CE) in *Oneirocritica* 1.36: "And to imagine that one is beheaded . . . is grievous for those who have parents and those who have children. For the head is like the parents due to its being the cause of life. And it is like children due to its face and its resemblance to them."[64]

The importance of the resemblance of a child to a parent (particularly a father) is illustrated by Gabael's reaction when he saw his relative Tobias for the first time: "Blessed be God, for I see in Tobias the very image of my cousin Tobit" (Tob. 9:6). The head bears the image of the family resemblance on the face.

The ancestor is the head, and the descendants are the seed.[65] This is where Paul differentiates woman's creation from familial descent on the basis of Genesis 2:24, where the husband and wife are one flesh instead of the wife being the seed. Since man is the origin of life for woman, he is her head. If man is the head of woman, and they are one flesh, then Paul concludes that the woman is his body. Paul is able to exploit the metaphor of "head" in his application of it to marriage, male and female, the relationship between Christ and the church, and the relationship between Christ and God the Father; he uses "head" to mutually interpret these relationships.[66]

3.5.2 The Headship of Adam over Humanity

Paul finds the stories in Genesis 1–3 to be deeply theological and authoritative, not only for the church's gender issues, but also for humanity in general and the relationship of Jesus to humanity. He continually draws insights about gender and answers to gender problems from Genesis 1–3. Adam is described by Paul in 1 Corinthians 15:45–49 as having a special relationship with the human race (cf. Rom. 5:12–21):

> So also it is written, "The first man, Adam, became a living person"; the last Adam became a life-giving spirit. However, the spiritual did not come first,

---

has it [so]" (introduction to *The Problem of Animal Generation in Early Modern Philosophy*, ed. Justin E. H. Smith [Cambridge: Cambridge University Press, 2006], 5).

64. Daniel E. Harris-McCoy, trans., *Artemidorus' Oneirocritica: Text, Translation, and Commentary* (Oxford: Oxford University Press, 2012), 89.

65. The reference to Christ as the "seed of David" may be familiar, but Paul also often speaks of the "seed of Abraham." "Seed" occurs in the sense of "descendant" fifteen times in the Pauline corpus (Rom. 1:3; 4:13, 16, 18; 9:7 [2×], 8, 29; 11:1; 2 Cor. 11:22; Gal. 3:16 [3×], 29; 2 Tim. 2:8).

66. This is a minor example of Paul's innovations as he worked out the implications of the new creation and the gospel. For Paul the innovator, see William S. Campbell, *Paul and the Creation of Christian Identity*, LNTS 322 (London: T&T Clark, 2006), 54–57.

but the natural, and then the spiritual. The first man is from the earth, made of dust; the second man is from heaven. Like the one made of dust, so too are those made of dust, and like the one from heaven, so too those who are heavenly. And just as we have borne the image of the man of dust, let us also bear the image of the man of heaven.

Adam was the prototype of both humanity and males because he was the first human, from which all other humans derived their identity. Adam was made directly from dirt, and that correlates with the "natural" or organic nature of humanity's being. Adam was not a living soul looking for a body, but first a body of dirt. Then God breathed life into Adam, and he became a living person.

Paul characterizes the identity of the human race as "dust" or "dirt." All of humanity bears "the image of the man of dust" (1 Cor. 15:49). All males and females equally bear this image. In contrast, Jesus is "from heaven" and is the source of spiritual life. All are invited to now bear the image of Jesus in the same way that we have borne the image of Adam. The relationship of humanity with Adam is called "headship," "natural headship," or "federal headship" by scholars and theologians and is described by A. A. Hodge:

> The federal headship of Adam presupposes and rests upon his natural headship. He was our natural head before he was our federal head. He was doubtless made our federal representative because he was our natural progenitor and was so conditioned that his agency must affect our destinies, and because our very nature was on trial (typically, if not essentially) in him.[67]

Hodge also described how some refer to natural headship in general terms: "We are said to have been in him as a 'root,' or as 'branches in a tree.'"[68] It is beyond my purpose to discuss federal headship, but this understanding of the natural headship of Adam as our progenitor is related to how Paul uses "head" and its related terms for Adam at creation, for Jesus, and for God.

Adam is the head of humanity because he is the source of biological life. Adam is not given supremacy, honor, authority, or reverence by humanity; rather, the relationship is one of identity derived from its origin, to which Paul gives a negative appraisal. Jesus replaces Adam as the head because Jesus is the spiritual life-giving source that fills the church, and the church forms

67. Hodge, *Outlines of Theology* (New York: Robert Carter & Brothers, 1863), 239.
68. Ibid., 238. But Hodge rejects that notion as "utterly indefinite" and "material and mechanical" because it fails to explain moral responsibility in sin.

an organic union with him (Eph. 1:22; 4:15–16; Col. 1:18). This relationship
reflects the Greek meaning of "head."

3.5.3 Headship between the Pairs in 1 Corinthians 11:3 (Man/Christ; Woman/Man; God/Christ)

Headship in 1 Corinthians 11:3–16 must be understood in the larger context of Christ as head of the human race in a way that is not equated with
authority. Note the parallels in 1 Corinthians 11:3:

Christ is the head of every man
Man is the head of woman // A husband is the head of his wife
God is the head of Christ

In idiomatic Greek, this describes the origin of life for man, woman, and
Christ. For Paul, these relationships signify important characteristics in the
identity of the three, which Paul relates to their literal heads, just as in Greek
familial language. This makes particular sense in view of the Christian community's description of itself as the family and household of God. Christ is
the source of man's life because he is the creator who formed man in Genesis
2:4–9. Man is the source of woman's life because she was created out of man in
Genesis 2:18–23. God the Father is the source of Christ the Son's life in eternity.[69]

Christ the Son's head bears the image of the Father, and his face reflects
God's glory. When we see Jesus, we see God. These concepts are central
for Paul's Christology, and the idioms help us interpret the relationship between the two other pairs. Paul utilizes the same terminology to explain

69. Therefore, the phrase "God is the head of Christ" came to be expressed in the doctrine
of eternal generation, which affirms Christ's identity with God the Father and his essential
equality with God the Father. It says nothing about subordination. This is confirmed by Cyril
of Alexandria (ca. 444):

Therefore of our race [Adam] became first *head, which is source* [κεφαλὴ γὰρ ὅ ἐστιν ἀρχή],
and was of the earth and earthy. Since Christ was named the second Adam, he has been
placed as *head which is source*, of those who through him have been formed anew unto
him unto immortality through sanctification in the spirit. Therefore he himself our *source
which is head*, has appeared as a human being. Yet he though God by nature, has himself *a
generating* head, the heavenly Father and he himself, though God according to his nature,
yet being the Word, was begotten of Him. *Because head means source*, he establishes the
truth for those who are wavering in their mind that man is the head of woman, for she was
taken out of him. Therefore, as God according to His nature, the one Christ and Son and
Lord has as his head the heavenly Father, having himself become our head because *he is
of the same stock* according to the flesh." (*Pulch* 2.3, trans. by Catherine Clark Kroeger,
"Appendix 3: The Classical Concept of *Head* as "Source," in Gretchen Gaebelein Hull,
Equal to Serve: Men and Women Working Together Revealing the Gospel [Grand Rapids:
Baker Books, 1987], 268, emphasis original)

cultic importance and to distinguish the appearance of the man's head and the appearance of the woman's head in worship, particularly when men and women pray and prophesy.

Most scholars have assumed that the topic of 1 Corinthians 11:3–16 is the authority of men and the subordination of women. This is partly because "head" is a metaphor for authority in Latin, English, and German, so the meaning of "authority" has seemed to be intuitive in the history of the interpretation of the passage. However, because male hierarchy has come under fire in Western society and the church, some scholars have recently made an effort to prove that the subordination of women is biblical by arguing for the eternal subordination of Jesus Christ to the Father based on the meaning of "head." In the recent discussion, this group of scholars argues for functional subordination but affirms ontological equality between male and female, and Jesus Christ and the Father.[70]

However, both premises fall apart before several problems. The three pairs are clearly meant to be parallel, but they are not parallel in terms of authority relationships:

- Every man is not functionally subordinate to Christ in the present age.
- There is no distinctive sense in which Christ would be the authority over a man but not over a woman.[71]
- No man experiences the degree or type of subordination to Christ that women experience to men.[72]
- The Father and the Son are ontologically equal, men and women are ontologically equal, but men are not ontologically equal to Jesus Christ.
- No man experiences the degree or type of subordination that Jesus would experience if he were indeed eternally subordinate to the Father.
- The pairs do not account for authority relationships between men.

70. For a recent overview and collection of articles on the discussion of subordinationism, see Dennis W. Jowers and H. Wayne House, eds., *The New Evangelical Subordinationism? Perspectives on the Equality of God the Father and God the Son* (Eugene, OR: Pickwick, 2012).

71. Payne points out that if man were under Christ's authority in a distinctive way that women were not, it would undermine Christ's universal lordship (*Man and Woman*, 130).

72. Charles Hodge cautions, "The subordination is very different in its nature in the several cases mentioned. The subordination of the woman to the man is something entirely different from that of the man to Christ; and that again is at an infinite degree more complete than the subordination of Christ to God" (*A Commentary on the First Epistle to the Corinthians* [Grand Rapids: Eerdmans, 1994], 206). However, Hodge cannot be suggesting that the men's subordination to Christ is "more complete" than Christ's conformity to God's will. Christ is one with the Father, but there is nothing complete about men's subordination to God. This illustrates how we are comparing apples to oranges.

The fact is that masters are not described by Paul as the heads of their slaves in the household codes, because in the Pauline corpus "head" is not synonymous with "master" or "authority."[73]

According to Scripture, the subordination of every man is eschatological: every man will finally be subordinated in the future when every dominion, authority, and power will be destroyed (1 Cor. 15:24–25) and every tongue will confess Jesus Christ as Lord (Phil. 2:11), but not until then. So at the present time, every man is not subordinate to Christ, and yet Christ is the head of every man.

Similarly, Jesus Christ is not explicitly subordinate to the Father at the present time. The only alleged scriptural support of the subordination of the Son to the Father is 1 Corinthians 15:28, but according to this verse, Jesus Christ is not subject to the Father during the present age, so it is not true that he is eternally subordinate. It is not until the very end of the age (future tense) that "the Son himself will also be subjected to the one who put all things in subjection under him, so that God may be all in all" (NRSV). Christ's "subjection" at the end of the age is, rather, a metaphorical description of the eschatological unity of all things that establishes order.

Some teach that the biblical subordination of women represents "headship" as a benevolent rule of men who try to follow the humility and servanthood of Christ.[74] However, the actual practice of "headship" would be universal, so it would also enforce universal male entitlement and subject women to exploita-

73. This is not to say that there could not be a document where the master of a household may be described as the source of life for the entire household, including slaves. However, that is not part of Paul's theology and should not be imported into it.

74. See, e.g., Raymond C. Ortlund Jr., "Male-Female Equality and Male Headship: Genesis 1–3," in Piper and Grudem, *Recovering Biblical Manhood and Womanhood*, 95–112. See also John Piper's definition of manhood and womanhood in "A Vision of Biblical Complementarity: Manhood and Womanhood Defined according to the Bible," in Piper and Grudem, *Recovering Biblical Manhood and Womanhood*, 31–59. Ortlund defines male headship this way: "In the partnership of two spiritually equal human beings, man and woman, the man bears the primary responsibility to lead the partnership in a God-glorifying direction" (95). Not only is this definition a modern construct that is inconsistent with the history of interpretation (which assumed the ontological inferiority of females), but also Ortlund fails to adequately account for the fact that the majority of men are not taking that responsibility, as if the inevitable outcome and experience of abuse were irrelevant to his theology: "Male domination is a personal moral failure, not a Biblical doctrine. . . . If we define ourselves out of a reaction to bad experiences, we will be forever translating our pain in the past into new pain for ourselves and others in the present. We must define ourselves not by personal injury, not by fashionable hysteria, not even by personal variation and diversity, but by the suprapersonal pattern of sexual understanding taught here in Holy Scripture" (102). But on the contrary, male domination is part of a biblical doctrine. It is called "total depravity." Modern men in the Western world protected themselves from experiencing similar abuses of the total depravity of other men by setting up Western democratic and legal systems.

tion and the abuse of power by men who do not recognize boundaries, nor Christ's authority.[75] This would be the norm rather than the exception, "For the gate is narrow and the road is hard that leads to life, and there are few who find it" (Matt. 7:14). The exercise of authority by males who do not obey Christ does not mirror God or glorify God, but instead it illustrates the fall (Gen. 3:16) and represents a dominion that will be destroyed (1 Cor. 15:24). These inconsistencies contribute to the argument that the word "head" has been misunderstood by traditional interpretation; the metaphor of "head" has been constricted, misapplied, and bleached in terms of its complex theological contribution.

The teaching that the authority of men and the subordination of women are biblical is an overrealized eschatology in which the execution of male authority far exceeds Christ's authority during his incarnation, or even the authority that he exercises over men in the present age. In this teaching, men exercise authority over women in a way that is not contingent on their submission to Christ—they do not earn it. On the other hand, Christ's humiliation, suffering, and obedience during his incarnation were the grounds for his exalted authority (Phil. 2:8–11; cf. Heb. 5:8–9). However, if the headship of Christ over man is understood as the source of his life/existence, then the analogy between the three pairs is parallel, and exploring it richly contributes to our understanding of Pauline theology.

3.5.4 Headship and Christ

Therefore, the understanding of humanity's relationship to Adam as "natural headship" further informs and constrains how we understand the concept in the Pauline corpus, including the headship between man and Christ, and Christ and God, in 1 Corinthians 11:3. Male headship may be understood in a way that is consistent with Paul's explanation of the natural headship of Adam and the headship of Christ. Similarly, Paul's explanation of the

75. In a world ruled by sin, the history of women's subordination tells of degradation and exploitation, and that should be the starting point of our understanding. However, Ortlund argues that the subordination of women is not degrading, saying, "What biblical headship requires and what slave-holding forbids is that the head respect the helper as an equal significant person in the image of God" (Ortlund, "Male-Female Equality," in Piper and Grudem, *Recovering Biblical Manhood and Womanhood*, 104). First, both wives and slaves should have been treated by Christians as helpers with equal significance in the image of God. If any form of slavery is biblical, it would not forbid ontological equality, but rather supports it. Second, the only way that a woman's subordination could avoid being degrading would be dependent on the man's biblical exercise of power, but even Christian men's exercise of power can never be presumed to be biblical, particularly if there are no checks or balances.

relationship between male and female and between husband and wife can be interpreted consistently with the historical understanding of the natural/biological headship of Adam. It is a familial relationship.

In 1 Corinthians 11:3–16, the understanding of headship focuses on the relationship between males and Christ, which is informed by the relationship between Christ and God. In Greek culture, the concept of the headship of a progenitor involved the representation and identity of the family. In Greek literature, the progenitor is the "head," and the "face" of the progenitor symbolizes the representation and identity of the descendants. Paul sees that the head or face of a son in turn represents the father. He extends the metaphor in this more literal sense in a chain of relationships. If "the head of Christ is God" (1 Cor. 11:3c) is understood as using language from natural headship and progenitor relationships, then this statement forms links with many statements in the Pauline corpus and the Gospel tradition of Jesus as God's Son.[76] It is interpreted with the culture's concept of the relationship of an only son to the father, which refers to "head," "face," and "image" as related metaphors. For Paul, Christ's head literally represents God's identity so that when we see the face/head of Christ, we see his Father and the Father's glory. This sense of Christ's representation of God's nature, glory, and image is a theme in both Paul and John:

> the light of the gospel that reveals the glory of Christ, who is the image of God (2 Cor. 4:4)

> the light of the knowledge of God's glory in the face of Jesus Christ (2 Cor. 4:6; cf. Phil. 2:6; Col. 1:15)

> Whoever has seen me has seen the Father. (John 14:9; cf. 12:45)

> We have seen his glory, glory like that of a father's only son, full of grace and truth. (John 1:14 CEB)

For Paul, Christ is God's image in the same way that humanity is Adam's image, which corresponds to "sonship," or σπέρμα. In church councils and confessions, the biblical relationship between the Father and Son has been summarized as "eternal generation."[77] Therefore, Paul has utilized and exploited the Greek concept of "head" to effectively flesh out theological aspects of Jesus's relationship with God.

---

76. We may refer to this relationship as "intertextuality."
77. See the Nicene Creed and the Westminster Confession.

3.5.5 Headship and Males

If Paul utilized and exploited the Greek concept of "head" to effectively flesh out the theological aspects of Jesus's relationship with God, the same may be said about Christ's relationship with men. Paul's argument for man's uncovered head in worship contains the same words—"head," "image," and "glory"—that form significant links with Genesis 1:27–28, Romans 1:18–32, and 2 Corinthians 3:7–18. It is profoundly meaningful that by worshiping appropriately and so giving God glory, men specifically reverse the decline of the gentiles into idolatry, as described in Romans 1:18–32, and display the image of God. By worshiping with unveiled faces, men manifest their spiritual transformation. When we see their heads, we are able to see Christ and God himself, because they bear the family resemblance. For men to cover the head is to deprive God of that glory. Paul associates the husband as the head of the wife with Christ as the head of the church, so that the services that Christ performed for the church become a model for how the husband acts toward his wife. Paul extends the metaphor of the progenitor as "head" and the descendants as the "seed" to apply it to woman's creation from man and the one-flesh relationship. If the husband is the head, then the wife must be his body if they are one flesh. This extension of the metaphor with the literal biological interaction of the head results in the head taking care of the body, so that the husband literally treats his wife like himself. Instead of claiming priority and authority, the husband serves the wife as if he were the woman and she were the man (his body).

3.5.5.1 Men and Christ as the Head in 1 Corinthians 11:3–16

In 1 Corinthians 11:3–4, Paul states that Christ is the head of man, which is to say that Christ is both the creator and the second Adam. He is the source of man's life and existence in a familial sense as well as through creation, though men are not generated in the same way that God generates Christ. Therefore, man's reflection of Christ's glory is differentiated from the way Christ reflects the glory of the Father. However, when a man prays and prophesies with his head uncovered, it draws attention to Christ in a way that honors him. The very appearance of the "creature" in worship demonstrates and motivates appropriate honor of the creator and the head of the new humanity, which is a reversal of humanity's failure to give glory to God through worship, described in Romans 1:21–23.[78]

---

78. Craig Keener rightly sees this as directly related to the image of God: "Humanity 'knew' God, but because they refused to 'glorify' him (1:21), they ended up exchanging his 'glory' and image for that of mortal, earthly creations (1:23). They were God's image (Gen. 1:26–27), but

But even more to the point, in 1 Corinthians 11:3–16, a man's spiritual transformation from Christlike glory to further such glory is on display for everyone to see when his head is uncovered: "And all of us, with unveiled faces, seeing the glory of the Lord as though reflected in a mirror, are being transformed into the same image from one degree of glory to another" (2 Cor. 3:18 NRSV).

This understanding suits the context in 2 Corinthians 3:7–18, where believers are bold and have freedom so that any veil is taken away, unlike Moses (Exod. 34:29–35). Even though the veil is spiritualized to be the law covering the hearts, the glorious ministry of the Spirit is visibly manifested by the man's appearance when he displays the image of God. Therefore, if we may bring these two Pauline passages from the Corinthian Letters together, we can see that Paul believes that spiritual transformation needs to be visibly displayed as a testimony in men. The glory that they display reflects on themselves and Christ, who is the source of their life in creation and new creation, the source of their renewed image of God, and the source of transformation into the family resemblance.[79] Therefore, Paul sees males as being under an obligation to uncover their head in worship, and if they cover their head while praying or prophesying, they are shaming their own literal head (1 Cor. 11:4, 14); but it does not follow that they shame Christ to the same degree or to a greater degree. Any shameful appearance of their literal head reflects more on themselves in their failure to glorify God (as in Rom. 1:8–32).

3.5.5.2 Man as the Head of Woman in Ephesians 5:21–33

The second passage that teaches about man as the head of a woman occurs in the household code in Ephesians 5:21–33.[80] There are two ways in

---

by corrupting God's image in worshiping things other than God[,] they gave up and lost his glory (cf. Rom. 3:23)" (*Romans*, NCCS 6 [Eugene, OR: Cascade, 2009], 34).

79. As Murray Harris observes, τὴν αὐτὴν εἰκόνα (2 Cor. 3:18) means transformation into "'the same image as we see mirrored,' that is, Christ as God's glory or God in Christ, rather than 'the same image as each other,' pointing to the family likeness of Christians" (*The Second Epistle to the Corinthians: A Commentary on the Greek Text*, NIGTC [Grand Rapids: Eerdmans, 2005], 315).

80. For a more technical discussion of the features of Eph. 5:21–33, see Cynthia Long Westfall, "'This Is a Great Metaphor!': Reciprocity in the Ephesians Household Code," in *Christian Origins and Greco-Roman Culture: Social and Literary Context for the New Testament*, ed. Stanley E. Porter and Andrew Pitts, ECHC 1 (Leiden: Brill, 2013), 561–98. See also Michelle Lee-Barnewall, "Turning κεφαλή on Its Head: The Rhetoric of Reversal in Ephesians 5:21–23," in Porter and Pitts, *Christian Origins*, 599–614. Lee-Barnewall maintains the meaning of "authority" for "head," but then she radically reorients it and calls for "a reevaluation of notions of status and privilege, a reevaluation that finds its basis in the example of Christ himself, the head of the body" (613), and comes to very similar conclusions.

the passage that Paul shows how a man should function as the head of a woman. The first is by the model of Christ, and the second is through looking at the implications of the metaphor of "head." This passage shows the key to Paul's development of the metaphor of "head" and its extension. This is the model with which men should teach about the nature of headship, but the instructions to the husbands have been neglected for a singular focus on wives' submission and the analogy of husband to Christ, without the proper understanding of the function of the grammar and syntax, or of how Paul defines the ways in which Christ and the husband are related. As a result, Paul's message has been distorted, and a false view of authority has been propagated in the church.

Let us first notice that the Pauline household code is embedded in Paul's command to be filled with the Spirit, which is followed by a number of activities that culminate in believers submitting to one another. Paul's use of grammar and syntax indicates that the submission of the wife to the husband is a direct application of the general function of mutual submission between believers.[81] The code has three sets of relationships: wives/husbands, children/slaves, and slaves/masters. Paul demonstrates how Christians submit to one another in the Greco-Roman household in these relationships, which are unequal in the world system. The household codes in the Greco-Roman culture concentrated solely on the obligations of the subordinate members of the household—wives, children, and slaves—outlining their duties such as obedience, honor, and submission to their authorities.[82] But Paul also places obligations and restrictions on the husbands, parents, and masters, who have the authority and power with the world system.

This passage on wives and husbands focuses on the husband. Christ's treatment of the church as his bride informs the husband's function as the head of the wife. This is particularly interesting in the analogy because the husband as a believer takes the role of Christ's bride and is therefore charged to treat his wife as he has been treated by his own head.[83] As Christ's bride, the church has received a number of benefits. First, Christ is identified as the church's Savior (Eph. 5:23), who gave himself up for her (5:25), so the husband

---

81. In the Greek, Eph. 5:18–23 is formally a single sentence, and the instructions to the wives in v. 22 are grammatically, syntactically, and lexically dependent on v. 21 (mutual submission) to even understand that submission is indicated. For a more detailed explanation of the structural analysis of Eph. 5:21–33 in terms of its relationship to Col. 3:13–4:1 and how it is embedded in the command to "be filled with the Spirit" in 5:18, see Westfall, "'Great Metaphor!,'" 573–78.

82. For an analysis and summary of the Greco-Roman household codes, see James P. Hering, *The Colossian and Ephesian* Haustafeln *in Theological Context: An Analysis of Their Origins, Relationship, and Message*, TR 260 (New York: Peter Lang, 2007), 9–60.

83. For a discussion of how this passage reverses gender stereotypes, see chap. 2.

is exhorted to lay down his life for his wife.[84] Then the husband is instructed to love his wife as Christ loved his church (5:25). Christ's love is illustrated by the sanctification of the church, which is described in terms of domestic chores normally performed by women: giving a bath, providing clothing, and doing laundry (including spot removal and ironing) (5:26–27).[85] Through the use of analogy and metaphor, Paul has told the husband to follow Christ by serving his wife's needs; this is a brilliant description of servanthood, how the first may be last, and how one may love one's neighbor as oneself when one is an authority in the world's power structures.

Paul then says essentially the same thing in Ephesians 5:28–33 by working with the implications of a husband being a head, which is very different from a progenitor serving as a head. If the husband is the head and husband and wife are one flesh, then his wife must be his body (Eph. 5:28). Note that the wife has now become the male in the metaphor. How does a man treat his own body? Again, the domestic chores described are typical of women's work: the husband provides food (cooking and serving are women's work) and "nurture," which is the word used for women who do child care (Eph. 5:29). The Greco-Roman distinctions between males working and providing in the high-status public sphere (rural, forensic, and political)[86] and females working and providing in the low-status domestic sphere are broken down, as Paul unmistakably assigns intimate domestic service to the husband.

Paul supports the head-body relationship with a citation from the climax of the creation account: a husband and wife "become one flesh" (Gen. 2:24). This passage provides the key for tracing Paul's adoption and adaption of the Greek word κεφαλή as he transfers the characteristics of a progenitor to both the husband and Christ in his relationship to the church (Eph. 5:31 // Gen. 2:24). Since the husband is his wife's source, he is her head, but since they are one flesh, she is his body instead of his seed. This breaks down the Greco-Roman philosophy about hierarchy and the separation between the genders in favor of an organic unity and biological interdependency. The interdependency that Paul explains involves how the husband continues to

84. The idea of sacrificing or dying for another believer is expressed here as the Johannine theme of laying down your life for your brother and sister, which is the quintessential act of imitating Christ (John 10:15, 17–18; 13:37–38; 15:13; 1 John 3:16).

85. For a discussion of the typical expectations for husbands and wives in the household, see Westfall, "'Great Metaphor!,'" 570–72.

86. Note Hierocles: "These therefore are to be divided after the accustomed manner; rural, forensic, and political works are to be attributed to the husband; but to the wife, such works as pertain to spinning wool, making of bread, cooking, and, in short, everything of a domestic nature" (*Household Management*, in Stobaeus, *Flor.* 4.85.21, in *Ethical Fragments of Hierocles, Preserved by Strobaeus*, trans. Thomas Taylor [1822, repr., Mobile, AL: Evergreen Books, 2011], digital edition).

be the source of his wife as a head, which answers Schreiner's key question about how the husband can be understood as the source of his wife.[87] Besides the evidence that man is the source of woman in the creation account, the wife is depicted by Paul as dependent on the husband for her life support (food, clothing, nurture, protection, and love) in the same way that the body is dependent on the head for food, water, air, and the senses of sight and hearing.[88] Paul closes the instructions to husbands with a paraphrase of Jesus's summary of the law and the prophets: "Each of you should love his wife as himself" (Eph. 5:33). But according to Paul's argument, this means that a husband should treat his wife as he treats himself as a man.[89] It is the Golden Rule in gender relationships.

The husband as his wife's head and the wife as his body in marriage became a profound mystery for Paul because he could use this metaphor as a paradigm for the church (Eph. 5:30, 32). This is the basis of one of his most powerful illustrations: the church is Christ's body, which derives its life from him (Eph. 4:15–16; Col. 2:19), shares his high position and authority (Eph. 1:22), and functions in unity and service as the different members of his body (1 Cor. 12:12–30). As his body, believers are completely identified with Christ and his human status; he made them heirs of God and joint heirs with himself (Rom. 8:17). The analogy between Christ and the husband should lead men to share authority, status, power, and resources, and bring freedom that is comparable to what their head, Jesus Christ, provided for them and intends for the rest of his body. Men should love women and treat them literally like themselves, not just as they imagine they would want to be treated if they were women. Therefore, Paul has applied Jesus's summary of the law and prophets to the marriage relationship: "You shall love your neighbor as yourself" (Matt. 22:39 // Mark 12:31 // Luke 10:27; cf. Matt. 19:19).

3.5.6 Headship and Females

Paul utilizes the Greek word κεφαλή in two passages as a metaphor for a person's origin and identity through ancestry and paternity. Eve received her life, her body, and her identity from Adam so that she was in his image in a way that was unique. Yet it was definitely a kinship relationship that was comparable to but closer than Adam's relationship with his descendants: she

87. See footnote 48 above and the corresponding quotation in the text.

88. See more details on the husband's provision for his wife as her source of life in Westfall, "'Great Metaphor!,'" 578–88.

89. The husband's love is not depicted as love for the significant other; it is not the love of an object, and this is an important distinction. It distinguishes between hierarchy and biblical unity.

was bone of his bones and flesh of his flesh (Gen. 2:23). According to Paul, all humanity shares a particular relationship with Adam; in this sense the creation of Eve has something more in common with the rest of humanity than with Adam, because her identity is directly taken from Adam's body. Adam is the source of life for all humanity and for Eve as well. Paul therefore is able to draw strong parallels between the culture's understanding of organic kinship between parents or progenitors and children and apply it to gender-specific apparel in worship (1 Cor. 11:2–12) and to the relationship between husband and wife (Eph. 5:22–31). In these two passages, he shares the culture's views of the correspondence between the metaphor of "head" and the cultural understanding of the function of the literal head. He uses that metaphor to interpret and apply the Genesis account, and he uses the Genesis account, the metaphor of κεφαλή, and a literal understanding of "head" to apply the kinship metaphor to women. It is important to recognize the complexity of the metaphor when it is applied to kinship: a person's head is literally their own head and represents, for example, their father's head, and his head is both his own head and theirs as well.

3.5.6.1 Woman and Man as Her Head in 1 Corinthians 11:3–16

The connection between head, face, image, and glory further explains Paul's connection of the woman's head to the concept of glory. The topic of 1 Corinthians 11:3–16 is about the head who receives glory during worship, not about authority of the men in the house church.

As stated above, a woman bears Adam's image (1 Cor. 15:49), and in Christ she also bears the image and glory of God, as does the rest of humanity. However, Paul also states that the appearance of men bears the image and glory of God in a way that is differentiated from the appearance of women, because a woman's appearance/beauty is the glory of man (1 Cor. 11:7). Paul directs that "man's glory" should be covered up or hidden during worship so that worship not be about honoring or glorifying either man or woman. Woman is the glory of man, and her hair is her glory; therefore she should cover it when in worship. Paul states that the hair is a woman's glory because it is her cloak/covering (1 Cor. 11:15). This is to say that a woman's hair functions like a beauty accessory (like a cloak) that enhances her appearance.[90] Cultures

---

90. This is a view held by many if not all cultures, including the Western culture. It could be argued that women's hair is an obsession in our culture as well, given the time, attention, and expenditure that women give their hair. Therefore, in the Greco-Roman culture, the ancient Near East, rabbinic literature, the Islamic culture, contemporary conservative Jewish culture, and in many anthropological parallels, women's hair is covered because it is considered to be seductive, and at the very least a distraction.

that veil believe that an honorable woman's hair should be reserved for her husband to look at and enjoy and thus not be seen in public.

Shaming the worshipers is also inconsistent with worship. In the culture, the laws about veiling reflect a pejorative evaluation of women, and of men as well (since they were susceptible to the seduction of an unveiled head). It was not directed toward the relationship between the individual husband and his wife. The laws and customs regulated and restricted the veiling of women in order to control them; on the one hand, they believed that veiling inhibited their women's ability to seduce other men, while on the other hand, an uncovered head told them whom they could solicit for sex without consequences.[91] Paul is arguing for a rationale to allow all women to veil, which was not consistent with the cultural practice and laws.[92] When he says that if a woman's hair is not covered, it should be shaved off,[93] he is expressing the seriousness of respecting God's glory by avoiding the distraction of women's hair, but he is also concerned that the church avoid shaming its members.[94] A man should not dishonor his own head by covering it, and a woman's head should not be dishonored by either uncovering it or shaving it. So there is only one option: allow every woman to cover her head.[95]

91. As Lloyd Llewellyn-Jones summarizes, veiling and its restrictions were grounded in a male ideology (*Aphrodite's Tortoise: The Veiled Woman of Ancient Greece* [Swansea: Classical Press of Wales, 2003], 1). However, women constructed their own self-perception and relationship to veiling.

92. There is a great deal of discussion devoted to whether head coverings or hairstyles are in view. For example, some argue that the problem is hairstyles: a disheveled head (like the leper in Lev. 13:45 LXX), in contrast with hair that is controlled and bound. For this view, see Payne, *Man and Woman*, 147–73, 180–87, 204–7; for a survey of the view, see 168n109. However, it is most likely that Paul is referring to all styles of veiling, which, though they may change from region to region, have the same common purpose. The position of this book, like Thiselton's position, still fits Payne's interpretation of the rest of the passage, except for his understanding of 1 Cor. 11:16 (166n100).

93. But Paul could also be subverting the practice of veiling and turning it on its head at this point. In Assyrian law, if someone sees a harlot wearing a veil, whoever sees her "must arrest her, produce witnesses, and bring her to the palace tribunal; they shall not take her jewellery away but the one who arrested her may take her clothing; they shall flog her fifty times and pour pitch on her head" (Middle Assyrian Law 40, in *The Assyrian Laws: Edited with Translation and Commentary* ed. G. R. Driver and John C. Miles [Oxford: Clarendon, 1935], 408–9). As Llewellyn-Jones says, "Practically speaking, it must have rendered her unfit for earning a living, since the removal of the pitch would necessitate the shaving off of the hair, leaving her disfigured for a long time" (*Aphrodite's Tortoise*, 124–25).

94. See §1.6.4. The shaved head did not signal a prostitute, because an uncovered head signaled a prostitute. Rather, a shaved head both destroys a woman's beauty and constitutes a serious violation against her.

95. Llewellyn-Jones offers an interesting hypothesis about the function of the veil that may be relevant: "The veil creates a portable form of seclusion that a woman is able to wear on her visits to the male public world" (*Aphrodite's Tortoise*, 4). If there was any question about

As shown in chapter 1 (above), in the context of the Greco-Roman culture, the veil represents honor, chastity, modesty, status, and literal protection from sexual harassment. In 1 Corinthians 11:5–6, Paul is concerned about shaming and disgracing women; this is shown particularly by the literal references to her head and the shame that a woman would suffer if her head were shaved.[96] Her literal head represents man's glory, and her literal head remains the focus. The wordplay could allow for the shame and dishonor of a woman's husband, father, or guardian to also be understood; it is consistent with the Greco-Roman culture and other cultures that veil. However, Paul does not directly address the shame of a husband because he is talking about all women, not just married women. He stays focused on a more generic relationship between man and woman that is grounded in creation and is applicable even if a woman is a slave and technically does not have a husband, a father, or a guardian who is her head.[97] Therefore, the generic focus of the regulation of gender-specific apparel is relevant to every woman in the same way that it is to every man (1 Cor. 11:3).

The language of the passage and Paul's conclusion suggest that someone wanted to either restrict or prohibit veiling in the Corinthian house churches, but that all women, some women, or an individual woman wanted to veil.[98] First, Paul briefly summarizes the creation account, stating that woman's creation out of and for man is the reason why woman is man's glory. Man is her head because she is created out of him, and her head consequently reflects or in some way expresses his glory. In the Genesis account, she was also his glory because she was specifically made to attract him, in contrast with all the animals (Gen. 2:18–23). In Paul's conclusive decision (signaled by "therefore," διὰ τοῦτο) he directs, "A woman ought to have authority over the head" (ὀφείλει ἡ γυνὴ ἐξουσίαν ἔχειν ἐπὶ τῆς κεφαλῆς),[99] followed by "Never-

---

the silence of women, the veil may have satisfied the proprieties while women spoke in prayer and prophecy.

96. See §1.6.9.

97. A woman who is a slave would not belong to her biological family's household. She would be a member of her master's household, but without biological relationship (unless, of course, the master was her father and her mother was also a slave). According to the non-Pauline social categories, her master would be her paterfamilias, but he would not be her head unless she was his daughter, granddaughter, etc.

98. See above, §1.6.6.

99. James Voelz confuses the English with the Greek in his analysis of the preposition ἐπί in 1 Cor. 11:10: "The conceptual signified [the idea] evoked by this signifier [the word ἐξουσία] cannot be that intended [cannot be just "power"], since one does not have power itself on one's head, but, rather, some symbol of power" (*What Does This Mean? Principles of Biblical Interpretation in the Post-Modern World* [St. Louis: Concordia, 1997], 171). In every other parallel occurrence of ἔχω ἐξουσίαν ἐπί [x], the preposition ἐπί means "over," as in "I have power/control

theless, in the Lord woman is not independent of man" (1 Cor. 11:10–11).[100]
Because women's hair attracts men, Paul directs that every woman should
have the right to veil her own head (presumably in opposition to someone's
objections),[101] but he carefully adds the caveat that this right should not be
extended in principle into some kind of independence movement for women.
He also says in verse 10 that they should have the right to veil their heads
"because of the angels." This could mean that a woman should be able to
exercise her own judgment in matters pertaining to women's apparel because
they are destined to judge the world and the angels, much as he has already
emphatically argued in 1 Corinthians 6:1–6.[102] This makes good sense with
his following caveat that she is not independent of man, particularly if we
assume that the women want to veil and men, or some men, are in some way
opposed to it. On the other hand, Paul could mean that the women need to
get their way about veiling because woman's beauty is so powerful that it
could inappropriately attract angels or distract them from worship.[103] This
would be consistent with the angels' sexual attraction to women and their
sexual relations with them in *1 Enoch* (cf. Gen. 6:1–4), and with a prevalent
belief that angels are present during worship. It makes sense with the thrust
of Paul's argument that during worship "man's glory" should be covered up.

Paul makes a careful statement of interdependency and reciprocity between man and woman to show that neither one is independent of the other.[104]
Here he does not argue that every woman is obligated to every man since
Adam was the source of Eve in creation; instead, he reminds his audience
that every man since Adam has had his source in a woman (1 Cor. 11:11–12).

---

over [*x*]." There is really no ambiguity in the Greek, but rather with assumptions about topic
and content. Note that the TNIV, the NIV 2011, and the CEB have represented the Greek text,
though the TNIV and pre-2011 NIV allow that it could mean "a symbol of authority" by giving
the variation in the footnote.

100. This second sentence is joined with a strong adversative conjunction (πλήν) to state a
contrast, qualification, exception, or contradiction.

101. If it is understood that women want to cover their heads and Paul is supporting them,
it solves the apparent contradiction in the passage that causes translators to make it mean the
opposite of what it says. Gordon Fee writes, "The real difficulty with the argument for us at this
distance emerges right here. What one expects next is for Paul to say that the woman therefore
should be covered. This is precisely why v. 10 historically has been so interpreted—because the
sense of the argument seems to call for it" (*The First Epistle to the Corinthians*, NICNT [Grand
Rapids: Eerdmans, 1987], 516).

102. See above, §1.6.6. But see Craig S. Keener, "Let the Wife Have Authority over Her
Husband (1 Cor. 11:10)," *JGRChJ* 2 (2001–5): 146–52, where he entertains the possibility that
Paul is saying a wife might have authority over her husband. Certainly, Paul says that a wife has
authority over her husband's body in 1 Cor. 7:4, but it does not fit the flow of the argument.

103. See §1.6.9.

104. See the discussion on reciprocity between men and women, §1.4.2.

Paul advocates not the ontological priority of men, or of women, but their mutuality. Therefore, the fact that man is the head of woman is not used here to argue for the subordination of women or the priority of men.[105] Rather, Paul argues that the glory of man should be diminished in worship and the glory of God should be magnified, and this is done, at least in part, by gender-specific apparel.

3.5.6.2 WOMAN AND MAN AS HER HEAD IN EPHESIANS 5:21–33

As discussed above, the reference to the wife's submission in Ephesians 5:22 is not prominent or even direct.[106] In the Greek, it is considerably softened because it is inextricably linked with mutual submission in verse 21. There is not a direct command, a direct address to women, or even a verb for submission in 5:22. Women's submission has to be inferred in 5:22 from the participle in 5:21, which indicates that it is interpreted by 5:21 and as part of the same sentence.

> 5:21 Ὑποτασσόμενοι ἀλλήλοις ἐν φόβῳ Χριστοῦ
> submitting to one another, in the fear of Christ

> 5:22 αἱ γυναῖκες τοῖς ἰδίοις ἀνδράσιν ὡς τῷ κυρίῳ
> wives to their own husbands as to the Lord

For the wife, headship is defined as patronage by referring to the benefits that she receives from her husband through the direct comparison with Christ's provision for the church. That is, Paul motivates wives to fulfill their part of mutual submission because their husbands supply them with their basic necessities of life.

Paul's reference to the husband as "head" in Ephesians 5:23 should be taken as Paul's allusion to the creation of Eve out of Adam. It is interpreted in the near context in verse 31 with the reference to "one flesh" from Genesis 2:24. Paul's inferences from the creation account are fully consistent with the first-century sociological reality of woman's dependence on man for life's necessities. In the traditional marriage in the Greco-Roman culture, the wife lost her identity in her family of origin and received her identity, protection, food, clothing, and shelter from her husband, which Paul correlates with

---

105. The only direct reference to authority is where Paul states that the woman should have authority over her own head (1 Cor. 11:10).
106. For a more detailed discussion of the household code in Ephesians, see Westfall, "'Great Metaphor!'"

Christ's provision for the church.[107] The church's dependence on Christ for its life and primary care was a good illustration of the sociological realities of a woman's dependence on her husband. Christ is represented as the patron of the church, and the church is represented as the beneficiary. The wife's role as the beneficiary and client of the husband is one of the most basic units in a complex Roman patronage system, whose scope stretched from the home to the relationship between the Roman emperor and the empire.[108] For that reason, Paul's understanding of "head" as the source of life's necessities collocates at points with concepts of Greco-Roman patronage and authority because of the concept of reciprocity. Paul's understanding of reciprocity for the client is best expressed in Romans 13:7: "So pay everyone what you owe them. Pay the taxes you owe, pay the duties you are charged, give respect to those you should respect, and honor those you should honor" (CEB).

Since the patronage system is in view, Paul's argument in Ephesians 5:23 is based on true benefits received, not on the order of creation or the basic nature of masculinity and femininity. For Paul, furthermore, Christ's role as the only Savior and benefactor of the church relativizes all patrons and other benefactors. Christ's role as servant (as in the actual activities of bathing, clothing, and laundering [including spot removal, bleaching, and ironing] in Eph. 5:26–27; cf. Phil. 2:1–11) relativizes any sense of entitlement from benefactors within the Christian community.

Therefore, the wife's obligation should be understood in continuity with the dominant culture's expectations for beneficiaries within the patronage system. The wife was obligated to respond to the husband's provision with the appropriate reciprocity of submission and gratitude and/or honor (Eph. 5:21–22, 33b).[109] There is little new information in the instructions to women, but the instructions to men are dramatically different in directness, expansion, and scope.

However, the identity and status of the wife should be transformed in the Christian community by Paul's commands to the husband, which are not consistent with the Greco-Roman patronage system, particularly its expectations of a patron. Instead, the husband is directed to serve his wife by doing

107. However, see chap. 1, n. 51, for the practice of marriage without *manus* (*sine manu*, "without the hand," versus *cum manu*), where the father retained authority over the woman. This points out the fact that women as well as men had multiple obligations or roles that legally and socially undercut, qualified, or overrode the authority relationships in the home between husband and wife. Every man was by no means a paterfamilias.

108. For an introduction to patronage in the Greco-Roman world, see D. A. deSilva, "Patronage," *DNTB*, 766–71. For a more in-depth description, see deSilva, *Honor, Patronage*.

109. Yet in the culture, the obligation of reciprocity shifted when the woman brought greater wealth into the marriage, and the power structure altered.

low-status work typical of women and slaves. Paul makes analogies between a wife and both the church and the man's body, both of which have a high status for Paul and his readers. Therefore, in Paul's theology of marriage, mutual submission is expressed in mutual service. This is an application of Paul's command to "outdo one another in showing honor" (Rom. 12:10 NRSV), where he applies different strategies to each gender. Neither partner is entitled or has priority, because every patron is reduced to functioning like a client. This is the dynamic within the entire section that deals with the household codes in Ephesians 5:22–32 and Colossians 3:18–4:1. In the pairs of relationships addressed, the wives, children, and slaves are to maintain behavior that is acceptable within the culture, while the directions to the husbands, parents, and masters are revolutionary. Paul places the responsibility and obligation for sociological transformation in the Christian community upon those who have power, while he reverses the culture's negative evaluation of those without power, which is consistent with Jesus's teaching.

The instructions to the women and the men interpret and are interpreted by the Genesis passage. The instructions to the woman are based on the act of creation of woman from man (Gen. 2:18–22), and the instructions to man are based on God's declaration that the husband and wife will be one flesh (Gen. 2:23–25). Paul's use of "head" and "body" metaphors have an organic association in both his theology of male and female and his understanding of Christ and the church. Woman draws her life from man, and the church draws its life from Christ. Ephesians 5 suggests that Paul sees the wife's relationship with the husband as an ongoing biological interaction whereby she receives life from the head, and she reciprocates with gratitude and honor expressed with submission. In the cases where the wife is an heiress, the traditional balance of the patron-client relationship and reciprocity was disturbed; in that case, women could be tyrants. However, in the community of God, if a man functioned as he was directed by Paul, the love, support, and service that a woman received would still create a reciprocal obligation, and a woman who was a believer would still have a mission to submit as appropriate in Christ in order to maintain the one-flesh relationship, and as a testimony to the unbelievers.

3.6 Woman Created for Man

One of the reasons why 1 Corinthians 11:3–16 seems difficult to follow in the Greek is the assumption that Paul is correcting women. It has not made sense to scholars that the creation of woman from man and the creation of woman for man (vv. 8–9) should support the conclusion that a woman should have authority over her head (v. 10). It is often assumed that the information "woman was created for man" (ἐκτίσθη . . . γυνὴ διὰ τὸν ἄνδρα) means that God created woman to be subordinate to man as a helper.[110] However, three things contribute to reconsidering the interpretation of the meaning of "woman was created for man" (11:9): first, the assertion that "woman was created for man" supports "woman is the glory of man"; second, the assertion is interpreted by the creation account in Genesis 2:4–25; third, it supplies the grounds for the conclusion "a woman ought to have authority over her head" (v. 10). "Woman is the glory of man" is actually a positive evaluation of women and indicates a high status, because she is both the image and glory of God, and she has such additional beauty that she is the glory of humanity.[111] She is the glory of man by virtue of the fact that she was created from him, and that is why her glory, her beauty, reflects on him. The fact that Paul supported a woman's authority over her own head indicates a positive evaluation. But is this positive evaluation of woman mirrored in the creation account?

One of the major themes in the creation account is God's negative evaluation of man being alone (Gen. 2:18: "It is not good for the man to be alone"), and God's elaborate demonstration of man's need for a suitable mate through giving him the task of naming the pairs of animals (Gen. 2:19–20). When Adam sees Eve, he is thrilled with her (Gen. 2:23). Therefore, we may infer that 1 Corinthians 11:9 means that man needed woman and knew it, which is a simple and straightforward summary of Genesis 2:18–23. The woman met a need and provided a service, which also invokes the principle of reciprocity in which the woman is the patron (helper) and the man is the client. In addition, man's attraction to woman is an essential dynamic between men and women that is built into the creation account.[112] In 1 Esdras 4:17, the statements "[women] bring men glory; men cannot exist without women" form part of the author's argument to prove the power of women over men.[113] This need and attraction is precisely the reason why certain cultures insist that respectable women wear a veil; these cultures place the responsibility and

110. A heavy interpretive load is placed on the preposition διά (in 11:9) by those who argue that this means the subordination of women, but Greek prepositions are minimal in their semantic contribution. The context of the text and the creation passage must determine the meaning of the preposition and the phrase.

111. See above, §1.6.9.

112. The "creation of woman for the sake of man" may be somewhat consistent with rabbinic and Islamic claims: in creation, "woman received nine parts of desire, and man only one," according to Ali ibn Abi Taleb, the first male convert to Islam and founder of the Shiite sect ('Amili, Muhammad bin Hasan al-Hurr al, Wasa'ilu sh-Shi'ah [Beirut: Dar Ihya'i't-'l-'Arabi, 1391], 14:40).

113. This study assumes that Paul was interacting with 1 Esdras, balancing out the argument for women's power with the creation account of woman's origin from man.

burden to control the men's response to woman's attraction on women and their attire and limit the power of women. In the Middle East, historically, men have responded to women's beauty as both a threat and a commodity, and they have controlled veiling to suit their own agendas. In contrast, Paul indicates that in the Christian community, it is the woman's right to veil, which transforms the symbol.

After making this point, Paul denies woman's independence from man, because if man was needy, and woman met the man's need, it would have certain repercussions within the first-century worldview. As stated above, the "helper" in Genesis 2:19 would be a patron, and the one who is helped would be a beneficiary. However, the obligation of reciprocity is offset because woman is not independent; she is also a beneficiary because she was created from man. On the other hand, every man is born from a woman (1 Cor. 11:12); thus men and women owe their life to each other and are mutually dependent. Rather than establishing and arguing authority and subordination in gender relationships in 1 Corinthians 11, Paul argues a mutual dependence between men and women. Furthermore, he reminds men and women that in the creation account, everything comes from God, and he is the patron who granted the gifts of life and partnership to both of them, so any claims to authority over each other are relativized.

The Pauline texts contain a theology of gender that is realized in how Paul explains the creation account with terms and symbols of the Greco-Roman culture and the idioms of the Greek language. Through applying the metaphor of "head" to Adam, Paul indicates that Eve has multiple identities like the rest of humanity after Adam. Women are the image of God, the image of Adam, and "the glory of man" as well. Paul's description of woman as "the glory of man" does not indicate subordination or a lesser glory, but rather refers to an additional glory: the power of her beauty over men. Neither can we project male priority into Paul's brief narrative in 1 Timothy 2:13–14, which states that Adam was formed first (v. 13). Instead, Paul teaches mutuality from the creation passage, because Paul depicts man as a beneficiary of benefits and needing the woman's help in terms that the culture would understand; however, woman was formed from man so that in the creation account man functioned as the woman's head (her origin of life) in Greek idiom; but then subsequently every man comes from woman so that woman is also the origin of life, which is what the name "Eve" means in Genesis 3:20. Therefore, through God's design, female and male are not independent of each other. There is no compelling reason to interpret Paul as contradicting, reinterpreting, or qualifying the authority of women in the creation account in Genesis 1:27–28 or in his use of the Greek idiom "head." Both male and female were created in God's image, and both were created for dominion that Paul indicates is exercised in terms of mutuality and reciprocity within appropriate cultural paradigms.

four

The Fall

The narrative of the fall in Genesis 3 has played a significant role in the biblical/theological discussion about gender alongside the creation account in Genesis. However, the gender discussion has tended to focus on the fall's implications for women and has neglected to fully and coherently address the implications for men. This study will begin to address that lacuna and then reinterpret the implications for women.

In the discussion of gender and the fall in the Pauline Epistles, 1 Timothy 2:14 is the central text. Paul connects his prohibitions of a woman teaching or dominating a man in 1 Timothy 2:12 with a brief summary of the fall narrative in verse 14, together with a reference to childbearing in verse 15. I will argue below that the reference to childbearing is constrained to have direct ties with the consequences of the fall: "Adam was not deceived, but the woman was deceived and became a transgressor. Yet she will be saved through childbearing, provided they continue in faith and love and holiness, with modesty" (1 Tim. 2:14–15 NRSV).

As with Paul's statement about the order of creation, the logic connecting the account of the fall with the two prohibitions placed on women in verse 12 must be inferred.[1] These Pauline statements have provided a lot of fuel for the gender discussion throughout the history of the church. The Genesis account describes the behavior of the woman in greater detail than Paul does, and it

---

1. In 1 Tim. 2:13–14, the summary of the creation and fall narratives is joined to the prohibitions with a γάρ, which indicates that it is support material for the prohibitions (v. 12) and most likely for the command that a woman should learn (v. 11). On the other hand, it could function as support material for the conclusion about childbirth (v. 15).

also has generated a lot of discussion on its own both in Jewish and Christian literature. That discussion of the fall together with 1 Timothy 2:14 has been given as the primary rationale for various restrictions of women in the church. The historical position of the church is that women are more easily deceived by nature, that they are possibly more susceptible to demonic influence, and therefore that women are not qualified to teach or lead the church—a position based on ontology.[2] In regard to sin, it is sometimes said that woman sinned first and is primarily responsible for the fall, and she often is assigned primary responsibility for Adam's sin as well. Therefore women in the church must bear the consequences for Eve's behavior through their subordination and various restrictions. On the other hand, 1 Timothy 2:15 has puzzled interpreters as to what being saved through childbirth means and how it is related to the prohibition, the Genesis account, and Pauline theology.

However, other Pauline passages about the fall may be used to interpret 1 Timothy 2:14–15. At least we can lay down parameters to better understand what Paul would likely mean and what he would be unlikely to mean. There has particularly been an issue with the interpretation of 1 Timothy 2:15. The statement that women will be saved by childbirth, if they behave in a godly way, seems to be in conflict with the Pauline theology that believers are saved by faith and not works. In such cases there are three basic options: (1) We may look for viable alternate interpretations in the language and grammar, the contexts of the text, the cultural situation, and Pauline thought. (2) We may accept it as Paul's distinction between men and women, with the result that Paul may be inconsistent or incoherent. (3) We may question Pauline authorship, though even in the case of pseudonymity, it was clearly meant to be understood in the context of the Pauline corpus. A fuller exegesis of 1 Timothy 2:8–15 will be given in chapter 9, but here I will discuss gender and the fall in terms of deception, the origin of sin, and Paul's conclusion that a woman "will be saved through childbirth."

4.1 Gender and Deception

Historically, most scholars have inferred how 1 Timothy 2:14 may be relevant to the prohibitions in 2:12: Eve displays a trait characteristic of all women

---

2. Now the historic view has been modified to avoid the historic rationale that women are ontologically inferior. See William Webb's discussion in *Slaves, Women & Homosexuals: Exploring the Hermeneutics of Cultural Analysis* (Downers Grove, IL: InterVarsity, 2001), 224–31. For a full argument that favors a contemporary version of this view and moderates the pejorative evaluation of women, see Daniel Doriani, "History of Interpretation of 1 Timothy 2," in *Women in the Church: A Fresh Analysis of 1 Timothy 2:9–15*, ed. Andreas J. Köstenberger, Thomas R. Schreiner, and H. Scott Baldwin (Grand Rapids: Baker, 1995), 213–67.

that disqualifies them from teaching or leadership, since all women are more vulnerable to deception than men. It has also often been inferred that women are drawn to false teaching and cults and will teach error.[3] Others have suggested that women are susceptible to demonic influence, interpreting the prohibition by associating it with the role of Satan in the temptation account and the reference to angels in 1 Corinthians 11:10 that alludes to Genesis 6:1–5. First, we must once again stress the fact that all these reasons given for the Pauline prohibitions are inferences largely drawn from the interpreter's past instruction, worldview, and other presuppositions. Paul simply gives a brief narrative of the fall without further explanation of his theology or the relevance of the narrative to the prohibitions, except for the conclusion in 1 Timothy 2:15. Second, the inference that all women are more deceived and susceptible to temptation has really been a statement about the priority, preeminence, and qualification of men for teaching and leadership in the church. Adam was not the one who was deceived; therefore men should be the teachers and leaders. However, if that is a valid interpretation, then to be consistent, Adam's behavior could be generalized for all men, and Adam would display a trait that is characteristic of all men: he was not deceived. Therefore, it is important to examine the topic of deception, teaching, and leadership in the Pauline corpus from the separate perspectives of male and female, as well as the effects of Jesus's redemption and the effects of sanctification on a person's susceptibility to deception.

4.1.1 Males and Deception

In 1 Timothy 2:14a Paul states that Adam was not deceived. If one finds that all women are prone to deception because Eve was deceived, to be hermeneutically consistent, one should also take the position that men are not prone to deception, because in the passage Adam's lack of deception is absolute and not a matter of degree. However, as it will be shown, Paul believes that all humans are in danger of deception, and he applies the paradigm of Eve's temptation to males.

In the Pauline corpus, Paul describes all believers as being in danger of deception by sin, by others, or by oneself (Rom. 7:11; 16:18; 1 Cor. 3:18; 6:9; 15:33; 2 Cor. 11:3; Gal. 6:3, 7; 2 Thess. 2:3; 1 Tim. 2:14; 2 Tim. 3:13; Titus 3:3).[4]

---

3. The percentages of women who are attracted to cults may often be higher than the percentages of men, but then again, the numbers of women in conventional religious groups are also higher than those of men. Rodney Stark claims that it is a generalization across cultures and time that women are more religious than men ("Physiology and Faith: Addressing the 'Universal' Gender Difference in Religious Commitment," *JSSR* 41 [2002]: 495–507).

4. Four verbs are used for "to deceive" in the Pauline corpus: ἐξαπατάω (Rom. 7:11; 16:18; 1 Cor. 3:18; 2 Cor. 11:3; 2 Thess. 2:3; 1 Tim. 2:14); ἀπατάω (Eph. 5:6; 1 Tim. 2:14); πλανάω (1 Cor. 6:9; 15:33; Gal. 6:7; 2 Tim. 3:13 [2×]; Titus 3:3); φρεναπατάω (Gal. 6:3).

In all of these texts, the deceived are grammatically either masculine singular or masculine plural in the Greek, which indicates that men certainly are the referents, though women could be included as referents as well.[5] Therefore, Paul is afraid that churches and individuals might be deceived regardless of gender. Paul wrote a description of temptation by sin in Romans 7:11, which appears to be autobiographical but probably is meant to apply generally to all humanity (Adam).[6] Paul (a male) alludes to the temptation account of Eve in Genesis 3 with some variation.[7] Probably in a paradigmatic statement that represents humanity's relationship to sin, Paul is the one who has been deceived: sin, like Satan, seized an opportunity, deceived him, and killed him. The result is Paul's description of a wretched man who is mired in a continual state as a prisoner to sin and death (Rom. 7:13–24). According to Paul, all unbelievers are blinded by Satan, or "the god of this world" (2 Cor. 4:4). As for believers, he specifically gives the account of Eve's temptation as an illustration for the entire Corinthian church, which he feared was in danger of being led astray (2 Cor. 11:3).[8] Therefore Paul would warn his readers: "Do not be deceived!" (μὴ πλανᾶσθε in 1 Cor. 6:9; 15:33; Gal. 6:7).[9] Furthermore, certain males are

---

5. Masculine singulars would not necessarily omit women from the reference, since the masculine was grammatically the default gender. It may be assumed that women are included in masculine plurals unless the context specifically indicates that women are not in view. In 1 Cor. 6:9, sexual immorality was more typical of men who chose to have sex with slaves, women or men in brothels or temples, or with each other. The Greco-Roman culture did not condemn men who acted this way. However, it would have been understood that any woman believer who voluntarily engaged in such behavior was even more deceived, since the culture roundly condemned this behavior in women. Paul clearly is addressing a person who chooses to have sex with someone who has had multiple sex partners. He was not passing judgment on slaves who were forced to have multiple sex partners or residents of brothels or temples who were prostituted and had no choice.

6. In Rom. 7:7–13, the suggested referents for the identity of "I" are Paul, the typical Jewish person, Israel when the law was given, Adam at the time of the fall, and the general unregenerate human predicament. In Rom. 7:14–25, however, the suggested referents are Paul before his conversion or Paul in his present experience as a Christian. Other possibilities include the general experience of a Christian, the typical Jewish person, the Christian who is living a defeated life, or the general unregenerate human predicament. For further discussion, see Cynthia Long Westfall, "A Discourse Analysis of Romans 7:7–25: The Pauline Autobiography?," in *The Linguist as Pedagogue: Trends in the Teaching and Linguistic Analysis of the Greek New Testament*, ed. Stanley E. Porter and Matthew Brook O'Donnell, NTM 11 (Sheffield: Sheffield Phoenix, 2009), 146–58.

7. As James Dunn says, "The echo of the Genesis account is certainly deliberate" (*Romans 1–8*, WBC 38A [Nashville: Nelson, 1988], 384). The connections: God's command has a similar role to the law, the deception, and the ultimate outcome of death.

8. As Paul Barnett says, "The very future of the Corinthians as an apostolic church is in jeopardy. . . . Under the symbolism of this allegory, Eve represents the church at Corinth" (*The Second Epistle to the Corinthians*, NICNT [Grand Rapids: Eerdmans, 1997], 501).

9. James too warned his readers not to be deceived (James 1:16).

depicted as false teachers who are self-deceived and themselves deceivers (cf. 2 Cor. 11:13–14; 2 Tim. 2:17–18; 3:6–8). Most important, in 1 Timothy, Paul states that without certain safeguards, male or female elders are in danger of (or prone to) falling into the devil's trap because of conceit or disgrace (1 Tim. 3:6–7). One cannot argue that Paul describes men as less prone to deception than women in the rest of the Pauline corpus or even in the Pastoral Epistles. Even though Eve was a woman, according to Paul the possibility of being tempted or deceived by Satan or sin is a universal experience. Eve's deception is a paradigmatic example of the human condition.

On the other hand, Paul saw certain groups of people or men as more prone to either knowing the truth or being deceived. In Romans 1–2, if it is given that Paul is contrasting gentiles with Jews, gentiles as a whole are viewed as being deceived, self-deceived, and deceiving others. They have failed to acknowledge God, as manifested in a chain of decisions or cultural developments culminating in godlessness and wickedness that make them the target of God's wrath (Rom. 1:18–32).[10] By contrast, Jews have the advantage of being entrusted with the oracles of God, though they are equally under the condemnation of sin for not practicing what they teach or following the law (Rom. 3:2). However, Paul does not restrict gentiles from teaching and leading even though he represents them as being more prone to deception than Jews. Similarly, he says it is true that "Cretans are always liars, vicious brutes, lazy gluttons" (Titus 1:12–13), yet if Titus rebukes them, they will be able to be sound in the faith.[11] Titus is still instructed to appoint elders and overseers in every town from among the believing population of Crete. Therefore, we see that even when Paul specifically believes and says that particular people groups are more prone to deception, self-deception, and being deceived, it does not disqualify individuals from those groups from teaching or leadership.

Paul teaches that by Christ's one powerful act, and by the Spirit, all believers are capable of overcoming deception (Rom. 7:7–8:11). Jesus Christ sets believers free from being captive to sin (6:6–7), and he meets righteous requirements that lead to life for everyone (5:18), so now sin has no real

10. James Dunn states that in Rom. 1:18–32, "The effect is to characterize human (Adam) unrighteousness from a Jewish perspective; that is, human unrighteousness typified by the Jewish abhorrence of idolatry and the degradation of Gentile sexual ethics" (*Romans 1–8*, 53).

11. William Mounce's comments are interesting from the standpoint of the gender discussion: "Paul obviously is not applying this saying to all Cretans; otherwise all Cretan Christians would fall under its condemnation, and Epimenides himself would also be a liar and therefore his saying false. Sweeping generalizations by nature do not always claim to be true in every situation; they are generally true. Paul is just trying to make a point" (*Pastoral Epistles*, WBC 46 [Nashville: Nelson, 2000], 398).

power over a believer. All believers are enabled to present the members of their bodies as instruments of righteousness (6:13–14). The law of the Holy Spirit gives life and sets a person free from the law of sin and death (8:1–2), which includes deception by sin, Satan, or demons (7:11).[12] Therefore, Paul did not believe that any believers were helpless in their susceptibility to deception, but that they could escape from deception by living in the Spirit and receiving correction.

In conclusion, one cannot say that Paul's assertion that "Adam was not deceived" (1 Tim. 2:14a) means that men in general are not deceived. On the contrary, in the Pauline corpus, deception is a human condition. Men who are not believers are deceived just like Eve, and Paul is afraid that men who are believers will be deceived just like Eve. Furthermore, Paul appears to believe that certain worldviews, cultures, and nationalities are more prone to certain sins that are linked with deception, such as gentiles being prone to idolatry, and Cretans being liars and gluttons. However, the weak, the foolish, the lowly, and the despised are not banned by Paul from teaching and leadership. Rather, in the context of correcting the Corinthian church for boasting about Christian leaders with worldly criteria (wisdom, power, status), Paul says that their entire calling in the gospel is based on God's reversal of those very criteria:

> God chose what is foolish in the world to shame the wise; God chose what is weak in the world to shame the strong; God chose what is low and despised in the world, things that are not, to reduce to nothing things that are, so that no one might boast in the presence of God. He is the source of your life in Christ Jesus, who became for us wisdom from God, and righteousness and sanctification and redemption, in order that, as it is written, "Let the one who boasts, boast in the Lord." (1 Cor. 1:27–31 NRSV)

Paul's point is that qualification for leadership comes from the model of Jesus Christ and the foolishness of the cross. Later in the epistle he teaches that the gifts of the Holy Spirit determine each person's function in the body. Since God loves to choose the foolish, the weak, the lowly, and the despised, we can expect surprises in his choices that challenge our worldly standards of what makes an ideal teacher or leader. Paul argues that he himself was exactly that kind of choice.

12. Grant Osborne speaks of five liberations in the larger context of Rom. 8:1–11: "a freedom from slavery to sin (6:16–22), a freedom from being taken prisoner (7:23), a freedom from condemnation (8:1), a freedom from the power of sin and death (8:2), and a final liberation of both creation and the individual at the eschaton (8:21, 23)" (*Romans*, IVPNTC 6 [Downers Grove, IL: InterVarsity, 2004], 194–95).

4.1.2 Females and Deception

What is the relevance of the fall narrative for the instructions to women in 1 Timothy 2:11–15? What is the logical relationship between the prohibitions against a woman teaching or dominating a man and the narrative of the deception of Eve by Satan? Until the twentieth century, the majority of scholars and interpreters have inferred that Satan's deception of Eve provided the reason or justification for such prohibitions.[13] Therefore, they made a concerted attempt to flesh out exactly how the fall justified these prohibitions. In short, motivated by the narrative of the fall, Paul's interpreters profiled women negatively in order to justify the application of the prohibitions in 1 Timothy 2:12 to all women. The inquiry was heavily influenced by Greek philosophy, particularly in the medieval period. This has resulted in a history of misogynist speculations about women in terms of their character, behavior, potential, and body that sound far more like Aristotle than Paul—if not even more negative—because they were imputing to women the blame, shame, and responsibility for the fall. However, in the twentieth century, the pejorative evaluations of women lost traction, in part because the education of women demonstrated their ability to use logic and critical thinking, and the use of statistics on gendered behavior overturned age-old stereotypes such as the charge that women were unspiritual and more interested in sex than men.

More recent discussions have proceeded with more caution in the evaluation of women. Though some scholars hold to a modified traditional view about women's susceptibility to temptation, others have looked for alternative interpretations. There are at least four views on the logical relationships between the prohibitions in 1 Timothy 2:12 and the deception of Eve in 1 Timothy 2:14:[14] (1) Eve's deception and actions in the fall are the reason for the prohi-

---

13. Many scholars have argued that the conjunction γάρ signals that Paul is giving a reason, but this does not reflect an adequate understanding of how the conjunction functions. See Mounce's discussion of γάρ in *Pastoral Epistles*, 131–35, where he briefly surveys Paul's uses of γάρ and concludes: the evidence that it introduces a reason in 1 Tim. 2:13 is overwhelming since its most frequent use is "to express cause or reason" (131). However, in every instance the logical relationship has to be inferred from the context, and γάρ itself does not "express cause or reason." Its minimal semantic contribution signals support material, which may include examples, types, quotations, and other forms of support as well as cause; it is comparable in flexibility to the relationship of a participle to a finite verb. Interpretations of specific texts cannot be determined by the "most frequent use." It is ironic that many of the scholars who have held this view also have tended to claim that one should never formulate theology from history/narrative in the Bible.

14. For a summary and evaluation of four total views, see I. Howard Marshall, *The Pastoral Epistles*, ICC (Edinburgh: T&T Clark, 1999), 465–67. He adds the views that (1) Eve is responsible for Adam's sin, and (2) vv. 13–14 provide "a universally applicable basis of the subordination of women to man" (ibid., 465). I have omitted both because they go beyond the

bitions against all women teaching men (or possibly anyone) because women are prone to deception; (2) Eve's deception and actions are an illustration (or typology) of all women apart from sanctification; (3) Eve's deception is an illustration of the deception among the women in Ephesus; (4) Eve's deception and transgression provide a correction of myths and/or false teachings that are circulating among the women in Ephesus. The third and fourth views are related to the situational context and are similar, but the traditional view that Eve's deception is the reason for the prohibitions will first be examined here.

Most scholars have suggested that Eve's role in the fall indicates that there is an ontological flaw in women that makes them susceptible to deception, and perhaps more likely to deceive others.[15] Some found particular significance in the fact that Satan approached Eve instead of Adam, which seems to indicate that women are more vulnerable to satanic attack than men. Furthermore, in Genesis 6:1–5, the "sons of God" saw that women were beautiful and took them as wives. The book of *1 Enoch* connects the "sons of God" with fallen angels, which is taken to indicate that women are vulnerable to other forms of spiritual attack from angels and demons. In 1 Corinthians 11:10, many have understood Paul to state that women ought to wear a veil "because of the angels,"[16] so that some conclude (based in part on a faulty assumption about the meaning of the veil) that women in the church continue to be susceptible to angelic (demonic) attack unless they are under male authority.

Paul did not hesitate to characterize all humanity as deceived and Satan as a deceiver, but he never explicitly says that all women believers have a special

---

issue of deception. Marshall omits the view that Eve could illustrate the deception of women (typology). He concludes that vv. 13–14 counter the false teaching in Ephesus.

15. A variation on this—held by Martin Dibelius and Hans Conzelmann, among others—is that the deception was sexual seduction, a view based on later Jewish interpretation (*The Pastoral Epistles: A Commentary on the Pastoral Epistles*, trans. Philip Buttolph and Adela Yarbro, ed. Helmut Koester, Hermeneia [Philadelphia: Fortress, 1972], 48). On that basis, they were able to propose considerable cohesion in 1 Tim. 2:11–15: sexual seduction led to sin so that "the question of salvation from divine wrath becomes an urgent one," and, influenced by Gen. 3:16, "where someone sins, through that he [or she] is saved." In contradiction to gnostic teaching (as in *Gospel of the Egyptians*: "How long will men continue to die? As long as women give birth"; and Saturninus's teaching: "Marriage and procreation come from Satan"), there is a "Christianization of the natural order" (48–49). Yet difficulties come with this anachronistic projection of seduction into the Greek word ἀπατάω ("to deceive" in 1 Tim. 2:14 in reference to Gen. 3:13), the confusion of the sin with the consequences, the failure to explain how the "natural order" would be natural for Paul since it is part of the consequences of the fall, and how participating in the "natural order" can be said to save women from divine wrath. Nevertheless, the possible connection of later gnostic teaching with the false teachers' prohibition of marriage (1 Tim. 4:3) is helpful.

16. See §3.5.6.1 on the angels in 1 Cor. 11:10. One position has been that the veil is a symbol of subordination that protects women from deception.

problem with deception, nor that women are Satan's favorite target or more likely to succumb to attack. In both Genesis 6:1–5 and 1 Corinthians 11:10, if the accounts indicate that women are vulnerable to angels, it is because of their beauty (their glory), not because they are ethically flawed. It is true that Paul said that there were some gullible women in Ephesus who were "overwhelmed by their sins and swayed by all kinds of desires, who are always being instructed and can never arrive at a knowledge of the truth" (2 Tim. 3:6–7 NRSV). However, Paul did not suggest that this was true of all the women in Ephesus; rather, they represent a type of woman.[17] Furthermore, in the context of 2 Timothy, the focus is on the far more depraved conduct of the type of men who are false teachers that prey on and victimize such gullible women (2 Tim. 3:1–9). In his brief and restrained summary of the fall narrative, Paul stops short of generalizing Eve's behavior as typical of women or profiling women negatively. But in the discussion of men and deception, we have seen that even if Paul had explicitly characterized all women as more foolish, weak, lowly, and despised, in the context of Pauline theology that may well qualify them to be God's instruments to shame the wise, the strong, and the privileged (1 Cor. 1:18–31). Paul's declaration that no individual or group is supposed to be able to boast in front of God should interpret and critique male claims of priority, authority, and honor in gender relationships in the Christian community.[18] The relevance of statistics demonstrating the relative strengths and weaknesses, qualifications, and mathematical aptitude of men versus women evaporate before Paul's clear teaching about how God calls believers into community and how God chooses his instruments to serve the church.

There must be no distortion about the nature of the deception in the fall narrative: Eve's deception is not a question of relative strengths and weaknesses, logic, or commitment to truth in formulating doctrine.[19] There is no

17. As Howard Marshall says, "To see a general devaluation of women here . . . is mistaken in view of the positive references elsewhere (1:5; cf. 3:14 by implication)" (*Pastoral Epistles*, 777).

18. In his analysis of 1 Cor. 1:26–31, Hans Conzelmann states, "The proclamation of the cross does not by any means replace unchristian self-glorification with self-glorification of a Christian kind, but with the renunciation of our own glory" (*1 Corinthians: A Commentary on the First Epistle to the Corinthians*, trans. James W. Leitch, ed. George W. MacRae, Hermeneia [Philadelphia: Fortress, 1975], 51). It is interesting that in 1 Cor. 11:3–16, the fact that women are the glory of man has been taken to mean that men's glory must not be compromised during worship.

19. Earlier, Thomas Schreiner argued that this indicates a difference in roles based on relative strengths and weaknesses: "Generally speaking, women are more relational and nurturing and men are more given to rational analysis and objectivity. Women are less prone than men to see the importance of doctrinal formulations, especially when it comes to the issue of identifying heresy and making a stand for the truth" ("An Interpretation of 1 Timothy 2:9–15: A

evidence of Paul believing that women were prone to any deception such that the work of Christ, the ministry of the Holy Spirit, and sound teaching could not rescue, sanctify, and correct them (Rom. 8:1–2). Paul emphatically taught that Jesus Christ frees humanity from the bondage of sin and the deception of Satan typified by Eve's actions. Women as well as men in the Christian community are in danger of deception, but the same remedies are available: biblical correction and teaching—the very remedies that Paul was implementing in both the epistle and the command for a woman to learn in 1 Timothy 2:11.[20] The suggestion that all women are disqualified from any service to the church because they are prone to deception or destined to repeat the pattern of the fall would mean that God's creation was inherently flawed or sinful and/or that the work of Christ and the ministry of the Holy Spirit were not sufficient for women.

On the other hand, Stanley Porter suggests that the fall narrative is an illustration of the condition of all women apart from the salvific and sanctifying work of Christ: "Even though Adam was first created, it was Eve or 'the woman' (here an anaphoric use of the article, 'the woman referred to above, that is, Eve') who was first deceived. The argument implies that all women as a result are 'deceived.' But the one who is 'saved' . . . is the woman who remains in faith and love and holiness."[21]

This view takes into account the context and contrasts between verses 14 and 15 in a way that reflects Paul's understanding of deception in the rest of the Pauline corpus. Since Paul is addressing women's issues, it may be relevant

Dialogue with Scholarship," in *Women in the Church: A Fresh Analysis of 1 Timothy 2:9–15*, ed. Andreas J. Köstenberger, Thomas R. Schreiner, and H. Scott Baldwin [Grand Rapids: Baker, 1995], 145). But Schreiner also argues that "susceptibility to deception" is characteristic of women and a "*moral* category" ("William J. Webb's *Slaves, Women & Homosexuals*: A Review Article," *SBJT* 6 [2002]: 62–63). Later, in a revision of "An Interpretation of 1 Timothy 2:9–15: A Dialogue with Scholarship," Schreiner has reversed his position, stating, "If Paul argued that women were deceived because of innate dispositions, the goodness of God's creative work is called into question" (endnotes to "An Interpretation of 1 Timothy 2:9–15," in *Women in the Church: An Analysis and Application of 1 Timothy 2:9–15*, 2nd ed., ed. Andreas Köstenberger and Thomas R. Schreiner [Grand Rapids: Baker Academic, 2005], 225n210).

20. There is a connection in Paul between ignorance and deception; the whole premise of 1 Tim. 1:3 is that Paul can correct and teach those who are being misled in Ephesus. He is continually urging elsewhere, "Do not be deceived!" In his review of Webb's *Slaves, Women & Homosexuals*, Schreiner states that Webb "turns susceptibility to deception into ignorance, lack of education, and inexperience, but this does not fit with the Scriptures, for deception is a *moral* category" (Schreiner, "Review Article," 63, emphasis original). Yet this implies that woman was created with a moral flaw because Eve was deceived before her transgression.

21. Porter, "What Does It Mean to Be 'Saved by Childbirth' (1 Tim. 2:15)?," *JSNT* 49 (1993): 93.

to say that all women are deceived apart from the sanctification provided by Jesus Christ and the Holy Spirit. There are significant links between verse 15 and the instructions to all women in 1 Timothy 2:9–10: the path out of deception (salvation) involves godliness and modesty (vv. 9–10, 15) together with instruction (v. 11). This view has many strengths, but it does not account for the contrast with Adam, who was not deceived, and it does not deal with the textual links to Genesis 3 and its consequences of the fall for women. Nor does it adequately explore the relevance of the situational context among the Ephesian women.

The epistles of 1–2 Timothy show that the Christian women in Ephesus were being deceived in a way that was unparalleled in the other churches addressed in the Pauline corpus. In 1 Timothy 1:3, Paul states that Timothy was left behind in Ephesus to correct a variety of false teachings, and the explicit purpose of the letter is to encourage him in that task. In both letters Paul repeatedly addresses a number of problems with false teaching that has spread among the women of Ephesus. There are several references to Satan and demonic activity in the deception of women, especially of widows, by false teachers (1 Tim. 4:1; 5:15; 2 Tim. 2:26; 3:6–7).[22] Some of the content of the false teaching includes the "prohibition of marriage" (1 Tim. 4:3), which could well have included the promotion of celibacy among married women.[23] It looks as though the widows were reluctant to marry because they were avoiding childbirth (5:11–15).[24] The older women were spreading godless myths (4:7), some of the widows were living for pleasure (5:6), and some widows had already turned away to "follow Satan" (5:15). False teachers had also wormed their way into the homes and preyed on gullible women (2 Tim. 3:6). Therefore, the problems of false teaching among the women in Ephesus include the misuse of narrative (myths, old wives' tales), deception with satanic and demonic activity, and issues with marriage and childbirth.[25] Certainly Eve was a good illustration of the nature of the deception (as in the use of typology), but there may be a stronger indication that Paul is correcting the content of the stories that were spreading and addressing some of the women's concerns that made them vulnerable to the content of false

22. But Paul also finds satanic activity trapping elders into "coming under his sway and sharing in his condemnation" (Marshall, *Pastoral Epistles*, 483).

23. Ibid., 541. Marshall writes that the "prohibition of marriage" (γαμεῖν) "presumably implies abstinence from sexual activity (within or outside of marriage)."

24. It is significant that in 1 Tim. 5:14, Paul wants women to marry, have children, and rule their households (γαμεῖν, τεκνογονεῖν, οἰκοδεσποτεῖν). He directly contradicts the false teachers, who are forbidding sex/marriage (γαμεῖν), by stating the direct outcome that the women will have children; childbirth is highlighted as an issue in 1 Tim. 2:15.

25. See §9.3.3.

teaching.[26] Therefore, a discourse reading of 1 Timothy strongly suggests that Paul is writing instructions to women in 1 Timothy 2:11–15 in order to deal with the specific problems among the women in the church community in Ephesus, and specific aspects of the false teachings were being addressed in verses 13–15.[27] As Howard Marshall says, "The likelihood is that a drastic measure is being taken to counteract the effects of false teaching."[28]

4.1.3 Summary

In summary, apart from 1–2 Timothy, men and women are equally prone to deception in the Pauline corpus. If anything, men typically are presented as those who are deceived like Eve and also as those who deceive.[29] Therefore, the fact that Adam was not deceived in 1 Timothy 2:14a cannot be considered as typical of men in Pauline teaching. In the letters to Timothy, Paul particularly identifies some types of men who are more prone to deception and self-deception, and as their victims, a type of woman who is gullible. The text in 1 Timothy 2:14 does not generalize Eve's deception as a pattern of all women, and the text does not demand such a generalization, particularly since Paul is simply summarizing the Genesis narrative. It is certain that the account of the fall is relevant to the command for a woman to learn and the prohibitions in 1 Timothy 2:11–12, but that relevance may be easily found in the context of the incorrect myths, false teaching, and deception among the women of Ephesus.

26. It is without question that women's narratives (myths, old wives' tales) were a significant part of the problem, which is consistent with the role of narrative among women historically. Richard Clark Kroeger and Catherine Clark Kroeger argue that gnostic myths (possibly from the second century) reverse Adam's and Eve's roles in the fall, and they demonstrate significant parallels to Paul's account of creation and the fall as well as the Ephesian situation, suggesting that the women in Ephesus similarly reversed the fall in a myth that was preserved in the gnostic oral tradition (*I Suffer Not a Woman: Rethinking 1 Timothy 2:11–15 in Light of Ancient Evidence* [Grand Rapids: Baker, 1998], 215–22). Howard Marshall counters, "If Kroeger has exceeded the evidence in reconstructing the Ephesian situation and Artemis cult on the basis of doctrines only found in later Gnosticism, there remain nonetheless strong indications that (1) women were involved in the heresy (and therefore teaching falsely); (2) that certain aspects of the traditional role of the woman (marriage, childbearing) were being challenged" (*Pastoral Epistles*, 466). However, the role of false myths should also be specifically included as a problem; it is unlikely that women were just teaching theological doctrines, but rather that they were embedding them in subversive stories.

27. As will be discussed in chap. 9, the problems among the women probably were located around the home and hearth, which fits the household-code content of 1 Tim. 2:11–15 and may guide us to a domestic venue for the instructions rather than a "public worship service."

28. Marshall, *Pastoral Epistles*, 466.

29. Ironically, one of the historic views in the church has been that Eve seduced Adam to sin, and that women are by nature deceptive. However, in the Pauline corpus, and particularly in the Pastoral Epistles, men are far more often depicted as false teachers and deceivers.

4.2 Gender and the Origin of Sin and Death

One of the more interesting problems, as far as potential contradiction within the Pauline corpus, lies in Paul's theology of the origin of sin. In Romans and 1 Corinthians, Paul describes the fall in some detail, and he states that sin and death entered the world through Adam so that he bears the responsibility. The fall of Adam is the basis for Paul's statement that all have sinned in Adam, which is directly connected with the salvific work of Jesus Christ as the second Adam. However, in 1 Timothy 2:14, he states that, in contrast with Adam, who was not deceived, "the woman was deceived and became a transgressor." The gender discussion has been dominated by assertions that Paul is stressing male priority through pointing out that woman sinned first and therefore bears the responsibility for the fall. Male priority and authority are thus established through the order of creation, the lack of deception on Adam's part, and the order of who sinned (or fell) first. Therefore, there seems to be a clear contradiction between the Pauline *Hauptbriefe* and the Pastoral Epistles on several counts.[30] Who bears responsibility for the fall? At what point did sin and death enter the world? In what way does a woman's status "in Christ" differ from a man's status in terms of the consequences?

4.2.1 Males and the Origin of Sin and Death

According to Romans 5:12–21, sin (ἁμαρτία) and death entered the world through Adam (cf. 1 Cor. 15:21–22).[31] The use of "human" (ἄνθρωπος) in Romans 5:12 and throughout the passage emphasizes the humanity of Adam rather than his maleness, probably in part because Paul is stressing that death

30. For example, Douglas Moo observes, "The fact that Paul attributes to Adam this sin is significant since he certainly knows from Genesis that the woman, Eve, sinned first (cf. 2 Cor. 11:3; 1 Tim. 2:14). Already we see that Adam is being given a status in salvation history that is not tied only to temporal priority" (*The Epistle to the Romans*, NICNT [Grand Rapids: Eerdmans, 1996], 319). Moo fails to note that 1 Tim. 2:14 does not use the verb "sin" (ἁμαρτάνω) but rather says the woman "came to be in violation" (ἐν παραβάσει γέγονεν), and there is no mention of sin in 2 Cor. 11:3, but only deception. Furthermore, the consequences given to Eve were explicitly for giving Adam the fruit, not for eating it herself. Notice how Moo takes a pejorative evaluation of Adam by Paul and understands it as a claim for male status rather than an indication of culpability.

31. Robert Jewett comments on the lack of speculative details in Paul's formulation, "which does not refer to the devil's wiles, to Eve's seduction of Adam, to angelic corruption of Eve or her descendants, to the perverse heart of Adam, to the cosmic powers, or to materiality itself as in later Gnostic speculations. . . . He simply explains that through Adam's sin, death came 'to all persons.' That death came as a result of Adam's fall is integral to the biblical narrative (Gen. 3:3–4, 19, 22), and Paul refers to it here as a kind of 'epidemic' sweeping over the world as a result" (*Romans: A Commentary*, ed. Eldon J. Epp, Hermeneia [Minneapolis: Fortress, 2007], 374).

spread to all people, both genders, because all sinned (ἥμαρτον) in Adam and after Adam. The argument is not focused on gender relationships, but the fact remains that Paul states that the man's one action is responsible for what we refer to as the fall—the entrance of sin and the rule of death in the world. Paul stresses that sin entered the world through one human, and that human was Adam.[32] Furthermore, death spread to everyone through Adam, and many died because of his violation (Rom. 5:12–14). But one righteous act and the gift of grace meet the requirements necessary for life (Rom. 5:15–18), so that the consequences of Adam's act are reversed in Jesus Christ.

Paul utilizes a range of words in Romans 5:12–21 to describe Adam's action and humanity's condition:

sin (noun): ἁμαρτία (6×)

sin (verb): ἁμαρτάνω (3×)

mistake/transgression: παράπτωμα (5×)

violation, act of going aside, crossing the line, in regard to the law: παράβασις (1×)

While all of these words are used to refer to Adam's action, they are not completely synonymous, and Paul does not use them interchangeably here or elsewhere in the Pauline corpus. "Sin" and "sinning" are used throughout the Pauline corpus to refer to acts of rebellion worthy of death, sin for which Christ died. "Mistakes/transgressions" are consistently used by Paul in referring to acts that require judgment and for which Christ died (Rom. 4:25; 5:15, 16, 17, 18, 20). However, παράβασις is a term that Paul and the book of Hebrews reserve for a violation or breaking of the law.[33] In Romans 5:14, Paul states that sin reigned even over those who had not sinned (τοὺς μὴ ἁμαρτήσαντας) in the same way as Adam's violation (τῆς παραβάσεως

32. Dunn comments, "Paul here shows himself familiar with and indeed to be a participant in what was evidently a very vigorous strand of contemporary Jewish thinking about Adam and the origin of evil and death in the world" (*Romans 1–8*, 272). Paul differs from Sir. 25:24, where culpability is assigned to woman: "From a woman sin had its beginning, and because of her we all die" (NRSV).

33. Παράβασις occurs only 5× in the Pauline corpus: (1) Rom. 2:23, "If you brag about the law, do you shame God through a violation of it?"; (2) Rom 4:14, "For the law brings wrath, but where there is no law there is no violation"; (3) Rom 5:14, "But death ruled from Adam to Moses, even over those who did not sin like the violation of Adam, who was a type of the one coming"; (4) Gal. 3:19, "So why the law? It was added because of violations"; (5) 1 Tim. 2:14, "Adam was not deceived, but the woman 'came to be in violation' [ἐν παραβάσει γέγονεν] because she was deceived." Similarly, the cognate παραβάτης occurs in Rom. 2:25, 27 and Gal. 2:18, referring to an individual who breaks the law.

Ἀδάμ; cf. Rom. 2:23; 4:15; Gal. 3:19; also Heb. 2:2; 9:15). According to James Dunn, "Adam's sin was παράβασις since it was an act of disobedience to what he knew to be a command of God (Gen. 2:16–17); hence NEB's 'by disobeying a direct command.'"[34] But this would indicate that, according to Paul, all violations are not the same; in the context of Romans, it most likely means that people without the law died, even though their violations technically did not break a law/command/rule that was given to them, as he indicates in Romans 4:15: "For the law brings wrath; but where there is no law, neither is there violation" (NRSV). When there is not any law, there technically is not any violation of the law. Therefore, Paul looks at extenuating factors in cases of violation, taking into account what is known or not known (or understood; cf. Rom. 7:7). In Adam's case, he sinned and transgressed in every sense because he violated a specific command that was given to him directly.

Romans 7:7–13 may throw light on Paul's theology, given the interacting knowledge of the law, sin, deception, and death. In seeming contradiction to Romans 5:14, people without the law/commandment are "alive" until they hear the law (7:9), and then the law actually provokes people to do what was prohibited (7:8).[35] Without the law "I" do not know what sin really is (7:7), but when the law is known, sin seizes an opportunity, deceives me, and puts me to death (7:11). There is a high level of intertextuality between this passage and Genesis 3, where the same elements of sin, deception, and death occur in relationship to the law, but the knowledge, actions, and consequences of two individuals (and two genders) are conflated into one process.[36]

In the Genesis account, Adam is confronted "because you have listened to the voice of your wife" (NRSV) and for direct disobedience to the command that was given to him (Gen. 3:17). However, though sin and death entered through a male, men in Christ who belong to the Christian community are not held to be culpable in a distinct way because of Adam's disastrous act. According to Paul, the consequences of Adam's action affect everyone: Paul stresses that sin and death enter the world through Adam, but also, labor

34. Dunn, *Romans 1–8*, 276.

35. Dunn states, "Paul asserts as a universal truth that sin is experienced only through the law, and in particular that the desire of covetousness is known only by virtue of the law which forbids coveting. Thus he picks up immediately the key phrase of v. 5, 'sinful passions which are through the law,' and breaks it down into two component parts: the law both provokes the actual experience of sin and makes the coveter aware that his desire is illicit" (ibid., 400).

36. According to Osborne, "The attack [of sin] takes the form of deception; it is not the law that is at fault but sin, which uses the law to seduce people like the serpent did in the Garden. . . . So in actuality the law has 'aroused' sinful passions (7:5) rather than curtailing them" (*Romans*, 178).

is multiplied for all humanity and the entire world is cursed because of his action (Rom. 8:20; cf. Gen. 3:17b–18). Adam's act has the same effect on all humanity, male and female, in terms of sin and death. Christ's one righteous act is fully effective in reversing the effects of the fall.

In Romans 8:1–17, Paul says that the process that renders us captive to sin and humanity's union with Adam are subverted by the righteous act of Jesus Christ and the law of the Spirit. Therefore, there is now no condemnation for those who are in Christ Jesus, because through Christ the law of the Spirit has freed the believer who is in Christ and in the Spirit from the law of sin and death. Those who have the Spirit may be led by the Spirit instead of their own selfishness (σάρξ). Consequently, the effects of the process are reversed: when a believer puts to death sinful actions, the believer is alive (8:13).[37] Therefore, believers have a choice to identify with the life and righteousness of Jesus Christ instead of Adam. Though the body is still dead because of sin, it will be given life, which refers to the promise of the resurrection (8:11).

In conclusion, Paul states unequivocally that sin (ἁμαρτία) and death entered the world through Adam, and the earth was cursed because of his act (Rom. 8:19–22).[38] There is nothing that directly contradicts those assertions in 1 Timothy 2:11–15. Paul's theological summary lines up with the consequences of sin given to Adam by God in Genesis 3:17–19: because of the sin of the man, the earth is cursed, labor is increased, and humanity would now return to the dust from which Adam was taken. We can also see that, to describe Adam's action, Paul uses various words belonging to the same range of meaning but that are not completely synonymous. The word "violation" (παράβασις) is reserved for breaking the law, and Paul differentiates between the gentiles who sinned without having the law and the nature of Adam's sin. This is particularly relevant for understanding what Paul says about Eve's action in 1 Timothy 2:14, because he uses the word "violation" rather than "sin" to describe what Eve did. Equally important, in Christ and through the Spirit, the effects of the fall are reversed, especially in terms of the role and power of sin and death.

37. Thomas Schreiner comments, "The paradox of Paul's thought must be noted in v. 13. Those who 'live' according to the flesh will 'die.' But those who 'put to death' the deeds of the body 'will live.' Victory is by means of the Spirit (πνεύματι), which means that believers conquer sinful passions by relying on and trusting in the Spirit to provide the strength to resist the passions that wage war within us" (*Romans*, BECNT [Grand Rapids: Baker, 1998], 422).

38. Paul does not mention Adam, but since he has been discussing Adam and the consequences of his action in the fall throughout Romans, that information has been activated for the readers, and they can be expected to supply it.

4.2.2 Females and the Origin of Sin and Death

When Paul writes directly on the topic of the origin of sin and death, he talks about how they entered the world through Adam's one action and how Jesus Christ reverses the fall through one action, but he does not mention the role of Eve. In 1 Timothy 2:8–15, the topic is not the origin of sin and death, but rather it is the correction of gender-specific problems in the Christian community in Ephesus. Men and women are addressed in turn. Men are corrected for anger and arguing (2:8), which is shown to be a problem among the false teachers and the community. Paul then gives more attention to the issues that concern women. Eve's behavior is relevant to the problems and concerns among the women whom he is addressing (2:9–15).[39]

There are several views about the nature of Eve's violation and how it relates to deception (v. 13), the command for women to learn (v. 11), and Paul's prohibitions (v. 12):[40]

- Woman is the origin of sin and death, as in Sirach 25:24, and is the source of Adam's sin.
- Woman is weak and therefore more susceptible to sin than men and more likely to teach error.
- Eve's temptation and fall were sexual, and she in turn seduced Adam.
- Women are created to be subordinate to men, Eve disturbed that order at the fall, and Paul is addressing unacceptable role reversal at Ephesus.
- Paul's account of creation and fall corrects the false teaching among the women at Ephesus.

I will examine Paul's probable understanding of the nature of Eve's violation, the possible relationship between deception and the transgression, and the consequences of Eve's action for women.

4.2.2.1 THE NATURE OF EVE'S TRANSGRESSION

The word that Paul uses (in 1 Tim. 2:14) to describe Eve's action in Genesis 3 is παράβασις: she came to be in "violation," or fell into "transgression," or

---

39. However, in the history of interpretation, the general topic is often given as "instructions in worship" or "instructions on prayer," with the effect that in some sense vv. 9–15 really are more about men, supporting male leadership and teaching, and that the narrative of the fall is about men's priority and authority in the church and home. This reflects the domination of the discussion by male scholars, who are subjectively more interested in how this is relevant to men rather than speaking to women's concerns.

40. For a breakdown of the views and examples of who has supported each view in the history of interpretation, see Marshall, *Pastoral Epistles*, 464–67.

"crossed the line." In Greek, it is not necessarily pejorative, but rather describes a deviation or a digression, though when it occurs in a legal context, it involves "overstepping," "transgression," or "error." In the New Testament, it is used elsewhere only in the Pauline corpus and the book of Hebrews to refer to a violation of the law, though in the Septuagint it also refers to breaking an oath.[41] In 1 Timothy 2:14, Eve's violation is highlighted by the use of the perfect tense: ἐν παραβάσει γέγονεν ("*had come* to cross the line, break the rule"). If we interpret this with the account in Genesis 2–3, the "line" or "rule" would be the command that God gave to Adam before Eve was created: "You may freely eat of every tree of the garden; but of the tree of the knowledge of good and evil you shall not eat, for in the day that you eat of it you shall die" (Gen. 2:16–17 NRSV).[42]

As Mignon Jacobs observes, as far as the text is concerned, the woman was not informed about the command, and her description of the command to the serpent shows discrepancies.[43] Therefore, there is some confusion on the woman's part about the command that Adam (who was with her) does not correct, and the woman is therefore deceived. It can be inferred that Paul finds the woman's case to be similar to the case of the gentiles in Romans 4:15: the command had not been given directly to her, and so she was confused and deceived; she was essentially without the law. What is more, in the Hebrew the command to Adam in Genesis 2:17 and 3:11, 17 is second-person masculine singular (e.g., לֹא תֹאכַל), which may account for some of Eve's confusion: the serpent asks, "Did God say [*to both of you*], 'You shall not eat [masc. pl.] . . .'?" (Gen. 3:1), which is not what happened; God spoke to Adam in the account before Adam knew that there would be a woman. Note that Eve's eyes were not opened until after Adam ate the fruit (Gen. 3:7), and God's concern with the woman's behavior in Genesis 3:11–13 appears to be with what she did to cause the man to eat the fruit.[44] Eve is the one who voluntarily admits to God that she also ate the fruit, but God does not highlight Eve's violation of eating the fruit as he does with Adam. Consequently, this careful reading of Genesis 2–3 renders the language

41. Παράβασις only occurs 3x in the LXX. In 2 Macc. 15:10, it has a similar meaning to breaking the law: "the breach of oaths." In the two other occurrences, this distinction is less certain though not ruled out. Psalm 101:3 (100:3 LXX) is translated as "I have hated transgressors [ποιοῦντας παραβάσεις]"; Wis. 14:31 is translated "it is the justice of sinners that always punishes the violations of the ungodly."

42. It may be significant that the second-person masculine singular, not the third-person plural, is used in the command to Adam.

43. Jacobs, *Gender, Power, and Persuasion: The Genesis Narratives and Contemporary Portraits* (Grand Rapids: Baker Academic, 2007), 47.

44. The command in Gen. 2:17 not to eat of the tree of the knowledge of good and evil is second-person singular in the Hebrew Bible and second-person plural in the LXX.

about Eve's role in the fall in 1 Timothy 2:14 coherent and consistent with the rest of Paul's theology: like the gentiles, she did not sin in the same way as Adam's transgression (Rom. 5:14), but when Adam fell, sin and death entered at that point, not at some point earlier. However, Eve's action demonstrates that she fully shared his culpability. In addition, the one-flesh relationship compounded the spread of sin and death, and so death reigned in her life as well.

Some translations render the phrase ἐν παραβάσει γέγονεν in 1 Timothy 2:14 as the woman "sinned" or "became a sinner,"[45] but it would be better to distinguish between Paul's vocabulary for wrongdoing and for sin in order to not confuse what is being said in his argument. The words for "sin," "sinning," and "sinful" are used in all three of the Pastoral Epistles (1 Tim. 1:9, 15; 5:20, 22, 24; 2 Tim. 3:6; Titus 3:11). It is significant that the vice list in 1 Timothy 1:9–10 includes fifteen different words or phrases for people who sin, but παράβασις is omitted from the list. In Romans, since Paul clearly states that sin did not enter the world until Adam's act, we should avoid inferring that Eve technically sinned first, in the sense of committing an irrevocable direct act of rebellion worthy of death. If the author of 1 Timothy wanted to state that Eve was responsible for the fall, it would have been clearer and more consistent with the Pauline corpus to have used "sin" (ἁμαρτία or ἁμαρτάνω) or "transgression" (παράπτωμα). Rather, Paul stresses that Eve became a person who crossed the line or violated the boundary that God set (ἐν παραβάσει γέγονεν) because of being utterly deceived (ἐξαπατάω). Therefore, the language does not compel us to conclude that sin (ἁμαρτία), as an irrevocable direct act of rebellion worthy of death, entered the world with Eve's action. If that were the case, it would be a direct contradiction of the Genesis account as well as the Pauline corpus because that would mean that death entered the world at that point. Therefore, translations, inferences, and interpretations declaring that Eve sinned first and was responsible for the fall unnecessarily place this verse in contradiction to the rest of Paul's theology.

4.2.2.2 THE RELATIONSHIP OF DECEPTION TO VIOLATION

If we read 1 Timothy 2:14 in the context of Paul's argument in Romans, we may be led to conclude that the writer believed Eve's complete deception

45. For Eve's action in 1 Tim. 2:14, the NIV, TNIV, NJB, and NLT use "sin" or "sinner," while the KJV, NKJV, NAU, ESV, NRSV, and NET use "transgression" or "transgressor." This suggests that while more formal equivalent versions maintain the distinction between "sin" (ἁμαρτία) and "transgression" (παράβασις), the word "transgression" is archaic, so that other versions see the word "sin" as more accessible and treat it as a synonym for "transgression." However, it would be better to find an equivalent in a more forensic/legal semantic domain. The CEB has it that Eve "stepped over the line," which is accessible English at a lower reading level and avoids confounding the terms.

may have placed her action in a category that amounted to ignorance, though her error had very serious consequences. But in contrast, Adam sinned because he had full knowledge (comparable to the law), had received a direct command, and was not deceived. It was a direct act of rebellion worthy of death, which is why with his one act, all sinned and death entered the world.[46] The language of 1 Timothy 2:14–15 is economical, careful, and restrained in comparison to Paul's description of Adam's responsibility for the fall in Romans 5. Both passages accurately reflect the account of the fall in Genesis 3.

In evaluating William Webb's suggestion that women in Ephesus were like Eve because of a lack of education and information,[47] Schreiner states, "The deception that leads to sin is not merely ignorance but a culpable state of affairs in which deception is rooted in a desire to displace God."[48] It is difficult to confirm Schreiner's statement in the case of Eve's deception before sin entered the world. The serpent suggests that being equal to God would be a goal, but Genesis 3:6 explains different motivations for Eve: "When the woman saw that the tree was good for food, and that it was a delight to the eyes, and that the tree was to be desired to make one wise, she took of its fruit and ate" (NRSV).

---

46. Others make a similar distinction yet suggest it indicates that Adam had been responsible as the leader and religious teacher. See Sharon Hodgin Gritz, *Paul, Women Teachers, and the Mother Goddess at Ephesus: A Study of 1 Timothy 2:9–15 in Light of the Religious and Cultural Milieu of the First Century* (Lanham, MD: University Press of America, 1991), 139; Donald Guthrie, *The Pastoral Epistles: An Introduction and Commentary*, TNTC (Grand Rapids: Eerdmans, 1957), 77; George W. Knight III, *The Pastoral Epistles: A Commentary on the Greek Text*, NIGTC (Grand Rapids: Eerdmans, 1992), 143–44; Douglas J. Moo, "The Interpretation of 1 Timothy 2:11–15: A Rejoinder," *TJ* 2 (1981): 204. The distinction is dismissed as insignificant because "it is hard to see how this argument would *function as a reason for men teaching women*" (Schreiner, "Interpretation of 1 Timothy 2:9–15," in Köstenberger, Schreiner, and Baldwin, *Women in the Church*, 143, emphasis added). Note that this passage is not about men; it is not a mandate for men to teach and dominate women. Rather, it supported a command for a woman in Ephesus to learn and a prohibition against a woman (wife) in Ephesus teaching or dominating a man (her husband). This is a reversal of the logical fallacy of "Negative Inferences" (D. A. Carson, *Exegetical Fallacies*, 2nd ed. [Grand Rapids: Baker, 1996], 101–3). Furthermore, the question of whether the instructions against false teaching and specifically the command and prohibitions would extend beyond Ephesus would have to be demonstrated; the burden of argument should be on the generalization. In addition, in the context in Ephesus, a woman could learn in the home when the men received spiritual formation from Timothy and could then pass it on to their wives (2 Tim. 2:2) in a culturally appropriate model. The distinction between Adam's sin and Eve's violation must be considered separately from the claim that the distinction indicates Adam as the leader and teacher by virtue of creation (as opposed to the fact that he had the relevant information).

47. Webb, *Slaves, Women & Homosexuals*, 227.

48. Schreiner, "Review Article," 63.

None of these three motivations are intrinsically wrong or indicate "a culpable state of affairs,"[49] particularly in the sense of primarily wanting to displace God and rebel against him. If that were the case, one might conclude that the fall had already happened before her action took place. Furthermore, the deception led to her crossing the line into disobedience, but according to Paul, sin had not yet entered the world. Nevertheless, her violation was disastrous, and she was fully accountable for the consequences.[50] A lack of information, an absence of education, a failure to think critically about consequences, and the failure to process teaching correctly through practice leave anyone open to error that can have disastrous consequences. Thus in 1 Timothy 2:11 Paul commands women to learn and supports that charge with a description of Eve's deception.[51]

Paul's emphasis in 1 Timothy 2:14 is on Eve being completely deceived, which is why she came to be in violation of God's command. There is nothing in the Genesis account or Paul's writing to suggest that Eve was "lording [it] over Adam" or "subverting his headship."[52] If anything, we have Adam's full complicity in the Genesis account, since he was "with" Eve the entire time during the deception and when she ate the fruit (Gen. 3:6). If he were in authority, all he had to do was say no. If anything, Adam appears to be using Eve's confusion to accomplish his own goals of rebellion and hopefully to escape blame because "she gave" him the fruit (Gen. 3:12). It is highly significant that in his attempt at self-justification he does not claim that she

49. Eve's assessment of the fruit is often compared to "All that is in the world—the desire of the flesh, the desire of the eyes, the pride in riches—comes not from the Father but from the world" (1 John 2:16 NRSV), and "But one is tempted by one's own desire, being lured and enticed by it; then, when that desire has conceived, it gives birth to sin, and that sin, when it is fully grown, gives birth to death" (James 1:14–15 NRSV). However, lust and sin should not then be imputed to her when the text does not explicitly suggest it.

50. One might speculate about what the consequences would be for Eve if Adam had not chosen to sin. However, that is beyond the scope of Paul's writings.

51. Contra Schreiner, who asserts, "Susceptibility [due] to deception into ignorance, lack of education, and inexperience . . . does not fit with the Scriptures"; and he insists that ignorance is not in play "because Paul did not say this" ("Review Article," 62–63). In response: first, Eve's ignorance is recorded in the Genesis account; second, Paul's summary of the fall supports his command in 1 Tim. 2:11 for women to learn. This indicates that women had a lack of education and Paul was addressing that as directly relevant to the deception of Eve. Furthermore, the entire discourses of 1–2 Timothy show a need for women to learn in order to correct their ignorance, lack of education, and inexperience that make them susceptible to false teaching in a way the men are not. In addition, as the false teaching is spreading among the women in the homes, Timothy is limited in his ability to teach individual women directly because of propriety in the culture, so that wives are to be taught individually at home, as in 1 Cor. 14:35.

52. See Schreiner, "Interpretation of 1 Timothy 2:9–15," in Köstenberger, Schreiner, and Baldwin, *Women in the Church*, 145; Schreiner, "Review Article," 62; Thomas C. Oden, *First and Second Timothy and Titus*, IBC (Louisville: John Knox, 1989), 100.

ate the fruit first, but that she *gave* him the fruit. Adam's action provides a contrast to Eve's action in Paul's discussion in Romans where he discusses Adam's thorough culpability. Adam was not deceived, but that is not to his credit; he was without excuse. He was the one who received God's command and became a sinner, a transgressor, and a violator with one action. The full Pauline theology and teaching on Adam's role in the entrance of sin and death into the world does not logically serve as a support for male authority or teaching in the Christian community. But Adam's strengths, weaknesses, or qualifications and lack of them were not relevant to the point that Paul was making: Adam is serving as a foil for the fuller description of Eve.

Paul's command for women to learn, his prohibitions against a woman teaching and dominating a man, and his description of Eve in the account of creation and the fall were first and foremost relevant to the women in Ephesus.[53] I have suggested that Paul's restrained narrative could be a correction of the myths and old wives' tales that are circulating among the women, and a correction of the false teaching, or some analogy to the situation in Ephesus. Whatever the purpose, its intention, together with the command for women to learn, is to remedy the problems, false teaching, and possibly the primary concern of women in the church that makes them susceptible to the false teaching. The chief concern of the women may be reflected in the conclusion of Paul's instructions. Paul has briefly described the key events that led up to the consequences of the fall for women in Genesis 3:16. Since the false teaching in Ephesus called for abstinence from marriage/sex and thus an avoidance of childbirth (1 Tim. 4:3), the point of his narrative could be in 1 Timothy 2:15, which is where Paul further interprets the Genesis narrative and the consequences of the fall for women.

4.2.2.3 FEMALES AND THE CONSEQUENCES OF THE FALL

In Paul's writing, Eve's action is paradigmatic for all believers as an illustration of how deception plays an important role in the process of falling into

53. This assumption should be the point of departure of any discussion, since so much of the material is unique to 1 Tim. 2:11–15. The material should be read as having primary relevance to the alleged recipient and the participants in the discourse. The location of this passage in the context of the discourse of 1 Timothy, which describes various problems and concerns among the women; the letter's self-description as a personal letter from Paul to Timothy, who is in Ephesus to correct false teaching; its location in the Pastoral Epistles; and its location in the narrative of the lives of Paul and Timothy—all these should be the starting point of interpretation. However, the history of interpretation has treated the passage as transcendent and normative for all women as if it were not primarily relevant to the women in the church at Ephesus. This historical-theological exegesis has therefore dominated the passage and has placed the burden of proof on any who would argue any particular relevance for Ephesus contrary to tradition. However, biblical exegesis places the burden of proof on those who would ignore the context.

sin and error. However, in Genesis 3:16, her action has direct consequences on women rather than all of humanity. For Eve, the consequences flowing from being deceived and falling into transgression affect her role in giving life to the human race: pregnancy, labor, and pain are multiplied, and the woman will crave a relationship with her husband in which she will be subjected to him. Furthermore, the consequences of Adam's action are added to those for the woman, so that women experience double jeopardy: death, increased labor, and a cursed earth as well as multiple issues with childbirth and subordination in marriage.

The negative consequences of Eve's action for women are therefore far more extensive than the consequences of Adam's action for men. In light of what Jesus Christ did for men, how can we understand the effect of Jesus Christ's work on the consequences of the fall for women? If there is no condemnation for those in Christ, then women should no longer bear a sense of guilt, shame, consequences, or restrictions for Eve's behavior any more than men do for Adam's behavior. If women are led by the Spirit, then they are identified with the life and righteousness of Jesus Christ; they are not identified with Eve's violation of God's command or any additional susceptibility to deception and sin. To be consistent, Paul's narrative summary of Eve's actions in the fall would not be the *reason* or justification for prohibitions or restrictions in the body of Christ, or else we would have to say that the actions of Eve were outside of the effects of the death of Jesus Christ. On the contrary, elsewhere Paul is crystal clear that there is neither male nor female in Christ (Gal. 3:28). All of us are children of God and fellow heirs. Christ has set us free and given us life instead of death. Nevertheless, believers still "fall asleep" because death is not yet defeated and the powers and authorities are not yet fully subjected to Christ. How does the "already and not yet" tension in Jesus Christ's reversal of the fall, and his function as the second Adam, change things for women, for their daily concerns, and for the extent to which women are still subject to effects of the fall? The evidence suggests that the women in Ephesus had these very concerns about Eve's role and the effects of the fall on women in marriage and in childbirth.

4.3 A Woman Is Saved through Childbirth

Perhaps this section should be titled "How Humanity Is Saved from the Effects of the Fall." We could explore how the Pauline doctrine of salvation by faith alone is applied to men, and how the work of Jesus Christ is understood to roll back the consequences of the fall for Adam. Consider the Pauline doctrine

of salvation by faith and the reversal of the fall through the work of Jesus
Christ as working assumptions with which we interpret the Pauline teachings on women. Paul clearly is concerned with reversing the consequences
of sin, death, and a cursed creation flowing from Adam and his sin. Was
Paul ever concerned with reversing any consequences of the fall flowing from
Eve's misstep? This study suggests that 1 Timothy 2:15 addresses the primary
consequence of the fall for women, which he has introduced with his brief
narrative on creation and the fall in 2:13–14.

The content and the relevance of 1 Timothy 2:15 to Paul's argument in
1 Timothy 2:9–15 have posed major interpretive problems for scholars: "But
a woman/wife/she will be saved through childbirth, provided they continue
in faith and love and holiness, with modesty."

What does it mean that a woman or wife or she will be saved through
childbirth? What does childbirth have to do with the instructions to women
in 1 Timothy 2:9–15?[54] Scholars present four views in trying to explain the
meaning of verse 15: (1) Women are saved (spiritually) by bearing children.
(2) Women are saved (spiritually) by Mary giving birth to Christ.[55] (3) Women
are saved (spiritually) by functioning in their God-ordained role of wife and
mother. (4) A woman will be brought safely through childbirth.[56] The fourth
view has had the least support, but it is the most likely reading in the context
of the epistle, the passage's ties with Genesis 2–3, and women's concerns
in Ephesus. As mentioned above, the evidence points to a major problem
among the women of Ephesus: the circulation of myths and false teachings
that concern marriage, sex, and childbirth. The references to Eve's role in
the creation and fall accounts in Genesis 2–3 are linked to the consequences
that God proclaimed to Eve, so that the reference to childbirth would be

54. There is even a question as to whether a "woman/wife" is the subject, since there is
no expressed subject with the future third-person singular "will be saved." The subject of
the verb σωθήσεται is unexpressed, which usually indicates a continuity of subject. However,
the conjunction δέ may indicate a return from the support material to the main point of the
argument, where the topic is "a woman"; it clarifies the relevance of the prohibitions and the
support material and reflects the continuity of a semantic chain.

55. This is the view of scholars such as Philip Payne (see *Man and Woman, One in Christ: An
Exegetical and Theological Study of Paul's Letters* [Grand Rapids: Zondervan, 2009], 429–31).
Three concerns are: he finds intertextual connections with the consequences given to the snake,
which are not convincing compared to the ties with Gen. 3:16; the reference to Mary is not
transparent; and he depends heavily on his grammatical analysis of the article as the "article
par excellence," which does not reflect how the article normally functions with nouns in Greek,
according to more recent linguistically based studies.

56. The discussion of the fourth view fits with the topic of gender and creation because it is
directly related to the consequences given to Eve. For that reason, I will not break down the various
views here. For a summary and critique of various views, see Porter, "'Saved by Childbirth.'"

most naturally understood as an allusion to Genesis 3:16:[57] "To the woman he said, 'I will greatly increase your pangs in childbearing; in pain you shall bring forth children, yet your desire shall be for your husband, and he shall rule over you'" (NRSV).

Until the advances of modern medicine, childbirth was the primary cause of death and disabilities for women, and often in the Roman Empire girls married at the age of twelve, which put them even more at risk.[58] The primary concerns of women historically have been fear of death or disability through childbirth, the ability to limit the number of children one was obligated to have, and infant mortality. This concern is expressed in women's practice of piety, religion, and magic. The reference to childbirth is the concluding and most prominent part of Paul's instructions to women, which makes sense if Paul was addressing a major legitimate concern that made women susceptible to false teaching.[59] However, a focus on the nature of women's spiritual salvation would have little relevance to the issues raised about the women in 1–2 Timothy, and a reference to women's God-given role would neither be understood nor be consistent with the pejorative associations with the process of childbirth.[60]

The multiple links in 1 Timothy 2:11–15 with Genesis 2–3 include the references to Adam and Eve, the order of creation, and the fall. These references

57. As Kenneth Waters states, "It is a clear application of God's pronouncement upon Eve in Genesis 3:16" ("Saved through Childbearing: Virtues as Children in 1 Timothy 2:11–15," *JBL* 123 [2004]: 705). This involves theories about intertextuality and discourse analysis. Paul's summaries of the creation, fall, and childbirth create multiple ties with Gen. 2–3. In the vocabulary of discourse analysis, the creation and fall narratives activate part of a "scenario" that includes the content of the consequences of the fall. As A. J. Sanford and S. C. Garrod say, "In order to elicit a scenario, a piece of text must constitute a specific *partial description* of an element of the scenario itself" (*Understanding Written Language: Explorations of Comprehension beyond the Sentence* [Chichester: Wiley, 1981], 110, emphasis original). It is highly unlikely that the mention of childbirth is coincidental.

58. As Craig Keener states, "The most natural way for an ancient reader to have understood 'salvation' in the context of childbirth would have been a safe delivery, for women regularly called upon patron deities (such as Artemis or Isis) in childbirth" (*Paul, Women & Wives: Marriage and Women's Ministry in the Letters of Paul* [Peabody, MA: Hendrickson, 1992], 118).

59. As Porter says, "Most plausible, it seems to me, is to take 1 Timothy 2:15 as a concluding statement of the entire section (1 Tim. 2:8–15)" ("'Saved by Childbirth,'" 93). Verse 15 receives the most development and interpretation by Paul. Sometimes the main point can occur at the end of the passage.

60. The alleged focus on a woman's spiritual salvation is random and off-topic apart from the fact that the content would raise doubts about how a woman is saved or even whether a woman is saved. This contradicts statements made by Jesus and Paul about the status of women who have not given birth to children, and it contradicts Paul's teaching on salvation by faith in Rom. 3:21–26 and the believer's life in the Spirit in Rom. 8:1–35. It may have ties with God's goals in 1 Tim. 2:1–3, but the function of the virtues is entirely different, and it seems to contradict the primacy of Christ's work in salvation in 2:4–7.

normally would constrain the reader's understanding of "childbirth" (τεκνογονία) to refer to the negative consequences of the fall in Genesis 3:16:
"To the woman he said, 'I will greatly increase your pangs in childbearing;
in pain you shall bring forth children'" (NRSV).[61] Childbirth was and is a
complex problem for women in terms of survival and quality of life, so that
the promise of safety while giving birth addresses a crucial felt need—and
the crucial felt need in the creation account. In spite of this, it is claimed that
σῴζω is a technical term for spiritual salvation in the Pauline corpus,[62] and it is
claimed that it would be a false promise because women still continued to die
in childbirth.[63] However, the claim that σῴζω is a technical term in the Pauline
corpus is not accurate. It misrepresents Paul's use of σῴζω, it misunderstands
his theology of salvation, and regardless, it is based on too small a sample of
the Pauline language for healing. The objection that women still died from
childbirth does not recognize the specific conditions of the promise in the
passage, and it invalidates parallel biblical promises of healing and rescue.

In the Greek Old Testament, the range of meaning for "save" (σῴζω) includes "delivery or rescue from trouble, danger, or illness."[64] It involves rescue

61. In discourse analysis, "constrain" refers to how the preceding context restricts the reader's
choice of the meaning of a word in its semantic range. For a more extensive argument for this
position, see Moyer Hubbard, "Kept Safe through Childbearing: Maternal Mortality, Justification by Faith, and the Social Setting of 1 Timothy 2:15," *JETS* 55 (2012): 743–62.

62. See, e.g., Porter, "'Saved by Childbirth'"; Thomas R. Schreiner, *Paul, Apostle of God's
Glory in Christ: A Pauline Theology* (Downers Grove, IL: InterVarsity, 2001), 284–86. Scholars
commonly claim that Paul does not typically use σῴζω to refer to rescue from this sort of danger, but rather uses σῴζω as a technical term for "deliverance from spiritual death" in contrast
to healing from illness (Douglas J. Moo, *James: An Introduction and Commentary*, TNTC
[Grand Rapids: Eerdmans, 1985], 181).

63. Schreiner objects, "Christian women are not always preserved in childbirth. Many have
died—presumably in Paul's day as well!" (*Paul*, 285). Porter has a more technical objection based
on grammar, which involves "the recognized grammatical categories of either some temporal or
some instrumental sense of the preposition διά with the genitive case. The temporal sense would
be one of duration: 'during the time of childbearing.' Although this is a grammatical possibility,
the major difficulty with this view is that the most convincing examples that grammarians cite
of the temporal use of διά have clear temporal words, for example, day, year, night (Acts 1:3;
5:19; 24:17; Gal. 2:1)" ("'Saved by Childbirth,'" 97). However, childbirth is a process that by
definition is associated with time in terms of hours (or even days), particularly from the woman's
point of view, so that the sense of duration is conveyed in English without specifying time, so
that "during childbirth" makes sense. More research could be done on the use of διά in Greek.

64. Johannes Louw and Eugene Nida give the range as "rescue" (21.18), "save" (21.27), and
"heal" (23.136) (*Greek-English Lexicon of the New Testament: Based on Semantic Domains*,
2nd ed. [New York: United Bible Societies, 1989]). As Keith Warrington argues, σῴζω "is capable of a variety of different meanings including 'preserve from danger, rescue, protect, heal,'
in various contexts. In other words, the identity of the salvation is determined by the situation
from which the sufferer is rescued; as has been suggested, for James, this may be broader than
sickness only" ("James 5:14–18: Healing Then and Now," *IRM* 93 [2004]: 351).

from dangers experienced by humanity such as sickness, warfare, and attack
(e.g., Pss. 6:2–4; 7:11; 67:21 LXX [6:1–3; 7:10; 68:20 ET]). Spiritual salvation is a metaphoric extension of this sort of literal rescue from danger. The
reference to literal rescue is so well established in Scripture that it would be
unusual, if not to say unbelievable, for Paul to eliminate it from his range of
meaning.[65]

Paul and other biblical writers used the metaphors of a woman in labor
and birth pangs to describe men who are terrified and in danger of dying
and to describe extreme threats to life.[66] For example, a woman giving birth
is comparable to the abject terror of kings with their armies in full retreat
from the presence of God, stunned, panicked, and frightened (Ps. 48:4–6).[67]
Jesus used birth pangs to describe the severe distress of the last days (Matt.
24:8) and was sensitive to the terrible distress and vulnerability of pregnant
women, nursing mothers, and mothers of children during the last days (Mark
13:17; Luke 23:29). Paul referred to childbirth as a metaphor for that threat
of attack, pain, suffering, and destruction from which humanity and creation
needed to be saved, not just spiritually, but also physically (Rom. 8:22–25;
1 Thess. 5:3–9). Paul understood the threat that childbirth posed for women,
and he used it as a paradigm for people who needed to be rescued.[68]

The claim that Paul used the word σῴζω (including its cognates) only for
spiritual or eschatological salvation is a misrepresentation of both his language
and the way that language works.[69] For example, the reference to salvation in
2 Timothy 4:17–18 is particularly significant: "But the Lord stood by me and
gave me strength, so that through me the message might be fully proclaimed
and all the Gentiles might hear it. So I was rescued [ἐρρύσθην] from the lion's

65. As Keener argues, "'Saved' means 'delivered' or 'brought safely through' more often in
ancient literature than it means 'saved from sin'" (*Paul, Women & Wives*, 118). Keener gives a
large number of examples from a spectrum of sources (130–31n24).

66. Interestingly, the metaphor of labor pains in childbirth is more often used as a metaphor
for men's fear and threat of death than for women's experience. It shows that the men who
wrote the Bible understood the threat.

67. The LXX translators rendered the Hebrew חִיל with the metaphor of birth pangs (ὠδίν/
ὠδῖνες) when in the context of male fear and human terror (e.g., Exod. 15:14; Deut. 2:25).

68. Contra Porter: "In the light of the above cumulative evidence and in particular in the
context of 1 Timothy 2:15, σωθήσεται is virtually guaranteed a salvific sense (the passive voice
is probably a divine or theological passive, that is, God is the agent of salvation). . . . As Houlden says, 'the salvation referred to must not mean physical safe-keeping in childbirth but that
assured on the Last Day'" (Porter, "'Saved by Childbirth,'" 94) (see also J. L. Houlden, *The
Pastoral Epistles: I and II Timothy, Titus* [London: SCM, 1976], 72).

69. As Hubbard insists, "It is often argued that Paul's prior or subsequent usage of σῴζω
in 1 Timothy is decisive for its meaning in 2:15. This is fallacious. Certainly the larger literary
context needs to be considered carefully, but words can be used in different senses within the
same context; in fact, it is rather common" ("Kept Safe," 745).

mouth. The Lord will rescue me from every evil attack and save [σώσει] me for his heavenly kingdom" (NRSV).

Being "saved" for God's heavenly kingdom is the other side of the coin of being rescued from the lion and evil; for Paul, it includes God's continued provision in present distress until he enters the kingdom.[70] In Philippians, similarly, Paul says that he expects salvation in the sense of rescue (σωτηρία) from his trouble and imprisonment through the Philippians' prayers and God's provision (Phil. 1:19). Paul uses σῴζω to describe an escape from fire in 1 Corinthians 3:15, which demonstrates his conscious metaphorical extension of eschatological salvation from a literal rescue. In addition, Luke uses σῴζω for Paul's healing of a man who was crippled (Acts 14:9) and reports him using it in speech to refer to rescue from a shipwreck (Acts 27:20).[71] These examples show that Paul used the same vocabulary for spiritual salvation as he did for God's provision and rescue in times of need.

It is misleading to say that Paul used "save" only for "spiritual or eschatological salvation," if one means that it has no pragmatic effects on the past and present. For Paul, salvation refers to God's pragmatic rescue of humanity from the past, present, and future consequences of Adam's sin. It includes rescue from present dangers, including "perishing" in this present life and being a slave to sin and death (Rom. 5:9–10; 7:25–8:1; 9:27–28; 1 Cor. 1:18; 2 Cor. 2:15; Eph. 2:5, 8; 2 Thess. 2:9–12; 2 Tim. 1:9). Furthermore, the expectation of the resurrection of the body shows that salvation is physical as well as spiritual.[72] The separation between spiritual/eschatological salvation and God's merciful provision for believers' needs in the present is a false dichotomy.[73]

It is important to note that in the early church, σῴζω was used to speak of healing that had both physical and spiritual aspects. In James 5:15–16, a person who is sick is told to send for the elders, whose faithful prayers will heal/save/rescue (σώσει) the sick/weak person, and the Lord will raise that person up.[74] Luke, who was Paul's close companion, demonstrates that God's

---

70. Hubbard draws parallels between 2 Tim. 4:17–18 and Ps. 21:21–23 LXX (22:21–22 ET) to show that σῴζω and ῥύομαι are used synonymously with rescue from the mouth of a lion ("Kept Safe," 748). It also suggests a textual relationship.

71. The quotation of Paul's speech about being saved from a shipwreck occurs in a "we passage."

72. On the other hand, Paul also uses ῥύομαι not only for being rescued from deadly danger (2 Cor. 1:10) and attack and persecution (Rom. 15:31; 2 Thess. 3:2; 2 Tim. 3:11; 4:17–18), but also for salvation, being rescued from sin and the coming wrath (Rom. 7:24; Col. 1:13; 1 Thess. 1:10). This is consistent with usage in the LXX.

73. See L. J. Kreitzer's discussion of the "dialectic between the present and the future, particularly as it relates to the concept of salvation" ("Eschatology," DPL, 257).

74. Warrington's argument that ἀσθενεῖ can refer to a "variety of conditions including spiritual weakness, physical weakness and sickness as well as less common meanings that relate

healing actions are not only in continuity with the salvation that God brings to humanity, but also both part of that salvation and evidence of the presence of the kingdom of God.[75] However, healing from illness and conditions of physical weakness is not a major theme in the Pauline corpus.[76] This does not mean that he would not address illness or physical weakness if it were a major concern. Rather, it indicates that we do not have a representative sample of the language that Paul would use to speak of healing. Therefore it is unconvincing to suggest that Paul would not use language to speak of healing and deliverance in a way that was typical of the Septuagint, the early church, and other Greek literature.

If there were concerns about childbirth that were contributing to the problems in Ephesus among the women, then it is likely that Paul would address those concerns. How likely was it that childbirth would have been an issue that fueled false teaching? Childbirth, or maternal mortality, has been a primary threat to women's safety, health, and life throughout history.[77] Therefore, the consequences of Eve's action are a primary concern to all women and those who care about them.[78] Women's religious beliefs

---

to other forms of weakness" is well taken and supports the range of problems in view in the psalms ("James 5:14–18," 347). However, a minority position argues that James 5:14–15 refers to being saved as restoring spiritual health alone. See M. Meinertz, "Die Krankensalbung Jak. 5,14f.," *BZ* 20 (1932): 23–36; C. Amerding, "Is Any among You Afflicted? A Study of James 5:13–20," *BSac* 95 (1938): 195–201; Charles H. Pickar, "Is Anyone Sick among You?," *CBQ* 7 (1945): 165–74; Daniel R. Hayden, "Calling the Elders to Pray," *BSac* 138 (1981): 258–66. See Ben Witherington's entire argument in "Salvation and Health in Christian Antiquity: The Soteriology of Luke-Acts in Its First-Century Setting," in *Witness to the Gospel: The Theology of Acts*, ed. I. Howard Marshall and David Peterson (Grand Rapids: Eerdmans, 1998), 145–66.

75. Healing is "an important part of what the salvation that comes from Jesus entails" (Witherington, "Salvation and Health," in Marshall and Peterson, *Witness to the Gospel*, 151). As John Nolland observes, "When the claim is made in [Luke] 10:9 that 'the kingdom of God has drawn near to you,' the immediate evidence of its presence is to be found in the healing of the sick that has taken place" ("Salvation-History and Eschatology," in Marshall and Peterson, *Witness to the Gospel*, 68). For example, in Luke 8:48, when the woman who had been suffering from hemorrhages touched the hem of Jesus's garment, she was saved (σέσωκεν) in the sense that she was made well (θυγάτηρ, ἡ πίστις σου σέσωκέν σε).

76. Most of Paul's references to illness concern a description of his own illnesses (2 Cor. 12:7–9; Gal. 4:13–14), with the exception of Epaphroditus (Phil. 2:26–27). Paul's topic in those passages is not healing. His lexical choices for God's healing varies (e.g., ἀφίστημι, ἐλεέω), so the sample is inconsistent and far too small to conclude that he would not use σῴζω in the sense that is dominant in the LXX and the contemporary use in the early church (James 5:15–16).

77. Hubbard also argues that 1 Tim. 2:15 should be translated thus: "But she will be kept safe through the ordeal of childbearing" ("Kept Safe," 743). He establishes the plausibility basis for his reading by describing the "grim first-century reality of giving birth to a child" (752–56).

78. It is still a primary cause of a variety of threats that women experience in the developing world when they do not have access to modern medical care. A website called Save the Mothers is a charity dedicated to prevent women's deaths from pregnancy-related causes. This strongly

and practices were dominated by childbirth and pregnancy-related issues.[79] Furthermore, the Christian women in Ephesus had a special connection between their former religious practice and childbearing. Artemis was the patron goddess of the city of Ephesus,[80] and she was literally the savior to whom the women went for safety and protection in childbirth.[81] Her role in the lives of women is illustrated in Greek mythology, where she serves as a midwife to her own mother.[82] C. L. Brinks writes, "She was the goddess who assisted women during the major transitions of their lives, from little girls to young women, from marriageable to married, and from marriage to motherhood. She was also the one responsible for the deaths of mothers and infants during childbirth."[83]

Artemis therefore not only was central to Ephesus as its protector and nurturer and dominated the public life of the city, but also was even more central for the women of Ephesus in their primary functions and concerns in the domestic sphere of the home.[84]

---

demonstrates that the use of "save" for deliverance or rescue from the threat of childbirth is still appropriate even in the language of the twenty-first century, and is understood as such simply with the constraint of the word "mothers." It states that 287,000 women die every year from pregnancy-related causes, 99 percent of them in the developing world. Also, during the twentieth century, more women died from childbirth than soldiers killed in both world wars. But this would be only a fraction of the death rate of women because of childbirth before the advent of modern medicine. See Save the Mothers, "What Are the Causes of Maternal Mortality?," http://www.savethemothers.org/learn-the-issues/overview-3.

79. Women's concern for protection is consistent with the practice of piety in the Greco-Roman world. As Witherington asserts, "The 'salvation' most ancients looked for was from disease, disaster, or death in this life" ("Salvation and Health," in Marshall and Peterson, *Witness to the Gospel*, 146). Much of women's religious practice typically includes stories and myths and the pervasive use of magic, charms, and rituals.

80. The venue of 1 Timothy is Ephesus (1 Tim. 1:3). Its patron goddess, Artemis, was primarily the protector and nurturer of the city and fulfilled a variety of functions for Ephesus that are associated with other deities. Her temple in Ephesus was one of the wonders of the ancient world and the basis for much of the city's economy (cf. Acts 19:23–40).

81. Callimachus (310–235 BCE) depicted Artemis as saying, "I will live in the mountains, but I will deal with the cities of men only when women who are distressed by the sharp labor pains of childbirth call for help" (*Hymn. Dian.* 20–22, my translation). Apuleius (ca. 120–160 CE) identifies Isis with Artemis/Diana: "or the sister of Apollo, who relieved the pangs of childbirth with your medicines, thus giving birth to so many people, and you are now worshiped in the shrines of Ephesus" (*Metam.* 11.2, my translation).

82. According to Greek myth, her father was Zeus, and after her mother, Leto, gave birth to her, Artemis assisted in delivering her twin brother, Apollo.

83. Brinks, "'Great Is Artemis of the Ephesians': Acts 19:23–41 in Light of Goddess Worship in Ephesus," *CBQ* 71 (2009): 777–78.

84. It is important to note that this is not a claim that Artemis is an erotic fertility goddess. Studies counteract the concept of Artemis as a fertility goddess because she is not erotic, but they usually fail to understand that the primary role of the goddess in the life of women who are legitimate wives and mothers would not be viewed as erotic by the culture that disapproved

Luke's account of Paul's ministry in Ephesus signals the importance of Artemis to the Ephesians and the Ephesian believers' tendency toward syncretism. In the riot recorded in Acts 19:23–41, Luke shows that Artemis was in direct competition with the gospel. The Christian community also showed a marked tendency toward syncretism in the practice of magic (Acts 19:18–20).[85] In such a context where the culture is dominated by the patron goddess of childbirth and the other stages of a woman's life, one can expect that there would be syncretism in the stories women told around the hearth (cf. 1 Tim. 4:7), and in their rites and rituals that permeated their daily life in the home. When a woman faced the crisis of childbirth, she would look for help and safety in the familiar remedies that were passed down from mother to daughter, grandmother to granddaughter, and friend to friend.[86] It cannot be overemphasized that these powerful ties bind women in the community and across the generations in most cultures. It should be no surprise to find that there were false teachings about marriage and childbirth and problems with myths among the women in first-century Ephesus.

Does the fact that women continued to die in childbirth indicate that Paul cannot promise safe deliverance for women through the process of childbirth? To answer yes would falsify the promise of healing through prayer in James

---

of viewing wives and virtuous women as sexual objects. Lynn LiDonnici convincingly argues that these functions were not primarily erotic categories:

> The figure of Artemis Ephesia in her role as city goddess was not eroticized. This feature may, in fact, be connected with her symbolic role as the legitimate wife, a figure to be respected and generally not represented in art in erotic contexts. Where we do see erotic scenes involving the female figure on vases and in sculpture, these figures are usually either hetaerae or images of Aphrodite. It should not then be surprising that few of the figures in erotic art have full, "matronly" breasts, given the division of the sexual roles for women implied in *In Neaeram* [by Demosthenes]. As early as Herodotus we encounter suspicion and surprise at the idea of a man being erotically obsessed by his own wife, and Roman sources regard the large families of the Jews and others as evidence of the men's weakness in not being able to stay away from their wives. While this particular objection may be a function of increasing health fears associated with sex, and in particular with procreative sex, it underlines the continuity into Roman times of sexual distinctions among categories of women that are different from our own. ("The Images of Artemis Ephesia and Greco-Roman Worship: A Reconsideration," *HTR* 85 [1992]: 409–10)

85. A large number of scrolls used for sorcery were surrendered by the believers in Ephesus after Paul had ministered in Ephesus for two years, if Acts 19:10 is taken as a temporal indicator for 19:18–20. Apparently it took time, effort, and strong evidence to convict the believers that the practice of Christianity was in direct conflict with their magical practices.

86. Hubbard, on the other hand, visualizes a young husband's syncretistic response when he sees his wife sickened from childbirth: "He runs to various shrines and temples pleading for mercy; perhaps he purchases an incantation and scrupulously enacts the ritual. In short, he prays to whatever god or goddess will hear him, as he watches his wife, in many instances, die" ("Kept Safe," 756).

5:14–15 on the same grounds: "Are any among you sick? They should call for the elders of the church and have them pray over them, anointing them with oil in the name of the Lord. The prayer of faith will save [σώσει] the sick, and the Lord will raise them up; and anyone who has committed sins will be forgiven" (NRSV).

These promises of safety in childbirth and healing through prayer are consistent with the many promises claimed by the men who wrote the psalms and prophetic books in expectation of some form of deliverance from battle, murder, abuse, and illness. Furthermore, rabbinic literature claims that there was a belief that piety could deliver women from effects of the curse, which is consistent with the Old Testament belief that God would deliver the righteous from trouble.[87] However, men still died in battle and were murdered and attacked, and Christians who prayed for healing still died from illness. These promises and claims are faithful confessions and expectations that God takes care of his people when they call on him and works things together for good for those who love God (Rom. 8:28). Therefore, safety and deliverance may take many forms that would be legitimate outcomes for the biblical authors, especially for Paul. He talked about being literally delivered from death and having confidence that "the Lord will rescue me from every evil attack and save me for his heavenly kingdom" (2 Tim. 4:18 NRSV), and yet tradition tells us that he was executed. The crisis of childbirth can be a danger to faith as well as to life, and the pain of labor can constitute an evil attack, particularly if women in Ephesus were prone to turn to magic, demons, or pagan gods for help.

It is important to notice that 1 Timothy 2:15 is not a global promise to all women any more than James 5:15 or the promises in the psalms are global promises to all people. Deliverance from the dangers of childbirth depends on perseverance in faith, love, holiness, and self-control. Furthermore, according to Paul, a woman's safety does not depend on her alone. There is an interesting shift to the plural: "a woman will be saved through childbearing, provided *they* continue in faith and love and holiness, with modesty" (1 Tim. 2:15 NRSV). "They" would normally refer to the closest relevant participants in the passage.[88] We find the antecedent to the singular verb "will be saved" in the woman/wife in verse 12, so that the shift to plural in verse 15's last clause could indicate the woman/wife *and* the man/husband in verse 12.[89] The reference to childbirth

87. See *b. Soṭ.* 12a. A similar theme occurs in *Pesiq. Rab Kah.* 22.2, where a woman's righteousness delivers her from barrenness, representing Israel's deliverance. The stories are later than the first century, but they demonstrate a trend in Jewish thought.
88. See also the more detailed exegesis of 1 Tim. 2:15 in chap. 9.
89. Most scholars have taken the plural to revert to the plural subject of "women" in 1 Tim. 2:9–10. However, it is not a convincing view, because there would be nothing to necessitate the

suggests that "man" and "woman" would be better translated as "husband" and "wife." This is also supported by the command that a "woman/wife" should learn in verse 11, the reference to Adam and Eve in verses 13–14, and the use of the singular "woman/wife" and "man/husband" with the prohibitions in verse 12. The command that a woman should learn suggests that she should be taught by her husband at home, just as Paul directed in 1 Corinthians 14:35. Furthermore, Adam and Eve represent the prototypical relationship of a husband and wife. Finally, the marital relationship would be the only situation in the culture in which a woman would have a chance to teach or control a man (one-on-one), other than a male slave. With the conclusion that deals with a woman's childbirth, there is a confirmation that the entire passage lies in the domestic sphere. Therefore, the marital relationship best accounts for the elements in the passage after Paul shifts from a focus on "women" to a focus on "a woman." The closest grammatical referents to "they" in verse 15 who must continue in faith, love, and holiness with self-control would be a husband and wife in verse 12, also typologically represented by Adam and Eve in verses 13–14.

Assigning joint responsibility to a husband for his wife's safety in childbirth would have been relevant, revolutionary, and effective.[90] Men controlled the size of the family[91] and the resources that could secure greater care, health, and safety during pregnancy and childbirth.[92] Furthermore, it was common for men to order their wives to have unsafe abortions as a form of birth control.[93] A

shift from singular to plural at that point, or to say how the salvation or well-being of a woman must be contingent on the piety of all the women in the church of Ephesus; a positive outcome would be hopeless, given the state of the gullible women in 2 Tim. 3:6. However, for further discussion on the antecedent of "they," see Waters, "Saved through Childbearing," 708–9. He does not consider the woman and man (wife and husband) as a theological possibility because it makes Eve's salvation dependent on both childbearing and her and Adam's piety.

90. What is happening to women in developing countries illustrates the experience of all women before the advent of modern medicine. One of the primary solutions of maternal mortality in the majority world is to change the care given by husbands. The husband is traditionally uninvolved in the process of childbirth mentally and physically, if not emotionally. For more information, see Thomas Froese, *Ninety-Nine Windows from Arabia to Africa and Other Roads Less Travelled* (Belleville, ON: Epic Press, 2009).

91. Controlling the size of the family involves either the unsafe practice of continuous (yearly) pregnancy to supply the family with workers and to ensure care in old age in a rural culture, or ordering an unsafe abortion to limit family size in an urban culture.

92. The women were completely dependent on their husbands during pregnancy for nurture and protection, and they were vulnerable to physical abuse and starvation or malnutrition. Studies have shown this to be a particular problem for pregnant wives of soldiers in third-world countries who are absent due to military action or duties: they are virtually abandoned and vulnerable at the point of crisis.

93. Abortion was a common practice in the Greco-Roman culture, contributing directly to maternal mortality and infertility (yet infant abandonment was also widely practiced).

husband's devotion to love, faith, holiness, and particularly sexual self-control in the marital relationship could save his wife from a large range of dangers that were and are associated with childbirth. Therefore, Paul's instructions would include both spiritual and practical support from a woman's husband that was countercultural and would make a concrete difference in a woman's plight as she faced childbirth.

This reading suggests that Paul is addressing women's concerns and experiences in an attempt to correct false teaching.[94] The concerns of women and their experiences have been missing from the history of the interpretation of what it means to be "saved through childbirth." Understanding 1 Timothy 2:15 as a promise that a woman will be brought safely through childbirth is a strong reading on six counts: (1) It recognizes links with Genesis 2–3, where the pain of childbirth is a consequence of the fall. (2) Childbirth was a primary health concern for women and their practice of religion. (3) Women in Ephesus were most likely to practice syncretism during pregnancy and labor, given the role of Artemis. (4) It addresses the probable content of the false teaching. (5) It contributes to the coherence of the passage. (6) It does not set the passage in contradiction to the rest of the Pauline corpus. As conceded elsewhere, theological self-contradiction and incoherence may not be a concern for those who interpret this passage, but neither is it inevitable.

In conclusion, 1 Timothy 2:14, with the Pauline discussion of Eve's role in the fall, has played a major part in the construction of gender, particularly in terms of the deception of women and the origin of sin. However, it has been shown that for Paul, deception was a human condition, and Paul showed that men, as well as women, generally followed the pattern of Eve's deception. Furthermore, Jesus Christ's work and the presence and leading by the Holy Spirit could effectively free all believers, male and female, from the cycle of deception. As for the origin of sin, Paul states that sin and death entered with Adam's one act, not with Eve's. However, Paul never suggests that the church should force male believers to suffer further consequences for

94. Taking into account women's experience in the biblical interpretation of passages that pertain to women should be differentiated from the feminist discussion of the elevation of gender identity in the knowledge of God, and linking women directly with the divine. The feminist discussion has debated the role that women's experience has in determining the religious and theological enterprise, specifying "experience of motherhood, menstruation, and other things related to women's bodies; experience of oppression, experience of connectedness; and experience of Spirit" (Linda Woodhead, "God, Gender and Identity," in *Gospel and Gender: A Trinitarian Engagement with Being Male and Female in Christ*, ed. Douglas A. Campbell, STS 7 [London: T&T Clark, 2003], 89).

Adam's act of overt rebellion; rather, the gospel invites men and women to accept the gift of justification and life from Jesus Christ, the second Adam. Chapter 9 (below) provides a fuller exegesis of 1 Timothy 2:9–15, but at this point I can say that Paul most likely is trying to correct women's issues at Ephesus with each point. The text particularly addresses the reversal of the consequences of Eve's behavior in the fall, results of maternal mortality and other complications resulting from pregnancy and childbirth (1 Tim. 2:15).

five

Eschatology

Probably most Christians have not considered how eschatology plays a crucial role in an attempt to construct a coherent Pauline theology of gender. Consideration of Pauline eschatology and the destiny of humanity as male and female provides a litmus test for any assertions about the purpose of creation. Pauline theology and the early church's eschatology saw a necessary relationship between creation, redemption/resurrection, and human destiny in the future. That is, Paul believed that through Jesus Christ's death and resurrection, God began to reverse the fall and work toward the restoration of creation, which will be completed at Christ's second coming. Therefore, the human destiny of male and female reflects the purpose of God's creation of humanity. Life in the Christian community is supposed to be an eschatological reflection of believers' status, seen in their ethics, their spiritual experience, and the ministry of the Holy Spirit. However, this eschatological fulfillment involves a continuing mission to the gentiles, so that Paul and his churches live as missionaries who contextualize the gospel for Greco-Roman culture and who live their lives according to the standards of this culture.

5.1 Pauline Eschatology and Transcendent Norms

Pauline eschatology reflects a considerable amount of material shared with his readers and the early church, and so it has connections, links, and allusions to other eschatological material in the New Testament. Paul's Letters indicate that he is drawing on a body of traditions that he taught his communities, including oral traditions about Jesus.[1] For example, he assumed that the Corinthian church shared a basic understanding of eschatology when he asked rhetorically, "Do you not know that the saints will judge the world?" (1 Cor. 6:2 NRSV). The book of Revelation explicitly states three eschatological convictions that are consistent with Pauline eschatology: (1) The believers will form a kingdom of priests who will rule the nations with authority (5:10; cf. 2:26). (2) The curse will be abolished (22:3). (3) Death will be abolished (21:4).

There is continuity in the eschatological hope between our origin, the fall, our redemption, our journey, and our destination. According to Paul and the other writers of the New Testament, the destiny of believers and the expectation of the second coming of Christ are to shape how believers live their lives in the present, as in 2 Peter 3:11: "Since all these things are to be destroyed in this way, what sort of people ought you to be in holy conduct and godliness, looking for and hastening the coming of the day of God, because of which the heavens will be destroyed by burning, and the elements will melt with intense heat?" Paul similarly wanted his churches to walk in the light of the future (1 Cor. 1:7–8; Phil. 3:20–4:1; Col. 3:1–4; 1 Thess. 5:6–11; 2 Thess. 2:13–15; Titus 2:11–14).

Eschatological hope made a difference in the relative status of believers in the church. To the extent that it has been implemented in the church and has influenced society, it has formed the basis of much social and political change, which typically started with significant changes for men. Much of this change begins with the Christian assumption of the dignity and value of all humans, and as a consequence it encourages them to achieve their God-given potential in skills and leadership, regardless of their background, their race, or the lack of other advantages. Paul emphatically states that women have the same eschatological hope without distinction (Gal. 3:28), but the realization of equivalent change in women's status in the church and society has been traditionally resisted on "biblical" grounds. Restrictions and prohibitions for women are based on alleged "transcendental norms" dictating the subordination of women. This has resulted in inconsistencies and contradictions in how Paul's eschatological passages have been read and applied to women, in sharp contrast with how they are applied to men.

Therefore, we must consider how eschatology confirms any "transcendent norms" for gender in terms of God's intentions at creation and of God's ultimate plan for men and women respectively. If transcendent norms could

---

1. The consensus of scholarship is that any letters by Paul were written before the Gospel accounts.

be identified, they would be useful tools with which to understand the categories of male and female in Pauline theology.[2] To be transcendent, a norm at creation would have to be consistent with any norm in the eschatological fulfillment of creation's purposes. The test is this: Is a given interpretation or inference drawn from Scripture consistent with Pauline transcendent norms that concern gender in the rest of the Pauline corpus? If it is found not to be consistent with the rest of Pauline theology, it would raise four questions for how we understand passages that form our Pauline theology of gender: (1) Did Paul change his mind? (2) Did Paul contradict himself? (3) Was an inconsistent verse or passage written by someone other than Paul? (4) Is this the only possible interpretation of an inconsistent verse or passage, or are there alternatives that could explain it? The underlying assumption of Galatians 3:28 is that in Christ, men and women will become what they are created to be. Conversely, women cannot become what they were not created to be.

5.2 Eschatology and Creation

In Pauline theology, there is continuity between what humans were created to be and the destiny of humanity. Human destiny was, ironically, foiled by Adam's action so that death reigned instead of humanity reigning. Jesus Christ reversed the act of the first Adam, so that humans reign instead of death reigning. Through Jesus Christ, humanity is being restored to its rightful status intended at creation and is beginning to rule over everything. God is working with believers, as God's new creation in Christ Jesus, to complete a destiny planned from the foundation of the world.

In Paul's discussion of the first Adam and the second Adam in Romans 5:12–20, he shows an intrinsic and ironic relationship between creation, Adam (the head of humanity), and ruling. Humanity was created to have dominion, yet Paul shows that Adam was the source of sin, judgment, and condemnation in the world, and "death reigned" (5:17a). But the second Adam, Jesus Christ, brought grace, justification, and righteousness. Consequently, those who receive those gifts "will reign in life through the one person, Jesus Christ" (5:17b). This is consistent with and dependent on the Genesis narrative: humanity was created to reign, but the fall of the first created human resulted in a horrible reversal so that death reigned instead. Jesus Christ reversed the fall so that humanity may be restored to its original purpose. As James Dunn

2. This picks up Thomas Schreiner's term "transcendent norm," which has a lot of currency in various circles, at least as a concept (*Paul, Apostle of God's Glory in Christ: A Pauline Theology* [Downers Grove, IL: InterVarsity, 2001], 408).

summarizes, "The risen Christ is the last Adam, prototype of God's new human creation, in accord with the original blueprint."[3]

Paul shows familiarity with Psalm 8:4–8 and applies it in a way similar to the author of Hebrews. In Hebrews 2:5–9, the author quotes Psalm 8:4–8 (cf. Gen. 1:26–28) to show that although humans were placed a little lower than the angels, God had the intention of restoring humanity to its rightful status, which is fulfilled through Jesus Christ: he is crowned with glory and honor and will rule over everything. Paul too alludes to and quotes Psalm 8:4–8 (1 Cor. 15:25, 27; Eph. 1:22), and he also indicates that humanity's purpose at creation will be realized in Jesus when we will reign with him (Rom. 8:17; 2 Tim. 2:12).[4]

Paul also believed that each believer is created anew by God and given a purpose and personal destiny consistent with both the purposes of creation and humanity's eschatological destiny. Anyone who is in Christ should no longer be evaluated, judged, or categorized by their outward appearance, "such as national origin, social status, intellectual capability, physical attributes, or even charismatic endowment and pneumatic displays" (2 Cor. 5:16).[5] In Jesus Christ, believers belong to the new creation that achieves the purpose of the old creation (2 Cor. 5:17; Gal. 6:15).[6] In Christ, as God's new creation, believers are God's work created to accomplish certain goals that "God prepared beforehand to be our way of life" (Eph. 2:10 NRSV).[7] Most commentators believe that "prepared beforehand" refers not just to the believer's work or personal goal, but to God's intention at the foundation of the world and his initial purposes for humanity.[8] In Philippians 1:6, Paul sees believers as being

3. Dunn, *The Theology of Paul the Apostle* (Grand Rapids: Eerdmans, 1998), 265.

4. Richard Middleton states, "Indeed, the creator restores them to their rightful status, for humanity was originally crowned with royal dignity (Ps. 8:4–8) to be God's vice-regent on earth (Gen. 1:26–28)" (*A New Heaven and a New Earth: Reclaiming Biblical Eschatology* [Grand Rapids: Baker Academic, 2014], 141).

5. Murray J. Harris, *The Second Epistle to the Corinthians: A Commentary on the Greek Text*, NIGTC (Grand Rapids: Eerdmans, 2005), 427.

6. "So if anyone is in Christ, there is a new creation!" (2 Cor. 5:17 NRSV). Harris writes, "The renewal of the individual in conversion prefigures the renewal of the cosmos at the end. . . . 'If anyone,' standing without qualification, must be all-embracing, excluding no one. . . . In status before God through Christ and in accessibility to all the spiritual benefits that flow from that status, 'there is neither Jew nor Greek' (Gal. 3:28; cf. Eph. 2:11–22; Col. 3:11). 'The dividing wall that formed a barrier' . . . separating Jew and Gentile has been demolished in the person and work of Christ (Eph. 2:14)" (ibid., 431–32). The parallel of male and female to Jew and gentile is explicit in Gal. 3:28.

7. Andrew Lincoln states, "'In Christ Jesus' [in Eph. 2:10] is shorthand for 'through God's activity in Christ.' Christ is seen as the mediator of the new creation just as much as he was of the original one (cf. Col. 1:16)" (*Ephesians*, WBC 42 [Nashville: Nelson, 1990], 114).

8. See Lincoln's summary of the consensus of scholars (ibid., 115).

God's work-in-progress, who are on a trajectory that is completed when they reach their eschatological destiny: "He who began a good work in you will carry it on to completion until the day of Christ Jesus" (TNIV).[9]

The relevance of the Pauline theology of creation and eschatology for gender is that Paul fully and explicitly includes men and women in humanity's final destiny. In Galatians 3:26–4:1, this destiny will be one of rule and authority, as God's children and equal heirs in Christ: "For in Christ Jesus you are all children of God through faith. As many of you as were baptized into Christ have clothed yourselves with Christ. There is no longer Jew or Greek, there is no longer slave or free, there is no longer male and female; for all of you are one in Christ Jesus. And if you belong to Christ, then you are Abraham's offspring, heirs according to the promise" (NRSV).

According to Paul, there is no differentiation in humanity's destiny on the basis of gender, race, or status. Women, as well as gentiles and slaves, have a shared destiny of authority and rule. If this is consistent with the purposes of God at the foundation of the world, with the creation of Adam and Eve, and with the new creation in Christ, then women could not have been created to be subject to men.[10] In other words, women cannot have a final destiny that was not their intended purpose or function at creation. Rather, it is a transcendent norm for men and women to share dominion. The loss of authority and rule for women is a consequence of the fall in Genesis 3:16, which symbolizes a general disruption and corruption of power in human relationships, including the loss of authority and rule for many men who have been subjugated, such as male slaves. Rather than supporting a "priority of Adam,"[11] Paul, in the Prison and Pastoral Epistles, argues for the entire church to adopt a missional and self-sacrificial adaptation to fallen social structures of the Greco-Roman world as a strategy to advance the gospel, similar to missionary strategy required in the Middle East today.[12] Arguing for the transcendent norm of the unilateral subjugation of women on the basis of these texts supports pseudonymous

9. Middleton summarizes, "Hope of the resurrection is thus able to inspire believers to expect that God's original purposes for human life will ultimately come to fruition, despite what suffering we experience in the present" (*New Heaven*, 30).

10. Some simply appeal to the word "helper" in Gen. 2:18 to support Paul's alleged subordination of women. However, in the Hebrew Bible and the LXX, the semantic range of "helper" (עֵזֶר, βοηθός) in Gen. 2:18 includes a helper who is a superior, particularly God as a helper, so that it cannot signal subordination. The appeal to "helper" treats the meaning of the English term as if it were the same as the Hebrew or Greek, and then it exploits the difference in a circular argument.

11. Thus Schreiner argues that the priority of Adam is the basis of Paul's "ban on women teaching and exercising authority over men" (*Paul*, 408).

12. Note, e.g., missional motivations in the household code in Titus 2:1–9. The social conduct of men, women, and slaves needs to be appropriate according to the culture so that the word of

theories for parts of the Pauline corpus, where an unknown writer supposedly sought to promote Greco-Roman gender stereotypes as a corrective of Paul's earlier radical teaching.[13] This is because, as apparent throughout the Pauline corpus, Paul believed that God was actively bringing women as well as men toward the completion of their destiny and reversing the fall.[14]

5.3 Eschatology, Resurrection, and the Representation of Christ

It has been the traditional position in historical Christianity that only men can represent Christ in church offices such as the priesthood or the pastorate because Jesus was male.[15] However, Paul saw profound eschatological significance in Christ's resurrection, which is relevant to this assumption.[16] He insisted that a belief in Christ's literal bodily/corporeal resurrection was crucial for the believer's faith.[17] In 1 Corinthians 15, he makes an extended

---

God will not be maligned, so that the people in the culture can find nothing bad to say about Christians, and to make the Christian teaching attractive.

13. This is Robin Scroggs's assumption in "Paul and the Eschatological Woman," *JAAR* 40 (1972): 283.

14. However, Paul may have fought false teaching about eschatology and the nature of authority in the Christian community that was related to gender issues. Philip Towner uses the term "over-realized eschatology" to refer to false teaching and practice based on incorrect eschatology (*The Goal of Our Instruction: The Structure of Theology and Ethics in the Pastoral Epistles*, JSNTSup 34 [Sheffield: JSOT Press, 1989], 95–124). The term should not be confused with a Pauline resistance to realizing features of the new age in the church in the way that it is used by Schreiner (*Paul*, 412). Based on his linking 1 Tim. 6:20–21 and 2 Tim. 2:15–18, Towner suggests that a heresy claiming that the resurrection already happened upset "the social equilibrium of the communities" and created an emancipatory tendency among the women (*Goal of Our Instruction*, 38). However, Paul's specific correction of women in 1 Tim. 2:9–15 focuses on the creation narrative rather than any beliefs about resurrection.

15. There is no explicit biblical support for exclusive male representation of Christ in the priesthood and pastorate. It is inferred, and yet it is one of the most pervasive assumptions against women in all forms of ministry.

16. As Dunn states, Paul's eschatology was not forward-looking; it was backward-looking, toward the resurrection of Christ and the gift and presence of the Holy Spirit:

Paul's gospel was eschatological not because of what he still hoped would happen, but because of what he believed had already happened. What had already happened (Easter and Pentecost) had already the character of the end and showed what the end would be like. Which also means that the character of the interim period as "eschatological" did not depend on the *parousia* alone, nor to any real extent on either the imminence or delay of the *parousia*. What mattered was the fact that "the powers of the age to come" (Heb. 6:5) were already shaping lives and communities, as would also in due course shape the cosmos. (*Theology of Paul*, 465–66, emphasis original)

17. Middleton states, "The New Testament clearly teaches not only that Christ was raised bodily from death but that all who share in Christ's death (by repentance and faith) will also share in his resurrection and new life" (*New Heaven*, 2). This is particularly true of Paul.

argument to the Corinthians to prove that Christ was raised and that believers should expect a resurrection from the dead.[18] For Paul, resurrection is the basis for the believer's hope. It is the first stage in bringing life into the world and conquering the power of death (1 Cor. 15:20, 22–23). Christ is the first-born, the firstfruits of the resurrection harvest. Paul prophesies that Christ will reign until he returns and the dead are raised (1 Cor. 15:23–25, 28; Eph. 1:20–22). Jesus was crucified in weakness, but his resurrection means that he now lives in power (2 Cor. 13:4).

Paul's emphasis that the believers share in Jesus Christ's resurrection means that they will share his life, the same glorious body, his inheritance, and his power (Rom. 8:10, 23; 1 Cor. 15:35–49; 2 Cor. 4:16–17; 5:1–4). When Christ appears a second time (Rom. 8:29), all believers will be resurrected bodily (1 Cor. 15:4–8, 12–19) and conformed to the image of God's Son. That is, their bodies will be like his glorious body (Phil. 3:21).[19] The fact that the body is "spiritual" does not mean that it is not corporeal, but that it is immortal rather than perishable. Now we suffer in our perishable bodies (2 Cor. 5:1–5), but when the children of God are revealed, they will be liberated into freedom and glory, which will be reflected in the liberation of the whole creation (Rom. 8:19–21).

The relevance of the Pauline theology of Jesus's resurrection and eschatology for gender and the representation of Christ is that in Christ, resurrected males and females equally share Christ's destiny. The resurrection bodies of men and women equally share his life, *the same glorious body*, the same inheritance, and the same power. Jesus's work fulfills the purposes of creation. Since God created humanity as male and female, it should not be assumed that male and female will cease to exist in the resurrected state, any more than we would assume that Jesus's resurrection body is not male. The point is that Paul believes that men and women equally share *the same resurrection body as Christ* regardless of their gender.[20] Notice that the male

18. This discussion is unparalleled in the rest of the New Testament. As Howard Marshall asserts, it is "the most sustained discussion in the New Testament of the resurrection of Christian believers" (*New Testament Theology: Many Witnesses, One Gospel* [Downers Grove, IL: InterVarsity, 2004], 164).

19. Paul maintains that there will be a significant change, agreeing with 1 John 3:2 that we do not know what we will be, but that we will be changed from what is perishable, and sown in dishonor and perishable weakness, to what is imperishable, and be raised a spiritual body in glory and power (1 Cor. 15:35–49). In Rom. 8:30, the process is described as glorification or sharing in Jesus's glory (cf. 2 Thess. 2:14).

20. As far as the difference between male and female is concerned, the Genesis account stresses the fact that man and woman are one body, one and the same bone and flesh. Paul plays on this mutual identity of male and female (husband and wife) in Eph. 5:25–32 to describe

believer's share in Christ's resurrection body is confirmed regardless of the significant differences in the condition of the male's genitals; a gentile or a eunuch did not have the same kind of genitals as Christ. Jewish Christians would have a very difficult time recognizing uncircumcised men or eunuchs as representing Jesus's masculinity in his incarnation. Most Jews did not believe that uncircumcised men could be included in the people of God, though women could be included without any physical alteration. According to Paul, our conformity to and share in Christ's body and new life are not inherently linked to gender or the condition of our genitals, either in creation, the life of the church, or resurrection. It follows that our representation of the resurrected Christ in ecclesial rituals or leadership is not biblically linked to the current condition of our mortal bodies; none of our bodies are like his yet, but every believer shares the same hope of being like him. It follows that our representation of Christ is based on our hope in him, and we share the same hope that we will be like him, male or female, circumcised or uncircumcised. There is no priority or entitlement for men and no hint of any primogeniture in gender relationships in Pauline eschatological fulfillment. But that should be no surprise: Paul relativizes Israel's firstborn status (Exod. 4:22) and argues for the gentiles to be grafted into the people of God without differentiation (Rom. 9–11; Gal. 3:28). Jesus is the one and only firstborn from before creation, and the firstfruits of the resurrection harvest.[21]

5.4 Eschatology and the Destiny of Humanity

Paul states that believers are adopted as children of God through faith in Christ (Gal. 3:26). He devotes an extended discussion to our expectations as children of God in Romans 8:14–21. Our adoption means that all believers are heirs of God and co-heirs with Christ (Rom. 8:17; Gal. 4:7). Our adoption is completed at the resurrection with "the redemption of our bodies" when Christ appears (Rom. 8:19, 23). At that point the children of God will be brought into freedom and glory, and the creation will be released from its bondage to decay (Rom. 8:21; Col. 3:4). The restoration of glory refers to a full recovery of humanity's state at creation: the grandeur and power of the image of God; "glory" represents humanity's final destination.[22] We will inherit the world

the one-flesh relationship between Christ and the church. We are all members of his body, and therefore one flesh with him.

21. While Paul freely uses the register of primogeniture for Christ, it is inaccurate to say that the same primogeniture register is used in Paul's language on the creation of Adam. Contra James B. Hurley, *Man and Woman in Biblical Perspective* (Grand Rapids: Zondervan, 1981), 207.

22. See R. B. Gaffin Jr., "Glory, Glorification," *DPL*, 348–50.

(Rom. 4:13) and the kingdom of God (1 Cor. 6:9; 15:50).[23] This promised inheritance includes a shared rule with Christ (Rom. 5:17; 2 Tim. 2:12), which is signified by language and symbols of regal authority in the eschatological language of the early church, including "rule," "judgment," "thrones," and "crowns." In Philippians 2:9–11, Jesus's attitude and experience are a model for believers, beginning with servanthood and suffering and culminating in resurrection, glory, and rule. Believers' identification with Christ and their share with his future are consistent with his fulfillment of both the law and the creation mandate on behalf of humanity. He became one of us so that we could become like him in function as well as form.

In summary, there is an essential link between the Pauline eschatology of human destiny and the purposes of creation. Humanity was created in the image of God, to exercise power and authority in his creation, and that is intrinsically linked to our destiny in Christ, the destiny that he shares with us.[24] Paul makes it clear that no believer is banned from that future because of inherent distinctions or divisions among humans, including race, status, and gender; in Christ, all are heirs of this inheritance and moving toward this future, which is the accomplishment of God's will and his purposes at creation. Therefore, the power and the authority that were the human destiny at creation were the original purpose for women as well as men, since it is their eschatological destiny. This is consistent with Genesis 1:27–28, which declares that both male and female were explicitly created in God's image, that God blessed both of them, and that God gave both of them dominion.[25] Any case or claim for male priority and entitlement in Christ fades before this transcendent norm. Rather, male priority is the result of the fall, which is the straightforward reading of the fall's consequences for women in Genesis 3:16: "Your husband . . . will rule over you." But in Christ this result is

23. Paul refers to the inheritance of the world and the kingdom in passing: we inherit Abraham's promise that he was heir of the world, and though the immoral and flesh and blood will not inherit the kingdom, it assumes that believers will inherit the kingdom. This probably indicates that information about the nature of the inheritance is shared from the oral tradition of the gospel (e.g., Matt. 5:3, 5, 10; 19:14; 25:34; Luke 6:20).

24. Some take 1 Cor. 11:7 as showing that Paul believes women are not created in God's image or that God's image is derived for women; this is refuted in §3.1.

25. Contra Schreiner, who states, "When God created Adam, he was called to rule the world for God and to subdue creation under God's lordship. . . . Christ has undone what Adam has wrought, and the rule over the world promised to Adam has begun to be restored through Christ's work. Those who are in Christ share in that rule by virtue of their union with Christ" (*Romans*, BECNT [Grand Rapids: Baker, 1998], 267). Schreiner errs in using the masculine singular to say "he" (Adam) was called to rule the world and implying that the promise of rule was given to him alone. In Gen. 1:27–28, God issues the mandate to rule explicitly "to them," male and female, not the male alone.

being overcome. The effects of a proper understanding of the eschatological future of dominion for humanity (both genders) should be to reject theological propositions about gender that compromise the understanding that women are human and that they were created to exercise dominion consistent with God's eschatological goal in Christ. If Paul indeed placed a ban on the legitimate exercise of authority by women, it cannot be a transcendent norm.[26] According to Paul, the eschatological future of women who are in Christ is the same as the destiny of humanity: the exercise of power and authority over the angels and the nations (including men).

5.5 Eschatology and Life in the Christian Community

There is a consistency between our destiny and our current responsibilities and the entire way that our present existence is framed. As L. J. Kreitzer asserts, "Any attempt to contrast what is 'present' with what is 'eschatological' in Paul's thought misrepresents his position—the two are dynamically interconnected."[27] According to Paul, believers are supposed to understand one another according to their eschatological status. They are supposed to conduct their ethical practice with kingdom standards. The presence of the Holy Spirit in all the various aspects of Christian life and community is the very presence of the future. All of these elements lead to an intrinsic existential difference in gender relations in the Christian community. However, Paul is willing to sacrifice personal status and rights for the sake of the gentile mission. Believers must adapt to the culture in their navigation of two distinct worlds in order to win people to Christ.

5.5.1 Eschatological Status in the Christian Community

According to Paul, the eschatological status of believers gives them freedom in the present. Whatever a believer's social status in the "world" (Greco-Roman culture) may be, the believer is not to submit to a yoke of slavery in the Christian community that compromises his or her position in Christ. The positions and functions of weak, foolish, lowly, and despised believers in the body of Christ show that their wisdom and power come from God. God's choice of people with low status literally nullifies the values and authority structure of the Greco-Roman culture while they remain within its structure.

---

26. The interpretation or understanding of αὐθεντεῖν in 1 Tim. 2:12 as a ban on a woman's exercise of legitimate authority that is consistent with pastoral care will be refuted in chap. 8.

27. Kreitzer, "Eschatology," DPL, 254.

Eschatological changes are already in place and form the believer's present experience.[28] Paul's primary assignment was to bring the riches of God to the gentiles, but he makes it clear that the same benefits are given to women and slaves. According to Paul, God has made us alive, raised us, and already seated us with him in the heavenly places (Eph. 2:4–6). In terms of present experience, believers are citizens of the kingdom and members of the household of God. God is creating one humanity by removing barriers and reconciling groups that are divided along racial, social, and gender lines (Eph. 2:15–16). Paul's goal was to

> make everyone see what is the plan of the mystery hidden for ages in God who created all things; so that through the church the wisdom of God in its rich variety might now be made known to the rulers and authorities in the heavenly places. This was in accordance with the eternal purpose that he has carried out in Christ Jesus our Lord, in whom we have access to God in boldness and confidence through faith in him. (Eph. 3:9–12 NRSV)

Paul prayed that consequently gentiles would now have the full power, comprehension, and wisdom that are available from God, who can even accomplish more than that for them (Eph. 3:13–21). In Galatians, Paul fights against any teaching that compromises or limits the equal and full participation of gentiles in the church community, and he extends full participation to women and slaves in Galatians 3:28.[29] Gentiles, women, and slaves are set free in their function as children of God and heirs in salvation history and in the church community (Gal. 3:22–29), and it should follow that they not submit to a yoke of slavery consisting of extra requirements, restrictions, or rules that compromise their status in exactly the same way as gentiles (Gal. 5:1).

Believers' lives are transferred to a different plane, and Paul claims that this changes the Christian community's appraisal of every believer. We are supposed to see one another as part of the new creation; our identity is not based on cultural standards. As Paul says in 2 Corinthians 5:16–17, "So from now on we will not evaluate anyone from a worldly point of view. We used to evaluate Christ that way, but we do not do it anymore. So, if anyone is in Christ, it is the new creation! The old is gone and the new is here!" According to Paul, the church does not typically attract the wise, the teachers of the law,

---

28. For a more extensive discussion of the role of experience in Pauline theology, see Cynthia Long Westfall, "Paul's Experience and a Pauline Theology of the Spirit," in *Defining Issues in Pentecostalism: Classical and Emergent*, ed. Steven M. Studebaker, MTSS 1 (Hamilton, ON: McMaster Divinity Press, 2008), 123–43.

29. For a fuller explanation of Gal. 3:28, see §5.7.

the philosophers of the age, the influential or the noble (1 Cor. 1:20, 26). But in Christ, the believers receive wisdom, teaching, understanding, influence, power, and spiritual status. However, they possess it in Jesus alone, so that the only thing that believers can boast about is the Lord (1 Cor. 1:31). God's choice of the foolish, weak, lowly, and despised "nullify the things that are" (TNIV) so that no one can boast in front of God (1 Cor. 1:27–28). Therefore, within the church there was supposed to be a true social reversal giving a message to the social power structures in the Greco-Roman culture. Of course, women, children, and slaves were typecast as foolish, weak, lowly, and despised, so that they would represent God's choice that nullified the culture's social and political power structures.

Therefore, the status of believers in the church community was markedly different from their status in society, as Paul makes clear in 1 Corinthians 1:20–31. The nullification of the "things that are" has both a present and an eschatological effect. At the present time, according to Paul, God's choice of the weak and foolish to be his people shames the strong and wise (1:27). God's choice of the lowly and despised is the very thing that nullifies the "things that are" (1:28). The world's wisdom and authority are coming to nothing in the present time (1 Cor. 2:6), so that for Paul the eschatological culmination is in some sense the climax of a process that is going on in the present through the church, which bypasses the authority and power structures of society. Of all things, the full participation of women, children, and slaves in the function of the church community epitomizes how God shames and displaces those who have a sense of entitlement within the social power structures of the culture.

5.5.2 Eschatological Ethics in the Christian Community

According to Paul, we walk in the shadow of the future. What we do ought to reflect our future: the believers' future should be reflected in their choices, actions, and function even now. For Paul, ethics, holiness, and holy behavior are an essential part of the eschatological Christian community. Our future hope defines our present-day reality. The character and the state of the believer are supposed to provide a distinct contrast with the rest of the world. Believers' ethics and behavior are supposed to be appropriate for heirs who will inherit God's kingdom. Furthermore, believers are obligated to practice future responsibilities in the present by literally learning to execute good judgment and by becoming teachers. In addition, God appoints every believer to build up the church in a specific way, and each of them will face judgment for how well or how poorly spiritual gifts, abilities, advantages, and privileges were used to accomplish God's goals. Eschatological ethics have serious repercussions for our understanding of gender.

Andrew Lincoln says that being "God's handiwork" refers to the new creation and being "created in Christ Jesus to do good works" (Eph. 2:10 TNIV). This indicates that "the whole of believers' lives, including their practical ethical activity, is to be seen as part of God's purpose."[30] Similarly, as a consequence of Christ's resurrection and ascension, Paul tells believers, "Set your minds on things that are above, not on things that are on earth, for you have died, and your life is hidden with Christ in God" (Col. 3:2–3 NRSV). Reality, priorities, and behavior for the believer are reframed by the eschatological identification with the resurrected Christ. The passage concludes, "When Christ who is your life is revealed, then you also will be revealed with him in glory" (Col. 3:4 NRSV). What is now hidden will be revealed in the future, but this eschatological identification is at the heart of the believer's life in the present.

Paul wanted believers' lives to be "blameless and innocent" and "without blemish." This is not simply forensic justification. Children of God are supposed to provide a very real contrast "in the midst of a crooked and perverse generation, in which you shine like stars in the world" (Phil. 2:15 NRSV). Interestingly, this is an outcome of the magnificent model of Christ's servanthood, suffering, and consequent exaltation to cosmic rule, described in Philippians 2:5–11. The imagery of "children of God" shining "like stars in the world" in 2:15 depicts developing a blameless and pure character and reflecting a state that exhibits the dignity of their new eschatological status.[31]

Believers are called to be holy (1 Cor. 1:2), and the goal (ἕως τέλους) of speech, knowledge, testimony, and spiritual gifts is that they be blameless when Jesus returns and have fellowship with him (1 Cor. 1:4–9; cf. 1 Thess. 3:12–13). According to Paul, ethical practice/holiness is directly related to a believer's current identity as an heir of the kingdom and the future expectation of inheritance. This argument is particularly well developed via Paul's discussion on sexual ethics in 1 Corinthians 5:1–6:20. According to Howard Marshall, one of Paul's points is that those who participate in the "obvious" sin of sexual misconduct will not inherit the kingdom of God (6:9).[32] In addi-

---

30. Lincoln, *Ephesians*, 115.

31. As Gordon Fee says, Paul "now turns to the final apocalyptic vision of Daniel (12:1–4) to describe their role in pagan Philippi. . . . It is probably the eschatological context of the Daniel passage that makes his own transition to their eschatological future so easy. But before that, he is concerned still with the 'already'" (*Paul's Letter to the Philippians*, NICNT [Grand Rapids: Eerdmans, 1995], 246–47).

32. See Marshall, *New Testament Theology*, 256.

tion, the fact that our bodies will be resurrected from the dead is a key part of Paul's argument for sexual purity (6:14). Within the same context, Paul states that those guilty of greed and cheating will not inherit the kingdom of God (6:10). A person may preach the gospel and yet be disqualified because of lack of self-control (1 Cor. 9:24–27). The believer's behavior in the world and in the Christian community must be evaluated according to what is consistent with and appropriate for the people of God who will inherit the kingdom.

Furthermore, believers have current obligations based on what will be expected of them in the future; they should be developing spiritual muscle (1 Cor. 6:1–6). Within the extended discussion on sexual ethics, Paul here prohibits litigation between believers. Rather than having believers sue one another in court, the church should find any believer who is wise and have that person act as a judge; someone in the community should be able to do it, since all are destined to judge angels. This is similar to the assumptions in Hebrews 5:12–14: "For though by this time you ought to be teachers, you need someone to teach you again the basic elements of the oracles of God. You need milk, not solid food; for everyone who lives on milk, being still an infant, is unskilled in the word of righteousness. But solid food is for the mature, for those whose faculties have been trained by practice to distinguish good from evil" (NRSV).

Believers are expected to grow in the faith to become teachers. This growth is directly related to ethical experience: every believer has a responsibility to train and develop the ability to make ethical decisions, not just for personal development and holiness, but to be a resource to the entire church community.

Finally, believers will be accountable for their failure to do what God created them to do. The quality and eternal value of what they do now will be determined at the future judgment, and what is worthless will be burned up (1 Cor. 3:10–15). Paul gave this eschatological declaration in the context of explaining his own call, work, and responsibility. He experienced a very controversial call from God: as an apostle to the gentiles, he felt a heavy responsibility to build the church. But he relativized his call and work as the equivalent to other workers who do their part in building up the church: "What then is Apollos? What is Paul? Servants through whom you came to believe, as the Lord assigned to each [ἑκάστῳ ὡς ὁ κύριος ἔδωκεν]" (1 Cor. 3:5 NRSV). This is Paul's language for the spiritual gifts or responsibilities that are given to each believer in order to build on the foundation that has been laid for the common good:

> To each is given the manifestation of the Spirit for the common good. (1 Cor. 12:7 NRSV; cf.12:8, 24; 14:7–9)

> According to the grace of God given to me, like a skilled master builder I laid a foundation. (1 Cor. 3:10 NRSV)

> We have gifts that differ according to the grace given to us. (Rom. 12:6 NRSV; cf. 12:3)

These responsibilities come according to the grace one receives, according to the measure of one's faith, and according to the will of the Holy Spirit, not according to gender. The bottom line is the believer's appointment/call. According to the verses above, the believer's appointment/call is not mediated through other people. Rather, it is primarily determined by experience. When 1 Corinthians 3:5–15 and 1 Corinthians 12–14 interpret each other, it is a serious warning for each believer to be very careful to use spiritual gifts to fully and properly produce work that will stand the test of God's judgment; God created us to accomplish the works that he prepared for us (Eph. 2:10). Any believer who either fails to do what God intends or fails in doing it for the right reasons with holy character will pay a profound price in the eschatological judgment. This is exactly the point of Jesus's parable of the talents in Matthew 25:14–30. Whatever believers have received from God must be invested in order to benefit him and accomplish his purposes, and if they refuse to do so, the consequences are severe. For Paul, the default place for investment was in the church, and yet many women have been restricted from using the majority of the gifts listed in the church because they involve speaking or leadership.

Understanding gender in the light of eschatological ethics necessitates certain important and relevant adjustments to traditional theology. On the one hand, it provides a serious warning against male ambition, competition, and entitlement. On the other hand, it reframes the traditional understanding of women's responsibilities in the eschatological community of God. Women are accountable to be wise enough to pass judgment on wrong behavior within the Christian community and to teach the Christian community. Women receive their appointments to build up the body of Christ exactly the same way that men do and with the same criteria. Women who do not exercise their spiritual gifts and abilities for the common good will be liable. Men who ban or restrict God's appointments in terms of how a woman will function in the church will be liable. No divine appointment for women may be ruled out on the basis of "transcendent norms" that are extrapolated and prooftexted by men engaged in a gender power struggle. Such power struggles miss the mark, and they involve building on the church's foundation with exactly the kind of wood, hay, and straw that Paul warned against when he criticized the Corinthians for pitting Christian leaders against one another in a power struggle (1 Cor. 3:11–15).

5.5.3 Eschatology and the Presence of the Holy Spirit in the Christian Community

For Paul, the gift of the Holy Spirit is the existential presence of God, as well as the experience and application of eschatological hope in the believer's life.[33] The Holy Spirit provides the experience that confirms our theology in terms of what has happened to us and for us in Christ, and what will happen when Christ appears again. The Holy Spirit gives believers the ability to conduct themselves according to kingdom ethics, to be a holy people. The Holy Spirit is the one who determines each person's appointment in the body of Christ as he wills. The baptism and fullness of the Spirit are the presence of the future,[34] and his lordship determines functions and offices in the Christian community that foreshadow the future dominion of God's people.

We have eternal life and will be resurrected because of what Christ did and his resurrection, but it is the Holy Spirit who actually gives us life (Rom. 8:2, 10; 1 Cor. 15:45; 2 Cor. 3:6). Jesus Christ is the firstfruits of the resurrection harvest, but the Spirit is the firstfruits of our future share (Rom. 8:23). We have redemption in Christ, but the Spirit is the seal/guarantee/down payment of "what is to come," including the completion of that redemption (2 Cor. 1:22; 5:5; Eph. 1:14). The believer receives the washing of rebirth and renewal from the Holy Spirit, who was poured out on us (Titus 3:5–6). The Spirit brought about the adoption of the believer and "testifies" with our spirit now that we are God's children (Rom. 8:15–16). Therefore the Spirit indicates that we are heirs and co-heirs of Christ (Rom. 8:17); the Spirit also guarantees our inheritance as heirs (Eph. 1:14). The Spirit pours God's love into our hearts, which gives us a hope that will not disappoint us (Rom. 5:5), and the Spirit prays for us (Rom. 8:27). The Spirit is the primary force in our ethical behavior; the Spirit frees the believer from sin and anticipates the future conquest of death (Rom. 8:2–4). Living by the Spirit produces Christian character in becoming like Jesus (Rom. 8:9–13; Gal. 5:16, 22–26), and the Spirit changes us from glory to glory (2 Cor. 3:17–18). The Spirit motivates speech and every confession of Christ as

33. For Paul's eschatological orientation of the Spirit's ministry, see Westfall, "Paul's Experience," in Studebaker, *Defining Issues in Pentecostalism*, 139–41.

34. According to Gordon Fee, the fact that the Holy Spirit belongs to the future is the key to everything in the New Testament (*Gospel and Spirit: Issues in New Testament Hermeneutics* [Peabody, MA: Hendrickson, 1996], 113).

Lord (1 Cor. 12:3), but ungodly unedifying speech grieves the Spirit (Eph. 4:30). The result of being filled with the Spirit is the practice of mutual submission as well as an overflowing verbal response in speech and song to one another and to God (Eph. 5:18–21). Mutual submission reflects the humble attitude of Christ in his incarnation and anticipates sharing his glory (Phil. 2:1–11). The Spirit sovereignly distributes manifestations of gifts, service, and workings to every believer for the common good of the Christian community (1 Cor. 12:1–30).

The Holy Spirit is the presence of the future. The significance of the Spirit for the gender discussion is the importance of experience, the effects of the Spirit's work, and the areas in which the Spirit is supposed to have control. Experience is very important in Pauline theology.[35] For Paul, the Spirit provides the direct experience of what we confess. His own experience on the Damascus road and of the gentile revivals informed and formed his theology and his reading of the Old Testament. The significance of the experience of the Spirit has played a role in the gender discussion. The effect of the Spirit on the believer is the development of Christian character, which is characterized by an outpouring of speech and song that confess Christ and edify the community. This primary evidence of the Spirit is consistent with the prophecy and ecstatic tongues that occurred when converts received the Holy Spirit, as recorded in Acts.[36] This contradicts various interpretations and understandings asserting that 1 Corinthians 14:34—"Women should remain silent in the churches; they are not allowed to speak"—refers to the absolute silence of women as a group in the Pauline house churches. Finally, the Spirit is supposed to have full control in the distributions of spiritual gifts to believers. There cannot be artificially constructed rules or biblical principles that override and restrict the Spirit's work in terms of whom he will use in various functions to edify the church.[37] This is a pragmatic question

35. For an extended discussion of the role of experience in Pauline theology that interacts with the relationship between gender and Pentecostal distinctives, see Westfall, "Paul's Experience," in Studebaker, *Defining Issues in Pentecostalism*.

36. Although some interpreters argue that only the apostles spoke in tongues at Pentecost, the context in Acts indicates that it was a meeting of believers (2:1), women were present (1:14), all spoke in tongues (2:1–4), the audience included pious men (ἄνδρες εὐλαβεῖς; 2:5), the content of the tongues spoke (λαλούντων) the wonders of God (2:11), and it fulfilled the prophecy in Joel 2:28, "Your sons and daughters will prophesy" (2:17).

37. See, e.g., Wayne Grudem, "But What *Should* Women Do in a Church?," http://cbmw.org/wp-content/uploads/2013/05/1-2.pdf. He lists 83 ministries and ranks the ministries on a cline of authority according to governing authority, teaching responsibility and influence, and public recognition and visibility; then he provides guidelines he hopes "will be helpful for many churches in coming to their own understanding of where to 'draw the line' on what they think appropriate for women and what they think to be inappropriate."

of lordship that critiques procedures whereby offices and functions in the church are determined along lines of gender rather than gifting by the work of the Holy Spirit.

5.5.4 The Relationship of the Eschatological Community to the World/Society

Paul's work among the gentiles was devoted to the formation of a subculture within the Greco-Roman culture. This was much more obvious in the gentile mission than in the case of Jewish Christianity, which saw itself in continuity with the history of the commonwealth of Israel and the dispersion. The subculture of the gentile churches deviated from the mainstream Greco-Roman culture in its values and norms of behavior, and Paul was in full opposition to the imperial theology that was a part of it.[38] Paul repeatedly offered blighting critiques of the "world," and he characterized the mainstream culture as living in "darkness" (2 Cor. 6:14; Eph. 5:8). He said that he waged spiritual warfare against the authority structures of the empire ("the powers of this dark world") as well as spiritual forces of evil (Eph. 6:12). There was no separation of religion and state behind the theology of the Roman Empire, which crucified Jesus Christ. The social, religious, and political systems that composed the Roman Empire in the first century were a threat to, and a target of, both the gentile mission and the Jewish mission.[39] However, the membership of the gentile churches had been fully identified with the Greco-Roman culture in a way that the Jews had not.[40]

Yet members of the Christian community lived in both worlds, for they infiltrated the Roman Empire. They had multiple identities, roles, and responsibilities that they needed to navigate with care, because even though they were heirs of the kingdom in the church, in the worldly society there were expectations, demands, and obligations that had to be met and entailed

38. For a description of imperial theology, see Cynthia Long Westfall, "Roman Religions and the Imperial Cult," in *Lexham Bible Dictionary*, ed. John D. Barry (Bellingham, WA: Logos Bible Software, 2015).

39. This statement summarizes the contribution of postcolonial biblical criticism. Postcolonial biblical scholars have made a convincing case for subversion tactics against empire in the New Testament. For an introduction to the discussion of empire in the New Testament, see Stanley E. Porter and Cynthia Long Westfall, eds., *Empire in the New Testament*, MNTSS 10 (Eugene, OR: Pickwick, 2010).

40. This is not to say that the Jews were not part of the Hellenistic culture, but that they saw themselves as a countercultural group, though certain Jews and groups of Jews were more integrated into the Greco-Roman culture than others. Therefore, Jewish Christianity was in continuity with the mainstream of Judaism, but the gentile mission created a counterculture within the Greco-Roman culture that was more problematic.

behavior often inconsistent with their true status in Christ. For Paul, there were at least three reasons why these expectations, demands, and obligations needed to be fulfilled. First, it was a primary goal for the church community to live at peace among the people and structures of the Roman Empire in order to thrive (1 Tim. 2:1–3). Second, survival was a goal, and it was important that the community did not flout the laws and core commitments of the Roman officials and local authorities in order to avoid being the victim of their sword (Rom. 13:1–7). Third, the expansion of the gentile mission was a primary goal, and there was no personal sacrifice that Paul was unwilling to make to win more people to Christ: "I have become all things to all people, that I might by all means save some" (1 Cor. 9:22 NRSV). Paul sacrificed social rights, power, and status that belonged to him in the eyes of the Roman Empire, to serve the gospel and follow Christ's example (Phil. 3:4–8), and he wanted his communities to make the same commitments and sacrifices.

Paul's Letters reflect how to live in a cutting-edge, foreign-missions setting. The letters urge the adoption of the respectable dress, norms, and customs of the target cultures, as well as its laws. The letters communicate to the people with language and symbols that they understand.[41] Like secret agents, Paul wanted his communities to fit in as much as possible; they did the same things that their neighbors did yet for eschatological reasons: they served another king and belonged to another kingdom.[42] Paul did not have the goal of empowering women and slaves in the social and political structures of the Roman Empire, but he was very interested in empowering and equipping them in the Christian community in every way. He wanted them to use their "calling" and resources in the world together with their spiritual resources to further kingdom purposes.

41. See Westfall, "Paul's Experience," in Studebaker, *Defining Issues in Pentecostalism*, 140–41, where I argue, "In crossing religious, social and cultural boundaries to reach the Gentiles, Paul provides the best example in the New Testament of the contextualization of the Gospels, both in Acts and in his epistles," and that contextualization is the eschatological fulfillment of the Abrahamic covenant.

42. Perhaps the role of women as "secret agents" is one of the best metaphors to explain the polemic against Christianity by Celsus. Carolyn Osiek and Margaret MacDonald summarize: "Was Celsus right? If we look beyond the polemic (though the polemic is part of the story!), largely, yes. Women did move in and out of houses and shops, taking risks and leading people—including children—to join the movement without permission from the proper authorities. They did so, it seems, while conducting their daily business. No doubt they sometimes remained largely invisible, but in other cases they met with real resistance both inside and outside of church groups. This combination of boldness, affront, and concealment is one of the most interesting and little understood features of the rise of Christianity" (*A Woman's Place: House Churches in Earliest Christianity* [Minneapolis: Fortress, 2006], 243).

5.6 Eschatology and the Household

The household was the place that best exhibited the tension and potential at the juncture of eschatology, the social structures of power in the culture, and mission. The behavior and subjugation of women and slaves were of supreme importance in the Roman Empire and its imperial theology. In the ancient Near East, women were subjugated because they were supposedly inferior to men, and they constituted a threat to men because of their sexual power, necessitating the continual need to control them sexually. Slaves were threats because they might turn on their masters or join a slave revolt. But in the Roman Empire, they both were also the basic building blocks of the Greco-Roman social web and authority structure and had a vital role to play. They both were the bottom tier of the patron-client relationship that culminated with Caesar. Subverting the authority of the household was tantamount to subverting the authority of the empire. Women were also the mothers of necessary soldiers and workers, and there was official anxiety about low birth rates. Therefore, the behavior code for women was a deadly serious concern: it was an ethical, social, political, and religious issue. The Greco-Roman "household codes" defined how the members in the household should operate, primarily defining the submission, obedience, and obligations of the household members to the male authority.[43] The Greco-Roman household codes were enmeshed with assumptions about ontological male superiority, and the inferiority of women and slaves, but these are inconsistent with the status of men and women in Christ that Paul taught in his churches. In the Pauline corpus the household codes represent the navigation of a minefield, both for the original author and for readers today. For stated missional purposes, he urged conformity with the Greco-Roman household codes that governed the behavior of those in subordinate roles. However, he subverted these codes by changing the subordinates' motivations, and by changing the behavior of those in authority without directly challenging their authority. The effect of the language of the Pauline household codes is to reverse the fall by reducing the household powers and authorities of the world to servanthood, and by assigning believers in subordinate positions a missional role, correctly referring to such as a "call" (κλῆσις in 1 Cor. 7:20).

43. For an overview of the household codes, see David L. Balch, *Let Wives Be Submissive: The Domestic Code in 1 Peter*, SBLMS 26 (Chico, CA: Scholars Press, 1981). See also James P. Hering's excellent analysis and summary of the discussion in *The Colossian and Ephesian Haustafeln in Theological Context: An Analysis of Their Origins, Relationship, and Message*, TR 260 (New York: Peter Lang, 2007).

Paul in fact subverted the Greco-Roman household codes by reframing the basis, purpose, and motivation for the behavior of social inferiors, and by adjusting and restricting the privileges of those who have power. Paul instructed believers to display righteous behavior within the dress, norms, and customs of the Roman Empire as pragmatic measures that serve the kingdom of God. Titus 2:1–14 indicates a missional intention for the household codes. The women are to be models of Greco-Roman expectations, "self-controlled, chaste, good managers of the household, kind, being submissive to their husbands" (2:5 NRSV). However, the reasons and motivations for their behavior were "so that the word of God may not be discredited" (2:5 NRSV). This reason is missional, not ethical or ontological. Similarly, the motivation for young men's behavior is apologetic: so that "any opponent will be put to shame, having nothing evil to say of us" (2:8 NRSV). The motivation for slaves is to make the gospel attractive, which is also missional: "so that in everything they may be an ornament to the doctrine of God our Savior" (2:10 NRSV):

> For the grace of God has appeared, bringing salvation to all, training us to renounce impiety and worldly passions, and in the present age to live lives that are self-controlled, upright, and godly, while we wait for the blessed hope and the manifestation of the glory of our great God and Savior, Jesus Christ. He it is who gave himself for us that he might redeem us from all iniquity and purify for himself a people of his own who are zealous for good deeds. (Titus 2:11–14 NRSV)

This passage beautifully expresses the "already but not yet" eschatological nature of "the present age" and how the believers' character formation and God's purposes were going forward as believers navigated their contradictory roles and duties in the world/Greco-Roman culture. Notice that the specific instructions to women in Titus 2:3–5 semantically echo the mission of every believer "to live lives that are self-controlled, upright, and godly" (Titus 2:12).

The added element of household management is an important qualification for leadership in the house church (1 Tim. 3:4–5, 12; Titus 1:5–6). Even the Greco-Roman household codes saw women as having authority in the domestic sphere, while men had complementary authority in the public sphere. It is interesting that Paul uses one of the strongest verbs of household authority for women's home management in 1 Timothy 5:14, οἰκοδεσποτεῖν, defined as "to be master of a house or head of a family" in Liddell and Scott's *Greek-English Lexicon*. A woman's management and leadership in the home included the proactive practice of hospitality in teaching, hosting

house churches, caring for needs (visitors, orphans, and widows), and evange-
lizing.[44] These functions represented the front line in the advancement of the
gospel; most of the activities of the Christian community took place in the
domestic sphere in the house church and the exercise of hospitality.[45] This is
often missed in the reading of Scripture because we see the church as a public
institution; however, the church met and functioned in the domestic sphere
while the New Testament was being written. It is inaccurate to read Paul as if
he did not allow women to have authority or that every reference to authority
must have a male referent; most women had multiple roles where they were
both in submission and in authority.[46] Managing the home and submission
to husbands were in direct continuity with the demands of the culture and
an essential for survival (as was obedience for slaves). The complementary
pairing of the practice of submission with the exercise of one's calling in the
world involved an eschatological understanding for the advancement of the
gospel that is part and parcel of a broader Pauline theology.

Paul's primary means of subverting the Greco-Roman household code was
the same as Jesus's method. Jesus taught that any leader among the disciples
had to become everyone's slave (Matt. 20:27; Mark 10:44). He demonstrated
it by performing the slave's job of washing the disciples' feet (John 13:3–16)
and by his entire mission: "The Son of Man came not to be served but to serve,
and to give his life as a ransom for many" (Matt. 20:28 NRSV). Paul taught
the same principle of mutual submission and service in Philippians 2:1–11.
He first exhorted submission in the Christian community, and then gave the
example of Jesus "taking the form of a slave" (2:7), and humbling himself
and becoming "obedient to the point of death" (2:8 NRSV). Every Christian
is to "do nothing from selfish ambition or conceit, but in humility regard
others as better than yourselves" (2:3 NRSV). This must be taken to heart
and practiced primarily by those who are advantaged socially, economically,
physically, and racially for it to have any effect on the Christian community.
Paul demonstrated how this would work in the master-slave relationship in
his letter to Philemon. Paul sees to it that the slave Onesimus submits to Philemon, the slave owner, an act that is in continuity with the Greco-Roman
culture. But Philemon is the one who must change everything in the power

44. See Osiek and MacDonald's chapter on "Women as Agents of Expansion," in *Woman's
Place*, 220–43, particularly the section "The Household and Conversion" (233–40).
45. For a description of the Pauline house church, see Robert Banks, *Paul's Idea of Community: The Early House Churches in Their Historical Setting* (Grand Rapids: Eerdmans, 1980).
46. Many aspects of women's work in the church involved being an "authority under authority," parallel with the Roman centurion and Jesus in his incarnate state (Matt. 8:8–9). As
Osiek and MacDonald say, "Some of these traces of influence have been precisely of women
acting as dutiful wives" (*Woman's Place*, 245).

relationship, so that Onesimus functions as an eschatological brother in every way (though presumably still a slave).

The household code in Ephesians 5:21–33 begins with the concept of mutual submission.[47] Then, similar to the requirement of Onesimus's submission, Paul reinforces the submission of women to their husbands in continuity with the Greco-Roman culture. However, the reason for submission is completely changed with an allusion to the creation account, where the husband is the wife's head as the source of her life and identity at creation.[48] The meaning of "head" as the source of life is consistent with the culture's understanding of the husband as the wife's patron, but it is not a stock metaphor for authority in Greek.[49] Therefore, Paul reframes the reason with the biblical understanding and changes the relationship to a metaphor, which he will exploit.

The primary focus in the Ephesian household code is on the husband's role. The language both reflects the model of Jesus's servanthood and exploits the metaphor of "head" to create a similar effect as in the episode where Jesus washed the disciples' feet. The fact that Jesus humbled himself and was obedient to the point of death is thematic in the servanthood passages, in that "he gave himself up for her"—"her" is the church and is parallel to the wife in the passage (Eph. 5:25). So Jesus is the model for the husband's role of protecting his wife. The rest of the passage is a fascinating study of role reversals in which Jesus gives his bride a bath and takes responsibility for providing bridal clothes that are treated for stains, laundered, and ironed (metaphors for sanctification). These metaphors for sanctification not only are a model of a husband directly serving the best interests of the wife in her well-being and development (cf. Phil. 2:1–4); they also depict Jesus Christ as doing women's work (stereotypical female domestic chores), which is comparable to washing the disciples' feet. Scholars have been confused about how a husband can sanctify his wife, but that is because they treat the information as abstract theology and miss the power, meaning, and association of the metaphors. In effect, Paul flips the patron metaphor of being the wife's head (protector and source of life). Instead of expecting or demanding client

47. See the discussion of the household code in Ephesians in Cynthia Long Westfall, "'This Is a Great Metaphor!': Reciprocity in the Ephesians Household Code," in *Christian Origins and Greco-Roman Culture: Social and Literary Context for the New Testament*, ed. Stanley E. Porter and Andrew Pitts, ECHC 1 (Leiden: Brill, 2013), 561–98.

48. For the meaning of "head" in the Greek language and in the kinship register, see §3.5.1 above.

49. For a full discussion of the patron-client relationship in the Greco-Roman culture, see David A. deSilva, *Honor, Patronage, Kinship & Purity: Unlocking New Testament Culture* (Downers Grove, IL: InterVarsity, 2006).

reciprocity (submission), the head supplies low-status domestic service to the body that is ordinarily expected from women or slaves. The head nurtures (as a mother/nurse cares for a baby), feeds, and cares for its own body. In effect, Paul has told the husbands to wash their wives' feet and much more. He has given an explicit application of Jesus's summary of the law: "In everything do to others as you would have them do to you; for this is the law and the prophets" (Matt. 7:12 NRSV). Paul applies Jesus's teaching literally to the men: "Husbands should love their wives as they do their own bodies. He who loves his wife loves himself" (Eph. 5:28 NRSV). Paul's caveat is that she *is* his body. The intertextuality between Ephesians 5:28 and the Jesus tradition is transparent.

In the Ephesian household code, Paul briefly indicates that wives should submit (in the context of mutual submission), and then, in great detail, he tells men to act just like women or slaves in their marital relationship. However, it is not a role reversal, because women never assume for themselves the role of master or head. In other words, there is never any question of a woman becoming an αὐθέντης (one who has "full power or authority over").[50] Paul prohibits this practice in 1 Timothy 2:12, which is a truncated household code. Instead, both wives and husbands are servants of each other, with only one Lord and master, who has full authority and power over them. The service requirement of the one who has social power and privilege in the world is completely consistent with Paul's Christology and his missiology, and it reflects how the equal eschatological status among the members of the Christian community can coexist in both worlds.

5.7 Eschatology and Galatians 3:28

Paul's statement in Galatians 3:27–28 is a brilliant formulation of the eschatological unity of our identity in Christ across the universal diversity, distinctions, and divisions of race, social status, and gender:

> For all of you who were baptized into Christ have clothed yourselves with Christ. There is no longer Jew or Greek, there is no longer slave or free, there is no longer male and female; for all of you are one in Christ Jesus.

However, it has been the focus of much discussion and controversy because of gender issues. On the one hand, it is sometimes utilized as an interpretive grid or a prooftext for all passages on women and as a manifesto for the

50. See LSJ, "αὐθέντης," 1:275.

equality of women.[51] On the other hand, others maintain that Galatians 3:28 applies to salvation or the mystical covenantal union in Christ, and not to the removal of role distinctions in the church.[52]

Often Galatians 3:28 is used to draw a parallel between the status of women in society and the status of slaves and the eventual abolition of the institution of slavery. For example, William Webb states, "On the surface, certain texts within the Bible appear to support slavery," but Scriptures such as Galatians 3:28, as well as 1 Corinthians 7:21; 12:13; Colossians 3:11; and Philemon 15–16, provided a "seedbed" in which the redemptive element would grow.[53] F. F. Bruce similarly states, "What this letter does is to bring us into an atmosphere in which the institution could only wilt and die."[54] According to Webb, Scripture modifies the original cultural norms as far as they will go in a way suggesting that future movement is possible and even advantageous in a subsequent culture.[55]

However, it must be clarified that the Pauline corpus was not directly addressing the Greco-Roman culture or overtly attempting to modify it. It was establishing the church, the kingdom of God, within the context of the

51. Ronald Allen and Beverly Allen call Gal. 3:28 "the feminist credo of equality" (*Liberated Traditionalism: Men and Women in Balance* [Portland, OR: Multnomah, 1985], 134), and Paul Jewett calls it "The Magna Carta of Humanity" (*Man as Male and Female: A Study in Sexual Relationships from a Theological Point of View* [Grand Rapids: Eerdmans, 1975], 142). Elisabeth Schüssler Fiorenza seeks to recover a "discipleship of equals." Galatians 3:28 "not only advocates the abolition of religious-cultural divisions and of the domination and exploitation wrought by institutional slavery but also of domination based on sexual divisions. It repeats with different categories and words that within the Christian community no structures of dominance can be tolerated. . . . It proclaims that in the Christian community all distinctions of religion, race, class, nationality, and gender are insignificant. All the baptized are equal, they are one in Christ" (*In Memory of Her: A Feminist Theological Reconstruction of Christian Origins* [London: SCM, 1983], 213). Note also Tatha Wiley's remark: "While men and women were Jew or Gentile, slave or free, male or female outside the community, these distinctions did not hold in the 'new creation' of the Christian community. The norms of the ancient world did not control relations in the *ekklēsia* or Christian assembly." She assumes the "radical equality" of the Christian community "embodied in the participation of members in the community and in shared leadership roles" (*Paul and the Gentile Women: Reframing Galatians* [New York: Continuum, 2005], 19).

52. See S. Lewis Johnson Jr., "Role Distinctions in the Church: Galatians 3:28," in *Recovering Biblical Manhood and Womanhood: A Response to Evangelical Feminism*, ed. John Piper and Wayne Grudem (Wheaton: Crossway, 1991), 154–64. Johnson summarizes: "The phrase 'in Christ' refers to the mystical and universal, the representative and covenantal union of all believers in the Lord. In the context of Galatians, the apostle simply affirms that every believer in Christ fully inherits the Abrahamic promises by grace apart from legal works" (163).

53. Webb, *Slaves, Women & Homosexuals: Exploring the Hermeneutics of Cultural Analysis* (Downers Grove, IL: InterVarsity, 2001), 84.

54. Bruce, *Paul, Apostle of the Heart Set Free* (Grand Rapids: Eerdmans, 1977), 401.

55. Webb, *Slaves, Women & Homosexuals*, 73.

Greco-Roman culture as distinct from that culture. It is true that some biblical principles later changed social structures because Christianity as a religion was becoming a political influence and eventually a power in its own right in the empire and in various later governments, forming the dominant culture in many parts of the world.[56] As a foundation of the dominant culture, the church later became a road to power, privilege, prestige, and wealth, though it was not so in the first century, when Paul wrote his letters to his churches. The majority of the scholars in Western Christianity have been members of the elite group within the dominant culture by virtue of their education and positions in the academy, if not by their birth. They fail to recognize, understand, and adequately account for the differences between the two horizons, or how the differences could affect interpretation. Therefore, traditional discussion concerning Paul's teaching on social change in the tradition of the Western church confuses and misunderstands the social dynamics of the gentile mission and its relationship to the dominant culture, because they are reading it from the viewpoint of the dominant culture. Paul's mission to the gentiles attempted to establish the church's unique eschatological identity and practice within a hostile dominant culture. At the time Paul wrote, the goal was not and could not be to change the social structures of the Greco-Roman world, but rather to establish God's church and to teach believers how to behave within God's household in a transformed way that does not conform to the social structures of the culture/world. However, he needed to advance God's mission within societal structures that neither he nor the church could control, and that tension must be recognized and explored.

The context of Galatians 3:28 is the entire argument of the book of Galatians, which explicitly defines what Paul meant by "there is neither Jew nor gentile." First, Paul clearly was concerned about the gentiles' salvation. His focus on gentiles shows that he is interested in the status of the disadvantaged members of the pairs: gentiles, slaves, and women. Paul's point in Galatians and in his entire mission to the gentiles was that gentiles have access to the same salvation as Jews, but without being circumcised and keeping the law, which was revolutionary. During his ministry he was devoted to working out the implications of this great theological insight, which should inform us about the implications of the equal salvation of the other two pairs of master-slave and male-female.

Second, the greater context is how Jew-gentile and male-female are entwined elsewhere in Pauline theology. One telling connection exists between Joel 2 and Romans 10:13, where Paul makes the explicit connection between

---

56. In Europe, parts of Asia, sub-Saharan Africa, and North and South America, Christianity has become the dominant culture.

the pouring out of the Spirit on "all flesh" and gentiles receiving the Spirit. In Joel and Acts 2:17, "all flesh" is defined as inclusive of age and gender (explicitly male and female), which was fulfilled on the day of Pentecost by Jewish participants. Paul extends the "all flesh" to be inclusive of Jew and gentile, unlike Luke's fulfillment in Acts 2:16–21.

Lewis Johnson states that with regard to women, "Paul is not speaking of relationships in the family and church, but of standing before God in righteousness by faith."[57] It appears that Johnson is trying to say that the change of a disadvantaged group's standing before God does not create "social change" in the relationships in the church. However, this is demonstrably false in the case of gentiles throughout the Pauline corpus and Acts; it can be shown to be untrue in the case of slaves as well within the context of the first-century church. Paul believed that the gentiles' "standing before God in righteousness by faith" transformed the relationships with the Jews and completely set the gentiles free, with pragmatic effects on their social standing within the people of God. Gentiles should resist any Jews who teach that they should be circumcised (Gal. 5:3) or that Christian Jews should eat separately from gentile Christians as if gentiles were unclean (2:11–14). Paul argues that the gentiles were set free for freedom, and they should actively resist Jewish teachers, teaching, and practices that compromise that freedom (Gal. 3–5). The principle that they were set free for freedom had potentially recursive pragmatic effects. The gentiles were set free to walk by the Spirit and were not to be taken captive by regulations and restrictions that are a yoke of slavery (Gal. 5:1). Although Johnson insists that the context in Galatians "contains no denial at all of role distinctions," again, that is not true in the case of how the gentiles functioned in the church, which is the people of God.[58] Whereas before gentiles were excluded from the people of God and any role among God's people, the appointment of leadership and the history of the early church show that gentiles were now qualified for every form of service and any position within the church; Paul's description of their freedom would not allow any such restriction. The teaching in Ephesians about God reconciling Jew and gentile in Christ and destroying the dividing wall of hostility between them is complementary to Galatians (Eph. 2:11–21). Paul's realization that there is "no longer Jew nor gentile" in Christ was far-reaching in its ramifications, not only in theology, but also in the pragmatic future and leadership of the church. In addition, it should not be missed that the new composition

57. Johnson, "Role Distinctions," in Piper and Grudem, *Recovering Biblical Manhood and Womanhood*, 160.
58. Ibid.

of the people of God posed a challenge to any social, political, and religious structures in Palestine that claimed a biblical basis.

Since the entire book of Galatians demonstrates in what way there is no longer Jew or gentile in the people of God, one may understand the relationships between slave and free as well as male and female to be interpreted and informed by the theological process that Paul applied to the gentile situation. Furthermore, the demonstration of his theological process would not be limited to the example in the Letter to the Galatians. The relationships between the other two pairs are meant to undergo parallel transformation with far-reaching implications similar to the gentile's righteous standing before God.

The insistence that there could not be similar sweeping changes in gender relationships within the church begs the question: the premise or presupposition about static gender relationships is the same as the conclusion. If that were true, women would be the only disadvantaged group that did not experience a status change among the people of God as a result of their "standing before God in righteousness by faith." Furthermore, the restrictions placed on women by the traditional church actually were a change from the way women functioned in the Old Testament. The restrictions that the church has traditionally placed on women's authority and ministries that involve public speaking prohibit functions that women had throughout the history of Israel.[59] The increased restriction on women was explicitly recognized in a legal textbook, a collection of canon law, published around 1140 CE:

> In the Old Testament much was permitted which today [i.e., in the New Testament] is abolished, through the perfection of grace. So if [in the Old Testament] women were permitted to judge the people, *today because of sin, which woman brought into the world, women are admonished by the Apostle to be careful to practice a modest restraint, to be subject to men and to veil themselves as a sign of subjugation.*[60]

This is an excellent example of how, in the history of interpretation, Paul's doctrine of grace resulted in literal freedom from the law for male

---

59. The increase of restrictions on women would particularly exclude the functions of a judge during the time of the judges (Judg. 4–5), the various functions and exercise of authority by women prophets (e.g., 2 Kings 22), and the teaching of women such as King Lemuel's mother (Prov. 31), which are included in Scripture.

60. Decretum Gratiani, causa 2, question 7, princ, in Catholic Church, *Corpus iuris canonici: Decretum magistri Gratiani*, ed. Emil Albert Friedberg (1879–81; repr., Graz: Akademische Druck- und Verlaganstalt, 1955), vol. 1, cols. 750–51, emphasis added. This was never given the status of an official collection, but it was widely used as the basis for canon law in the Catholic Church until 1918.

gentiles in the church, but an increase in law/restrictions for women, so that Paul's vocabulary was turned on its head by inconsistent hermeneutics. Furthermore, while Jesus's sacrifice and the new covenant were understood to result in justification for men in regard to Adam's act, it resulted in greater culpability and increased consequences for women in regard to Eve's act. Jo Ann Bynum states, "Unless this patriarchal attitude is contained, religion will be presented to the womenfolk as an oppressive mystical experience, an opium which sedates us."[61] Limiting Galatians 3:28 to one's standing before God is unwarranted in light of the changes Paul argues for in the surrounding context, directly eliminating evaluative distinctions between Jew and gentile.

Yet Galatians 3:28 does not erase the diversity that is represented by the pairs.[62] In fact, Paul's entire argument in Galatians and the Jerusalem Council insists that the gentiles should still be gentiles *and* members of the people of God instead of being forced to become Jews. Similarly, the Jews were not to become gentiles. There remained a distinctiveness and diversity of the people of God.[63] What this means is that the opposite in the pair can no longer be labeled as "the other," because our unity and identity are in Christ.[64] This is similar to the diversity in unity of spiritual gifts.[65] Therefore the distinction between male and female is not erased into some homogenous identity, but it does not follow that there are "role distinctions" in the church that are determined by gender, any more than distinctions should be determined by racial or social status. For one thing, "role distinctions" are a euphemism for role restrictions of the disadvantaged party; in the traditional paradigm, men have no "role distinctions" because they can theoretically fill any service

61. Bynum, foreword to *Gender and Ministry in Early Christianity and the Church Today*, by Adolphus Chinedu Amadi-Azuogu (Lanham, MD: University Press of America, 2007), x.

62. Kathy Ehrensperger correctly insists, "[Paul] is supporting the differing identities of the others and sharply opposing the attempt to homogenize and universalize one particular identity at the expense of another. And he explains that to relate to each other in Christ implies welcoming each other in faith, as Christ has welcomed them" (*That We May Be Mutually Encouraged: Feminism and the New Perspective in Pauline Studies* [New York: T&T Clark, 2004], 200).

63. See, e.g., Mark Nanos, *The Mystery of Romans: The Jewish Context of Paul's Letter to the Romans* (Minneapolis: Fortress, 1996), 9. There are some essential issues here in the gentile-Jew controversy. It is often assumed that Paul taught Jews not to keep the law. But a new view has suggested that both gentiles and Jews retained their identity in the Pauline model.

64. As Ehrensperger says, "The oneness of God's people, the oneness in faith, then implies the difference of people because their oneness is a reflection of the oneness of God, who is the one God for all only as they are different" (*Mutually Encouraged*, 154).

65. Contra Elizabeth Castelli's evaluation of Paul, which concludes that he tries to eradicate differences including gender and seeks to reinforce his own position of absolute authority by encouraging his churches to imitate him (*Imitating Paul: A Discourse of Power* [Louisville: Westminster John Knox, 1991]).

slot in the church, even kitchen duty and nursery if they are willing to do it.[66] Pragmatically, only women have assigned and specific "role distinctions" in the church. However, there is not a single female identity that makes all women suitable for a uniform set of roles, any more than there is one male identity.[67] Gender profiling is no more acceptable than racial profiling. Paul clearly taught what the role distinctions in the church were supposed to be based on: gifts distributed by the Spirit. As was demonstrated in 1 Corinthians 11:3–16, when a woman exercises a leadership gift such as prophesying, her distinctive identity as a woman is maintained as a part of that ministry.

5.8 Is There a Problem with Overrealized Eschatology?

There is a tendency to make a distinction between our eschatological identity and purpose and our present status in the area of gender, by warning against an "overrealized eschatology."[68] This position insists that the church must presently keep women subject to men in the household and the church in order to be biblical. It assumes that men are created with a God-given right to exercise authority, women are created to be subject to men, and that "in this present age" it is ethically wrong for women to "exercise authority" over men by holding offices in the church.[69] Such an argument needs to be answered: it misunderstands the purposes for gender at creation and is in direct contradiction with

66. As Amadi-Azuogu states, "All the levels of ministry are taken to be compatible with the male gender," but in addition, any levels or roles that are not characterized as leadership are also compatible with the male gender (*Gender and Ministry*, xxiii).

67. The idea that all males are the same and all females are the same is an artificial construct, according to recent feminist studies. Ehrensperger writes, "There is no one and the same female identity, there is no one and the same male identity. Moreover, what 'female' and 'male' actually means is not something that we can define once and forever and for all; instead, it is a matter of continuous and new negotiations across fluid boundaries. Feminist research emphasizes that real diversity and the proper recognition of difference definitely provide a presupposition for real relationship of equals" (*Mutually Encouraged*, 192).

68. Schreiner, e.g., argues that a change in women's status in the church would be "overrealized eschatology." He goes on to say, "Those who understand that the present evil age is fleeting, however, will have a new perspective on all events. They will avoid trying to make earth into heaven. They will not fall prey to overrealized eschatology but will set their hopes on the future, on the consummation of all things, on the day when moral perfection will be theirs. They will not become consumed with roles and stations in this world, even though they will seek to do as much good in this world as possible. The present world order will never be perfectly cleansed of evil, and thus any utopian schemes will be jettisoned" (*Paul*, 412). What he says is true of the world order/society, but not "all events." The community of the people of God is meant to reflect the kingdom of God: some of our work in building the church is permanent (1 Cor. 3:10–13), and we live our lives together in the light of our status in the kingdom (2 Cor. 5:16–17).

69. In this view, a primary presupposition is to see church offices as "having authority" rather than as serving. This will be discussed in chap. 8.

Pauline eschatology. The criticism against women in positions of authority as "overrealized eschatology" should not be used to support resistance to any progressive reversal of the fall in social, racial, or gender categories, particularly a reversal already supported in some way by the dominant culture.

5.8.1 Overrealized Eschatology and Women

First, the application of the label "overrealized eschatology" to the practice of women's teaching and leading/serving according to their spiritual gift is a misuse of the term, which refers to incorrect/false eschatological teaching, such as the belief that the resurrection has already occurred (2 Tim. 2:18). However, full "accessibility to all the spiritual benefits that flow" from the believer's status before God in Christ would not be overrealized eschatology, but rather is consistent with Paul's thorough application of his theology of salvation by faith to gentile males.[70] Paul's meticulous working out of the ramifications of salvation by faith alone and how the gentiles' eschatological membership in the people of God affects religious and social practice in the community of God provides the hermeneutical pattern for similar ramifications across gender and social lines.

Second, the notion that women are created to be subordinate fails to recognize that women's eschatological future must be consistent with their purpose at creation. It confuses the effects of the fall on women with what is normative and an expression of God's will.

Third, this view confuses temporal missional strategy with transcendental norms. It does so by conflating church and society rather than recognizing the existence of two worlds that are in conflict and in competition in terms of authority and theology. In his letters, Paul distinguishes between roles and status in the church on one hand, and roles and status in the society at large on the other hand.

Fourth, this view does not allow women to read a vast number of biblical passages about their spiritual responsibilities literally or to apply them in the same way that men do. A woman's literal/straightforward application of a biblical passage would not be overrealized eschatology if

- the passage is addressed to all believers;
- the passage has been understood, applied, and modeled in the same way by men;

70. This is Murray Harris's description of being a "new creation" (*Second Epistle to the Corinthians*, 431).

- the application is missionally appropriate—that is, it stays within the bounds of what the current culture allows or approves.

We will continue to see that a consistent hermeneutic cuts across many restrictions that have been placed on women and will call into question traditional gender theologies and practices.

5.8.2 Overrealized Eschatology and Men

On the other hand, the theology claiming that males have a God-given sense of responsibility and leadership that requires the subordination of women is, in fact, an overrealized view of authority in general and a misunderstanding and misapplication of the Pauline passages about gender and authority. Paul addresses similar claims in his correction of the Corinthians' overrealized eschatology about authority in 1 Corinthians 4:6–14:

> I have applied all this to Apollos and myself for your benefit, brothers and sisters, so that you may learn through us the meaning of the saying, "Nothing beyond what is written," so that none of you will be puffed up in favor of one against another. For who sees anything different in you? What do you have that you did not receive? And if you received it, why do you boast as if it were not a gift? Already you have all you want! Already you have become rich! Quite apart from us you have become kings! Indeed, I wish that you had become kings, so that we might be kings with you! For I think that God has exhibited us apostles as last of all, as though sentenced to death, because we have become a spectacle to the world, to angels and to mortals. We are fools for the sake of Christ, but you are wise in Christ. We are weak, but you are strong. You are held in honor, but we in disrepute. To the present hour we are hungry and thirsty, we are poorly clothed and beaten and homeless, and we grow weary from the work of our own hands. When reviled, we bless; when persecuted, we endure; when slandered, we speak kindly. We have become like the rubbish of the world, the dregs of all things, to this very day. I am not writing this to make you ashamed, but to admonish you as my beloved children. (NRSV)

Neither Jesus Christ nor Paul aspired to exercise the kind of dominion that is claimed by those who currently support men's priority and authority with Paul's teaching.

It is overrealized eschatology and error to claim that the Bible or Paul teaches that every man is by nature an independent paterfamilias over his wife and children. This is inconsistent with both Paul's teachings (above) and the context of the first-century Greco-Roman culture. The modern Western nuclear family did not exist in the Greco-Roman culture. Few men attained the status of a paterfamilias.

This was the status of men in Roman culture who were elite and so entitled within the extended family. Even if one allows an understanding of "head" as "authority," the patriarch in the extended family would be the only "head" in the first-century context. This individual would roughly be the equivalent of a "godfather" in contemporary literature and films about the Mafia. Particularly given the number of slaves in Italy (as much as one slave to three free people), one may suggest that the majority of men and their wives functioned in some kind of a subordinate role within the Greco-Roman household. There were numerous checks and balances on the power of a male over his wife within the extended family and the alliances of marriage. Male slaves never had any legal authority over their "wives" and children; they were not even legally married, so in that case the master would be the woman's "head" if authority was what Paul intended in 1 Corinthians 11:3 and Ephesians 5:23–30. A claim of the absolute authority of every man over his wife would indeed be a challenge to the Greco-Roman social order and consist of an authority for men that would exceed the Greco-Roman model of power. Paul's readers would not have understood such a claim, nor could many apply it.

In addition, some churches, educational institutions, and organizations have actually asserted in doctrinal statements that all men are in authority over all women. There is no precedent for this claim, given a careful interpretation of Paul's teaching or practice in the Greco-Roman culture. Rather, Paul urged believing women to rule their household (1 Tim. 5:14). He commanded believing slaves to obey their masters without excluding female slave owners (Eph. 6:5; Col. 3:22; Titus 2:9). He also commanded believing children, including males, to obey their mothers (Eph. 6:1–3; Col. 3:20). The Greco-Roman society and the underpinning philosophy recognized and supported these authority relationships of women over men, acknowledged various other positions of power and influence that women held, and knew of circumstances, such as wealth, that gave women power. In the first century, Paul's statements would not have been understood to remove women believers from these responsibilities or to defuse any power; rather, Paul advanced his mission through women's patronage and their households, which were *the* venue for Pauline house churches.

It is overrealized eschatology to suggest that a man's role is equivalent to the authority of the ascended Christ over the church on the basis of Ephesians 5:22–24. This passage consists of instructions to women, not to men, and even in the instructions to women, Christ's ultimate incarnate act as Savior and sacrifice is in view. In the instructions to the men, Jesus Christ is the model for men in the most sacrificial aspects of his incarnation and servanthood. Males are never commanded to model themselves according to Christ's authority over the church as he is seated at the right hand of the Father, nor does Paul adopt the Roman ideal of aggressive masculinity and ambition.

Furthermore, it is overrealized eschatology to equate the male role with the sovereign authority of God the Father on the basis of 1 Corinthians 11:3, yet the arguments that support male headship as authority assume this analogy. Some assert that male headship is essential because it directly expresses and supports the sovereignty of God. Apart from the gender issue, basing human roles in the church directly on the relationships in the Trinity, or vice versa, has no clear basis in Pauline teaching. All authority that believers possess is shared with Christ and is realized in Christ. It is not based on an ontological ranking equated with any privileged identity with the Father. That is reserved for Jesus Christ alone, an identity that all believers share through grace.

The exercise of male rule and dominion over the church subjects more than half the members of the church, women (usually more than 50 percent of the membership), who according to Paul's gospel are equal heirs; they have the same future of ruling with Christ as all believers have. But, what is more disturbing, it equates leadership in the church with imposing subjugation rather than serving—yet the true measure of leadership is to become a slave to everyone, which is both Christ's and Paul's model. Undermining this principle is the primary fallacy behind the overrealized eschatology of those who argue for only male leadership in the church. The claim that the unilateral exercise of authority in models of "male headship" is "servant leadership" creates an oxymoron on virtually every level.

The roles and behavior of believers in the church were supposed to reflect their eschatological status just as their wisdom and understanding in the present reflected their eschatological responsibilities; in fact, Paul's argument in 1 Corinthians asserts that it is the believers' ethical responsibility to change their present behavior and take appropriate authority in the light of their future. Caution is in order if eschatological change causes problems with the advance of the mission, such as damage to the church's reputation. But if the eschatological presence and witness of the Holy Spirit designate that someone should function as a pastor, teacher, or leader for the common good, it is ethically wrong for the person who is called to refuse to obey the Spirit, and ethically wrong for the church to say "I have no need of you" by restricting the function of anyone solely on the basis of gender, race, or social status. The traditional theologies and practices of gender, on the one hand, support an "overrealized eschatology" in the current role of men, and, on the other hand, fail to practice a coherent hermeneutic consistent with the eschatological destiny of women.

six

The Body

Gender, as it relates to male and female bodies, probably includes some of the most misunderstood parts of Paul's theology in the history of the church. Not surprisingly, there is a marked tendency for cultural beliefs and personal experiences about the body and sex to heavily influence one's understanding of Pauline biblical theology. Understanding how Paul's use of "flesh" relates to the physical body has always been an issue. The early connection between the physical body and sin was influenced by Platonic dualism; consequently, Paul's writings were used to promote celibacy and the denigration of women. However, Paul's concern with certain aspects of the male body and the female body is of interest, as Paul wrote quite a bit about sexuality; he did not adopt the Greco-Roman view of the body, but rather brought Jewish sexual ethics to the Greco-Roman culture. We will see that Paul had a deep appreciation for the power of the sex drive and the meaning of the sexual relationship, while at the same time he made a case for celibacy as an option for undistracted ministry. I will conclude with a brief summary of Paul's teaching on sexual ethics. Paul's teaching on sexuality and the body has been a battleground, but there is a coherent train of thought that unites his writings.

6.1 Gender, the Flesh, and the Body in Paul

The theological traditions about gender have been heavily influenced by certain interpretations of Paul's use of the word "flesh" (σάρξ) in passages such as Romans 8:3–8:

For God has done what the law, weakened by the *flesh*, could not do: by sending his own Son in the likeness of sinful *flesh*, and to deal with sin, he condemned sin in the *flesh*, so that the just requirement of the law might be fulfilled in us, who walk not according to the *flesh* but according to the Spirit. For those who live according to the *flesh* set their minds on the things of the *flesh*, but those who live according to the Spirit set their minds on the things of the Spirit. To set the mind on the *flesh* is death, but to set the mind on the Spirit is life and peace. For this reason the mind that is set on the *flesh* is hostile to God; it does not submit to God's law—indeed it cannot, and those who are in the *flesh* cannot please God. (NRSV, emphasis added)

Here the flesh weakens the law, is sinful, is condemned by Jesus, is the opposite of the Spirit, and leads to death and hostility with God. In summary, those who are under the influence of the flesh cannot please God.

Similarly, Galatians 5:19–21 attributes a representative range of human evil to the flesh:

Now the works of the *flesh* are obvious: fornication, impurity, licentiousness, idolatry, sorcery, enmities, strife, jealousy, anger, quarrels, dissensions, factions, envy, drunkenness, carousing, and things like these. I am warning you, as I warned you before: those who do such things will not inherit the kingdom of God. (NRSV, emphasis added)

Here the Pauline meaning of "flesh" is related to human sin and evil.[1] Johannes Louw and Eugene Nida define it as "the psychological aspect of human nature which contrasts with the spiritual nature; . . . that psychological factor in man which serves as a willing instrument of sin and is subject to sin."[2] R. J. Erickson defines it as "rebellious human nature."[3] However, the opposite of a focus on the Spirit is a focus on the self, independent of God. Self-centeredness or selfishness is what places humanity in rebellion because human nature was originally designed for worship.[4]

1. Johannes Louw and Eugene Nida show that σάρξ has a broad range of meaning: flesh, body, people, human, nation, human nature, physical nature, life (*Greek-English Lexicon of the New Testament: Based on Semantic Domains*, 2nd ed. [New York: United Bible Societies, 1989], 2:220). Σῶμα has a broad range of meaning in Greek generally and in the Pauline corpus: body, physical being, church, slave, reality (ibid., 2:240). In other words, Paul uses the range of meaning of the word appropriately and consistently with normal usage, and it can refer to the physical body.

2. Louw and Nida, *Greek-English Lexicon*, 1:322–23. They contrast σάρξ with the Spirit in semantic domain 26.7. But see James Dunn's discussion in *The Theology of Paul the Apostle* (Grand Rapids: Eerdmans, 1998), 62–73.

3. Erickson, "Flesh," *DPL*, 304–5.

4. Robert Jewett similarly sees σάρξ as a power that is differentiated from sensual passions or human weakness: "The associations with sin, passions, law, and death demand an interpretation

There is a strong Christian tradition that equates sinful "flesh" with the human body, associating it with sin and evil, and this understanding is perpetuated by what "flesh" means in English.[5] Furthermore, Paul's condemnation of the "flesh" has been taken historically to condemn sexuality and the sex drive, and even has led to a widespread belief that heaven is an escape from bodily existence rather than the expectation of physical resurrection. However, Paul's use of the Greek term "flesh" (σάρξ) is distinct from his use of the Greek term for "body" (cf. the quotation with σάρξ from Gen. 2:24 LXX with the Pauline substitution of σῶμα in Eph. 5:29–31).[6] Paul speaks of the physical body of a man having sex with a prostitute (1 Cor. 6:13, 16, 18) and of the physical bodies of a husband and wife having sex (1 Cor. 7:4), and he refers to the physical body to describe the head-body relationship between a husband and wife and between Christ and the church (Eph. 5:23, 28, 30).[7] Therefore, in the Pauline corpus, the sin and evil associated with the "flesh" should be differentiated from the physical body and the sexual act. A Platonic dualism of "spirit and flesh" and a negative view toward sexuality have been imposed on Paul yet are inconsistent with his Jewish mind-set.[8] This dualistic

---

of flesh as the power that drives perverted systems of honor and shame, leading captives into lives of unrelenting competition to gain advantage over other persons and groups" (*Romans: A Commentary*, ed. Eldon J. Epp, Hermeneia [Minneapolis: Fortress, 2007], 436). See also Douglas J. Moo, *The Epistle to the Romans*, NICNT (Grand Rapids: Eerdmans, 1996), 47n36, where he describes a spectrum of meaning, including "a much more negative (or ethical) meaning: human life, or the material world considered as independent of, and even in opposition to, the spiritual realm" (e.g., Rom. 7:5; 8:8; 13:14; Gal. 5:13–18).

5. This tradition has appeared to convey dualistic overtones by associating materiality with evil (see Dunn, *Theology of Paul*, 64). On the other hand, the NIV/TNIV translates σάρξ as "sin nature."

6. Σῶμα has a broad range of meaning in Greek generally and in the Pauline corpus: body, physical being, church, slave, reality (Louw and Nida, *Greek-English Lexicon*, 2:240). Dunn suggests that we utilize terms such as "embodiment" and "corporeality/corporateness" to show that the meaning of σῶμα in Paul's work goes far beyond the physical to "denote the person embodied in a particular environment" in a social sense, and relates it to a corporation where individuals as bodies work together in harmony for a common purpose (*Theology of Paul*, 56–57).

7. Contra Thomas Schreiner, who says that Paul uses it for the sexual union, "which at the least signifies the physical union between a man and woman" (*Paul, Apostle of God's Glory in Christ: A Pauline Theology* [Downers Grove, IL: InterVarsity, 2001], 141). Paul utilizes the phrase σάρκα μίαν from Gen. 2:24 LXX in Eph. 5:31 and 1 Cor. 6:16 to refer to the sexual/marital union, and then he significantly chooses σῶμα to interpret the phrase. In Eph. 5:22–31, when speaking about the head-and-body relationship between a husband and wife and Christ and the church (Eph. 5:23, 28, 30), though, he uses σάρξ in v. 29 in reference to nurturing and feeding one's own body. The same pattern occurs in 1 Cor. 6:18–20; Paul chooses to use the word σῶμα in his commentary.

8. See, e.g, Gerhard Delling, *Paulus' Stellung zu Frau und Ehe*, BWANT 4/5 (Stuttgart: Kohlhammer, 1931). Paul's Jewishness has been an object of recent study. See Oskar Skarsaune and Reidar Hvalvik, eds., *Jewish Believers in Jesus: The Early Centuries* (Grand Rapids: Baker

theological understanding developed rather quickly by the patristic period to demand a choice between sexuality and spirituality.[9]

Since, historically, theology and biblical exegesis have been the domain of men, the theological rejection of sexuality set up their choice between the spiritual option of celibacy or women. At its worst, it entailed an explicit rejection of the female body and its functions. When this was combined with Greek philosophy, not only were women ontologically weaker (essentially flawed), but also normal sexual attraction to women was seen as sinful. Women's bodies, as well as natural and normal female functions, even became nauseating to some. Theologians and church leaders who were sexually attracted to women sometimes projected their own sexual desires onto women as a group and thus concluded that in contrast to men, who were more spiritual by inclination, women were temptresses like Eve, obsessed by sex, and worldly and wicked by nature and inclination. Although the Reformation sponsored a corrective that elevated the family over celibacy, a strong stream of interpretation of the passages that deal with women perpetuated attitudes and practices in the church that were born in an environment essentially hostile to women and their bodies. This also developed together with a positive evaluation of men and their bodies, in part because Jesus was incarnated as a male. However, Paul's view of the church and gender both enhances the view of the female body and relativizes the evaluation of the male body.

6.2 The Body as Male/Female

Paul discussed certain issues that pertain to the male body and other issues that pertain to the female body. Circumcision, a primary issue in Paul's ministry, was a gender-specific issue that concerned the male body and shook the early church to its foundations, changing its future course irrevocably. It directly

---

Academic, 2007); John Howard Yoder, *The Jewish-Christian Schism Revisited* (Scottdale, PA: Herald Press, 2008).

9. So argues Will Deming, *Paul on Marriage and Celibacy: The Hellenistic Background of 1 Corinthians 7*, SNTSMS 83 (Cambridge: Cambridge University Press, 1995), 224. Dunn summarizes,

> In the "Hellenization" of Christian thought the negative overtones of fleshliness became more and more attached to human bodiness, and not least to the creative function of sexuality. What Paul had objected to—the denigration of sexual relations *per se*—became a feature of Christian spirituality in late antiquity. Concupiscence, sexual desire, came to be regarded by definition as wicked. Virginity was exalted above all other human conditions. Original sin was thought to be transmitted by human procreation. The results of such denigration of sexuality continues to distort Christian attitudes to gender till this day. (*Theology of Paul*, 73)

impacted social relationships and the structure of leadership in the church. Other male issues that Paul discusses include the role of the gymnasium, the ideal beauty of the male body, and the emotion of anger. Issues concerning the female body include its beauty and attraction.

6.2.1 The Male Body

The male body was a primary battleground for Paul and his opponents. Circumcision was the central issue in the conflict between Paul and the "Judaizers," and it served as a synecdoche for Jewish identity and observing the law of Moses. However, it is clearly a gender issue because it concerns male genitals and the Jewish purity laws; Paul's concern about the circumcision of gentiles reflects his pragmatic concern for the salvation of gentile males and their participation in the people of God. In contrast, as Elisabeth Schüssler Fiorenza observes, the common initiation ritual of baptism indicates that women became full members of the people of God with the same rites and duties as Jewish converts.[10] Other issues that Paul treated and/or confronted were masculine bodily discipline and men's anger. One can argue that Paul's sexual ethics were directed at males, since there was almost complete continuity in the culture's sexual ethics for women, but this will be discussed in the next section.

6.2.1.1 CIRCUMCISION

Circumcision is a male issue, a Jewish "covenantal rite centered on the male genitals."[11] The biblical practice requires the surgical removal of the foreskin from the penis of a male infant on the eighth day after birth, based on Genesis 17:13, and it was the sign of the Jewish/Abrahamic covenant with God. In a study on the practice of circumcision in the context of the Roman Empire, Ra'anan Abusch writes, "While not unique to the Jews, circumcision of the male genitals not only constituted one of their most distinctive practices, but also served as a particularly visible mark of difference. This physical demarcation was especially acute in a society in which public nudity

---

10. Schüssler Fiorenza, *In Memory of Her: A Feminist Theological Reconstruction of Christian Origins* (London: SCM, 1983), 210.

11. This is a succinct summary of circumcision from the back cover of Elizabeth Wyner Mark, ed., *The Covenant of Circumcision: New Perspectives on an Ancient Jewish Rite* (Hanover, NH: Brandeis University Press, 2003). As Tatha Wiley observes, gender is at the heart of the Galatian conflict, and Paul's opponents' position "threatened the redemptive equality symbolized by baptism and made real by its performance" (*Paul and the Gentile Women: Reframing Galatians* [New York: Continuum, 2005], 15).

both during work and at play was prevalent and in which the perfection of the unaltered male physique was prized."[12]

Jews were legally allowed to perform circumcision as a religious rite under the Roman Empire, but non-Jews ridiculed them for this practice and regarded it as genital mutilation, placing it in the same category as castration. Therefore, circumcision had a stigma attached to it in the Greco-Roman world, and it was a very painful process for an adult male.

Circumcision in Greco-Roman Culture. Among the Jewish population, difficulty with maintaining the practice of circumcision first became a particular issue during the Hellenistic period, because of the influence of the Hellenistic culture on Jews who wished to assimilate into the dominant culture. In addition, there was a period when circumcision was illegal: Antiochus Epiphanes had ordered the inhabitants of Judea to no longer circumcise their infants. Consequently, some Jewish males tried to disguise their circumcision, as Nissan Rubin describes: "By stretching vestigial penile skin tissue to cover the glans penis, a man who desired to pass beyond Jewish communal boundaries to join non-Jewish society could remove the identifying mark of Jewish identity."[13] This practice is probably what Paul was referring to in 1 Corinthians 7:18 when he said, "Was anyone already circumcised when he was called? He should not try to remove the marks of circumcision." Furthermore, according to Luke, Paul had Timothy circumcised as an adult out of consideration for the Jews in the area, so in the Acts account Paul appears to recognize that circumcision and the law are valid for Christians of Jewish descent (Acts 16:3).[14] Therefore, circumcision was a distinctive boundary between the Jews and gentiles, and in the Jewish mission there were thousands of Jews who still kept the law.

Circumcision in Early Christianity. Until the gentile revival in Antioch (Acts 11:19–29) and the success of Paul and Barnabas's first missionary journey raised the issue (Acts 13–14; cf. 14:27), there appears to have been an assumed understanding in the Jerusalem church that salvation for a gentile entailed conversion to Judaism (including circumcision). At some point, the leaders of the church in Antioch did not require the gentile male converts to be circumcised, and that was the practice of Paul and Barnabas in their missionary

12. Abusch, "Circumcision and Castration under Roman Law in the Early Empire," in Mark, *Covenant of Circumcision*, 75.

13. Rubin, "*Brit Milah*: A Study of Change in Custom," in Mark, *Covenant of Circumcision*, 87–88.

14. In Acts 21:20–26, there is a tacit denial by Luke in v. 21 that Paul ever taught Christian Jews not to circumcise their children or to neglect the law, and a claim that Paul led a life in which he obeyed the law of Moses.

journey. The fact that a council had to be called to consider the matter would indicate that until that point (15:6), the gentile converts of the Jewish mission, such as Cornelius and his household, had converted to Judaism and kept the law when they believed (15:5). "Judaizers" from Jerusalem came to Antioch and confronted the uncircumcised gentile men by challenging their spiritual status (15:1).[15] The basis for the practice in Antioch, Paul's theology, and the decision of the Jerusalem Council was Paul's and Barnabas's experiences and the experiences of gentile believers when they were confronted with the gospel: "All the signs and wonders God did among the gentiles through their activity" (15:12). One of the motivating factors in the council's decision to no longer require the gentiles to be circumcised was articulated by James: "It is my judgment, therefore, that we should not make it difficult for the gentiles who are turning to God" (15:19).

This was a momentous decision that, in one fell swoop, eliminated the primary purity requirement for males for full participation in the church. Although the issue was whether an uncircumcised male believer could be saved, the elimination of circumcision created social and spiritual privileges for the uncircumcised male from which he was excluded in Judaism. It made him equal to a Jewish male in status and practice in the church, though it would not change his status and participation in the structures of Judaism, such as the synagogue and admission to the temple. This created change and upheaval for the entire church, not just the private religious practice and spiritual standing of uncircumcised men. The purity restrictions that kept Jews separate from gentiles were removed so that Christian Jews were affected in

---

15. Sandra Hack Polaski provides an example of reader-oriented criticism when she asks the question that most contemporary women probably ask when they read Paul: "Why is *circumcision*—and not some other characteristic of Jewish practice—the synecdoche of Law/Jewishness in Paul's letters? Why not, for example, kosher laws?" (*A Feminist Introduction to Paul* [St. Louis: Chalice, 2005], 15, emphasis original). The accounts of Luke and Paul agree that the entire issue was forced on gentile believers. According to them, the "Judaizers" from Antioch chose circumcision as the primary marker of Jewish identity that they insisted on, which is the context of the conversation (Acts 15:1–2; Gal. 2:2; 5:2–3). They started the thread of the argument when they told gentile converts in Antioch point-blank, "Unless you are circumcised according to the custom taught by Moses, you cannot be saved" (Acts 15:1 NRSV). The omission of women from the conversation must be answered with the first-century understanding of Jewish identity, rather than Paul's oversight of women. The issue was over the ritual of initiation that was a commitment to observing the other aspects of the law. The ritual of initiation for gentile proselytes to Judaism was circumcision and immersion for males and immersion only for females. The "new perspective" on Paul argues that the disagreement was over the identity markers and initiation of gentiles into the membership of God's people. The more interesting question is: Why is it, exactly, that Paul, himself a Jewish male, "circumcised on the eighth day" (Phil. 3:5), is so adamant about prohibiting the ritual for the Galatian believers? Luke's answer is that the common experience of salvation became definitive, and that led to the other changes.

basic areas such as dining and hospitality, and ultimately positions of authority within the church. Any practices of the church that correlated with Jewish religious structures and practices were altered, including any spatial restrictions in access to God, the priesthood, and even apostleship.

Now an uncircumcised male could potentially be in a position of leadership and authority in the church over a male Christian Jew, which removed the male Jew's prized spiritual advantages and privileges that he possessed, according to Jewish tradition and its understanding of the law.[16] The fact that the privileged position of the religious Jewish male was treasured is indicated in the Pharisee's prayer in Luke 18:11–12 and expressed in the well-known *berakah* (blessing) from the Babylonian Talmud: "Praised are You, ETERNAL . . . God, who has made me an Israelite, who did not make me a woman, who did not make me a boor."[17] Paul continued to work through and fight for the implications of this significant change in the church, and his letter to the churches in Galatia demonstrates some implications of the simple decision to not require gentile males to be circumcised in order to be saved. The letter from the Jerusalem Council and Paul's Letters indicate that the removal of the requirement of circumcision had enormous consequences: it meant that gentile converts would not be required to keep the law of Moses.

Were there any implications in this change for women?[18] There would be a subsequent change in the expectations for the daily lives of the women converts. As Sandra Hack Polaski points out, the kosher food laws belong to the realm of women's concerns in their daily lives, while circumcision is a visible sign and frequent reminder to men.[19] But furthermore, when Paul is discussing the implications of gentiles not keeping the law, he states, "There is neither Jew nor Greek; there is neither slave nor free; there is neither male nor female"

16. In Rom. 3:1, Paul appears to echo the complaint of the Jews in the church over their loss of privilege: "So what's the advantage of being a Jew?" Jews had the advantage of being trusted with God's revelation (3:2), but ultimately that did not privilege them by making them more righteous, according to Paul (3:9–20).

17. See *b. Menaḥ.* 43b, in *The Three Blessings: Boundaries, Censorship, and Identity in Jewish Liturgy*, trans. Yael H. Kahn (New York: Oxford University Press, 2011), 4.

18. Tatha Wiley attempts to understand Paul's assertions in their historical context when she asks, "What did circumcision signify for men? For women? What obligations did it impose? What effect on the assembly would its acceptance bring? What changes for the new members?" (*Paul and the Gentile Women*, 10).

19. However, Polaski also asserts, "Paul speaks, as is typical for males of his day, as a man to men, and draws his imagery from male experience. Women readers or hearers are left to extrapolate for themselves what might be the analogous images or teachings" (*Feminist Introduction to Paul*, 15). On the contrary, Paul does give attention to other aspects of the law and draws out implications, but not as fully as he does in the issue of circumcision. It may be argued that it is suitable for the church to follow Paul and further extrapolate the implications as Paul did.

(Gal. 3:28). When this statement is read in the context of the entire Galatians discourse and the gentile-Jew debate to which it belongs, it shows how Paul saw that the implications of the radical change he initiated stretched across gender lines as well as social lines. It is highly unlikely that Paul would see no ramifications beyond women's eschatological position in Christ, since a major part of his life was dedicated to working out the practical implications of the Jew-gentile debate. The priorities and the hermeneutics that Paul applied to the Jew-gentile debate can and should be extended to the gender issue.[20] Apart from the explicit parallel that Paul draws in Galatians 3:28, the role of Paul's experience of the gentiles' conversion has significant correspondences with the role of evidence and experience of the nature, gifts, capacities, abilities, performance, and spiritual life of women. In the Greco-Roman worldview, women by nature were inferior or incapable in all of these areas, and traditional gender restrictions were coherent with that worldview. However, since experience caused a shift in theology concerning gentile males and circumcision, so the evidence and experience of women's abilities and gifting should have similar ramifications.[21]

6.2.1.2 BODILY DISCIPLINE

Paul interacts with the values and experiences of masculine Hellenism when he utilizes language of the gymnasium, both as spiritual illustrations and, at least in one case, as a competing value.[22] When Paul talks about boxing/fighting (1 Cor. 9:26; 1 Tim. 6:12), running a race in a stadium (Gal. 2:2; 1 Cor. 9:24; Phil. 3:13–14), the laurel wreath (1 Cor. 9:25; 2 Tim. 2:5), and athletic training (1 Cor. 9:25; 1 Tim. 4:10), he is making a connection with his readers through a central aspect of the Greco-Roman culture. The gymnasium was an essential element of the Hellenistic city, where males exercised in the nude in order to develop the Greek ideal of a beautiful body. Two things are of interest. First, all readers, male and female, are invited to enter into a masculine mentality when Paul uses athletic competition to illustrate spiritual reality. It might be assumed that Paul's metaphors exclude women, but the women who take all Scripture as profitable for their own

20. Paul did not seem to think that a defense of God's authority and honor required the continued advantages, privileges, authority, and status of the Jews in the church community, so the argument that men should have authority over women on the grounds of God's authority does not follow.
21. We have now come to a time in the Western world when we have rejected long-established views on the body, gender, and the differences between male and female because of a number of factors, including modern education and modern disciplines such as scientific research, social science, and anthropology. We occupy an interesting position in which we may critically understand Paul's theology of gender within his Jewish and Greco-Roman context.
22. See E. M. Yamauchi, "Hellenism," *DPL*, 383–88.

training are invited, for their own spiritual benefit, to identify in a constructive way with the male world from which they are excluded. Second, men were thought to be disciplined and females undisciplined; but self-control is a godly value that is important for all to attain, and these word pictures help women as well as men. On the other hand, Paul minimizes this essential element of masculine Greco-Roman culture in comparison with the importance of godliness (1 Tim. 4:8).

6.2.1.3 ANGER MANAGEMENT

The management of anger is a human problem, but the experience of anger is directly related to hormones that are different in male and female bodies. In 1 Timothy 2:8, Paul singles out anger and arguing as a problem among the males at Ephesus. This is often overlooked because the instructions to women and the prohibitions in 1 Timothy 2:9–15 have interested commentators more, so their focus tends to be on how the topic of prayer in 2:8 is related to the instructions to women. However, there are complementary instructions, to men first and then to women, addressing gender-specific issues that are part of the false teaching at Ephesus (1:3–7). Paul addresses men's issues first, saying that he wants them to pray everywhere "lifting up holy hands without anger or argument" (2:8 NRSV). Therefore, we may trace the themes of anger and arguments through the epistle and suggest that they typify the problems in false teaching among the men in Ephesus.[23] Anger and arguments are a direct threat to the goal of prayer in 2:2 for "a quiet and peaceful life" and are a major theme in the Letters to Timothy (1 Tim. 1:3; 3:3; 6:3–5; 2 Tim. 2:14, 23–24). First Timothy 6:3–5 is particularly informative:

> Whoever teaches otherwise and does not agree with the sound words of our Lord Jesus Christ and the teaching that is in accordance with godliness, is conceited, understanding nothing, and has a morbid craving for controversy and for disputes about words. From these come envy, dissension, slander, base suspicions, and wrangling among those who are depraved in mind and bereft of the truth, imagining that godliness is a means of gain. (NRSV)

Anger is addressed at some length in Ephesians 4:25–5:2. As Andrew Lincoln states on 4:26–27, "The readers are to avoid anger at all costs, and if they do become angry, they are not to indulge their anger, and thereby sin, but are instead to expel it immediately. The reason given for this counsel is

---

23. Craig Keener observes, "Paul first addresses the men in the Ephesian churches, who are apparently involved in conflict inappropriate for worshipers of God" ("Man and Woman," *DPL*, 590).

that anger which is indulged gives the devil opportunity to exploit its effects" (cf. 2 Tim. 2:26).[24] In Ephesians 4:31, Paul continues with a similar vice list that is associated with anger: "Put away from you all bitterness and wrath and anger and wrangling and slander, together with all malice" (NRSV). This is similar to the vice list of the works of the flesh in Galatians 5:19–21, particularly "enmities, strife, jealousy, anger, quarrels, dissensions, factions, envy, drunkenness, carousing" (vv. 20–21 NRSV). In Ephesians 4:32–5:2, the vices of anger are to be replaced with virtues of kindness, compassion, and forgiveness, and believers are to walk in the way of love like Christ, who gave himself up for us. This passage has multiple ties with the instructions to husbands in the household code, where husbands are commanded to love their wives as Christ loved the church, as the Savior who gave himself up for her, which is Paul's solution for harshness, anger, rage, and disputing.

It is telling that male commentators have not been interested in focusing on anger as an issue in Paul's view of men in the same way that they have focused on Paul's view of women in a large number of issues. The angry man and the legendary effects of testosterone are cultural stereotypes, but perhaps the issue has lacked convincing documentation until recently. A Harvard study has shown that nearly 10 percent of American men have intermittent explosive disorder (IED): "If the Harvard researchers are correct, almost 1 in 10 adult men routinely display wildly disproportionate aggression, and are so angry that they're likely to damage property, or threaten or injure others. (The researchers estimate that only half as many women suffer from IED.)"[25] While some may argue that this is a recent phenomenon due to cultural developments that discriminate against men, similar patterns of behavior may be detected in other cultures and other time periods. Men murder more and commit more crimes and acts of violence than women. The Pauline words about anger are applicable to women as well, but Paul addressed it as a male-specific issue in Ephesus, and one may consider it still to be a male-specific problem today.

6.2.1.4 SUMMARY

The issues regarding the male body are not usually identified as gender-specific ones. Since most commentators were male, the male experience was treated as if it were the human experience. However, Paul's theology and hermeneutics were both influenced and revealed by how he dealt with the issue

24. Lincoln, *Ephesians*, WBC 42 (Nashville: Nelson, 1990), 313.
25. Kevin Hoffman, "Why So Angry?," *Men's Health*, April 10, 2013, http://www.menshealth.com/health/why-so-angry.

of circumcision. Paul was a true champion for the gentile male and removed
a serious obstacle to the spread of the gospel. On the other hand, he was just
as critical of issues that concerned the Greco-Roman male body, including
the ideal of the beautiful male body and the problem of anger among men.
The way Paul addressed the issue of circumcision ("There is neither Jew
nor gentile") and worked out the theological implications in detail should
be paradigmatic for working out the theological implications of there being
neither male nor female in Christ in Galatians 3:28. Paul made them parallel
issues in a context where he was specifying the implications. Gentile men have
benefited from his radical work for two millennia, and it is time to complete
Paul's work for women. But as for men, we need to effectively address male
anger and take responsibility for aspects in the culture that are feeding it and
making it worse: video games, pornography, violent music, films, and televi-
sion have become toxic.

6.2.2 The Female Body

Paul is relatively reticent about the female body, which is surprising, given
the literature about the female body in Jewish sources, Greco-Roman culture,
and church history. The issue of male purity and circumcision was central,
but the issue of female purity is virtually unaddressed. However, the gender-
specific female issues of beauty and adornment corresponded to issues among
men such as anger and being argumentative.

6.2.2.1 PURITY

Paul does not address ritual purity for the female body in the gentile
churches. Ritual purity for the female body is important in Judaism because
of the Levitical laws about menstruation (Lev. 15:19–24), spotting (15:25–30),
and the blood flow following childbirth (12:1–8). When a woman has any
vaginal discharge of blood, she is unclean, which means that she is not to
touch anything sacred or go to the temple (12:4). Anyone who touches her is
unclean until evening (15:19). The woman's bed and anything that she sits
on are unclean and can contaminate others. Anyone who is made unclean
by this contact will have to take a bath, wash clothing, and remain unclean
until evening (15:21–23). These purity laws meant that women were unable
to perform priesthood duties because they would be disqualified for much of
their adult lives. However, there may not have been widespread comparable
ritual purity practices for women in the gentile cultures of the Greco-Roman
world, in spite of the fact that women's menstruation and the process of
childbirth were a sign of women's physical mutability and inferiority in Greek

philosophy.[26] There is never a Pauline discussion about women that is comparable to the controversy of circumcision. The Pauline discussion on ritual purity that would have affected women most directly concerned food, since women were responsible for food preparation. Paul indicated that no food is ceremonially unclean for the gentile church (Rom. 14:14, 20; 1 Cor. 8:4, 8; 10:2–26), but he allowed that some might feel ceremonially defiled by food sacrificed to idols, or a particular kind of food (Rom. 14:14), in which case, eating it would be wrong for them.[27]

The house church was not sacred space, but also, Paul claims that God's people sanctify others, such as an unbelieving spouse or children. Therefore, though women were a dangerous source of contamination in Judaism, they (and male believers) were a source of holiness in the Pauline mission. Ceremonial purity, which separated those who are impure at table fellowship, was a major issue among the Jewish Christians, but Paul insisted that Jewish and gentile Christians eat together (Gal. 2:11–14). The elimination of circumcision canceled the other sources of ritual impurity caused by the body. This has a direct application to the priesthood of the believer and the representation of Christ: having the same genitals is eliminated as a factor. Neither uncircumcised male genitals nor female genitals were an issue when it came to full membership in the church, the priesthood of the believer, or full participation in the people of God.

6.2.2.2 BEAUTY AND ADORNMENT

The Pauline corpus is interested in women's physical appearance as the primary gender-specific issue.[28] It critiques the Greco-Roman cultural standard of beauty and supports the choice of modesty, but also portrays feminine beauty and physical attraction positively. The physical appearance of women is important across cultures in the ancient Near East and the Greco-Roman culture. There are both expectations of beauty and the felt necessity to control women's sexuality and limit their power of seduction over men. On the one hand, women's appearance and sexuality have been their primary road to any

26. However, there is some evidence about prohibitions of sex during menstruation and beliefs about magical and dangerous properties of menstrual blood. See William Loader, *The New Testament on Sexuality* (Grand Rapids: Eerdmans, 2012), 79–80.

27. See Mark Reasoner, "Purity and Impurity," *DPL*, 775–76.

28. Sharlene Hesse-Biber writes, "A woman . . . is judged almost entirely in terms of her appearance, her attractiveness to men, and her ability to keep the species going" (*Am I Thin Enough Yet? The Cult of Thinness and the Commercialization of Identity* [New York: Oxford University Press, 1996], 17). She is addressing contemporary issues in the Western culture, but her summary is timeless.

190 Paul and Gender

power that they may wield; on the other hand, these are also the primary reason for harsh restrictions, confinement, suspicion, punishment, and rejection.[29]

A woman's response to the public appraisal and judgment of her appearance and her own relationship to her body image generally proceed down two paths that are not necessarily mutually exclusive. The first path has the goal of being attractive. Women tend to prioritize adornment and enhancement of their appearance with hairstyles, clothing, jewelry, and cosmetics. Cultural ideas and ideals about the nature of feminine beauty are both imposed on women and exploited by them. The second path has the goal of being safe. Women may choose (or be compelled) to restrict those who are allowed to view their appearance because they believe that their body's inherent power to attract men poses a threat to them. In cultures expecting a veil or some style of formal covering that conceals the woman's body, it is common for women to count the covering as safety, security, honor, and freedom from being judged negatively or positively for their appearance.

The issue of beauty and the appearance of women is addressed in 1 Timothy 2:9–10 and 1 Corinthians 11:3–16 (as well as 1 Pet. 3:3). The passage in 1 Timothy 2:9–10 directly addresses the goal to be attractive. "In the same way, I want women to enhance their appearance with clothing that is modest and sensible, not with elaborate hairstyles, gold, pearls, or expensive clothes. They should make themselves attractive by doing good, which is appropriate for women who claim to honor God" (CEB).

Notably, Paul does not criticize women's goal to be attractive.[30] In fact, he legitimizes women's desire to adorn themselves and make themselves beautiful. However, as Howard Marshall says, the standard of beauty "is to be guided by deeper spiritual realities."[31] The first-century beauty practices included elaborate hairstyles, immodest clothing, expensive jewelry, and other accessories, all of which "might be both showy and extravagant as well as sexually enticing."[32] Paul encourages women to make themselves attractive within the parameters of modest and appropriate clothing. He argues that the greatest adornment is doing good, which reflects appropriate character that is consistent with the Christian profession.[33] The fact that here Paul does not tell women to wear veils indicates that the directives in 1 Timothy 2:9–15

29. See above, §1.6 on veiling.
30. As translated above, κοσμεῖν ἑαυτάς refers to making themselves beautiful or to adorning themselves in the context of clothing and jewelry (1 Tim. 2:9).
31. Marshall, *The Pastoral Epistles*, ICC (Edinburgh: T&T Clark, 1999), 448.
32. Ibid., 449. Paul's criticisms are held in common with Stoics and other philosophical moralists.
33. This creates an indirect mandate for Christian men to cultivate an attraction to godly women for the right reasons rather than supporting the cultural standards of beauty.

are not specific instructions for worship, but rather general guidelines for a woman's appearance and apparel.

Paul addresses women's goal of being safe in 1 Corinthians 11:3–16 in the context of public worship.[34] In that passage, Paul also acknowledges that woman is the glory of man (11:7), and that a woman's hair is "her glory" (11:15). In the context of cultures that veil, these statements reflect not only the climax of the Genesis account, where Eve is the "glory" of Adam (which is *very* good in Gen. 1:31; cf. Gen. 2:23–24), but also the transcultural view that a woman's appearance is so beautiful that it is dangerous: a woman's beauty brings honor or shame to her father and husband and to herself. Paul advocates for women wearing veils during worship so that they will not be shamed when they pray or prophesy by presenting themselves in a way that solicits sexual attention. Paul tries to ensure that their beauty will not detract from the worship of God, or especially from their own leadership in praying and prophesying.

Paul also refers to the beauty of a woman's appearance in his imagery of the church as the bride of Christ in Ephesians 5:25–27: "Husbands, love your wives, just as Christ loved the church and gave himself up for her, in order to make her holy by cleansing her with the washing of water by the word, so as to present the church to himself in splendor, without a spot or wrinkle or anything of the kind—yes, so that she may be holy and without blemish" (NRSV).

As Andrew Lincoln says, this is "the image of a young and lovely bride" who has "regal glory and perfect splendor."[35] Her bridal clothes are without spot or wrinkle, with the effect that she is radiant. However, the bride's beauty is similar to the woman in 1 Timothy 2:10, who makes herself attractive with doing good. She is sanctified as the water of the word washes her; her bridal clothes are supplied by Jesus Christ, and she is holy and blameless.

One of the outcomes of Paul's and Peter's teaching on women dressing modestly and appropriately is that they are asking women to lay down what has been their primary source of power over men. There is no room for manipulation or seduction in the church. Believers are to be a people characterized by servanthood, which may confront some of the darker side of traditional marriages. Another outcome is that women are to meet their desires to be attractive with a complete reversal of values. This may be one of the things that women need the most at this time. The church is in desperate need of

34. Each of these points is fully argued and supported in chap. 1, and will not be repeated or documented here.
35. Lincoln, *Ephesians*, 377.

developing an adequate theology of the body for women. Young women are being driven to eating disorders by their desire to be attractive in terms of the cultural standards and in competition with actresses and models. Paul seems to recognize the driving force behind the phenomena. There needs to be much more discussion about the symbolism of clothing, and there must be authentic spiritual vitality in a rigorous pursuit of godliness that goes far beyond pleasing men. The painful reality may be that Christian men similarly influenced by the media will not find a woman who adorns herself with good works attractive. Christians need a wake-up call to rewire their sexual orientation by rejecting narcissism and ideals of beauty that are unnatural, unhealthy, and ungodly. Young women desire a relationship with a man (cf. Gen. 3:16), and in some cases the attempt to fulfill this desire is killing them through eating disorders.

6.3 Sexuality

As William Loader states, "The early Christian movement as it developed within Judaism was heavily influenced by Jewish assumptions," and if anything, Jesus enhanced their strictness further.[36] Judaism was generally positive toward sexual desire, given that God created the body parts.[37] Yet the law contained an extensive list of sexual wrongdoings and (among other rules) forbade a woman becoming a prostitute, intermarriage outside of Israel, incest, same-sex intercourse, and infanticide. There were some similarities between Jewish, Greek, and Roman values and customs concerning marriage. Marriages were arranged between families, and the intention was to produce offspring, control inheritance, and support the old and sick. The widespread belief held that "the purpose of marriage was the procreation of legitimate heirs who would inherit and continue the name, property, and sacred rites of the family."[38] Traditional views stressed marriage as an obligation and responsibility, particularly for the man. The most important common feature and expectation was that the wife must be chaste, and chastity for the female was rigorously enforced.

In contrast, the males were not as limited as women were sexually, except in the case of access to other Roman citizens' wives and daughters. In the

36. Loader, *Sexuality*, 3–4.
37. According to Edward Ellis, the Jewish literature is generally positive or neutral toward sexual desire, but "most condemn excessive, overpowering, or misdirected desire and advocate self-control" (*Paul and Ancient Views of Sexual Desire: Paul's Sexual Ethics in 1 Thessalonians 4, 1 Corinthians 7, and Romans 1*, LNTS 354 [London: T&T Clark, 2007], 18).
38. Roy Bowen Ward, "Musonius and Paul on Marriage," *NTS* 36 (1990): 286–87.

Greco-Roman culture, men had sexual access to the slaves in the household and to prostitutes, male and female. Loader states, "Roman males were to be the very opposite of passive: strong, active, assertive, soldiers, and the sexual capacity was one of their weapons of subjugation."[39] They seemed to view sex as penetration of a passive partner. Greek and Roman literature includes a great amount of affirmation of sexual love, and erotic art, decorations, and fetishes were publicly displayed, surely in full view of Christians as they walked the streets. The Greek and Roman philosophers were more ambiguous toward sex, many advocating self-control, while the Pythagoreans insisted that sex should only be for procreation.[40]

6.3.1 The Bond of Sex

Paul has often been misrepresented and misinterpreted in his views on sex. Both Jesus and Paul view the sexual act between a man and a woman as mystical and powerful. Genesis 1–2 is foundational for Paul's views on sex, from which he bases his understanding of what we are as male and female. Like Jesus (Matt. 19:4–5), he appeals to Genesis 2:24 to argue that the male and the female become one flesh. Jesus boldly asserts that when a husband and wife become one flesh, they are sealed in the sexual act, and that it is God who actually joins them together. Paul speaks of the union in the sexual act as becoming one flesh even outside of the marital relationship (1 Cor. 6:16), and in Ephesians 5:28–31 it is discussed in terms of the marital relationship. His understanding of the bonding that is involved in sex is more explicit in his discussion of sex outside of the marital relationship in 1 Corinthians than it is in Ephesians.

Paul believes that sex creates a bond between male and female with every act of sexual intercourse: "Don't you know that anyone who is united with a

39. Loader, *Sexuality*, 87.
40. The Stoic-Cynic debate assumed marital obligation as an axiom: "The responsibilities of a father, a householder, and a citizen ensured and required that the married man became active in the social, political, and economic life of the town" (Anthony Thiselton, *The First Epistle to the Corinthians: A Commentary on the Greek Text*, NIGTC [Grand Rapids: Eerdmans, 2000], 487). Therefore, the Latin poet Ovid's view follows logically: "There could be no erotic pleasure [*amor*] between husband and wife because it was a relationship of duty." Larry Yarbrough summarizes Musonius the Stoic, who argued that sexual or erotic desire (ἀφροδίσια) in marriage was only justified for the purpose of impregnation, but that sex for the purpose of erotic pleasure was unlawful, even in marriage (Musonius, *Is Marriage a Handicap for the Pursuit of Philosophy?* 85.56). The divine purpose demanded individualism, so that Epictetus could say that marriage for love was good, but it may distract from the better (*Diatr.* 4.1.147). See O. Larry Yarbrough, *Not Like the Gentiles: Marriage Rules in the Letters of Paul*, SBLDS 80 (Atlanta: Scholars Press, 1985), 97.

prostitute[41] is one body with that person? The Scripture says, 'The two will become one flesh'" (1 Cor. 6:16). The discussion of having sex with a prostitute is viewed from the perspective of a male client and a female prostitute. The use of the masculine gender may be taken as the default (especially in the case of being united with a prostitute), and it is a given that patronizing prostitutes in Corinth was a predominantly male activity; yet the theology and restrictions would apply to women as well. An honorable woman's sexuality was severely restricted in the culture, while men had the option of accessing prostitutes (in a temple or in a brothel) or forming liaisons with women (or men) who were marginalized for various reasons and had multiple sex partners.[42] According to Paul, the bonding that takes place in the act of sex becomes destructive to participants in sexual relations outside of the marital relationship. It specifically violates the nature of oneness and the unity with Christ (as opposed to a purity violation or collaboration with evil). On the other hand, Paul asserts that the permanent sexual union/marriage between a believing spouse and an unbeliever results in the sanctification of the spouse (1 Cor. 7:14), and their children are holy.

In both continuity and contrast, Ephesians 5:28–31 develops the understanding of the unity created by the sexual union in the marital relationship.[43] Here a combination of metaphors that Paul has used elsewhere are joined in a new way. Christ as the head of the church (and the church as his body) is combined with the metaphor from 1 Corinthians 11:3–16 of the husband as the head of the wife,[44] and the sexual union of one flesh from Genesis 2:24. The inference is that the wife is the husband's body, making the union formed or sealed by the sexual relationship even closer:

> In the same way, husbands should love their wives as they do their own bodies.
> He who loves his wife loves himself. For no one ever hates his own body, but he

41. The word πόρνη is usually glossed as "prostitute," but in the Greco-Roman period it is used for any woman who has sex outside of marriage, not exclusively for prostitutes.

42. It is troubling that the plight of the slave is omitted from Paul's discussions about sex, because female and male slaves were forced to be sexually available to their owners. Paul targets one form of sexual behavior, and perhaps he hopes that applications will be drawn by Christian slave owners. Similarly, many of the prostitutes were slaves. David Garland depicts the prostitute "as a confederate of evil, a member of the dark, death-dealing forces at war against Christ" (*1 Corinthians*, BECNT [Grand Rapids: Baker Academic, 2003], 233). This probably misses the point and does not necessarily reflect the realities of prostitution in the first century or in other times.

43. Disputed in the Pauline canon, Ephesians weaves a number of Pauline metaphors into new associations in describing the relationship between husbands and wives in Eph. 5:21–33.

44. While there are many disagreements on what "head" means, in this context it is plausible to see that Paul has coined this metaphor from the Genesis account, where man is the source of life for woman, and has correlated it with Christ, who is the source of life and nourishment for the church.

nourishes and tenderly cares for it, just as Christ does for the church, because we are members of his body. "For this reason a man will leave his father and mother and be joined to his wife, and the two will become one flesh." This is a great mystery, and I am applying it to Christ and the church. (Eph. 5:28–31 NRSV)

In Pauline literature, the sexual union is described as a bond in marriage that appeals to the climax of the creation in the Genesis account: Eve made from Adam.

6.3.2 Sex and the Natural Order

Paul also appeals to the natural order for support (cf. 1 Cor. 11:14). In Romans 1:20, he says that even God's invisible qualities can be understood through what has been made. He characterizes sex between a male and female as "natural relations" (τὴν φυσικὴν χρῆσιν), a function in accordance with nature (Rom. 1:26–27).[45] The male and female genitals correspond to each other, and the sexual joining of male and female is considered by Paul to be an adequate indication of the purpose of creation for humanity without any need of specific revelation.

6.3.3 The Power of the Sex Drive

Paul has a realistic view of the sex drive. He does not underestimate its power, and he treats the sex drive as if it were equal for men and women. He believes that the majority of people would most likely not succeed in being celibate. If they do not get married, they may become involved in sexual immorality—that is, any sex outside of marriage: "Because of sexual immorality, each man should have his own wife, and each woman should have her own husband" (1 Cor. 7:2). He instructs married couples to engage in an active sex life, interrupted only for special times set aside for prayer. He believes that the sex drive is particularly vulnerable to attack by Satan: "Don't refuse to meet each other's needs unless you both agree for a short period of time to devote yourselves to prayer. Then come back together again, so that Satan might not tempt you because of your lack of self-control" (1 Cor. 7:5). The sexual relationship between the husband and wife is explicitly mutual and

45. See Douglas Moo's discussion of the significance of the word "natural" (*Romans*, 114–15). He concludes, "It is clear that Paul depicts homosexual activity as a violation of God's created order, another indication of the departure from true knowledge and worship of God." William Countryman tries to argue that the reference here is not to sin but to physical impurity, and Paul does not require gentiles to observe the Jewish purity rules (*Dirt, Greed & Sex: Sexual Ethics in the New Testament and Their Implications for Today* [Minneapolis: Fortress, 2007], 108–16).

evenhanded, where each has authority over the other's body, as in 1 Corinthians 7:3–4: "The husband should meet his wife's sexual needs, and the wife should do the same for her husband. The wife does not have authority [ἐξουσιάζει] over her own body, but the husband does. Likewise the husband does not have authority [ἐξουσιάζει] over his own body, but the wife does."

Paul's Letters are remarkably free from Greek cultural ideas drawn from Aristotle and others about the essential differences between men and women as demonstrated in the sexual act. He contradicts the Greco-Roman belief that the man shows dominance through penetration and the wife is submissive through being penetrated; in Paul's model, both exercise authority and have power while they are equally mastered by the other, as in Song of Songs. Paul stands in stark contrast to a blog post by Jared Wilson that appeared during the summer of 2012.[46] Wilson promoted an Aristotelian view of the male and female body, affirming Douglas Wilson's statement that describes sex as an act of male authority and female submission: "However we try, the sexual act cannot be made into an egalitarian pleasuring party. A man penetrates, conquers, colonizes, plants. A woman receives, surrenders, accepts."[47] This description of sex is completely antithetical to the teaching in the Bible and the Pauline corpus on the act of sex; it is, however, very close to how Plato and Aristotle understood and described the act of sex. It also reflects the theology behind a long history of Christian abuse of power through oppressive systems such as colonialism and imperialism, and the attendant rhetoric that the colonizers can exploit the colonized as a benevolent act.

Paul tells the unmarried to marry if they cannot control themselves, because "it's better to marry than to burn with passion" (1 Cor. 7:9). In the First Letter to Timothy, the younger widows apparently were vowing celibacy in service to the church, but instead they tended to be idle; some were going house to house and gossiping, and some had "turned aside to follow Satan" (1 Tim. 5:11–15). In his view, it was inevitable that their sexual drive would prove stronger than their dedication to Christ, so that instead they should marry, have children, and run a house (5:14). To some extent, marriage looks like a stop-gap measure for Paul, and primarily a solution to a problem, but the instructions in 1 Corinthians 7 have to be read as specific interactions with the Corinthians' questions and sexual behavior, and it should be placed in the context of his more theological remarks about marriage and sex elsewhere.

46. Jared C. Wilson, "The Polluted Waters of *50 Shades of Grey*, Etc." These and other statements about rape raised a public outcry that resulted in the blog being removed from the website after several days of attempts by Wilson to justify his statements.

47. Wilson, *Fidelity: What It Means to Be a One-Woman Man* (Moscow, ID: Canon Press, 1999), 86–87.

6.3.4 Summary

Even though Paul was single, and perhaps was the unintentional inspiration for monasticism, he had a deep appreciation and respect for the power of sex to bind men and women together, and he took the power of the sex drive seriously. In Ephesians, he uses that powerful union to explain the relationship between Christ and the church, and that union in turn informed his view of marriage. However, the power that created the bond in marriage was portrayed as equally destructive when it occurred outside of a relationship that was not permanent. In other words, promiscuity was an incomprehensible contradiction in the face of the bonding that takes place with the sexual act.

6.4 Marriage and Singleness

Paul was an unblushing advocate of an active sex life within marriage, but his long discussion of sex, marriage, and singleness in 1 Corinthians 7:1–40 begins with a remark that seems to state the opposite: "Now, about what you wrote, it's good for a man not to 'have sex' with a woman" (7:1). This statement, together with the later discussion about the benefits of being single, appears to place a higher value on virginity or celibacy than marriage.[48] It seems to cast a condescending light over his following instructions about marriage. However, it is more plausible that he was answering a series of questions from the Corinthians, and this remark reflects their position: "Now, about what you wrote: 'It's good for a man not to "have sex" with a woman.'"[49]

Regardless, Paul gives instruction to the unmarried, advising that it is good for them to remain unmarried as he is, "because of the present crisis" (1 Cor. 7:8, 26). The Stoic view in the Stoic-Cynic debates on marriage is often seen to influence Paul's views on the advantages of celibacy.[50] He contends that unmarried men and women are "free from concern" and can devote themselves to being concerned about serving the Lord, but married people's interests are divided because they are concerned about pleasing their spouses (7:32–35).

---

48. As Loader argues, it certainly cannot mean that sexual intercourse is sinful (*Sexuality*, 453).

49. Thiselton writes, "Without doubt the allusion to abstinence from physical intimacy (the context implies that the reference is to that within marriage) comes not from Paul, but from Corinth (7:1). It is part of the topic indicator of explicit response to the letter from Corinth" (*Corinthians*, 494).

50. For discussions on the Stoic influence on Paul, see Deming, *Paul on Marriage and Celibacy*; Vincent L. Wimbush, *Paul the Worldly Ascetic: Response to the World and Self-Understanding according to 1 Corinthians 7* (Macon, GA: Mercer University Press, 1987); Wimbush, "The Ascetic Impulse in Ancient Christianity," *ThTo* 50 (1993): 417–28; Yarbrough, *Not Like the Gentiles*.

Paul himself was celibate (7:7–8), and he believed that people who were gifted to stay single, as he was, could live a more ordered life (7:35), experience less worry (7:32), be less troubled (7:28), and have a happier life (7:40).[51] Therefore, he encourages unmarried people to stay single, if possible, because of spiritual and pragmatic advantages (7:32–35). Paul's treatment of men and women is once more mutual and evenhanded throughout 1 Corinthians 7, which is in contrast with the cultural expectations for men and women.[52]

6.5 Sex and Children

Some of Paul's statements on the issue of childbirth and children have points of relevance to the topic of sex, marriage, and gender. According to 1 Corinthians 7:14, the children of a believer are holy or sanctified (ἅγιος) even if the spouse (the other parent) is an unbeliever. In some way, Paul states that all children of believers are consecrated for God. This may be, in part, a cryptic reference to the Christian prohibition of abortion and infanticide, indicating that only God has the right of life and death over a child, since the practice of abortion was widespread in the Greco-Roman world. Furthermore, infant exposure was a common practice. For example, the Roman culture gave the father the power of life and death over his children (*patria potestas*), particularly in the case of the newborn. The father had the choice to accept or reject a newborn in a ceremony in which the infant was placed in front of him. If he picked up the infant, it was received into the family, and if he did not pick it up, it was exposed.[53] In some circumstances, such as divorce, a husband's death, or illegitimacy, a mother would choose to expose her infant. Infant exposure was a common cultural practice throughout the Mediterranean world, as a method of family planning and also as a means of eliminating the weak and deformed. As is often the case in other cultures, healthy male children were preferred, and so female children were more often exposed.[54] Although the

---

51. So summarizes Jerome Murphy-O'Connor, "The Divorced Woman in 1 Corinthians 7:10–11," *JBL* 100 (1981): 59.

52. Contra Schüssler Fiorenza, who highlights tensions in the Pauline texts. She notes the liberating effects where Paul gives permission to remain unmarried, but challenges his characterization of marriage as a life of divided loyalties: "One can only wonder how Paul could have made such a theological point when he had Prisca as his friend and knew other missionary couples who were living examples that his theology was wrong" (*In Memory of Her*, 226).

53. Cicero, *Att.* 11.9.

54. A fourth-century-BCE poet generalizes, "Everyone raises a son even if he is poor, but exposes a daughter even if he is rich" (*Posidippus*, 11E, cited by Stobaeus, *Flor.* 77.7) (Mark Golden, "Demography and the Exposure of Girls at Athens," *Phoenix* 35 [1981]: 316). This practice continued to be common, as indicated in an Oxyrhynchus papyrus bearing a letter from

probability of death for an exposed newborn was very high, exposed infants might be raised by others. Some were made slaves (many of those were used in the sex trade), but some were raised with a free status and even adopted. Jewish practice was in direct conflict with the surrounding culture over the issues of abortion and infanticide, forbidding such practices in any form. The early Christian movement followed the Jewish ethical practices and teaching, roundly condemning abortion and infanticide.

The fear of death in childbirth and high infant mortality affected the practice of religion and molded the relationships between parents and children. The fear of a woman's death in childbirth was pervasive, and it was heightened in the Greco-Roman world by death during pregnancy, which often was due to botched abortions. Much of women's religious pagan practice was dominated by concerns with fertility, protection during pregnancy, and the assurance of a safe delivery. The use of prayers, charms, rituals, and various magical objects to deal with childbirth permeated daily life, and there were obligatory observances not only for the woman, but also for others who were concerned with various aspects of the process, including the extended family as well as the midwife and attendants. This probably is the context for 1 Timothy 2:15 and the preceding narrative about creation and the fall. Women would be prone to syncretism in this crucial area and susceptible to false teaching.

6.6 Separation, Divorce, and Remarriage

Paul believes that the marriage bond is meant to be lifelong (Rom. 7:1–3; 1 Cor. 7:10–11, 39). However, a spouse's death, desertion, or adultery breaks the covenant bond (Rom. 7:2–3). These three options were common in the first century, especially for a Christian married to an unbelieving spouse. Paul deals with the different cases pragmatically and without the legalism that has characterized the policies of church traditions. In principle, a believer is commanded not to desert a spouse (1 Cor. 7:10). However, Paul says, someone who does choose to separate from a spouse should not initiate a divorce and remarry (7:11–13). But if a spouse breaks the covenant bond by adultery or desertion, a believer is free to remarry, which indicates that the believer may initiate divorce proceedings: "The brother or sister isn't tied down in these circumstances" (7:15). But a believer is forbidden to commit adultery, and one who commits adultery faces excommunication from the church (5:5, 9–11).

---

an absent husband to his pregnant wife: "If you have the baby before I return, if it is a boy, let it live; if it is a girl, expose it" (P. Oxy. 744).

These instructions aid a believer in navigating difficulties and options in a number of scenarios that characterize difficult marriages.

Paul's position is further clarified in 1 Corinthians 7:27–28 for those who have been divorced for whatever reason: "If you are married, don't get a divorce. If you are divorced, don't try to find a spouse. But if you do marry, you haven't sinned."[55] If the marriage bond has been shattered because a believer was at fault, the believer should come under discipline (excommunication in terms of exclusion from the fellowship), but then may be restored to fellowship when repentant (2 Cor. 2:5–10). In such a case, Paul has often been interpreted to forbid remarriage, but in this passage, celibacy is not by any means suggested as a form of repentance or a punitive measure for sexual misconduct. Celibacy is a gift of self-control that few will possess. He is concerned about unmarried people (divorced or never married) falling into sexual immorality because of their natural sexual needs, and those who already have a record of incontinence are particularly at risk. Paul frankly acknowledges that some of his readers have previously been sexually immoral, participants in same-sex intercourse and adulterers (1 Cor. 6:9–10); his answer for the temptation of sexual incontinence is marriage with an active sex life (7:2–7).

6.7 Sexual Immorality (Rom. 1:26–27; 1 Cor. 6:12–19)

The only sexual options for Paul are marriage with "natural relations" (male-female) or abstinence (1 Cor. 7:9). Marriage therefore refers to one man and one woman exclusively. Paul's discussion of sexually immoral behavior focuses on all sexual acts that are committed outside of the bond of marriage. Lust is not as much an explicit sin of sexual immorality in the Pauline corpus as it is in Jesus's teaching. Rather, burning with passion is presented in 1 Corinthians 7 as a problem typical of the human condition and concerns and directly affects self-control or the lack of self-control. Those who are abstinent must control their sexual desire, and if they cannot, it is better to get married (7:9). Married people should have regular sexual relations so that they will not be tempted by Satan to lose self-control (7:2–5). Similarly in 1 Thessalonians 4:3–5, believers are instructed to exercise sexual self-control: "For this is the will of God, your sanctification: that you abstain from fornication [πορνεία]; that each one of you know how to control your own body in holiness and honor, not with lustful passion, like the Gentiles who do not know God" (NRSV).

55. See Colin Brown, "Separate: Divorce, Separation and Re-marriage," *NIDNTT*, 3:535–43.

Sexual immorality/fornication, πορνεία, was an inclusive term for extra-marital sex.[56] It includes premarital sex, adultery, sex with prostitutes, "unnatural sex," and same-gender sexual relations, though same-gender sexual relations are often treated as a separate category. Paul regards extramarital sex as the antonym of sanctification, which is the will of God and therefore a primary goal of the Christian life.

6.7.1 Devotion to God or the Pursuit of Happiness?

Paul's priorities stand in stark contrast with those who do not know God. Sexual satisfaction or release and meaningful love relationships with a life partner are not a priority, a goal, or a right for those who are devoted to God. Sexual immorality involves a lack of control, uncleanness, the loss of honor, and participation in degrading and dishonorable conduct (cf. Rom. 1:26–28). Paul identifies and addresses the issue of sexual exploitation and wronging others sexually in 1 Thessalonians 4:3–7: "For this is the will of God, . . . that no one wrong or exploit a brother or sister in this matter, because the Lord is an avenger in all these things, just as we have already told you beforehand and solemnly warned you. For God did not call us to impurity but in holiness" (NRSV).[57]

Paul does not see sexual immorality as a victimless sin, but rather as one in which both participants as well as any extended family are ultimately victims.[58] In 1 Corinthians 6:18, he places "sexual immorality" in a unique category in that it is a sin with serious spiritual consequences for each participant: "Every sin that a person can do is committed outside of the body, except that

---

56. For a Jew, πορνεία included not just prostitution, but all sexual activity that was forbidden by the law of Moses.

57. In 1 Thess. 4:4–6, the admonishment is "for each of you" (ἕκαστον ὑμῶν) not to wrong or exploit a "brother" (ἀδελφόν) in this matter. A case may be made for the wronged party in view to be either a male sexual partner and/or a woman's husband, father, or guardian, meaning that a female who was sexually exploited would not technically be considered to be the one wronged or dishonored. However, this should be taken here as the default use of the masculine singular, where ἀδελφόν stands for whoever is exploited or wronged by the sexual act (to whom it may concern), which often extends beyond a single person to the honor of the family, including parents, spouse, children, and beyond.

58. However, in the case of a prostitute (or a woman with multiple sex partners) in 1 Cor. 6:15–18, Paul is not addressing the sexual exploitation of prostitutes or women, but considers the dire consequences from the perspective of a male Christian client. In 1 Thess. 4:4–7, Paul's focus is on the effects on the body of Christ and the impact of sexual misconduct on other Christians. However, it should be recognized that the readers and culture shared the belief that women should not engage in prostitution or extramarital sex, and that such acts were degrading and dishonorable, but gentile readers would not necessarily share the belief that the same standards applied to men.

those who engage in sexual immorality commit sin against their own bodies."
Therefore, any immoral sexual act would result in both personal harm and
wronging or exploiting the sexual partner. Furthermore, Paul states that men
who perform sexual acts with each other are "in their own bodies paid back
with the penalty they deserved for their mistake" (Rom. 1:27), suggesting that
there are negative physical consequences that are a natural penalty, at least to
the same-gender sexual act among males.

6.7.2 The Damage of Temporary Sexual Bonds

Paul connects sinning against one's own body with a violation of the
nature of sex, which is to become one body with a sex partner (1 Cor. 6:16;
cf. Gen. 2:24). Forming a sexual bond that is not permanent creates some
form of spiritual and/or physical damage—perhaps a tearing.[59] Furthermore,
the unity that the believer has in Christ is violated by the unity formed with
someone who has multiple sex partners. Paul argues that when you have sex
with someone, as a member of Christ's body, you unite Christ and his body
with that person: "Don't you know that your bodies are parts of Christ? So
then, should I take parts of Christ and make them a part of a prostitute?"
(1 Cor. 6:15). This could possibly be a concern with defiling the body of
Christ with a prostitute's impurity, but it is more likely a deeper concern
with compromising the relationship of faithfulness to Christ with a relationship that throughout the Old Testament is the quintessential metaphor
of unfaithfulness.

6.7.3 Continuity and Discontinuity with the Greco-Roman Culture

Christian sexual ethics would have made the biggest difference for men.
I have suggested that the vice lists that decry anger were primarily targeting
an issue for males. Cultural studies suggest that the vice lists against sexual
immorality would also be primarily targeting and changing male behavior,
because there was considerably more sexual freedom for males in the ethics of
the culture. William Loader states, "In some ways the change for men in the
alternative society is more radical than for women. Making them responsible
for their own sexuality removes from them the traditional self-understanding
that they must control women and can blame them."[60]

---

59. As Cameron Diaz's character, Julie Gianni, expresses in the 2001 film *Vanilla Sky*: "When
you sleep with someone, your body makes a promise whether you do or not" (*Vanilla Sky*,
directed by Cameron Crowe [Hollywood, CA: Paramount Pictures, 2001]).
60. Loader, *Sexuality*, 361.

This is an understatement. In fact, Christianity undercut essential patri-archal rights by requiring men to be faithful in the same way that the culture had required women to be faithful.[61] It condemned divorce, incest, and marital infidelity, and discouraged polygamy.[62] Christianity provided ethical continuity and equality for women. It prized female chastity, but women with any status were already required to be chaste. Now if their husbands converted, Christian women's status, security, and satisfaction in their marriage were much higher.

6.7.4 Sex and Slavery

There is an issue in the Pauline community concerning the sexuality of slaves.[63] The obedience of slaves is addressed in the household codes, and Paul repeatedly mentions their status, showing that they are essential members of the Christian community, and "there is no free or slave." However, there must have been tension due to the sexual status and situation of slaves. Given the Greco-Roman practice of the first century, male and female slaves were par-ticipating in what Paul describes as sexual immorality and unnatural sexual relations. They would appear to be in an ethical double bind in the Christian community. Betsy Bauman-Martin suggests that in the case of the commands to slaves in 1 Peter, slaves of unbelieving masters were already not submitting to their masters: they were already subverting the normal patriarchal system by becoming Christians and attending Christian meetings. In her view, it fol-lows that they were also refusing to submit sexually. The advice is to submit to the consequent persecution, which is "suffering for behaving correctly" (1 Pet. 2:20).[64] However, this overestimates the power of a slave, especially a woman slave. We may assume that masters continued to use and abuse Christian slaves who had no choice, and it is possible that the community held them to be without fault, or faithful within their circumstances. Life was messier in the Pauline communities than we sometimes acknowledge. But notice that

---

61. This is not to say that individual women were not guilty of sexual immorality, but that the culture uniformly condemned women who were not chaste, but did not have the same expectation for men.

62. See Rodney Stark, *The Rise of Christianity: How the Obscure, Marginal Jesus Movement Became the Dominant Religious Force in the Western World in a Few Centuries* (San Francisco: HarperSanFrancisco, 1997), 104. He argues that the higher status of Christian women resulted in a higher rate of conversion.

63. Jennifer Glancy has suggested that scholars have overlooked the gender of slaves; see Glancy, *Slavery in Early Christianity* (Oxford: Oxford University Press, 2002); Glancy, "Obstacles to Slaves' Participation in the Corinthian Church," *JBL* 117 (1998): 481–501.

64. Bauman-Martin, "Feminist Theologies of Suffering and Current Interpretations of 1 Peter 2:18–3:9," in *A Feminist Companion to the Catholic Epistles and Hebrews*, ed. Amy-Jill Levine and Maria Mayo Robbins, FCNTECW 8 (New York: T&T Clark International, 2004), 71.

Paul's teaching on the veil in 1 Corinthians 11:2–16 insists that a woman who prays and prophesies in the church should be allowed to wear a symbol that was a cultural icon for honor, chastity, and protection. As far as it was in his power, Paul at least symbolically protected women slaves who were believers from being sexually used by those in the Christian community who submitted to his guidance and leadership.

The interpretation of Paul and his theology of the body has had a tortured history. A lot of this happened because of what we now label "reader-oriented criticism." Early on, Christian interpreters and teachers projected views of Greek philosophy onto the Pauline texts, including Platonic dualism and the Pythagorean rejection of sex for any purpose but procreation. Paul's use of the word "flesh" became equated with the physical body, and celibacy became spiritually privileged. Male interpreters projected their own sexual urges onto women, and they combined this with a rejection of the (supposedly) inferior woman for the superior choice of celibacy. This entire trend is completely antithetical to what Paul actually said about sex and the body.

The Christian pastoral community, biblical scholars, theologians, and church historians need to think carefully and thoroughly about the way forward in our theology of the body. We are desperately in need of a coherent biblical theology and worldview that engage a heavily sexualized culture in this key area. It should be not only about sexual ethics, but also about dealing with crucial related issues that Paul highlighted: sexual immorality, anger, and perceptions of the body and beauty. These continue to be central issues that should be addressed carefully and are among the foremost priorities of the Western Christian community.

seven

Calling

The concept of every believer's call or calling to ministry is fundamental to most Christian traditions and central to the function of the churches. The majority of Protestants' concept of ministry is based on the claim that there is no biblical distinction between the laity and professional clergy in regard to God's call to service or his provision of specific gifting from the Holy Spirit for every believer. This is closely related to the priesthood of every believer, whereby the Old Testament role of priest is transformed and filled first by Jesus Christ in his work as mediator and his provision of sacrifice. Then it is filled by every believer's spiritual service of worship so that the church consists of priests who anticipate the kingdom of God. The present chapter will demonstrate how these passages are understood in regard to men's roles in the church. It will demonstrate that they have been applied to women with hermeneutical inconsistency that confuses and inhibits the service required of all believers and invalidates these core doctrines for women as believers. Paul's understanding of the role of experience in determining call and gifting is crucial to the discussion because while a man's experience constitutes his call, a woman's comparable experience of call is often negated and unsupported. First, the heart of this study is an attempt to disambiguate the concept of call, service, and priesthood of the believer in regard to gender. Second, it will

Most of the material in this chapter appeared in Cynthia Long Westfall, "On Developing a Consistent Hermeneutical Approach to the Application of General Scriptures," *PriscPap* 24 (2010): 9–13.

study call, service, and vocation alongside gender distinctions. Third, it will examine Paul's command in 1 Corinthians 14:34 for women to be silent in the churches in light of its immediate context, the larger context on spiritual gifts, and the discourse of the letter as it affects women's calls and their service.

7.1 Gender, Call, Service, and the Priesthood of the Believer

Paul's theology of spiritual gifts plays a crucial role in determining the call and service of each believer. The passage on spiritual gifts in 1 Corinthians 12–14 gives the most detail about the gifts, including their variety and functions in the church, and reflects the Holy Spirit's primary role in the distribution of these gifts. Ephesians 4:7–13 shows that there is a direct relationship between the gifts provided by God and positions of leadership and ministry in the church, including the list of apostles, prophets, evangelists, pastors, and teachers in verse 11. Historically, however, the church has followed a hermeneutical approach in which an interpretation of the prohibitions against women in 1 Timothy 2:12 has taken priority over their exercise of most of the spiritual gifts outlined in Ephesians 4:11, Romans 12:1–8, and 1 Corinthians 12:28. The interpretation of 1 Timothy 2:12 functions as an a priori assumption that operates as a hermeneutical grid over these and other passages. The understanding of 1 Timothy 2:12, according to many scholars and church leaders, is that it prohibits women from teaching or exercising authority at some level in the church, public worship, and possibly in any Christian context where an adult male is present.

The broad spectrum of opinion concerning what exactly is prohibited in what context contributes to the confusion, both for women who are trying to navigate their call and for the churches, organizations, and individuals who are trying to apply the prohibition. Furthermore, women find that they hit unanticipated glass ceilings because they are dealing with embedded theologies that are far more restrictive and confusing than what is actually articulated or overtly permitted in Scripture. I also will show how there is hermeneutical inconsistency and confusion when a woman attempts to read and apply Romans 12:1–8. My contention is that anyone studying Scripture, whether woman or man, needs to apply sound hermeneutical principles consistently when studying Romans 12:1–8. Inconsistencies in the hermeneutical approach applied in regard to women result in theological inconsistencies.

7.1.1 Romans in the Context of the Pauline Corpus

Paul lays out templates for the believer's function in the church in three letters: 1 Corinthians, written about 55 CE; Romans, written about 57 CE;

and Ephesians, written 60 CE or later.[1] The Epistle to the Romans provides a particularly interesting test case for Paul's theology of ministry regarding spiritual gifts and gender. It is one of the least occasional of his epistles: he is not dealing with a large number of specific group or personal problems as he did in the Corinthian Epistles or the Pastorals, though tensions between Jews and gentiles certainly are addressed.[2] It is also somewhat systematic in argument, with the most explanation and clarity; Paul had never visited Rome, and he did not assume a high level of shared information with the church in Rome. If there had been essential constraints on women in the exercise of spiritual gifts, this would have been the time for Paul to make such constraints clear. He did not do so.

Romans provides a significant contrast with 1 Timothy in several ways. This letter was written to a group in a place Paul had never visited, but 1 Timothy claims to be a private, intimate letter to a member of his ministry team, which by nature assumes a high level of shared information.[3] In such private letters, invariably key information for outsider interpretation is omitted, because the recipient understands the context.[4] Read on its own terms, 1 Timothy is highly occasional, embedded in a particular context in Ephesus.[5] In the letter, Paul is addressing a number of specific issues and problems caused by false teaching, including a variety of problems among the women. The authorship of 1 Timothy has been challenged on the basis of content and grammar, and its authorship is thought by some to date to the second century. If authentic (by Paul), 1 Timothy was written as much as eight years after Romans was written (most likely between 63 and 65 CE), so

---

1. In the case of Ephesians, this is probably where the letter "places itself" in the Pauline narrative, though it is not highly situational. It is beyond the purposes of this study to discuss its status as a disputed letter.

2. One may infer that there is an acute problem between the Jews and the gentiles in the church, reflected in Rom. 14:1–15:33. See Joseph A. Fitzmyer, *Romans: A New Translation with Introduction and Commentary*, AB 33 (New York: Doubleday, 1993), 638.

3. For a discussion of 2 Timothy as a private letter versus a fictitious letter, see Cynthia Long Westfall, "A Moral Dilemma? The Epistolary Body of 2 Timothy," in *Paul and the Ancient Letter Form*, ed. Stanley E. Porter and Sean A. Adams, PSt 6 (Leiden: Brill, 2010), 225–29. The recipient issues are similar in both epistles. See also chap. 9.

4. One of the key principles of relevance theory is that a writer/speaker does not share more information than is necessary.

5. Most scholars technically treat 1 Timothy as fictitious: they believe that it purports to be a private letter, but that it is intended to be read by an entire church, and possibly accessed by the entire Christian community. This assumption is quite important in supporting a universal reading of the prohibitions against women in 1 Tim. 2:12, but there is no grammatical evidence that the letter is fictitious, given the conventions of letter writing. Personal letters were not necessarily private, and greetings to another individual, a family, or a community at the end of a personal letter were standard.

it cannot be assumed that it contains information that the readers in Rome would have known and could have used as an interpretive grid.[6] Furthermore, the alleged interpretive grid in 1 Timothy 2:12 contains a number of significant interpretive problems that disqualify it from being given preference over content in Romans in determining doctrine and praxis.[7] Three hermeneutical principles are shared by most traditions that hold the Bible as authoritative: (1) We do not base a doctrine on one verse.[8] (2) We do not base a doctrine on a verse or passage with interpretive problems.[9] And (3) we give weight to the clearer teaching.[10] Romans not only serves as providing a clear passage on believers' function in the church; it also is particularly useful for determining the effect of gender because Romans 16 is notable for the number of prominent women in the Christian community whom Paul singles out and commends.

7.1.2 Romans 12:1–8 in Its Contexts

From the start I articulate three assumptions about the passage. First, while most commentators suggest that Romans 12:1–2 introduces the whole exhortation in the following four chapters, it is also part of a unified thread in 12:1–8,[11] and 12:9–21 is also closely related. Second, parallel passages in 1 Corinthians 12 and Ephesians 4:11–15 elucidate Paul's theology of spiritual gifts and can be used legitimately to interpret each other. Third, regardless of one's translation theory, in the Greek, ὑμεῖς ("you" plural) and ἀδελφοί

6. As Craig Blomberg argues, "Interpreting Scripture with Scripture, the 'analogy of Scripture,' or adopting what the ancients called the 'rule of faith' (*regula fidei*) is always legitimate when the additional passage being used to interpret a given text would have been known to the text's author" (Blomberg, with Jennifer Foutz Markley, *A Handbook of New Testament Exegesis* [Grand Rapids: Baker Academic, 2010], 229). Assuming that Paul would have said the same thing eight years earlier to a group rather than an individual is circular. We argue as well that the issues and problems are shared information between the author and readers.

7. Wayne Grudem asserts, "We should never use one part of Scripture to draw conclusions that deny or contradict other parts of Scripture" (*Evangelical Feminism and Biblical Truth: An Analysis of More Than One Hundred Disputed Questions* [Sisters, OR: Multnomah, 2004], 405).

8. As William Klein, Craig Blomberg, and Robert Hubbard give as a key point, "Theology must be based on the Bible's total teaching, not on selected or isolated texts" (*Introduction to Biblical Interpretation* [Dallas: Word, 1993], 388).

9. "Obscure texts whose points may be ambiguous" carry less weight. "Where metaphors or narratives leave conclusions more ambiguous, we dare not force them to overrule texts that speak more clearly or didactically" (ibid., 389).

10. "Clearer teaching must carry more weight than obscure texts whose points may be ambiguous" (ibid., 388–89).

11. While λέγω ("I say") in Rom. 12:3 is emphatic, as well as "every one of you," the verse is joined to 12:1–2 with γάρ ("for"), indicating that 12:3–5 not only is connected to or flows out of 12:1–2, but also supports 12:1–2.

("siblings") refer to both women and men. This is made explicit and emphatic in 12:3: the following instructions are addressed to every single one of the believers (παντὶ τῷ ὄντι ἐν ὑμῖν).

> I appeal to you therefore, brothers and sisters, by the mercies of God, to present your bodies as a living sacrifice, holy and acceptable to God, which is your spiritual worship. Do not be conformed to this world, but be transformed by the renewing of your minds, so that you may discern what is the will of God—what is good and acceptable and perfect. For by the grace given to me I say to everyone among you not to think of yourself more highly than you ought to think, but to think with sober judgment, each according to the measure of faith that God has assigned. For as in one body we have many members, and not all the members have the same function, so we, who are many, are one body in Christ, and individually we are members one of another. We have gifts that differ according to the grace given to us: prophecy, in proportion to faith; ministry, in ministering; the teacher, in teaching; the exhorter, in exhortation; the giver, in generosity; the leader, in diligence; the compassionate, in cheerfulness. (Rom. 12:1–8 NRSV)

7.1.3 Romans 12:1–2: Priesthood of the Believer

The exhortations in Romans 12:1–2 are couched in terms of worship, so that the believer is depicted both as the priest who serves and offers the sacrifice and as the sacrifice that is being offered.[12] Worship in the Old Testament, including the sacrifice and the priesthood, is now being fulfilled with the inauguration of the new age.[13] As Stanley Grenz observes, "The believer has the privilege and responsibility to engage in priestly functions such as offering spiritual sacrifices to God (Heb. 13:15; Rom. 12:1; 1 Pet. 2:9)."[14] The sacrifice involves the totality of one's life; we are now to be God's possession. We are to resist conformity to the world's norms and standards and experience transformation by the renewing of our minds.

12. Robert Jewett states, "The metaphors of bodily sacrifice and reasonable worship as a fitting response to grace . . . suggest the basis of their cooperation with Paul . . . in priestly service to the gospel of God" (*Romans: A Commentary*, ed. Eldon J. Epp, Hermeneia [Minneapolis: Fortress, 2007], 724). Similarly, for Douglas Moo, Rom. 12:1 describes the priesthood of the believer: "Christians are all priests (1 Pet. 2:5; Rev. 1:6; 5:10; 20:6), forming together the temple where God now reveals himself in a special way" (*The Epistle to the Romans*, NICNT [Grand Rapids: Eerdmans, 1996], 754).

13. As Thomas Schreiner asserts, "The worship and sacrifices of the OT can no longer be confined to the cult [practice of worship]. . . . [Paul] understands the OT cult as now being fulfilled because the new age is inaugurated. In other words, Paul's understanding of the cult is fundamentally eschatological" (*Romans*, BECNT [Grand Rapids: Baker, 1998], 646).

14. Grenz, *Theology for the Community of God* (Grand Rapids: Eerdmans, 1994), 555.

One of the common arguments used to support prohibiting women from the priesthood or pastorate is that Old Testament priests were male.[15] Here, however, we have the priesthood of believers in a ministry/gift context, and there is no longer Jew or Greek, slave or free, male or female in the priesthood. This is consistent with the argument in the book of Hebrews: now that Christ has offered himself as a once-for-all sacrifice for our sin and guilt, all believers stand on the same ground before God; each believer is to follow Christ into the holy of holies, functioning as priests (Heb. 10:19–25). If the Old Testament teaching role really did belong to the priests rather than the prophets, as has been argued,[16] then the teaching role would be extended across the racial, social, and gender lines as well. As a part of the doctrine of the priesthood of the believer, evangelicals have held that every believer is responsible to share knowledge, though every believer does not have the gift of teaching.[17]

The priesthood of the believer is differentiated from the qualifications for elders or deacons.[18] However, here there is an explicit relationship between all functions in ministry and the priesthood of the believer: the functions flow out of the priesthood in Romans 12:1–8. Every member of the church shares in the church's ministry and mission. Every gift is presented as a possibility for consideration as each reader determines one's own measure of faith with sober judgment. According to the doctrine as it has developed, every Christian has equal *potential* to minister before God. Where there is a priesthood of believers, there is no spiritual aristocracy or hierarchy.[19]

7.1.4 Romans 12:1–2: The Call to Authenticity and Transformation

The exhortations in Romans 12:1–2 involve a call to authenticity. The presentation of the body is the whole person; it includes who we are as uniquely

15. See, e.g., Craig L. Blomberg, "Women in Ministry: A Complementarian Perspective," in *Two Views on Woman in Ministry*, eds. Stanley N. Gundry and James R. Beck (Grand Rapids: Zondervan, 2005), 133. Most of the leaders in the gentile mission would have been uncircumcised gentiles whose maleness was neither like Christ nor like the Levites by Jewish standards. The qualifications for priesthood in the Levitical system are completely different from the qualifications for the pastorate and particularly for the believer as priest.

16. Ibid., 137.

17. Bruce L. Shelly, *What Baptists Believe* (Wheaton: CB Press, 1973), 25–32.

18. Grudem, *Evangelical Feminism*, 404–5.

19. As Gordon Lewis and Bruce Demarest state, "The priesthood of believers means that no leaders (bishops, ministers, or elders) can demand that others confess sins to them for divine forgiveness. No leader can add to the mediatorial provisions of Jesus Christ as implemented by the Holy Spirit. As priests, church members have not only equal privileges but also equal responsibility to exercise in love their different spiritual gifts for the good of all" (*Integrative Theology* [Grand Rapids: Zondervan, 1996], 3:274).

created by God, where we have been, and where we are now in our life journey.[20] This is a point at which experience is an essential part of the equation.
Exactly what is sacrificed is that which is lodged in the configuration of our
heritage, time, and place, which was predetermined by God as optimal for our
relationship with him, according to Paul's speech in Acts 17:24–28.[21] Every
believer in every age is God's workmanship, created in Christ Jesus for good
works (Eph. 2:8–10).[22] Paul's mission to the gentiles encompassed a respect
for the culture and the background of those who were not Jews; he brought
the gospel to them where they were. First-century gentiles placed their body
on the altar as a living sacrifice, and God created something new and revolutionary. This must continue to be the paradigm for the priesthood of the
believer; the believer's experience, the nature of the sacrifice, and spiritual
service will transform persons within biblical boundaries as the gospel crosses
new frontiers of time and culture. Paul demonstrated that there was a great
deal of flexibility within those boundaries.

Jesus and Paul also demonstrated that, within religion, human traditions
develop that will be tested and corrected at the crossroads of faith, time,
culture, and experience. In this process, the believer is not to be conformed
to the pattern of this world—as J. B. Phillips translated, "Don't let the world
around you squeeze you into its own mold!" (Rom. 12:2 Phillips).[23] For Paul,

20. Schreiner states, "The word 'bodies' here refers to the whole person and stresses that
consecration to God involves the whole person. . . . Genuine commitment to God embraces every
area of life, and includes the body in all of its particularity and concreteness" (*Romans*, 644).
Moo suggests that "Paul probably intends to refer to the entire person, with special emphasis
on that person's interaction with the world. Paul is making a special point to emphasize that
the sacrifice we are called on to make requires a dedication to the service of God in the harsh
and often ambiguous life of this world" (*Romans*, 751).

21. If it is claimed that some of us (born after 1970) are the unwitting products of a feminist
agenda and environment, I can reply that Jesus's sacrificial death is the product of oppressive
institutional terrorism.

22. What has changed? For women, the change in the past 150 years has been dizzying. A
new map has been established through a proven track record involving possibilities in society
and in evangelicalism, roles in the church and parachurch ministries. Why has the change occurred? The last fifty years have seen progressive corrections of myths and folklore about women
in terms of intellectual and physical abilities, corrections based on statistics. Coeducation has
played a crucial role: doors to higher education slowly opened, and women operate as peers
in the classroom. Women's attendance in seminary has undergone a revolution. When women
take traditional biblical studies and ministry courses such as Hebrew and Greek, exegesis,
hermeneutics, and homiletics, the professors often perceive that they excel.

23. However, Elisabeth Elliot applies "Don't let the world squeeze you into its own mold" to
resisting feminist theology, avoiding self-assertion, and embracing a feminine role ("The Essence
of Femininity: A Personal Perspective," in *Recovering Biblical Manhood and Womanhood: A
Response to Evangelical Feminism*, ed. John Piper and Wayne Grudem [Wheaton: Crossway,
1991], 394–99, 532). I have trouble with her appeal to a jungle tribe's view of gender roles as an

his encounter with Jesus Christ resulted in nonconformity to the patterns of the world that surrounded him—not only the patterns of Greco-Roman culture and the patterns of Judaism, but also the patterns of Jewish Christianity. When Paul urged his churches to follow him as he followed Christ, he modeled a life that held few shibboleths, and none that he was unwilling to leave behind. He was a person who broke the molds.

A call for a man to place his body on the altar looks entirely different in the twenty-first century from how it looked in the first century. A man's spiritual service of worship legitimately reflects vast changes in government, technology, finances, vocation, and lifestyle. The transformation to which God calls us continually moves beyond cultural patterns that constrain us. A call for women to place who they are on the altar should also look significantly different now than it has at various points in the past. A growing number of women are born and bred to reflect a significantly expanded set of personal potentials and possibilities for a number of different reasons. Some women have subsequently been educated, tested, trained, certified, elected, and proved to function in an expanding variety of different roles of responsibility and leadership.[24] Within those accomplishments, women who are believers are able to take verses seriously such as "Whatever you do, do everything for the glory of God" (1 Cor. 10:31 NRSV); this is not invariably about self-assertion or selfish ambition. Women's personalities, abilities, potential, and development are not inherently broken; they are an essential part of each woman's authenticity. This is what a woman is required to place at God's disposal at the altar, and this feeds into a woman's measure of faith with which she thinks about her gifts. As in the story of the talents in Matthew 25:14–28, women are under a sacred obligation to use all of what God has given them and every advantage to serve him. Women must resist any effort to squeeze their strengths, gifts, and abilities into a mold that hides them in the ground and quenches the Holy Spirit. A woman's God-given role and service in the twenty-first century must be constructed by the dynamic transformation of Romans 12:1–2 rather than conformity to a pattern that has been constructed by religious tradition from another time, place, and culture.[25] This is the only

---

indication of their importance, but she found a voice, and her ability to speak to crowds and write prolifically was an illustration of change.

24. According to Neela Banerjee, women now make up 51 percent of the students in divinity school ("Clergywomen Find Hard Path to Bigger Pulpit," New York Times, August 26, 2006, http://www.nytimes.com/2006/08/26/us/26clergy.html?th&emc=th&_r=0). However, the 51 percent includes students in all seminary degree programs, not just the master of divinity degree.

25. In specific dialogue with Dorothy Patterson, who states, "I knew that [the Bible] was authoritative and, if authoritative, true, regardless of culture or customs, or perceived relevance. . . . [God] expected me to adapt myself to the consistently and clearly presented principles found in

way we will "discern what is the will of God—what is good and acceptable and perfect" (Rom. 12:2 NRSV).

7.1.5 Romans 12:3–5: The Call to Diverse Service in Unity

The next verses, Romans 12:3–5, emphasize unity in diversity. They display additional principles for navigating a believer's calling. Again, this is clearly addressed to every member of the community. As Thomas Schreiner observes, "Every believer has been given a measure of faith and is called on to estimate himself or herself in accord with this apportioned faith."[26] Each believer is to think soberly and sensibly in regard to one's own gift. In addition, believers have different gifts "according to the grace given to us" (Rom. 12:6a NRSV); thus we should expect to see variety among the church members: prophesying, serving (ministry as a deacon),[27] teaching, exhorting, giving, leading, and showing mercy (Rom. 12:6–8). The other lists of gifts in 1 Corinthians 12:28 and Ephesians 4:11 have some overlap but also additional gifts, so that this is a representative variety. Note also that leadership gifts and verbal gifts are distributed by God's grace, and according to 1 Corinthians 12:11 they are specifically distributed by the Holy Spirit. Paul is urging each believer to evaluate personal gift and calling realistically according to his or her *faith* and *grace*; that is, there is a responsibility to determine ministry through the experience of the recipient via observation and careful consideration. In other words, it is up to each individual to identify one's own calling, and there is no calling without experience.

A man's personal call to the pastorate and other ministry is treated with due respect and seriousness in the seminaries. There is a reluctance to question or contradict a man's sense of his own call, even if he appears to lack the gifts and social skills deemed appropriate for ministry. John Piper serves as an excellent paradigm for a call to the pastorate: He *sensed* a call to ministry

His Word. God did not expect me to interpret His principles in light of my gifts and intellect, but He admonished me 'to be conformed to the likeness of His Son' (Romans 8:29), including gifts and intellect and creativity" ("The High Calling of Wife and Mother in Biblical Perspective," in Piper and Grudem, *Recovering Biblical Manhood and Womanhood*, 365). Patterson is seeing a false dichotomy between herself as God's new creation in a specific time and place and the image of Jesus Christ. Paul's customs, culture, perceived relevance, gifts, intellect, training, and creativity all contributed to his call and his radical fulfillment of it.

26. Schreiner, *Romans*, 651.

27. Moo states, "Probably, then, Paul thinks of a specific gift or service that qualifies a person to fill the office of 'deacon,' a ministry that apparently involved especially organizing and providing for the material needs of the church" (*Romans*, 766). Some argue that "deacon" implies an office, but Jewett suggests that a specialized sense of office is doubtful, and it focuses on the function rather than the functionary (*Romans*, 749).

while he was at Wheaton, which he describes as "my heart almost bursting with longing."[28] Then, in 1980, he *felt* an *irresistible* call to preach.[29] When a man negotiates his call to ministry, he utilizes emotions and experience in accordance with his faith and the grace that he is given.[30]

However, the role of variety and experience in the realization of calling is either explicitly or effectively discounted for women. When a woman determines her call by the same model, using the same criteria, if she comes to the same conclusion as Piper, she is told that her navigational system is broken. A woman is often told that it is invalid for her to utilize experience and emotions in discovering her call, since she may come up with the "wrong" conclusion.[31] This is ironic, because women learn the procedure directly from the unified witness, teaching, and example of men in the pulpit, adult Sunday school teachers, professors of Bible classes, theologians, and writers of commentaries. The procedure and criteria appear to reflect a biblical understanding of Romans 12:1–8, and other passages. However, many traditions will restrict the potential possibilities for women, and have a range of restrictions based on the implications of the prohibitions against women in 1 Timothy 2:12, the command for women to be silent in the church in 1 Corinthians 14:34, and the subordinate role of women. Therefore, it has been assumed that it is not biblical for a woman to be called for serving as a deacon, teaching, exhorting (men), or leading—and in many traditions prophesying would be ruled out. Giving would also be a questionable call, since a husband would (traditionally) be responsible for her finances. In the end, if a woman has attempted to submit to traditional authorities, she may be completely sure that her call is biblical only if her heart leads her to show mercy—unless her church is also hostile to the social gospel.[32] Thus there has not been much variety or rich

28. John Piper, *The Supremacy of God in Preaching* (Grand Rapids: Baker, 1990), 18.
29. For John Piper's books (some of them coauthored), see http://www.desiringgod.org/books.
30. This is not far from the Wesleyan Quadrilateral, where theology's sources are Scripture, tradition, reason, and experience.
31. Grudem states, "God never calls people to disobey His Word. Our decision on this matter must be based on the objective teaching of the Bible, not on some person's experience, no matter how godly or sincere that person is" (*Evangelical Feminism*, 481). Of course, an experiential response to Rom. 12:1–8 where a woman determines that she is called to be a leader is directly based on obedience to the Bible. Grudem does not go so far as to invalidate the experience completely, but he says that there would be a mistake in understanding the meaning of those experiences.
32. Even the gift of "showing mercy" has had a spotty reputation among conservative traditions. During much of the twentieth century, the "social gospel" and social justice were rejected by traditions that claimed to have a very high view of Scripture. Thomas Schreiner finds that relational and nurturing character qualities consistent with showing mercy make a person susceptible to deception and more liable to doctrinal error and heresy ("An Interpretation of

diversity in opportunities for women to serve in the church; the metaphor of the diversity of the body in 1 Corinthians 12:12–31 has been drastically reduced for more than half the congregation,[33] though the range, variety, and significance of gifts are a primary point in all the passages on gifting.[34]

If a woman's experience and emotions are negated in this process of obedience to God, not only is any sense of call compromised, but also the essence of following Jesus and the imitation of Christ become qualitatively different than they are for a man. When experience, emotions, and personal responsibility are removed from the equation, she must go to an authority or mediator to perceive her call for her, to hear God's voice, and to figure out what her function is. Each woman is incapacitated in determining her gift according to the grace given to her. The "plain" sense of Romans 12:1–8 is canceled.

In practice, a man's experience and emotions are treated as normative in his call to ministry, but a woman's emotions and experience are treated as suspect and can be invalidated if they lead her to a place that is outside of wherever the male authorities draw the line delimiting the appropriate sphere of ministry for women. Historically, the line has been drawn in every conceivable place. But, in the two passages that explicitly address the basis of the function of ministry, there are two primary determinants of gifts and function: the realistic estimation of the individual, and the Holy Spirit, who gives gifts to every individual just as he determines (1 Cor. 12:11). This argues against the theology of "drawing a line" and creating a priori rules of how God works that cancel out the clear theology of the passages on gifting in regard to women.

The consequences of "drawing the line" across the application of these passages to women is that a "hermeneutic of suspicion" is pervasive among conservative evangelicals, and it has been used to interpret and judge a woman's identity and abilities as well as her behavior. Women who are extroverts may be suspect and considered unbecoming.[35] That which is pragmatically prohibited

---

1 Timothy 2:9–15: A Dialogue with Scholarship," in *Women in the Church: A Fresh Analysis of 1 Timothy 2:9–15*, ed. Andreas J. Köstenberger, Thomas R. Schreiner, and H. Scott Baldwin [Grand Rapids: Baker, 1995], 145).

33. In some traditions that mandate women's silence in the church service, one might say that the church has determined that half the body must function as an ear.

34. As Jewett observes concerning Rom. 12:6, "Some of the gifts mentioned have particular relevance for the Spanish mission project, but their main function is to stand for the hitherto unacknowledged range and significance of the charismatic gifts collectively present in the various Roman congregations" (*Romans*, 746).

35. A woman speaker on the radio was teaching teenage girls, on the basis of Prov. 31, that they should not be extroverts if they want to cultivate a biblical femininity. Perhaps she was simply addressing rude and aggressive behavior, but extroversion and introversion should be understood as legitimate personality traits for both genders, which are relatively essential to the

tends to flow to the least common denominator, as if it would be safer to apply a more severe restriction of women than one's own theology would warrant.

As far as men are concerned, their participation in the exclusion of women from leadership circles, church positions, and places of influence, and the rationale behind it, should be a matter of deep concern if we are to honor Romans 12:3–6. James Dunn suggests, "The emphatic warning against inflated thinking (v. 3) recalls the similar warning against Gentile presumption in 11:7–24 (particularly 11:20), but also the similar theme of the earlier diatribes against Jewish presumption (chaps. 2–4): the 'us' over 'them' attitude which Paul saw as the heart of Jewish failure and as a potential danger for Gentile Christians must not be allowed to characterize the eschatological people of God."[36] An "us" over "them" attitude similar to that which characterized relationships between the Jews and gentiles is embedded in much of the language, the inferences, and the outcomes of those who teach that men are to have priority and authority over women in the church. Men in positions of authority and influence in the church should seriously consider the fact that Paul asserted that the same issues were at play among males and females, as well as slaves and free, as there were among the Jews and gentiles (Gal. 3:28). Claims of priority and entitlement should sound completely out of place in the light of the Pauline corpus. The criteria of emotions and personal experience that are referred to in Romans 12:1–8 are recognized as an indication that men are called to the ministry and positions in the church. Therefore, it is problematic to claim that the same experiences and emotions of women are invalidated as criteria for their call to ministry and positions in the church, since the passage addresses all believers.

7.1.6 Romans 12:6b–8: Gifts Given to Meet the Needs of the Body

When the different lists of spiritual gifts are compared, a direct relationship between the gifts and the function of leaders or offices in the church is seen. Romans 12:6–8 lists seven gifts: prophecy, serving (διακονία), teaching, exhorting, giving, leadership (which has a lexical association with elders and deacons in 1 Tim. 3:4, 12; cf. 1 Thess. 5:12), and mercy. This is not an exhaustive list. In 1 Corinthians 12 we find a somewhat different list, which includes apostles, prophets, teachers, miracle workers, healing, service (helps), administration, tongues, interpretation of tongues, wisdom, knowledge, and faith. Ephesians 4:11 adds two more gifts: apostles, prophets, evangelists, pastors, and teachers,

---

person's identity. Each trait may be identified with inappropriate behavior, and extroversion is consistent with the profile of the woman in Prov. 31.

36. Dunn, *Romans 9–16*, WBC 38B (Nashville: Nelson, 1988), 720.

and specifies that these gifts are given to prepare God's people for service so that the body of Christ may be built up (4:12). In 1 Corinthians 12:21–26, Paul says explicitly that the gifts are provided so that one part of the body cannot say to the others, "I have no need of you," and that God has combined the members of the body so that greater honor should be given to the parts that lack it.

When a man looks at Romans 12:6–8, he sees a nonexhaustive list of possibilities through which he may interpret himself and his calling. They are written to suggest virtually unlimited opportunities of application. When a young woman who has not been coached in the traditions that restrict women reads Romans 12 for the first time, in the light of her life's potentials and possibilities, she responds with the same uninhibited faith that God may use her in any one of these categories, because she sees women functioning in similar ways all around her. Women's core competencies, personalities, and paths are as varied, distinctive, and unique among one another as are men's.

However, the application of these passages to women has had a spotty history. It has often been asserted that giftedness follows gender lines, but that tends to be a one-sided argument, since there are never any restrictions placed on men, nor are any gifts identified that are exclusively feminine. Men are free to consider any gift as a possibility and are particularly commended if they serve in the nursery or wash the dishes after the church potluck. On the other hand, there has historically been flat denial that a woman could exercise the majority of these gifts in the church based on whether they involve authority, speaking, or passing judgment, based on 1 Timothy 2:12.[37] Others acknowledge that a woman could be gifted in teaching but restrict her to exercising the gifts with women and children or for evangelism.[38] However, the gifts are specifically given to build the body, the church; therefore, the general restriction cannot be a norm that one draws from the passage.

Men are saying to gifted women, "I have no need of you," which is a violation of Scripture (1 Cor. 12:21–26). Consequently, women who show themselves to be gifted in areas other than service, showing mercy, giving, and faith are prey to being underutilized, misused, or even treated with hostility. The principles governing the exercise of spiritual gifts are clear when applied to men, but they are not understood or applied with any rigor or consistency to women.

On the other hand, some churches have recognized women's giftedness in a variety of areas and fully utilize women in the ministries of the church.

37. Exercising gifts "in the church" refers to Paul's description of the exercise of gifts in 1 Cor. 12 and 14, as opposed to contexts that did not exist in the first-century church, such as teaching children in Sunday school.
38. Grudem, *Evangelical Feminism*, 452.

However, if they draw the line before allowing the woman to exercise the kind of authority that a man with the same responsibility would exercise, they open the door to certain forms of exploitation. Women respond to the church's needs by becoming volunteers, staff, and home missionaries. Some of the most sacrificial church ministries that I know of have been run by women. If the church constricts their role, then the congregation can believe that they have held the biblical line, but, consequently, they may also take advantage of women because of their lack of power in the church structure. There have been cases of sexual harassment and spiritual abuse in some churches because the women are relatively defenseless against those who are in authority.[39]

Thomas Schreiner says, "Once believers have identified their gifts they should strive to excel in the gifts they have been given and devote themselves to the body by exercising those gifts. . . . They should not spend too much time in serving when their primary gift is teaching."[40] Most women in conservative churches who are gifted in the "gray zones" that involve leadership, teaching, or other verbal gifts probably find this principle nearly impossible to follow; they fall into the practice of concentrating on ancillary roles of practical service, such as serving in the nursery and offering hospitality. It is the path of least resistance, and they are performing the actions that are most appreciated.

7.1.7 Summary

I have shown how using a certain interpretation of 1 Timothy 2:12 as an interpretive grid lays a veil over other passages; for example, women are not permitted to interpret or apply Romans 12:1–8 in the same way as the men who teach them and lead them by example. In essence, they are not allowed sound hermeneutical principles that are applied consistently. A passage becomes something else; in some cases, based on gender considerations, the principle that is asserted is the exact opposite of the one that the passage espouses or illustrates. The priesthood of the believer becomes circumscribed so that it has nothing to do with the function of ministry. A man knows that he is created in Christ Jesus for good works. He knows that his calling is based on who God has created him to be in terms of his personality and spiritual gifting/skills,

---

39. This is one of the most tragic outcomes that I have seen in a context where women have had many opportunities for ministry, but leadership and authority are reserved for males. It constitutes a system in which women lose every conflict regardless of the righteousness or justice of the given situation. Elders should receive support from each other, and accusations against elders should not be easily accepted (1 Tim. 5:19), but when support is consistently given to men who are in conflict with women and where there is exclusively male leadership, the situation is toxic.

40. Schreiner, *Romans*, 657.

where he has been, and where he is now in his life journey. A woman's sense of calling can be regarded with suspicion and hostility if, for example, she has a leadership personality and/or a significant set of leadership skills and abilities. The starting point for a man's call is his own discernment together with his emotions and experience. However, a woman's discernment, emotion, and experience must be tested and qualified against possible prohibitions. A man can approach spiritual gifts as spiritual possibilities, but a woman may be unsure of what she is allowed to do. She becomes immobilized.

I have consistently said that it is an *interpretation* of 1 Timothy 2:12 that is inappropriately applied as a hermeneutic grid on these passages. I question its use in interpreting Romans 12:1–8 on spiritual gifts because the Roman church could not have used it as an interpretive grid. Furthermore, I repeat that we should not base a doctrine on one verse, we should not base a doctrine on a verse or passage that carries interpretive problems, and we should give preference to the clearer passage in Romans and let it assist us in interpreting the less clear passage in 1 Timothy. It is a serious enough problem that sound hermeneutical principles are not being applied consistently to Romans 12:1–8 in regard to women. This results in some serious theological ramifications. Is this inconsistent application bringing life, freedom, and grace to women in Christ, or is it placing women under law? The rejection of human restrictions on the practice of faith is central to the Pauline corpus: "It is for freedom that Christ has set us free. Stand firm, then, and do not let yourselves be burdened again by a yoke of slavery" (Gal. 5:1). If Paul was so deeply troubled about Judaizers requiring circumcision, what would he think about the intentional restraint and immobilization of the Spirit's gifts for ministry? Pragmatically, the use of 1 Timothy 2:12 involves a sort of "hermeneutic imperialism" that cancels out the clear teaching of Romans 12:1–8; 1 Corinthians 12:1–29; and Ephesians 4:7–13. The effects of this practice result in complex patterns of injustice. Ultimately, it generates a different theology for women than for men.

7.2 The Relationship between Marriage and Calling

Sometimes the call to spiritual service in the church is confused with the woman's call to vocation. One of the interpretations of 1 Timothy 2:15, given by Thomas Schreiner, is that the phrase "a woman will be saved through childbirth" indicates that women will experience eschatological salvation by functioning in their God-given role of wife and mother.[41] He treats "childbearing"

41. Schreiner writes, "Women, Paul reminds his readers, will experience eschatological salvation by adhering to their proper role, which is exemplified in giving birth to children"

as a synecdoche for the appropriate role for women. Schreiner sees a parallel between the woman's "domestic and maternal roles" and the man's role of teaching and exercising authority in the church. He argues that these roles are mutually exclusive in that "a woman should not violate her role by teaching or exercising authority over a man."[42] Schreiner claims this does not mean that a woman is saved by good works, but that women will not be saved if they do not practice good works such as "bear[ing] children in accord with their proper role," which is the evidence that salvation is genuine.[43] He suggests that 1 Timothy 4:11–16 is a parallel, where Paul instructs Timothy, "Pay close attention to yourself and to your teaching; continue in these things, for in doing this you will save both yourself and your hearers" (1 Tim. 4:16 NRSV). Schreiner claims, "What Paul means is that abiding in godly virtues and apostolic instruction are the necessary evidences that one has been saved."[44]

The first problem with Schreiner's argument is that the woman's supposed vocational domestic and maternal roles drawn from Genesis 2–3 would be parallel to the man's vocational role. However, it is explicit in the context that man's vocational role was farming, not teaching and exercising authority in spiritual service.[45] There are additional questions arising from Schreiner's analysis that concern the topic of gender and call.

- Does "childbearing" correlate as a function with men teaching and leading?
- Is "childbearing" or the process of childbirth an appropriate synecdoche for the role for women?
- Does Paul commend women for functioning in their role of wife and mother?
- Does Paul explicitly teach that a woman's choice to marry and to function as a wife and mother is the best context to provide evidence that salvation is genuine?

("Interpretation of 1 Timothy 2:9–15," in Köstenberger and Schreiner, *Women in the Church*, 120).

42. Ibid., 118.
43. Ibid.
44. Ibid., 119.
45. If being a wife and mother is the proper role for a woman based on Gen. 1–3, then the proper role for a man is farming, made clear by the instructions in the garden (Gen. 2:15, 19–20) and a description of the consequences of the fall (3:17–19). The narrative depicts agriculture as Adam's vocation. Nothing is said in Gen. 2–3 about aspects of spiritual service, which Paul distinguishes from one's breadwinning vocation. Beyond that, the strict division of labor in primitive rural agriculture is implausible; women and children labor on farms with the husband and father. Proverbs 31 describes the virtuous woman buying a field and planting a vineyard. In times of war, the women take over the farming completely.

These questions highlight one of the many serious interpretive problems in 1 Timothy 2:8–15.

7.2.1 Women and "Childbearing" versus Men Teaching and Leading

Would "childbearing," which refers to the actual process of giving birth to a child,[46] be an appropriate Pauline description for a woman's function in "a public worship context" or a woman's function in the Christian community?[47] This is an important question, because most analyses of 1 Timothy 2:8–15 say that the passage provides instructions for public worship. If the text were taken at face value and one accepted Schreiner's definition of the terms and the context, this would indicate that women should not be teaching or exercising authority in the public worship service, but instead they should somehow be going through the process of giving birth in the context of the worship service. Schreiner attempts to sidestep a literal understanding of the text according to his own terms by suggesting that the physical process of giving birth to a child is a synecdoche for the woman's role that differentiates women from men who teach and lead.

The assumption of biological essentialism in determining two sets of functions for humanity was common among the Greek philosophers and in the Greco-Roman culture. However, Paul's description of service in the church defies the culture's beliefs about essentialism as far as race, slaves, and women. While he correlates the head-body relationship of the husband and wife to Christ and the church, the distinction between male and female immediately breaks down in relationship to Christ. Christ is the head, and Paul represents the believers literally and metaphorically by a rich diversity and variety in the measure of faith assigned by God, gifts, services, activities, and body parts (Rom. 12:3; 1 Cor. 12:4–6, 12–27; Eph. 4:11), all of which cannot and must not be reduced to two sets of distinct roles, which is Paul's primary point in 1 Corinthians 12. Furthermore, the function of each part of the body is determined directly by the Holy Spirit, not by any biological essentialism reckoned as inherent in the Hellenistic beliefs about race or gender or social status. In addition, the literal process of a woman's childbirth is not analogous to the spiritual gifts of teaching and leading. The process of giving birth is a bodily function that neither directly edifies the church nor is done on behalf

---

46. Schreiner, "Interpretation of 1 Timothy 2:9–15," in Köstenberger and Schreiner, *Women in the Church*, 116. Schreiner asserts, "The noun τεκνογονίας emphasizes the actual giving birth to a child, not the result or effect of childbirth." He takes this position when he disputes the view that 1 Tim. 2:15 refers to Mary giving birth to Jesus.

47. Ibid., 91.

of the church (cf. 1 Cor. 14:3–5, 17). The corresponding functions of the man would be the ejaculation of sperm in terms of a bodily function, and as far as suffering pain and the threat of death for the sake of the existence and growth of the family, it might be comparable to a man fighting a battle in which he lays down his life to protect his home.

7.2.2 The Connotations of Childbirth in the Pauline Corpus

Childbirth and the natural functions of being a mother have both negative and positive connotations in the Pauline literature. The process of giving birth is an inappropriate synecdoche for either a woman's role or her function in public service in 1 Timothy 2:8–15, because the references to the fall remind us that negative effects on the process of childbirth and the increase in the number of births are primary consequences given to women in Genesis 3:16. In 1 Timothy 2:14 the reader is directed to Genesis 3 by the summary of the deception and transgression of Eve. Therefore, the process of childbirth has the negative connotations of the threat of pain and death. It would not serve well as a positive summary of a woman's contribution (particularly in that context), and something that is commonly referred to as "a curse" can hardly be analogous to a man's exercise of his spiritual gift.

On the other hand, Paul uses the process of childbirth and related bodily functions as metaphors for service, but they describe his nurturing function as an apostle who was a leader and a teacher. He compares his painful relationship with the Galatian churches to childbirth: "My little children, for whom I am again in the pain of childbirth until Christ is formed in you . . ." (Gal. 4:19 NRSV). He compares his service and nurture of the Thessalonians to a wet nurse or a lactating mother:

> As you know and as God is our witness, we never came with words of flattery or with a pretext for greed; nor did we seek praise from mortals, whether from you or from others, though we might have made demands as apostles of Christ. But we were gentle among you, like a nurse tenderly caring for her own children. So deeply do we care for you that we are determined to share with you not only the gospel of God but also our own selves, because you have become very dear to us. (1 Thess. 2:5–8 NRSV)

Paul notably finds that women provide a better model for apostolic leadership than the typical male model of leadership in the Greco-Roman culture, which he indicates is characterized by flattery, greed, people-pleasing, and a lack of gentleness. A Thessalonian reader would not conclude that women would violate their feminine role by assuming a Pauline style of leadership. On the other hand, one may conclude from Paul's criticisms of his competition in leadership throughout the Corinthian correspondence, and particularly his description of the "superapostles" in 2 Corinthians 11, that those who embraced and exemplified the typical male model of leadership in the Greco-Roman culture should be disqualified from leadership.

7.2.3 The Nature of Paul's Commendation of Women

In the rest of the Pauline corpus, Paul usually does not commend individual women for performing stereotypical women's functions, as was common in the culture. In the Greco-Roman culture, though there were exceptions, it was not considered proper to give women public recognition.[48] Therefore, a woman could accomplish feats and function in a variety of roles for which a man would be commended, but on her tombstone, she would be commended for conforming to the stereotypical roles of wife and mother and for spinning wool. However, Paul is countercultural because he commends women in the same way as men and for the same things for which he commends men.[49] Romans 16 is far more significant than is sometimes recognized, not just for assigning church offices to women, but also for the number of women mentioned by name and the nature of the commendations.[50] Not only are individual women commended by name as a deacon (v. 1), a patron (v. 2), a fellow prisoner (v. 7), and an apostle (v. 7),[51] but also a number of them are

48. Inscriptions give honor to women patrons, for example. This simply shows the difference between the ideal and the reality.

49. Jewett writes, "The crucial role of feminine leadership visible . . . in Romans 16 is an impressive indication of the social revolution associated with the early church, quite apart from the Pauline missionary movement" (*Romans*, 961).

50. Jewett states, "In view of the fact that so many women are included on this list, it is clear that this mutuality [in granting recognition to those greeted] extends across sexual barriers. In this context, to greet is to honor and welcome one another" (ibid., 952). J. E. Lendon explains the role of greetings in an honor-shame culture: "When one man honoured another in the Roman world, he granted him a quantum of honour, which, provided that the bestower was sufficiently distinguished himself, the aristocratic community at large then accepted that the recipient possessed. . . . A great man's laudatory remarks—or speeches—in public, his greetings on the street, prompt admission at his levee, his kisses, all such things were honours, closely watched by contemporaries, and added to the recipients' honour" (*Empire of Honour: The Art of Government in the Roman World* [Oxford: Clarendon, 1997], 48–49).

51. Every one of these terms has been criticized, and they are often translated so that they do not appear to refer to women in church offices; yet, such criticism and translations have been theologically driven by the assumption that Paul would not permit women to fill these offices. For example, Jewett states, "Although earlier commentaries interpret the term διάκονος as a subordinate role, it now appears more likely that she functioned as the leader of the congregation" (*Romans*, 944). "The modern scholarly controversy over [Junia] rests on the presumption

commended as fellow workers (συνεργός)[52] and those who work hard (κοπιάω)[53] (vv. 3, 6, 12; cf. Phil. 4:3).[54] In Rome, Paul commends only women for working hard, though κοπιάω is a word that he most often uses for his own apostolic work. It is highly significant that Paul states in 1 Corinthians 16:15–16 (cf. 1 Thess. 5:12): "Now, brothers and sisters, you know that members of the household of Stephanas were the first converts in Achaia, and they have devoted themselves to the service of the saints; I urge you to put yourselves at the service [ὑποτάσσησθε: be subject, subordinate yourselves] of such people, and of everyone who works and toils [τῷ συνεργοῦντι καὶ κοπιῶντι] with them" (NRSV).

This demonstrates that when Paul applies leadership terms to women, he expects the churches to "submit" to them. Paul even commends Priscilla, together with her husband, Aquila, for risking her life (literally, "neck") on Paul's behalf (Rom. 16:4), an act that is typical of male heroes, including Jesus Christ (Eph. 5:23), Paul (2 Tim. 4:17), and Epaphroditus (Phil. 2:30), and is to be reciprocated in the church with honor and recognition.[55] The exception is his commendation of Rufus's mother for being a mother to him (Rom. 16:13), but as seen in 1 Thessalonians 2:7, the literal function as a mother is not mutually exclusive to leadership: it rather indicates that she had given Paul hospitality and patronage by treating him like he was one of the family.[56] Therefore we may conclude that in the Pauline corpus, particularly in the *Hauptbriefe*, either Paul does not believe that women being in leadership in the church violates their role as women, or he is not concerned if they are acting contrary to cultural expectations. Certainly he is not concerned about violating cultural mores by giving them recognition. Consequently, Schreiner's interpretation of 1 Timothy 2:15 about teaching and leading violating a woman's role throws the author of the Pastoral Epistles into contradiction with the evidence in the *Hauptbriefe*.

---

that no woman could rank as an apostle, and thus that the accusative form must refer to a male by the name of Junias or Junianus" (ibid., 961).

52. The noun συνεργός is used 12× in the Pauline corpus for members of the Pauline ministry team.

53. The verb κοπιάω is used 14× in the Pauline corpus for ministry/service, with one or two exceptions. But it is used most often for Paul's own apostolic work on behalf of the churches.

54. In Rom. 16, three women are commended for working hard; in Phil. 4:3, two women are commended and referred to as fellow workers. In the context, the two women were exhorted to get along with each other, but Paul softens the correction with his strong commendation.

55. Jewett argues that risking one's neck alludes explicitly to risking death by decapitation (*Romans*, 958).

56. Ibid., 969. See also 1 Tim. 5:2, where Paul tells Timothy to treat older women or female elders as mothers, which involves respect, obedience, and honor. In the same way, he is to treat older men or male elders like fathers.

7.2.4 Marriage and the Lord's Affairs

Schreiner correctly connects the statement in 1 Timothy 2:15 with the false teaching among the women and the later directions for widows to remarry. But is he correct in understanding Paul as saying that adhering to the "God-given role of wife and mother" is the way in which women experience salvation?[57] Is this consistent with the teaching in 1 Timothy or the rest of the Pauline corpus? The elephant in the room is the apparent contradiction between Paul's instructions in 1 Timothy that widows should marry and his desire expressed in 1 Corinthians that widows should not remarry. The instructions to Timothy concerning the widows' remarriage are in 1 Timothy 5:14: "So I would have younger widows marry, bear children, and manage their households, so as to give the adversary no occasion to revile us" (NRSV).

Although this verse may appear to support Schreiner's interpretation of 1 Timothy 2:15, it is cited by many as a blatant contradiction to Paul's instructions in 1 Corinthians 7, where he advises the unmarried and the widows not to marry because they will be obligated to please their husbands instead of the Lord (1 Cor. 7:32–35, 39–40):

> I want you to be free from anxieties. The unmarried man is anxious about the affairs of the Lord, how to please the Lord; but the married man is anxious about the affairs of the world, how to please his wife, and his interests are divided. And the unmarried woman and the virgin are anxious about the affairs of the Lord, so that they may be holy in body and spirit; but the married woman is anxious about the affairs of the world, how to please her husband. I say this for your own benefit, not to put any restraint upon you, but to promote good order and unhindered devotion to the Lord. . . . A wife is bound as long as her husband lives. But if the husband dies, she is free to marry anyone she wishes, only in the Lord. But in my judgment she is more blessed if she remains as she is. And I think that I too have the Spirit of God. (NRSV)

The contrast between the two sets of instructions is marked. It is particularly important for this study to observe that in 1 Corinthians 7, Paul specifically distinguishes between the role of wife and mother and "the affairs of the

---

57. Schreiner's proposal that "being saved by childbirth" means that women experience salvation by adhering to their role as wife and mother involves a great deal of inference and an even more questionable understanding of salvation. Schreiner's comparison with 1 Tim. 4:14–16 ("Interpretation of 1 Timothy 2:9–15," in Köstenberger and Schreiner, *Women in the Church*, 119) fails as a parallel, since in 1 Tim. 4:12–16, Paul's instructions to Timothy—on reading Scripture, preaching, teaching, and particularly paying attention to his life and doctrine—are central to Paul's statement to Timothy that he will save himself and others. This is not the same as the statement that women will be saved through a bodily function and pious behavior.

Lord."[58] His preference is that women, whether they are virgins or widows, stay unmarried so that they can devote themselves to "the affairs of the Lord" rather than pleasing a husband, which typically entails childbirth and running a home.

However, in 1 Corinthians 7:2, 8–9, he gives an important exception to his view that people are better off if they do not marry; he taught that in most cases, people should marry:

> But because of cases of sexual immorality, each man should have his own wife and each woman her own husband. . . . To the unmarried and the widows I say that it is well for them to remain unmarried as I am. But if they are not practicing self-control, they should marry. For it is better to marry than to be aflame with passion. (NRSV)

If people lack sexual self-control when they are single, they should get married, which ends up being the norm.[59] The situation concerning the widows in Ephesus is an example of a case in which people should marry. Conversely, in order to be blessed while single, one needs to concern oneself with the Lord's affairs, which amounts to a call to full-time service for a woman. For example, a true widow "has set her hope on God and continues in supplications and prayers night and day" (1 Tim. 5:5 NRSV).[60] A true widow is therefore occupied with the Lord's affairs—with pleasing the Lord (1 Cor. 7:32–35).

58. Because Paul distinguishes between "the affairs of the Lord" and the function of wife and mother, Schreiner's attempt to reconcile his view with 1 Cor. 7 is unconvincing: "Paul is hardly attempting to be comprehensive here. He has elsewhere commended the single state (1 Cor. 7). He selects childbearing because it is the most notable example of the divinely intended differences in role between men and women" (ibid., 118). Paul is not concerned with distinguishing gender differences in 1 Cor. 7. I maintain that in 1 Tim. 2:8–15, Paul is dealing with differences being manifested in false teaching and ethical behavior rather than creating or reinforcing differences. Men are exhibiting problematic behavior that is typical of men, and women/widows are exhibiting problematic behavior that is typical of women.

59. As David Garland says, "Paul's first reaction to the maxim in 7:1b reveals that he is no misogamist and that he has a realistic appraisal of human beings as sexual creatures. He recognizes that the sex drive is a powerful force that can pose a great danger if it is not properly harnessed" (*1 Corinthians*, BECNT [Grand Rapids: Baker Academic, 2003], 257).

60. George Knight interestingly sees the widow's supplications as personal in order to meet her own needs (*The Pastoral Epistles: A Commentary on the Greek Text*, NIGTC [Grand Rapids: Eerdmans, 1992], 219). Howard Marshall appears to be in agreement: "In the context the prayers would appear to be an expression of dependence on God rather than intercessions for the church" (*The Pastoral Epistles*, ICC [Edinburgh: T&T Clark, 1999], 588). However, is there any reason to limit a widow's prayer to concern for herself alone versus a pastoral concern for God's people (as in Samuel's obligation in 1 Sam. 12:23)? Marshall wishes to avoid any reciprocity for being on the widows' list, but is that a valid objection? Could not a woman see intercession for the people as part of her obligation and call, as Samuel did?

However, according to 1 Timothy 5:3–16, widows in Ephesus were exhibiting behavior that was not devout and lacked self-control. Certain circulating false teaching forbade sex and marriage, possibly with the goal of avoiding childbirth (4:3). Some widows were idle and going from house to house, gossiping and being busybodies; some were living for pleasure, and some had already turned away to "follow Satan" (5:15). Paul was convinced that a widow under the age of sixty would, in general, have sensual desires that make her want to marry. Therefore, he says that he does not want them to pledge themselves to full-time ministry by going on a list to receive church support. In view of the problematic ethical patterns among the widows at Ephesus, he says that he wants widows to marry, have children, and run a household.

His instructions to Timothy are basically the same as in 1 Corinthians 7:2, where he says that, in general and because of immorality, each man should have his own wife, and each woman should have her own husband. In 1 Timothy 5, he still leaves the possibility open for the truly pious widow who has a full-time devotion to service, but she will always be the exception, not the rule. However, Schreiner's interpretation of 1 Timothy 2:15 truly places 1 Timothy in conflict with 1 Corinthians 7 and even with the context of 1 Timothy, because he has incorrectly glamorized and prioritized the vocation of being a wife and mother in a way that is inconsistent with Pauline theology. According to him, a woman's choice to marry and be a wife and mother would be the best example of adhering to her proper role, in which she may show the evidence of salvation: she would therefore be saved through childbirth. However, Paul explicitly says, "When [the widows'] sensual desires alienate them from Christ, they want to marry" (1 Tim. 5:11 NRSV). This hardly refers to an ethical condition that reflects the evidence of salvation; it is similar to Paul's concession to marriage in 1 Corinthians 7:32–35, only it is more pejorative.[61] Marriage for Paul, whether in the *Hauptbriefe* or the Pastoral Epistles, is a distraction from service but a pragmatic necessity, given the reality of human sexuality.

7.2.5 Summary

Schreiner has suggested that a woman's adherence to her proper role is parallel to a man leading and teaching. In his view, however, the woman's "proper role" is equivalent to her vocation and normal responsibilities of functioning as

61. Marshall asserts that "their sexual impulses form a temptation that leads them from devotion to Christ. . . . This might mean that they fall into sexual sin[,] which is inconsistent with Christian ethics. But this is apparently excluded by the fact that they wish to marry . . . , unless the sin is entering into marriage with an unbeliever . . . , having made some kind of vow to serve Christ" (*Pastoral Epistles*, 599).

a wife, bearing children, and keeping house. Schreiner has confounded the Pauline categories by representing men's responsibilities in terms of their spiritual service and gifting by the Holy Spirit and representing women's responsibilities in terms of their typical vocation. The process of giving birth is a female bodily function, not a gift of the Spirit, and the process was negatively impacted as a consequence of the fall, which is the immediate context of 1 Timothy 2:15. The process of childbirth as constrained by the fall cannot serve as a synecdoche for a woman's spiritual responsibilities in the church, but when Paul's references to childbirth are positive, they are metaphors for his own apostolic ministry. Paul does not commend women for staying in their "proper role," but on the contrary, Paul states that marriage distracts women from the Lord's affairs, as it also does for men. Equating childbirth with ministry excludes women from functioning in the body of Christ as Paul describes in 1 Corinthians 12 and replaces it with the consequences of the fall.[62]

7.3 Women in Service or in Silence?

Within the most detailed description of each believer's manifestation of the Spirit through a variety of gifts and calling in 1 Corinthians 12–14, Paul directs women not to talk in church.[63] Historically, this has been taken to mean that women are not allowed to participate verbally in the worship service. Therefore, they would not be allowed to offer any service that is verbal or to lead in prayer while the church is gathered in worship. The injunction for women to keep silent is in 1 Corinthians 14:34–35 (but I include the context of v. 33):

> For God is not *a God* of confusion but of peace, as in all the churches of the saints. The women are to keep silent in the churches; for they are not permitted

62. Schreiner's suggestion that the process of childbirth represents a woman's role in a positive sense shows a lack of understanding and empathy concerning the terror that the process has held for women through most of history. Part of the reason why it is difficult to appreciate the disastrous consequences of the fall in childbirth is that modern medicine has brought so much of this aspect of women's lives under control. Western interpreters need to step outside of the realm of their own experience to connect with the perspectives, concerns, and real threats of the first century. See §4.2.2.3.

63. Philip Payne has convincingly argued that 1 Cor. 14:34–35 is an interpolation (*Man and Woman, One in Christ: An Exegetical and Theological Study of Paul's Letters* [Grand Rapids: Zondervan, 2009], 252–61; see also Payne, "Fuldensis, Sigla for Variants in Vaticanus, and 1 Cor. 14:34–35," *NTS* 41 [1995]: 240–62). Gordon Fee has similarly argued that it is an interpolation (*The First Epistle to the Corinthians*, NICNT [Grand Rapids: Eerdmans, 1987], 699). Their argument is not easily dismissed. Nevertheless, the text may be analyzed as a discourse, based on the extant manuscripts that we possess, with the caveat that this passage has evidence of significant interpretive text-critical issues in those manuscripts.

to speak, but are to subject themselves, just as the Law also says. If they desire to learn anything, let them ask their own husbands at home; for it is improper for a woman to speak in church. (NASB)[64]

However, the atomistic reading that women are not allowed to speak at all in the house church creates a number of problematic contradictions within the text of 1 Corinthians at several levels.[65] As interpreters have started to read the text itself more carefully within its immediate context and within the context of the entire discourse of 1 Corinthians, a growing consensus has it that the passage has been misunderstood and misapplied historically. This letter addresses a number of questions and problems that were occurring at Corinth, but we have the text only as one side of a dialogue.[66] If we try to understand 1 Corinthians 11:33–35 in terms of what was happening in the bigger picture, we need to create that bigger picture with a combination of the signals in the text, the way the text interprets itself, and relevant features in the culture. I will begin the discussion with an examination of the social context of the house church, next look at the issue of women/speech at the discourse level of 1 Corinthians, and proceed to look at relevant features in 1 Corinthians 12–14. Then I will consider the preceding verses in the passage in which the instructions about women occur in 14:26–33, and finally look at features within the text itself that constrain and clarify its meaning. In addition, I will examine the function of the concluding section in 14:36–40.

In many studies, interpreters assume that the relevant contexts for interpreting 1 Corinthians 14:34–35 lie in the household codes in Colossians 3:18 and Ephesians 5:22–24, and in the prohibitions in 1 Timothy 2:12.[67] However, it

64. Here I revert to a highly formal equivalent translation in order to avoid "spinning" the meaning of the passage, though I do support the CEB translation: "Like in all the churches of God's people, the women should be quiet during the meeting. They are not allowed to talk. Instead, they need to get under control, just as the Law says. If they want to learn something, they should ask their husbands at home. It is disgraceful for a woman to talk during the meeting."

65. An atomistic reading treats verses as if they are unconnected and sometimes as if the interpretation lies outside the passage. Some of our traditional understanding of principles in the Pauline Epistles has come from treating the letters as flat documents consisting of theology and rules; thereby the letters have been mined to create various systematic theologies that then impact the reading of the text, rather than the other way around.

66. As Anthony Thiselton acknowledges, "The translation and exegesis is immensely complex. Contextual factors are vital, including presuppositions about what the addressees were *assumed* to understand by language of which we know only Paul's part of the dialogue" (*The First Epistle to the Corinthians: A Commentary on the Greek Text*, NIGTC [Grand Rapids: Eerdmans, 2000], 1146, emphasis original). This is true particularly of letters.

67. See, e.g., D. A. Carson, "'Silent in the Churches': On the Role of Women in 1 Corinthians 14:33b–36," in Piper and Grudem, *Recovering Biblical Manhood and Womanhood*, 144, where the meaning of "subordinate" is linked to Ephesians and Colossians, and "permit" is linked

is the scholarly consensus that 1 Corinthians was written before the Prison Epistles and the Pastoral Epistles. Furthermore, the context in 1 Corinthians 14:34–35 is public worship, not the household. The prohibitions in 1 Timothy are not repeated here, though Paul's desire for a woman to learn in quietness and submission (or self-control) in 1 Timothy 2:11 is very similar. Thus 1 Corinthians 14:34–35 may provide an interpretive key for 1 Timothy 2:11–12, but it would be anachronistic to import information from 1 Timothy 2:11–12 into 1 Corinthians 14:34–35. Something written as much as nine or more years later cannot be assumed to be a relevant context. Rather, priority should be given to interpreting the passage in its immediate contexts, and understanding the terms "silence" and "submission" in 1 Corinthians 14:34–35 consistently with how those same terms are used and defined in the immediate context.

7.3.1 The Context of the House Church

Both scholars and laypeople often speak about worship services referred to in the Pauline corpus as if they were large groups in public meetings that took place in public buildings similar to a synagogue or a pagan temple; in fact, sometimes little differentiation is made between our own experience of church services and a church service in the first century. References and supplied subtitles speak of "public worship" as the context for passages such as 1 Corinthians 11, 1 Corinthians 12–14, and 1 Timothy 2:8–15. However, it is the scholarly consensus that the Pauline Christian communities worshiped in house churches. Therefore, corporate worship took place in a home, which was a domestic environment that lay within the woman's sphere of influence and responsibility. Early Christian corporate worship was not a private affair by modern standards, but primarily that is because of the different cultural standards for privacy and personal space. The home was part of the domestic sphere and definitely not public space in the sense of a forum or synagogue.[68] The use of the home and the central feature of the fellowship meal created an informal environment that contributed to unusual intimacy

---

with 1 Tim. 2:12. See also ibid., 152, where the passage is read as a restriction of women's authority in the light of 1 Tim. 2:12.

68. This interacts with David Balch and Carolyn Osiek's discussion of the first-century home and private and public space (*Families in the New Testament World: Households and House Churches* [Louisville: Westminster John Knox, 1997], 17). They point out the lack of privacy in the home and society, but the home was still a family environment. The concepts of "formal" and "less formal" worship or the "sacramental" and "nonsacramental" are closely associated with the concept of "public" versus "private." These concepts must be tested by the fact that the church's practices originate in a nonformal environment, though domestic worship certainly had a structure.

for the Christian worshipers.[69] To some extent, house churches were intimate
because the number of worshipers was limited by the size of the rooms; some
of the largest rooms might accommodate twelve to fifteen people reclining,
though it is possible that they would make adjustments to get more people
into the meeting.

The location of the church in the domestic sphere indicates that women
served in a number of functions. The operation of the church in the private
home and the sharing of the fellowship meal (cf. 1 Cor. 11:20–34) entailed
the exercise of hospitality, the preparation and serving of food, and possibly
other rituals of domestic worship that normally took place in the household.
The domestic arrangements of food preparation and service and any other
arrangements either were done by the woman/wife who managed the home
or were done under her direction. Domestic worship in both the Jewish and
gentile cultures included responsibilities and services that are comparable
to those performed by priests in public service in the Jewish temple. When
comparable rituals took place in the home (involving food associated with
worship, lighting candles, incense, purity regulations), normally they were
performed by women.[70] It was later, when worship was moved to public church
buildings, and particularly when Christianity was legalized, that rituals such
as the preparation and service of food (the Eucharist) became honorific privileges of position and power.[71]

Women who owned large homes were active in hosting house churches, as well
as in other aspects of work in the ministry. A case in point is that of Priscilla,
who was influential in ministry and teaching through offering hospitality to Paul

69. See Balch and Osiek's discussion of the symbolism of meals (ibid., 45–46). They conclude, "In ancient Mediterranean culture, the banquet represents prime space and time for the
symbolization of social relationships, both hierarchical and vertical, including those with the
deceased and with divinity. It is no wonder that it became an important locus for the symbolization of Christian social relationships" (ibid).

70. Yet the origins of the practice of the Eucharist/Communion are a meal in the home; the
preparation and service of meals was the work of women and slaves. The movement of Christian worship from private space to public space may have resulted in the removal of women
from certain functions that would have been a given in domestic worship. This is most simply
illustrated in the contrast between women's role in the preparation and serving of a common
meal, and then the replacement of a sacramental offering of the elements of the Eucharist by
a male priest. In Protestant circles, serving Communion has been rather zealously guarded as
a function for male deacons, who hold an honorific position in the churches. Men gradually
filled all functions and roles defined in public worship as "liturgical." This is partly because the
"role" of the Christian leader became equated with the identity of the male Levitical priests
who served in the temple priesthood.

71. The public worship that developed after the first century seems to be molded on a con-
flation of public practices in the Jewish temple and certain features of Greco-Roman public
worship rather than early domestic worship in the household.

and Apollos (Acts 18:1–3, 24–26). In addition, she and her husband hosted house
churches in their home in Rome, Ephesus, and most likely Corinth (Rom. 16:3;
1 Cor. 16:19). Chloe also seems to have led a house church in Corinth (1 Cor.
1:11). Nympha had a house church in her house, and no husband was named
(Col. 4:15). Lydia, the first convert mentioned in Europe, hosted Paul's mission
team and the house church in Philippi during Paul's second missionary journey
(Acts 16:14–15, 40). In addition, it is most likely that Phoebe also sponsored a
house church, and so she was referred to as a patron (Rom. 16:1–2). Women
who functioned as patrons and opened their homes and shared their table
and food with the Christian community were crucial to the churches' success,
and Paul showed his appreciation for their patronage and hard work.[72] Most
of the house churches were likely sponsored by couples, but even in that case,
the woman would be responsible for the food and arrangements, given the
definition of roles in the culture, but her inclusion at the table means that she
would participate in the conversation during the meal. In cases where women
were omitted from the conversation, either women or slaves would provide the
labor, but the women would be spatially segregated for the meal.[73]

So, when we read 1 Corinthians 14:33b–35, we should do so in the context of meeting in a private home, perhaps at the table of a woman such as
Priscilla, who is hosting the meeting by providing food, shelter, and comfort
for an intimate gathering of believers. In that role, she and Aquila would be
the "founders of the feast" and receive appropriate recognition and honor.
This was a prominent couple who had earned the gratitude of "all the gentiles," and Paul tended to place Priscilla's name first when he honored them
as a couple, perhaps because she excelled in offering hospitality effectively
in order to teach and preach the gospel (Rom. 16:3–5; cf. Acts 18:18–26).[74] If
they followed the Greco-Roman custom, they would preside over the group
that meets in their home, but the other women might have brought additional
food and probably would pitch in and work together on completing the meal,
organizing and serving it, and cleaning up, typically entertaining themselves

72. See Paul's honor and recognition of women for their work and leadership in Rom. 16;
Phil. 4:2–3.
73. In earlier Eastern Greek tradition, women would have been present with men only in
family circles and would be absent from formal dinners (David Balch, "Paul, Families, and
Households," in *Paul in the Greco-Roman World: A Handbook*, ed. J. Paul Sampley [Harrisburg,
PA: Trinity Press International, 2003], 274). However, Roman practice included women being
seated next to their husbands, and the fictive kinship relationship in the church community
leaves little doubt that women were included in the space and the conversation in Corinth.
74. On the other hand, it is often suggested that Priscilla had a higher social standing than
Aquila. However, in Acts 18:2, Luke introduces Aquila first. It is only later that the order of
the names is reversed.

and each other in the process, often loudly.[75] However, this is not just a dinner party, but rather a gathering that has rituals and an informal agenda that Paul describes in 1 Corinthians 14:26–33. There had to be order and the sharing of important content. This is the context in which Paul tells the women not to talk during church. We will look at additional relevant aspects of the women's culture when I examine the text more closely.

7.3.2 The Context of 1 Corinthians

Every verse in the Bible should be read in the context of the entire book in which it occurs. The entire book has a structure, and an integral part of understanding the message of the Bible is knowing how a given sentence, phrase, or word is functioning in the author's narrative or argument. Our primary interest should be in the main point, not in the supporting material.[76] Also, authors often define their terms and provide the context in which information must be understood. Words can mean many things, and only the context determines and selects which meaning is intended. The task of the reader is to understand the book as coherent communication.

7.3.2.1 First Corinthians 11: Appropriate Apparel

Much could be said about how the earlier part of the letter impacts the understanding of 1 Corinthians 14:33b–35, but I will focus on the most relevant material in 1 Corinthians 11:2–16. Usually the point of the passage is obscured in traditional interpretations by arguments about "head," assumptions about the meaning of the veil, and by the traditional application of the passage, which is well summarized (though not supported) by Kenneth Bailey:

This passage tells women that
1. they are to live under authority,
2. keep their heads covered in public, and
3. understand that they were created to serve men![77]

75. If it was the case that the "sisters" would work together in the house church, then in at least Roman domestic arrangements there would be movement of the women between the servile areas of the house and social area: "Servile areas of the house, rooms where cooking, washing, and working occurred, were socially 'dirty,' marginalized, pushed away to the far corners of otherwise beautiful spaces" (Balch, "Paul, Families, and Households," in Sampley, *Paul in the Greco-Roman World*, 273). Activity and talking in the servile areas of the house might reach a level of disruption in smaller homes.

76. In many ways, mining the biblical text to create systematic theology has distorted our understanding of the text.

77. Bailey, *Paul through Mediterranean Eyes: Cultural Studies in 1 Corinthians* (Downers Grove, IL: InterVarsity, 2011), 297.

However, whatever theology one constructs from the support material,[78] the main point of the passage is that believers should wear gender-appropriate apparel when leading or ministering during worship: when women lead the congregation in praying or prophesying, they should cover their heads; when men lead the congregation in praying or prophesying, they should not cover their heads. This passage in turn constrains 1 Corinthians 14:33b–35: when Paul tells women not to talk during church, he does not mean that women should not lead in prayer or exercise the spiritual gift of prophecy.[79] He has given the proper conditions under which leading in prayer and prophecy should take place, and both genders have restrictions.

7.3.2.2 FIRST CORINTHIANS 12–14: SPIRITUAL GIFTS

The section in which the instructions for women to be quiet are located is within 1 Corinthians 12–14, which is an extended discussion on spiritual gifts and their operation in the church. We have looked at Romans 12:1–8, all of which is relevant to our understanding of what would be meant when Paul instructs women not to talk during church. The instructions in 1 Corinthians 12–14 are even clearer and directly constrain and interpret the instructions to women in 1 Corinthians 14:34–35. While the instructions in Romans 12:1–8 emphasize the believer's responsibility to determine and exercise one's gift, the instructions in 1 Corinthians 12 emphasize how the congregation is to appropriately honor each individual's gift.

Much can be written on the content, but I will give a brief summary of relevant points in 1 Corinthians 12–14.

- The Spirit distributes a variety of gifts (12:4–6).
- Each believer has a particular manifestation of the Spirit that the Spirit decides to give to each one (12:7a, 11, 27).
- The manifestation of the Spirit is for the common good (12:7b).

---

78. I could build on earlier arguments about the "head" and the "veil," but the interpretation of 1 Cor. 14:34–35 is not dependent on the earlier arguments. However, for discussion on the "head," the "veil," and authority, see chap. 3.

79. Although some argue that women's leading in prayer and prophecy should take place in contexts other than a church service, or that Paul's instructions in 1 Cor. 11:3–16 are only a concession. See Carson's critique of these views ("'Silent in the Churches,'" in Piper and Grudem, *Recovering Biblical Manhood and Womanhood*, 145–46). But in brief, the function of prophecy is linked to the directions for meetings in 1 Cor. 12, and the immediate context in 1 Cor. 11:17–34 addresses the Lord's Supper in the meeting. The shift in 11:2 and the relationship to the following texts indicate a worship service. The idea that Paul would regulate prayer and prophecy but then forbid it is incoherent.

- The manifestations consist largely of verbal functions, which include prophesying (12:8–10, 28–29).
- The social and ethnic divisions among the members illustrate the unity in diversity of the body, but at the same time the diversity is redistributed so that the identity of the individual is now relative to the type of gift that the Spirit has distributed rather than to ethnicity, social status, or gender (12:12–14).
- No part of the body can say to another part, "I have no need of your service/ministry" (12:21).
- All the different parts and individuals should honor and value one another's call to service and show concern for one another (12:24–26).
- The believer's exercise of a spiritual gift and the congregation's treatment of each individual and the variety of gifts are governed by love (1 Cor. 13).
- The purpose and the value of gifts are edification of the hearers (14:3–5, 17).
- Prophecy should be the gift that each individual and the congregation value most highly.
- Those who prophesy should have relatively high status (14:1–5).

Prophecy is constricted and described by Paul not only as strengthening, encouraging, and comforting, but also as convicting and judging as the prophet uses the mind and understanding and *instructs* the others who learn from the prophet (κατηχέω: "catechize, teach by word of mouth"; μανθάνω: "learn"), in contrast to speaking in tongues (14:3, 14–15, 19, 24, 31).[80]

Chapters could be written on each of these points and how various interpretations of 1 Corinthians 14:34–35 have invalidated every one of these points that Paul has made in the immediate context, with the effect that women are placed outside of the function of the body of Christ as Paul describes it in the passage as a whole. However, women prophets were identified in the church

80. Paul's contrast between prophecy and tongues demonstrates that Wayne Grudem's restrictive definition of the function of prophets and prophecy contradicts Paul's description of prophecy in the text in question: "A spontaneous 'revelation' made prophecy different from teaching" ("Prophecy—Yes, but Teaching—No," *JETS* 30 [1987]: 15). He ignores the significance of κατηχέω and 1 Cor. 14:19 and incorrectly restricts prophecy to only spontaneous revelation (1 Cor. 14:30). Grudem fails to exegete the extensive material in 1 Cor. 14 that defines prophecy in great detail. This is a good example of inappropriate restriction of a word's meaning, driven by theological considerations. He is actually interpreting 1 Cor. 14:34–35 by 1 Tim. 2:12 instead of by Paul's own discussion in 1 Cor. 14, where he defines the term in detail and gives it priority over all the gifts available—points that Grudem overlooks.

(e.g., Acts 21:8–9), and Paul indicates the appropriate manner in which women prophesy in the worship service (1 Cor. 11:5). Women must be included in all aspects of service and ministry outlined in 1 Corinthians 12–14 by virtue of the fact that they are specifically depicted as having the "greatest" gift (1 Cor. 14:1, 5, 25), which Paul depicts as being invaluable to the church as well as unbelievers. Paul encourages everyone in the church at Corinth to desire to exercise the gift of prophecy in the meeting (14:1). In fact, he states that it would be a positive thing if everyone literally prophesied when an unbeliever entered the church because that person would be "called to account by all," male and female (14:24–25).[81]

7.3.2.3 First Corinthians 14:26–33: Being Quiet and Self-Controlled

It is essential to understand 1 Corinthians 14:34–35 as part of a larger passage or unit in the discussion of spiritual gifts, which is 1 Corinthians 14:26–35. In that passage, Anthony Thiselton argues, "controlled speech in traditions of speech-ethics" provides the background.[82] This consists of a concern with personal self-control, speaking in turn, and order with firm boundaries as opposed to shouting, talking all at once, and lack of self-discipline in speech.[83] These concerns can be traced through the passage. Those who speak in tongues should be limited in number and speak one at a time; but if there is no interpreter, they should keep quiet in the church (14:27–28). Prophets should be limited in number, and they should also speak one at a time; but Paul allows for interruptions or overlapping of prophecies, in which case the first speaker should sit down (14:29–33). The others in the congregation (male and female) are responsible for evaluating the prophecy.[84] Paul is emphasizing talking one

---

81. Notice that there does not appear to be a concern about a violation of masculinity by women prophesying to a male unbeliever within the context of the group meeting, even though the content of prophecy is characterized as instruction so confrontational that it can drive a man to his knees (1 Cor. 14:24–25). This is in contrast to private, intimate, one-on-one instruction and domination in view in 1 Tim. 2:12.

82. Thiselton, *Corinthians*, 1131–32. See also William R. Baker, *Personal Speech-Ethics in the Epistle of James*, WUNT 2/68 (Tübingen: Mohr Siebeck, 1995). Baker traces "controlled speech" as an ethical issue in Wisdom literature, the Old Testament, the Apocrypha, the Pseudepigrapha, Qumran, rabbinic literature, Greco-Roman texts, Philo, and parts of the New Testament.

83. See, e.g., Pss. 50:19; 59:7; Prov. 17:27; Plato, *Leg.* 701C; Josephus, *J.W.* 2.8.6; 1QS 10.24–25; Philo, *Spec.* 2.195; *Abr.* 21.29.

84. Contra Carson, who suggests that women are excluded from "the others" who judge the prophecy (οἱ ἄλλοι διακρινέτωσαν; 1 Cor. 14:29) ("'Silent in the Churches,'" in Piper and Grudem, *Recovering Biblical Manhood and Womanhood*, 151–53). See also Wayne Grudem, *The Gift of Prophecy in 1 Corinthians* (Washington, DC: University Press of America, 1982), 245–55. Carson argues that "Paul's point here . . . is that they may *not* participate in the oral weighing of such

at a time and being self-controlled so as to maintain order instead of disorder in speech, which is the purpose of the passage.

7.3.3 First Corinthians 14:34–35: Women Should Not Talk during Church

In 1 Corinthians 14:34–35, the overriding concern is therefore order (see 14:33, 40), which is defined as each individual talking/exercising their spiritual gift one at a time and other individuals keeping quiet (σιγάω, v. 28) and self-controlled (ὑποτάσσω, v. 32) while someone else is talking, unless they receive a specific revelation/prophecy. Quiet and self-controlled behavior is the rule/law (νόμος, v. 34) that maintains order in the Christian congregations, and in other contexts of Greco-Roman culture and Second Temple Judaism.[85]

Disorder is therefore characterized as everyone talking at once. In this context, Paul breaks the pattern he has set in 1 Corinthians 12–14 by referring to a group by its social/cultural/gender status (cf. 12:13) rather than by gifting. He tells women as a group not to talk during the church meeting, but to be quiet (σιγάω, v. 34) and self-controlled (ὑποτάσσω, v. 34), which is constrained by verses 28 and 32 to refer to precisely the same behavior as those with the gifts of tongues and prophecy through verbatim repetition.[86] That is, they are not supposed to be talking while someone else is sharing a hymn, a word of instruction, a revelation/prophecy, a tongue, or an interpretation (v. 26); that is the rule or the principle (v. 34), not just in all the churches, but also in Qumran, later rabbinic practice, and similar Greco-Roman contexts.[87] Paul is

---

prophesies" ("'Silent in the Churches,'" in Piper and Grudem, *Recovering Biblical Manhood and Womanhood*, 151). However, that is a minor point, neither the topic nor close context for 14:34–35, and nothing from the phrase is repeated in those verses; in other words, there are no ties between the phrase about evaluating prophecy and Paul's instructions for women. Nor is it consistent with Paul's suggestion that women learn and ask questions at home.

85. Here νόμος has its most common meaning, "rule, principle, norm." There is no citation from the Old Testament, though perhaps there is an allusion to the topic of the restraint of speech. Because women are mentioned, some want to suggest that Gen. 2–3 must be in view, but there is nothing about women's silence in speech in the creation and fall accounts.

86. Verbatim repetition forms powerful cohesive ties in tracing topics and minor semantic chains in close contexts (Michael Hoey, *Patterns of Lexis in Text*, DEL [Oxford: Oxford University Press, 1991], chap. 3). Because women are asked to submit, it is sometimes assumed that this passage is about submission to husbands. However, the meaning of ὑποτάσσω must be understood as lexical repetition constrained by the self-control of the prophets (cf. Thiselton, *Corinthians*, 1153).

87. Contra Grudem, who insists, "We must remember first, however, that there simply is no evidence in vv. 33b–35, or in the rest of the letter, or in any writing inside or outside the Bible, that indicates that disorder among women was a problem specifically in the Corinthian church" ("Prophecy," 20). Grudem fails to recognize the role of relevance and constraint in the interpretation of language; the immediate context provides the evidence, and restricting the

not referring to the orderly exercise of spiritual gifts one at a time, but rather addressing the disorderly conduct of talking while someone else is speaking. This is confirmed in verse 35 by Paul's further constraint and explanation of what he means: "If there is anything they desire to know, let them ask their husbands at home. For it is shameful for a woman to speak in church" (NRSV).

Learning and asking questions are not spiritual gifts or ministries determined by the Holy Spirit.[88] This constrains the behavior by the women that is being addressed to refer to something other than what he has just described as the orderly exercise of spiritual gifts, including the silence and self-control of the prophets and those who have the gift of tongues (even though Paul indicates that someone with the gift of tongues or a prophet could break the same rule by speaking out of turn [14:27–32]). Paul allows that perhaps the women have a good reason for talking while others are speaking, if they are talking about the topic and asking questions because they lack information.[89] If that is the case, then Paul instructs the men to homeschool their wives (and perhaps other women in their household) so that they have enough knowledge to understand the prophecy, teaching, and other content.

7.3.4 First-Century Women and Conversational Styles

Why would Paul single women out for violating the principle? Why did he not talk to men as well, since men are also known to talk while others are talking?

---

data to vv. 33b–35 is not legitimate interpretation. He finds that the anachronistic prohibitions in 1 Tim. 2:12 provide more evidence than the immediate context plus general observations on the behavior of women and women's culture. This is an example of an unwarranted demand for proof; for Grudem, one would have to find some inscription or text that addresses disorder among women in the Corinthian church. Ironically, the traditional understanding of the misbehavior of the women in veiling would be evidence of such a disorder.

88. Neither would the women's speech necessarily be error or "chatter" per se, though producing "chatter" is not an improbable characterization of much of the women's conduct. However, that nature of speech cannot be based either on the semantic range of λαλέω (1 Cor. 14:34), nor the constraint by Paul, who suggests (for the sake of argument) that they may be talking about the topic and asking questions about the content: that is not chatter. Contra, e.g., Gaston A. Deluz, *A Companion to 1 Corinthians*, trans. G. E. Watt (London: Darton, Longman & Todd, 1963), 215; Catherine Clark Kroeger and Robert Clark Kroeger, "Strange Tongues or Plain Talk?," *DSar* 12 (1986): 10–13. But neither do I support James Moffat, who inaccurately asserts, "Worship is not to be turned into discussion groups" (*First Epistle of Paul to the Corinthians*, MNTC [New York: Harper, 1938], 233). The problem is not learning through asking questions, which is a well-established Greco-Roman model of education. Worship is not antithetical to models of education.

89. This is a first-class condition, so that Paul is assuming (for the sake of argument) that women are talking while others are talking because they want to learn something about the topic or ask questions. See Stanley E. Porter, *Idioms of the Greek New Testament*, 2nd ed., BLG 2 (Sheffield: Sheffield Academic, 1999), 256.

The answer lies in the typical behavior of women in what is in many ways a semi-segregated culture, when they gathered not only in the home, but also in other contexts. Remember that Christians met in small, intimate house churches organized around fellowship meals, where women were busy with food preparation, serving food, and cleaning up, regardless of their spiritual gift. That alone creates an environment where women naturally tend to be noisy and talk among themselves to facilitate their work and enjoy each other as they work. But beyond that, women could be disruptive when they got together in public contexts as well. Chrysostom singled out the women and addressed this very problem:

> Then indeed the women, from such teaching keep silence; but now there is apt to be great noise among them, much clamor and talking, and nowhere so much as in this place [the cathedral]. They may all be seen here talking more than in the market, or at the bath. For, as if they came hither for recreation, they are all engaged in conversing upon unprofitable subjects. Thus all is confusion, and they seem not to understand, that unless they are quiet, they cannot learn anything that is useful. For when our discourse [sermon] strains against the talking, and no one minds what is said, what good can it do them?[90]

Kenneth Bailey discusses similar experiences in forty years of living in Egypt, Lebanon, Jerusalem, and Cyprus, both in terms of the behavior of women in public worship as well as his personal experience of teaching women in small groups.[91] He describes multiple factors that could have contributed to the phenomena: "Attention-span problems, limited knowledge of Greek, accent issues, language levels of Greek in use, lack of amplification for the speakers, along with chatting as a methodology for learning are all involved."[92]

I can add my own experiences of homeschooling and teaching in the inner city, which involve problems due to a lack of socialization in a group-learning context, and the problem of an individual's limited knowledge or the capacity to learn in a group.[93] Homeschooled children and street people can sometimes fail to behave in an orderly manner in a classroom environment or during delivery of a sermon because they either are not trained in or refuse to submit to behavior that is standard for others who have been through a conventional school system. In an inner-city Sunday school where I encouraged questions,

90. John Chrysostom, "Homily IX (1 Tim. ii. 11–15)," *NPNF*[1] 13:435.
91. Bailey, *Paul*, 412–17. Bailey's descriptions of Egyptian Christian women having a fifteen-second attention span and typical learning styles in oral cultures are very helpful.
92. Ibid., 416.
93. When I discussed this passage with one of my daughters, she, without being prompted, immediately started to supply numerous examples of street people and people with mental disabilities disrupting sermons and Sunday school, very similar to Bailey's anecdotes.

sometimes one person who was mentally disabled continually interrupted the teaching to demand answers to very basic questions. In such cases I would say, "Those are good questions! Let's meet after class, and I'll take as much time as you want to get all your questions answered." This sort of combination of antisocial behavior and ignorance manifested in asking questions cannot be equated to the exercise of any spiritual gift. I suggest that there is a correspondence with the lack of socialization and the underdeveloped abilities of women in the first-century Greco-Roman world.

Women may have received some education, but it was virtually always at home, and generally a complete absence of formal education or comparable experience results in difficulties in attention span and group behavior. In addition, it is likely that the women in the lower classes experienced a greater degree of arrested development and learning disabilities due to malnutrition, sexual abuse, and general lack of mental stimulation.[94] We may add to these the possibly universal female practice of "overlapping" in speech ("chiming in" while someone else is talking).[95] These factors—together with the holiday atmosphere of taking a break and meeting together with other women for the preparation, sharing, and cleanup of a meal—would normally result in quite a conversational buzz at the very least, which may or may not have been on topic but certainly would create disorder. Distracting and disruptive side conversations during a meeting cannot be equated with exercising a spiritual gift. Even to this day such behavior is common in women's cultures in the majority world, and particularly in the Middle East. Therefore, I have drawn a convincing picture of a number of ways in which women specifically may have created confusion and disorder during an informal meal in a home through conversational styles that were (and are) characteristic of women in comparable contexts.

7.3.5 The Function of 1 Corinthians 14:36–40 as a Conclusion to 1 Corinthians 12–14

Paul abruptly shifts to a more polemical tone with pointed rhetorical questions that many assume are directed at women and function as a conclusion

---

94. Malnutrition and lack of stimulation continue to be problems for females in the majority world. For instance, UNICEF put out the following report concerning gender and malnutrition in India: "Malnutrition limits development and the capacity to learn. . . . Anemia affects 74 percent of children under the age of three, more than 90 percent of adolescent girls and 50 percent of women. . . . Girls are more at risk of malnutrition than boys because of their lower social status" (UNICEF, "Malnutrition," http://unicef.in/Whatwedo).

95. For a discussion of women and "overlapping" in contrast with men's speech, see Deborah Tannen, You Just Don't Understand: Men and Women in Conversation (New York: Morrow, 1990), 188–215, esp. 201.

for 1 Corinthians 14:34–35. However, two things must be considered: verses
36–40 form a unit, and the unit clearly concludes chapter 14 with a summary,
making reference to tongues, prophecy, and doing things decently and in order
(vv. 37, 39–40). The previous material on spiritual gifts and love provides a
context for all of the confrontations in chapter 14, so that this passage also
serves as a conclusion for 1 Corinthians 12–14, before the topic shifts in 15:1.
Paul has sharply confronted and corrected a number of groups in chapter 14,
and in verse 36 he addresses all of them with a masculine plural "you" (ὑμῶν,
ὑμᾶς).[96] So his sharp rhetorical questions in verse 36 are not directed at women
alone, but rather he is talking to all of the Corinthians whom he has just corrected.[97] He is anticipating that there may be objections to everything that he
has said about tongues, prophecy, and everyone not speaking at once.

7.3.6 Summary

It is common for people to regard Paul's instructions for women not to
talk during the worship service in 1 Corinthians 14:34–35 as a serious challenge for anyone who argues for women in ministry and leadership. However,
very few scholars argue that the silence for women should be understood as
absolute. The question is this: What provides the context for understanding
the nature of the silence, or what Paul meant when he said that women are not
to talk? The preferred contexts for interpreting Paul's instructions for women
are not material from Pauline texts that were written after 1 Corinthians, as
those texts were not available to the first readers. Rather, the context of the
situation of worship in house churches, the context within the letter, and
the context of the culture of women are most relevant for determining the
meaning of the passage. The contexts indicate that Paul expects women to
participate in prayer and the legitimate exercise of spiritual gifts. However,
he then addresses specific problems that are causing disorder and confusion
during worship. As in the instructions to those who speak in tongues and those
who prophesy, Paul is instructing women not to talk at the same time others
are talking during worship, but instead to be quiet and self-controlled, which

96. See Ben Witherington III, *Women and the Genesis of Christianity* (Cambridge: Cambridge University Press, 1990), 98, 259; Fee, *Corinthians*, 710; Thiselton, *Corinthians*, 1161–62.
97. Contra Carson, who asserts, "Paul's point in 14:36 is that some Corinthians want to
'deny or refute' what Paul has been saying in vv. 34–35" ("'Silent in the Churches,'" in Piper and
Grudem, *Recovering Biblical Manhood and Womanhood*, 151). The objectors have to include
men, since Paul uses a masculine-plural pronoun. While his corrections of the misunderstanding
and misuse of tongues and his attempts to regulate those who speak in tongues and prophets
would clearly raise objections, it is less likely that men in the Greco-Roman culture would defend
women's behavior, but not object to the correction of their own behavior.

is the rule of conduct in all of the traditions of speech ethics. Paul directs men to teach their wives at home so that they will not be dependent on getting their questions answered by talking among themselves or by whispering to their husbands during worship.

In conclusion, women should interpret and apply instructions to all believers with the same hermeneutics as men. The passages about determining the function of each believer in the church and the call to ministry are general instructions for all believers. The priesthood of the believer applies to all believers, so that the function, race, social status, physical condition, and gender of priests in the Old Testament are not requirements or prerequisites for any ministry in the Christian community. The Holy Spirit determines who gets what gift; a theological system that filters and restricts the gifts for a given group compromises the authority of the Holy Spirit. Each individual is responsible for identifying one's own gifts in the same way and with the same criteria. Each person's "call" to service is determined by personal experience, which includes not only work experience but also emotions, such as one's passion for a given ministry and guidance through prayer. The gifts are given to edify the entire church, and no one should say to another, "I have no need of you." If God sends the church women who are apostles, evangelists, pastors, and teachers to equip it and the church refuses to accept them, they will all pragmatically function as prophets against the church and the theological system that refuses the gifts—actually, according to Romans 12:6, such behavior is literally refusing God's "grace given to us."

eight

Authority

The Greco-Roman world inherited and reinforced the Greek philosophy of a society structured by rank and status, and the Greek philosophers generally reinforced privilege and the social pyramid.[1] Virtue tended to be equated with social conventions and the social expectations of the Greek aristocracy and elite. It involved honoring the superiority of the upper strata and the wealthy, such as military generals, officeholders, doctors, and judges. Eventually the concept of virtue was embodied in the ideals of the Roman Empire. The Roman Empire's values included serenity, order, and stability in civic life and the household, but these values were realized through relatively rigid social structures known as the patronage system, which is concerned with rank, friendships, benefaction, honor, reciprocity, and gratitude. The imperial cult, as founded by Octavian, can be understood as an intersection between polytheism and the patronage system within the Roman Empire.[2] A person's honor came from knowing one's place within the social system and functioning

1. For a more extensive discussion of Paul's critique of the ideas and ideals of the Greco-Roman culture, see Mark Strom, *Reframing Paul: Conversations in Grace & Community* (Downers Grove, IL: InterVarsity, 2000). For his discussion of the social pyramid, see 64–67.

2. Octavian Augustus laid down the framework of the imperial cult through his claims and the roles that he assumed: "During the transition from Republic to Empire, without seeming to change anything, Augustus and his family entered into a special relationship with every possible legal, religious, and social institution of the city of Rome. It was a patronage relationship of identity, responsibility and generosity that was expressed in part though granting Octavian Augustus numerous offices derived from the Republic and city and included titles such as 'Father of the Country,' and minting coins with the images of the family" (Cynthia Long Westfall,

appropriately, but a quest for personal honor and status was a noble goal, and the male ideal was to attain the position of a paterfamilias with as many men as possible subjugated to his patronage.

By the middle of the first century, concepts of power and hierarchy were embedded within the imperial theology, and the culture's ideology of gender was indivisibly linked to the power and authority of the entire hierarchy of the Roman Empire. Jesus explicitly rejected the Greco-Roman leadership models and the manner in which those in authority exercised power and authority over those under them (Matt. 20:25–28 // Luke 22:24–27). Paul also confronted and rejected the Greco-Roman culture's conventional human wisdom, the imperial theology of power, authority, and the ideology of status (1 Cor. 1:18–31).

On the other hand, Paul adopted and adapted aspects of the Greco-Roman household, yet with God as the paterfamilias, or patron, and promoted reciprocity among the members of the household. Thus Paul relativized the authority structure in the church by casting every leader as a slave of both God and the community, while he still advocated conventional reciprocity for benefits received among those functioning as clients, who received benefits from others.[3] All leaders served while the community submitted, so that leadership could cross what we have held as conventional Greco-Roman boundaries of gender or social status without usurping or claiming authority, but the community properly submitted to the conventional authority structures. We will look at the leadership roles of men and women in that context.

However, the Pauline corpus has historically been incorrectly interpreted as positively supporting the hierarchy and power of the imperial government and adopting, reinforcing, and pragmatically extending the hierarchical authority and power structure of men over women in the Christian community.[4] Meanwhile, the influence of Christianity on Western political and social systems eventually diminished hierarchical authority between men and moved toward shared power and away from class systems, with basic human rights guaranteed

---

"Roman Religions and the Imperial Cult," in *Lexham Bible Dictionary*, ed. John D. Barry [Bellingham, WA: Logos Bible Software, 2015]).

3. This accounts for the lack of consistency that Michael White observes in Paul's use of theological reflections on the paterfamilias ("Paul and *Pater Familias*," in *Paul in the Greco-Roman World: A Handbook*, ed. J. Paul Sampley [Harrisburg, PA: Trinity Press International, 2003], 470–72). When Paul is stressing authority, God is the paterfamilias; when he is stressing reciprocity, anyone could be the patron to whom the community owes appropriate honor and gratitude.

4. Biblical interpretation has been controlled by those who have had relative power and privilege in the Western culture; thus the subjective influence of class, power, and wealth was not recognized as being far different circumstances from the first-century participants who were marginalized. Postcolonial criticism has provided a healthy corrective to the view that the Bible supported the Roman Empire. For an overview, see Stephen D. Moore and Fernando F. Segovia, eds., *Postcolonial Biblical Criticism: Interdisciplinary Intersections* (London: T&T Clark, 2005).

and privilege based on merit. As the form and philosophy of government shifted from imperial hierarchy to democracy in the West, the ideology of gender remained hierarchical. Consequently, since men were no longer under a comparable hierarchical authority either in government, society, or family, the hierarchical structure based on gender was changed and transferred to the nuclear family, which was more isolated from societal and political structures because of changed notions of privacy. Therefore, male authority in the household came to be applied to every man and husband in a way that was far more absolute than it was either in the Roman Empire or particularly in Paul's household codes, and that authority has lacked checks and balances in the churches and religious traditions that continue to advocate it.[5]

8.1 Gender, Authority, Power, and Status in the Greco-Roman Culture

As stated above, hierarchy in gender was an essential component of relationships in the Roman Empire, and the household was the foundational building block of the patronage system, which was the backbone of its authority structure.[6] In the marital relationship, the husband was the patron and the wife was the client. The children and slaves were similarly in a patron-client relationship with the paterfamilias and his wife, who managed the household. Individuals who were not slaves normally occupied multiple roles in the patron-client system.[7] In common with the Roman centurion in Matthew 8:9, each male or female was a person under authority and thus obligated to do what

5. The hierarchical relationships in gender are extended because in the current model in the Western world, the family is a nuclear unit so that the checks and balances, accountability, and authorities for the man are removed. Rather than the more complicated obligations, obedience, and accountability to extended families, and the multiple obligations of slaves, each married man now is held to be practically the only authority in his household and over his wife, and the structure of the church is often thought to be obligated to avoid compromising a husband's authority and a wife's submission. In this model, the only effective check on a husband's power over his wife is the law of the land. In addition, historically the authority of male over female was held to be not only based on ontological inferiority, but also an essential consequence of the woman's role in the fall, so that there was often something of a penal nature to some of the discussion. While the Greco-Roman culture recognized that a woman should have authority in the family when she contributed more to the family in status and wealth (based on reciprocity and the patron-client model), in a hierarchical or complementarian understanding of women's subjugation, the man is the authority based on what he is rather than what he provides for the family.

6. As White describes, there was a "basic conception of the family as a microcosm of the state" ("Paul and *Pater Familias*," in Sampley, *Paul in the Greco-Roman World*, 471–72).

7. Even this statement must be qualified, for a slave could own a slave, and a slave could become free. However, freedom did not release a person from the patron-client system. Often relationships of patronage continued with the former owner, and new relationships could form.

they were told, and each had persons under them who were obligated to obey their commands.[8] The hierarchical relationships of gender were embedded in a system far more complex than is generally recognized in biblical studies, which usually seems to assume a nuclear household and fails to recognize the mother's authority in the Greco-Roman family. Authority in the household and society did not invariably follow lines of gender, since a woman could be a head of a household (materfamilias), a mother of sons, a patron of men, a master of male slaves, and a supervisor of male servants.

The Greco-Roman understanding of gender was based on the teaching of the classical Greek philosophers.[9] The concepts of philosophers such as Plato, Stobaeus, and particularly Aristotle continued to be influential in the rhetoric discussing gender. Stoic philosophers similarly discussed marriage and gender as complementary aspects of power and authority, but defined them as more mutual. The influences of the classical philosophers may be seen in Philo, while Paul had more in common with Stoic philosophers. The classical Greek philosophers argued for and practiced a semi-segregated culture with a well-defined distinction between the male in the public sphere and the female in the domestic sphere, and a hierarchical relationship between the two whereby the man was the ruler and the woman was ruled. Yet even within the classical rhetoric, the female had multiple roles, for it was her responsibility to rule in the domestic sphere, and that sphere included male and female slaves as well as children. Furthermore, positions in society and membership in elite groups correlated with authority.

In the first-century Greco-Roman world, many of the barriers between the public and domestic spheres were more fluid than during the Greek classical period, but the rhetoric remained fairly consistent. Furthermore, since it was part of the rhetoric that was used to maintain the Roman hierarchy, the behavior of women in an identifiable group could come under scrutiny and be used to charge a religion or social organization with sedition. These dynamics serve as a context to understand the authority structures that Paul was addressing and also his missional concern with carefully ordered household relationships as integral to the Christian community's reputation and survival. However, it must be recognized that when Paul directed hearers to submit to parents and masters, these categories were by no means exclusively male in the classical Greek rhetoric and the Greco-Roman culture, and a failure to respect the

8. It is interesting and significant that Matthew (8:9–10) depicted the centurion's exercise of power in the military as analogous to faith in that he was able to transfer his own experience of the exercise of power to Jesus and his capacity to exercise spiritual authority.

9. For a more extensive discussion of Greco-Roman philosophy and the rhetoric of gender, see §1.3.1.

authority of one's mother, a materfamilias, or any female οἰκοδεσπότης who ruled the household would be considered equally seditious.

8.1.1 The Rhetoric of Gender, Authority, Power, and Status

Ancient rhetoric was one of the political instruments of the Greek and Roman elite used to establish and maintain power. The gender rhetoric in the Roman Empire was consistent with that of the classical Greek philosophers, even if the actual practice of gender relationships was less structured and varied regionally across the empire. The ancient writers belonged to the elite and, generally, the noble class. It should not be assumed that the members of the Christian community occupied the same positions of authority and privilege as the Greek and Roman elite.

8.1.1.1 GENDER AND AUTHORITY IN CLASSICAL PHILOSOPHY

The classical philosophers regarded men as fit to rule and women as fit to be ruled, but they also described more complex power relationships in the social system where women exercised power and authority. Plato talked about women's "one task" or "social service" as submission to male authority.[10] Yet in some relationships, a woman appropriately filled the slot of a ruler. He described six groups as having the right to rule: parents over children, noble over ignoble, older over younger, masters over slaves, stronger over weaker, and the wise over those without understanding.[11] Some women would have belonged to all six groups of the ruled. A woman slave would have virtually no power, not even over her own children. All women may have been excluded from the groups composed of the stronger and the wise, but some would have been included in the other four groups that ruled. On the other hand, a man could belong to all six of the groups that were ruled and therefore be under the authority of other men and probably under the authority of certain women as well. Therefore, even during the most conservative period of practice, the Greek philosophers acknowledged the authority of men in marriage and the family, but in the complex social and power structures, women also ruled over men in various social forms.

8.1.1.2 GENDER AND AUTHORITY IN STOICISM

In Stoic philosophy, Hierocles was very positive about the benefits of marriage and optimistic about women's character and contribution. He defined

10. Plato, *Resp.* 4.433a, c–d.
11. Plato, *Leg.* 3.690a–d.

a division of labor and authority between a husband and wife, where the husband exercised authority in men's affairs (public) and the wife exercised authority in women's affairs (domestic). He concluded, "But the beauty of a household consists in the conjunction of man and wife . . . who . . . exercise a becoming authority over their house and servants."[12] While Hierocles is more positive about women than the classical philosophers, they hold a similar view about the wife's exercise of authority in the domestic sphere. Nevertheless, he speaks of a husband and wife as sharing all things and sharing each other's bodies. Paul's description of marriage reflects, strengthens, and extends the Stoic view of mutuality in marriage.

8.1.2 The Reality of Gender and Authority in the First-Century Roman Empire

The New Testament is in dialogue with a Greco-Roman rhetoric of power that formed the standards and values by which individuals and groups were judged. However, the rhetoric about gender was composed by the elite and reflects a male hegemony of power and privilege that few men experienced fully. It should not be assumed that most of the men in the Christian community belonged to all six of the groups that ruled, according to Plato's list. Furthermore, it should not be assumed that most of the women in the Christian community were subordinate in all their relationships with men or in the household, because this was not true of the classical period or of the first-century Greco-Roman culture. In addition, women in the society were not as segregated or secluded as they were during the classical period in Greece, though Philo talks as if classical gender segregation was still an ideal.[13]

The early church had a reputation for being a religion composed of slaves and women. While that was an attack on the status of the movement, the reality of the presence of slaves must figure into the equation of power and gender, particularly if they were believers in the same household. If male slaves were in the household, women exercised authority over them and even over adult men in the extended family or business. Men who were slaves were under the authority of the master and mistress and had no legal authority

12. Hierocles, *Concerning Marriage*, in *Political Fragments of Archytas, Charondas, Zaleucus and Other Ancient Pythagoreans*, ed. and trans. Thomas Taylor (Whitefish, MT: Kessinger, 2003), 100.

13. Philo's remarks about women's seclusion in *Flacc.* 89 are recognized as inconsistent with conditions in first-century Alexandria. See Mary Rose D'Angelo, "Gender and Geopolitics in the Work of Philo of Alexandria: Jewish Piety and Imperial Family Values," in *Mapping Gender in Ancient Religious Discourses*, ed. Todd Penner and Carolyn Vander Stichele, BIS 84 (Leiden: Brill, 2006), 85–86.

over their own wives or children; in fact, they were not allowed to have a civil marriage. Adult males and their wives were under the authority of both their parents and the paterfamilias (if, as was often the case, they were different individuals), and the wife might have been under the rule of her mother-in-law in the domestic sphere more than under the rule of her husband. On the other hand, there is indication that the authority of the paterfamilias over the life and death of the members of his household was eroding in the first century.

Often the household codes are read and translated as if every adult male was the husband, the father, and the master, and women were subordinate to men as a group. This is because it is common for Paul to be read as if he is writing to establish and support the power of the father in the Western nuclear family, but this is not the case.[14] He was writing to believers who were navigating a complex structure of authority and obligations that could involve a number of different roles involving authority and subordination. Paul was addressing individuals in the power structures (their calling) in which they lived—husband, wife, or single, parent and/or child, free or slave. Men could be fathers and masters, but many were adult children and under an obligation to obey both their parents and a paterfamilias; some were slaves, and some could be both a slave and a master. Virtually all male believers would be clients within a complex patron-client system. Although women were often under the control of a husband or a male guardian, they could also be slave owners and a materfamilias,[15] or they could be slaves with no control over their own families or their own bodies. Rather than establishing a form of male authority that would reconstruct Greco-Roman society, Paul was instructing the Christian community to operate within the conventional authority structures in the society.

However, within the church, the authority structure was far different than in the home and in the public venue for both men and women. The early church almost spoke a different language: men and women were brothers and sisters as equal heirs. Any sense of rule based on categories of position and privilege is removed. God is the believer's only patron, and Jesus Christ is the only mediator. No one but God was a father to the community. On the other hand, Paul could be a father to the churches that he planted or function as a

14. Any understanding of the household codes in terms of the nuclear family is an example of reader-oriented criticism. As White observes, "The term *familia* was not limited to the 'nuclear family' consisting of parents and children, as it is commonly applied to the modern world. . . . The *familia* normally included parents and children, along with other relatives (agnates and cognates), the domestic slaves, and a coterie of other dependents, freedmen, or clients" ("Paul and *Pater Familias*," in Sampley, *Paul in the Greco-Roman World*, 457).

15. For a description of households and marital arrangements in which the women held authority, see ibid., 458–59.

mentor even while he made himself a slave to all. A leader is to respect all the older believers like their own fathers and mothers (1 Tim. 5:1–2), while the leaders described themselves with low-status titles such as "slave," "servant," and "shepherd."

8.2 Paul's Theology of Authority, Power, and Status

Paul is often used to support a theology of strict hierarchy in the government and the home in a way that stands in contrast to Jesus's criticism of the authority structures in the gentile world. However, the major themes of Paul's theology of authority are overlooked in such cases, for Paul and Jesus are not far apart in their evaluation of the power structures of the Roman Empire. Paul critiques the power structures of the Roman Empire and the Greco-Roman basis of status more severely than Jesus does. He taught that leadership was not personal authority but rather humility and sacrificial service. Power and authority came from demonstrations of God's power rather than control.

8.2.1 Paul and Jesus on Authority

Paul understood Jesus's humble status and service as the model to emulate in Christian ministry. Jesus described his own character as "gentle and humble in heart" (Matt. 11:29). Paul claims to follow the same model in his dealings with the Corinthian church: "I myself, Paul, appeal to you by the meekness and gentleness of Christ—I who am humble when face to face with you, but bold toward you when I am away!" (2 Cor. 10:1 NRSV).

Paul recognizes that Jesus did not please himself, but instead was insulted by the people with whom he identified (Rom. 15:3). Paul asks believers to exhibit the same attitude and behavior toward other believers: "We who are strong ought to put up with the failings of the weak, and not to please ourselves" (Rom. 15:1 NRSV).

In addition, Paul claims that putting up with insults was the pattern of his life as an apostle, and that it should be the pattern of all apostles (1 Cor. 4:8–13; 2 Cor. 6:3–10; 11:21–33). If there is a contrast between Jesus and Paul, it lies in the fact that Jesus was imprisoned, dishonored, beaten, and crucified in his passion, whereas Paul was imprisoned, dishonored, and beaten throughout the course of his ministry. The Corinthian church felt that Paul was not an impressive charismatic leader by the standards of their culture.

Jesus spoke of leadership among his followers as taking the role of a servant/slave, which is based on the anticipation of his own example in his life and in death as a common criminal:

But Jesus called them to him and said, "You know that the rulers of the Gentiles lord it over them, and their great ones are tyrants over them. It will not be so among you; but whoever wishes to be great among you must be your servant, and whoever wishes to be first among you must be your slave; just as the Son of Man came not to be served but to serve, and to give his life a ransom for many." (Matt. 20:25–28 NRSV)

Paul characterizes Jesus's incarnation as exhibiting the same model of obedience, which was extended to suffering and death:

Christ Jesus, though he was in the form of God, did not regard equality with God as something to be exploited, but emptied himself, taking the form of a slave, being born in human likeness. And being found in human form, he humbled himself and became obedient to the point of death—even death on a cross. (Phil. 2:5–8 NRSV)

In the preceding context, Paul specifically applies Jesus's model as paradigmatic for all believers in their treatment of each other:

If then there is any encouragement in Christ, any consolation from love, any sharing in the Spirit, any compassion and sympathy, make my joy complete: be of the same mind, having the same love, being in full accord and of one mind. Do nothing from selfish ambition or conceit, but in humility regard others as better than yourselves. Let each of you look not to your own interests, but to the interests of others. Let the same mind be in you that was in Christ Jesus. (Phil. 2:1–5 NRSV)

The mutual submission that Paul described and Jesus modeled was not simply among peers of the same class, race, and gender. It was not exclusive of any authority relationships that might be in place among believers, whether they were social roles or leadership roles in the church communities. In Jesus's case, his model of literal servanthood was demonstrated when he, as the one with superior status, washed the disciples' feet (John 13:1–17).[16] Paul describes his ministry to his churches as functionally becoming a slave to all, and he describes adopting the role of those with lesser status in order to more effectively minister to them:

16. Kathy Ehrensperger asserts that, according to Paul, "When it comes to conflicting situations, however, those in the 'stronger' position have to accommodate. . . . Paul clearly demands mutuality in relationships of equals, but he is well aware that even if there are only slight inequalities, it is still primarily the identity and integrity of the weaker ones that the Christ-believers need to respect" (*That We May Be Mutually Encouraged: Feminism and the New Perspective in Pauline Studies* [New York: T&T Clark, 2004], 187).

For though I am free with respect to all, I have made myself a slave to all, so
that I might win more of them. To the Jews I became as a Jew, in order to win
Jews. To those under the law I became as one under the law (though I myself
am not under the law) so that I might win those under the law. To those outside
the law I became as one outside the law (though I am not free from God's law
but am under Christ's law) so that I might win those outside the law. To the
weak I became weak, so that I might win the weak. I have become all things
to all people, that I might by all means save some. I do it all for the sake of the
gospel, so that I may share in its blessings. (1 Cor. 9:19–23 NRSV)

Paul teaches this kind of mutuality and accommodation in many ways and
in many contexts.[17]

The examples of both Paul and Jesus describe leadership in the Christian
community in terms of servants and slaves. Both Jesus and Paul modeled working hard at menial labor on behalf of others. They also subjected themselves
to dishonor and mistreatment. Their model of leadership cannot be glossed
over or bleached into describing exercise of unilateral benevolent power.[18]
Their example of servitude was literal in the way it was meant to function,
rather than a part of ritual or metaphor.

8.2.2 Authority and the Pauline Narrative

We tend to read Paul as a triumphant power broker who dominated his
recipients in a structured and authoritative way, from a position of undisputed
power. This is largely because the gentile church that emerged from his mission eventually dominated Christianity, and his writings to his churches form
such a large part of the New Testament. However, during his life he was in
conflict with the leadership from Jerusalem, he faced beatings and imprisonment by the Roman Empire, he fought factions within his own mission, and
he died feeling deserted.

Paul formerly used his status, education, and power to persecute the church,
but he repented from his former methods of authoritative force and followed
Christ's gentleness and humility. In his experience on the Damascus road,
Paul was confronted with the fact that the Lord and creator became poor,

17. Ehrensperger points out that the teaching in Rom. 14–15, the teaching on the "weak
in faith" and the "strong," shows that inequalities of power are involved in the relationship
rather than quality of faith, and that this teaches mutuality and accommodation (ibid., 183).

18. Men have historically exercised control over women through their advantages that correlate with the criteria that Paul rejects, and they label domination and control as "servanthood"
when they are supposedly using their advantages for what they determine to be the good of the
women. In this paradigm, servanthood is redefined as exercising power and authority that is
similar to the Greco-Roman model yet with little if any correlation to slavery.

suffered, was humiliated, and then was crucified by the governing authorities. God's choice of Paul as his apostle to the gentiles also overturned Paul's presuppositions about authority. It showed Paul that God could choose a person who was "a blasphemer, a persecutor, and a man of violence" (1 Tim. 1:13), someone at open enmity with God, to accomplish God's purposes. In his dealings with the churches, Paul's authority was based on the charismatic "signs of a true apostle" (2 Cor. 12:12), reciprocity, and forms of persuasion that reflected Hellenistic patterns but rejected the use of force and power that was inherent and respected in the imperial system.

Paul was effective in planting churches in virgin territory, but his methods of leadership could work to his personal disadvantage. His churches rebelled against him. For example, the church at Corinth was critical because he failed to perform as an ideal leader according to the culture's standards, so they could be proud of him. Paul tried to persuade them of countercultural values, promising or threatening that his ministry was backed by God's power and demonstrations of the Spirit. Jewish-Christian antagonism toward him led to his arrest as he made a humble attempt to appease James and quell rumors (Acts 21:20–33). The Prison Epistles and Pastoral Epistles contribute a narrative showing that he feared an erosion of influence through competitive leaders preaching the gospel to make his chains worse. False teachers were gaining a foothold and Paul sent members of his mission team to deal with the situations, but the open enmity of certain people caused him harm. According to 2 Timothy 4:9–16, he faced death with very little support.

8.2.3 Paul's Critique of Greco-Roman Authority

Paul's teaching about leadership was consistent with the narrative of his life. It is a direct critique of the Greco-Roman social pyramid and the values on which honor in the culture was based.[19] According to Paul, authority and power in the Christian community were based on the nature of the foolishness of the gospel, the sovereign choice/election of God, and the demonstrations of power by the Spirit. God treats all believers in the same way that he treated Paul: he "saved us and called us with a holy calling, not according to our works but according to his own purpose and grace" (2 Tim. 1:9 NRSV). If God could call and use Paul, he could call anyone. The weakness of the leaders demonstrated God's power. The distribution of the gifts was therefore

19. As Richard Horsley correctly observes, Paul's situation and purpose are not the same as the general formulation and use of Greco-Roman rhetoric ("Rhetoric and Empire and 1 Corinthians," in *Paul and Politics: Ekklesia, Israel, Imperium, Interpretation; Essays in Honor of Krister Stendahl*, ed. Richard A. Horsley [Harrisburg, PA: Trinity Press International, 2000], 78).

paradigmatic of God's choice and grace, and they were random in terms of the usual cultural expectations. God's instruments were slaves of righteousness. The positions in the church were elders, caregivers (so-called overseers), and servants (deacons), and his apostles (ambassadors) were slaves.

Paul explicitly and vehemently opposed the Greco-Roman concepts and system of authority as a model for leadership in the church. He urged his church communities to do the same by resisting conformity to the world (Rom. 12:2). Such change is part of a "great reversal" where the "turning of the ages" occurred at the cross, at which point "all human standards of evaluation are overturned."[20] This is most clearly expressed in Paul's correspondence to the Corinthians and to the Thessalonians.[21] He rejects leadership that is based on Greco-Roman concepts of wisdom, power, and status (1 Cor. 1:18–31). His teachings are the polar opposite of Plato's argument that the weak should be ruled by the strong, the ignoble by the noble, and the ignorant by the wise. When Paul rejects the status markers of his heritage, privileges, and attainments in Judaism, he rejects the biological essentialism and the social pyramid of the Greco-Roman system as well (Phil. 3:1–11). He therefore rejects all the values on which status and authority in the culture were based. Paul's criticism of the superapostles shows a reversal of the culture's concepts of honor and the character traits that defined an ambitious leader and patron. He replaces them with the meekness and gentleness of Jesus Christ as well as his servanthood and sufferings (2 Cor. 10–11). Paul speaks against leaders who enslaved, exploited, and took advantage of the Corinthian church. He describes these leaders as pushing themselves forward and slapping church members in the face (2 Cor. 11:20) or as pleasing people, flattering, masking greed, looking for praise, and asserting their prerogatives (1 Thess. 2:6).

---

20. Richard B. Hays, *First Corinthians*, IBC (Louisville: John Knox, 1997), 30.

21. Paul asserts that God chose the "foolish," the "weak," and the "lowly" or the "low class" to shame the "wise," the "strong," and the "upper class/influential" (1 Cor. 1:27–28). Similarly, Paul describes his presentation of the gospel in Corinth as being without wisdom, weak, and fearful yet as demonstrating the Spirit and the power of God (2:1–4). Along with that, Paul intentionally rejects exercising the authority and the power that are due to the position of an apostle (9:1–12). Paul asserts that he makes himself a slave to all people so that he can save them (9:19–22), and this includes being weak in order to reach weak people. In every way he describes himself as taking a position of powerlessness and a position that is marginalized and outside of the world's authority structure in order to be qualified as a partner in the gospel (9:23). In 1 Thess. 2:5–8, Paul illustrates taking the low position in ministry when he contrasts how he and his ministry team could have approached the Thessalonians from a position of authority and power as Christ's apostles, but instead they chose to be gentle, like a nursing mother caring for her children. Therefore, he describes his approach to church planting and leadership with stereotypical behavior of slaves and women, claiming that his behavior vindicates both his motives and the outcome (2:1–4).

However, Paul reinforces the obligations of reciprocity for all believers who received benefits from anyone, which he applies effectively on his own behalf and on behalf of others. Paul instructs the Romans to "Pay to all what is due them—taxes to whom taxes are due, revenue to whom revenue is due, respect to whom respect is due, honor to whom honor is due" (Rom. 13:7 NRSV). This was the essence of grace and the obligation of gratitude. God's people were to pay or at least acknowledge their debts to humanity, and since they owe their very life to God, they become his slaves. Paul claims a unique relationship with the Corinthian church: "For though you might have ten thousand guardians in Christ, you do not have many fathers. Indeed, in Christ Jesus I became your father through the gospel" (1 Cor. 4:15 NRSV).

Paul uses this kind of relationship as leverage in his other arguments as well. He exhibits a complex understanding of reciprocity in his communication with Philemon on behalf of Philemon's slave Onesimus. Paul acknowledges that Onesimus may have an obligation to Philemon, but Paul asks Philemon to charge it to his own account, which may indicate that Philemon supported Paul: "If he has wronged you in any way, or owes you anything, charge that to my account. I, Paul, am writing this with my own hand: I will repay it" (Philem. 18–19a NRSV). However, Paul balances his own obligations by reminding Philemon of his own obligations: "I say nothing about your owing me even your own self" (Philem. 19b NRSV). He reminds church members to exercise reciprocity in their treatment of the leaders who work hard for them—they owe their submission to these leaders (1 Cor. 16:16; 1 Thess. 5:12)—and Paul honors all who function as patrons to him and to the church. He claims that Priscilla and Aquila risked their necks for him, which adds to a considerable debt that he owes this couple, which he takes seriously (Rom. 16:3–4). Paul's instruction to wives to submit in Ephesians 5:22–24 is based on reciprocity, as are his instructions to submit to governments in Romans 13:1–7. The caveat is that instructions to recipients of benefits to submit based on reciprocity are not used by Paul to empower patrons or support hierarchy, but only for the clients to render what is due.

In summary, Paul rejects the authority structure of the Roman Empire as a model of authority in the church.[22] He teaches that leadership and service are

22. Contra both feminists and traditional scholars who associate Paul with patterns of male hierarchy and domination. The difference is that the traditional evaluation is positive and uses Paul to legitimate hierarchy, and the feminist evaluation of Paul is generally negative and finds him guilty of promoting oppression. For example, Elizabeth Castelli asserts that Paul created a clear hierarchical separation between the apostles and the community, without equality or reciprocity in his description of himself as the planter and the architect and of the Corinthians as a field and building (*Imitating Paul: A Discourse of Power* [Louisville: Westminster John Knox, 1991], 105). Both feminists and traditional scholars take the tradition of how Paul is interpreted and confuse it with his actual letters. As Beverly Roberts Gaventa suggests, "Paul

based on God's election, call, and gifting alone, not on biological essentialism or works; no group was born to lead or earned the right to lead in the church. Furthermore, the words "leadership" and "authority" in the church need to be defined carefully and according to Paul's terms. He avoids describing leadership as anything other than slavery or in similar terms that represented leadership in all forms as low-status menial labor. "Servant leadership" truly meant slavery to Paul, and it could never be a claim to the cultural norms of privilege, priority, status, power, or authority. Those who held positions of authority in the culture's power pyramid were expected to function as stewards of their power, yet modulated into the role of servants and slaves. Paul does not bestow or support hierarchical privilege, but instead teaches believers how to live within the Roman social and political system with kingdom values. On the other hand, every believer had the obligation to submit in principle, and even more so with reciprocity for actual benefits received. The slave's position and obligations in the Roman Empire remain the most consistent model for every believer's understanding of service within the Christian community. On the basis of that model, no believer would be excluded from the positions of service in the church, all of which are low in status.

8.3 Men and Authority

Paul's rejection of the Greco-Roman social pyramid and the superiority of the wise, noble, and powerful condemned the male hegemony that was integral to the entire system and emblematic of the Roman Empire, which crucified Christ. The foolishness of the cross and God's choice of the weak, despised, and foolish (1 Cor. 1:28–31) had the effect of commending women and slaves, who were the archetypes of the bottom of the pyramid, while Paul announced God's intention to shame the wise and influential and render them power-less. The goals, values, and character qualities of the ideal elite male were invalidated. The basis of honor changed, and any virtues that remained were available to all believers; in many cases the virtues were stereotypical female qualities and roles. This nevertheless was good news for men, because the Christian community freed both elite men and men who aspired to improve their status from a rigid structure that placed an enormous amount of pres-sure on them to perform and compete for honor.[23]

---

presents himself as the authority who does not conform to standard norms of authority" (*Our Mother Saint Paul* [Louisville: Westminster John Knox, 2007], 14).

    23. Paul resists and condemns the attitude that claims any position or power over another believer in the Christian community on the basis of class, intelligence/education, strength, or

8.3.1 Reversals of the Masculine Role for Leadership

For men, there were a number of reversals from the cultural ideal of masculinity. Anything that the culture regarded as qualifications for power or leadership was a gift from God and a responsibility, but it was not the basis of any leverage for power or status over another believer. Various positions of influence in the community were based on the "demonstration of the Spirit's power" rather than a person's own power (1 Cor. 2:4).[24] Paul believes that the Spirit's power is displayed best when he is weak, afraid, and shaking (1 Cor. 2:3). He does not want the success of the gospel to depend on his own techniques of persuasive speech.

Paul contrasts his weakness and lack of rhetoric with the arrogance, boastful qualifications, and polished speech of his opponents. Paul is actually well qualified according to their standards, but he claims that these standards are no longer valid. Instead of competing with them, Paul insists that the test is the power of the Spirit, and he concludes, "For the kingdom of God is not about talk but about power" (1 Cor. 4:20).[25] The power that Paul is talking about is not a masculine character quality, but rather confidence in the miraculous. Similarly, the gifts of the Spirit are manifestations of the Spirit so that service and functions in positions of authority including pastor, evangelist, and administrator are grace that is determined by the Spirit (Rom. 12:5, 8; 1 Cor. 12:11, 29; Eph. 4:11). As Paul states, "We have this treasure [of our ministry] in clay pots so that the extraordinary power might be from God and not us" (2 Cor. 4:7, cf. 4:1).

Paul's description of the work of the flesh and the fruit of the Spirit offers an interesting contrast between the culture's view of masculinity and the manifestation of the Spirit in character and behavior. The "works of the flesh" involved behavior more typical of the kind associated with male competition, particularly striving for honor and control as well as exploiting any sexual double standard: "Now the works of the flesh are obvious: fornication,

---

wealth. This encompasses particularly any assumed ontological differentiation on which human wisdom or culture evaluates worth.

24. This is true of the manifestation of the Spirit for every believer. However, here Paul is most likely referring to the charismatic demonstration of the miraculous "signs, wonders, and miracles" that identify him as an apostle and that he claims he performed among them with "continuous endurance" (2 Cor. 12:12). However, Luke records no specific miracles in Corinth (Acts 18), though Paul's vision in Acts 18:10 would qualify as a sign. Nevertheless, Luke records various signs, wonders, and miracles done through Paul that both identify him as an apostle and should be considered as typical of his ministry.

25. Later in 2 Corinthians, Paul asserts that he will brag only about his weakness, and that when three times he asked God to take away a problem, illness, or disability, the reply was "My grace is enough for you, because my power is made perfect in weakness" (12:9).

impurity, licentiousness, idolatry, sorcery, enmities, strife, jealousy, anger, quarrels, dissensions, factions, envy, drunkenness, carousing, and things like these. I am warning you, as I warned you before: those who do such things will not inherit the kingdom of God" (Gal. 5:19–21 NRSV).

While these qualities and activities would be understood as vices for women as well, as far as men were concerned, some of them were desirable or necessary for masculinity and embedded in the cultural system of power and privilege.[26] On the other hand, most of the "fruit of the Spirit" would not have been necessarily desirable or mandatory virtues for men: "By contrast, the fruit of the Spirit is love, joy, peace, patience, kindness, generosity, faithfulness, gentleness, and self-control. There is no law against such things" (Gal. 5:22–23 NRSV). Love, joy, peace, and kindness were little valued as masculine qualities, but generosity, faithfulness, and self-control were in high esteem.

In conclusion, Paul confronts and reverses many of the Greco-Roman culture's standards for masculinity and success. Honor and power were obtained through God's grace and only by the manifestation of the Spirit rather than by personal striving. In 1 Timothy 2:8, Paul explicitly confronts men for anger and arguing, which was a major problem in Ephesus. On the other hand, Paul's opponents were men who competed with him according to the culture's standards.

8.3.2 Does Paul Teach That Leadership in the Church Should Be Exclusively Male?

There is no question that men were called and are called to every aspect of ministry and service outlined in the New Testament. This is true in spite of the fact that the Greco-Roman culture's ideology of masculinity and male leadership ran directly counter to the biblical call to humility, gentleness, and servanthood/slavery.[27] Furthermore, in practice the choice of men for leadership runs counter to God's choice of the weak, foolish, and despised

26. Conventional masculinity essentially involves some form of combat, competition, and striving. As James Nelson observes, we still live in "a society where masculinity seems never achieved once and for all and always needs proving" (*Body Theology* [Louisville: Westminster John Knox, 1992], 68).

27. Paul, Jesus Christ, and God have been misrepresented by secular and particularly Greco-Roman ideals of masculinity and leadership. Lisa Isherwood argues that the misrepresentation is "fashioned from some pre-Christian thinking and some dualistic metaphysics. . . . The image of a Christian god that has no need of anything and no vulnerability has been prevalent despite the central symbolic of incarnation and crucifixion"; thus God becomes "the one who is no-relational, self-sufficient, powerful and, in short, hard" (*The Fat Jesus: Christianity and Body Image* [New York: Seabury, 2008], 21). See also Nelson's critique of phallocentric theology (*Body Theology*, 94). While some will be uncomfortable with their assumption that God is

and counter to the fact that the biological makeup of males has a higher association with combat, competition, anger, domination, murder, and all other forms of crime. However, as Paul's call illustrates, male leadership may display God's grace and power as well as dramatic redemption and spiritual transformation when it operates on biblical principles.

What should be considered strange, given the mismatch between masculinity (cultural and biological) and the biblical description of leadership in the church, is that the traditional teaching and praxis of the church have been that only men may exercise authority by leading and teaching in the church community. Yet the dominant teaching in the Pauline corpus and the teaching of Jesus exposes several problems with the traditional position.

The first problem is that the traditional concept of authority in the church does not reflect Jesus's or Paul's teaching. Rather, it has developed into the exercise of elite power and status, and the possession and control of education and wealth.[28] The concept of authority in the church has traditionally been correlated with the "rule" of a husband over his wife in Genesis 3:16, and it is taught that a woman in authority in the church would be a violation of her husband's rule. However, the way Jesus and Paul have defined leadership excludes the concept of rule; instead, true leadership embraces slavery and placing oneself last. God chooses the weak, the foolish, the powerless, and the despised to shame the advantaged, and there can be no disqualification of the disadvantaged because of real or imagined failings. Therefore, the status of a leader who is God's slave does not violate the role of submission in societal relationships.

The second problem is that the power behind legitimate authority in the church comes from the manifestation of the Holy Spirit, not from the personal power of any individual. God's grace is manifested in personal weakness.

The third problem is that the manifestations of the Spirit, on which positions in the church should be based, are given to all as the Spirit wills, not according to any other criteria.

As the fourth problem, Paul is concerned that believers not get "puffed up" in relationship to their own leadership or in regard to each other; that

---

vulnerable, there should be no question that our primary model is the incarnate Christ, who was vulnerable in every human sense.

28. The tradition of interpretation has been heavily influenced by the later development legalizing Christianity. The transfer of worship from the house church to public space and the development of the church into a road to power resulted in positions in the church having substantial power in the empire. In the present times, the powerful role of the church and Christianity, particularly in the United States, is taken almost as a right by some scholars. Therefore, positions in the church are associated with elite positions of power, status, and income, and church and societal controls are conflated in a way completely foreign to the first-century context.

is a sign of a false apostle. Men's claim of priority over women must raise questions about men being "puffed up" from various claims of the God-given right to rule by virtue of their inherent qualification. Such claims sound far more consistent with classic Greek philosophy than Pauline theology.

The claim that only men can hold "positions of authority" in the church is based on a non-Pauline understanding of both the nature of ministry and the nature of spiritual authority. For the most part, this claim is based on the Pauline prohibitions for women in 1 Timothy 2:12. However, prohibitions and restrictions for women do not constitute positive mandates for the behavior of men; that is an exegetical fallacy. The traditional interpretations, inferences, restrictions, and practices built on that one verse create inconsistencies, contradictions, and incoherence between Pauline texts and within Pauline theology.[29] Men in leadership who have a goal of practicing biblical authority should study and implement Paul's theology of authority and embrace his example, which continues to be countercultural and in opposition to the traditional male leadership model.

8.4 Women and Authority

In the Greco-Roman culture, women were the archetype of what was considered foolish and weak, in contrast with men, who were upheld as wise and strong.[30] Platonic thought also contrasted the ideal with anything that changed, was flexible, or was in flux, and women—who experienced menstruation, childbirth, lactation, and menopause—typified change.[31] The traditional view that Roman women should not exercise authority was still intact at the inception of the Greco-Roman world, as Cicero shows: "Our ancestors determined that all women, on account of the inferiority of their understanding, should be under the protection of trustees."[32] Furthermore, Octavian attempted to legislate a supposed return to traditional Roman values in women's roles and

29. The context of "public worship" is assumed from the command for men to pray in every place in 1 Tim. 2:8, but prayer "in every place" in the context of the first-century practice of prayer would mean all forms of prayer at all times, public and private. Furthermore, the prohibitions in 1 Tim. 2:12 apply to a woman (singular) teaching a man (singular). This signals private, one-on-one instruction, which involves an intimacy that could appropriately take place only in the household in the Greco-Roman culture. Furthermore, it is followed by a summary of the classic passage on marriage (2:13–14) and concludes with a reference to delivery during childbirth (2:15).

30. For more detailed information on the Greco-Roman ideology of gender, see chap. 2.

31. Platonic thought influenced later theology to question whether women could be made in the image of the absolute, unchangeable God.

32. Cicero, *Mur.* 27. http://perseus.uchicago.edu/perseus-cgi/citequery3.pl?dbname-Perseus LatinTexts&getid-18query-Cic.%20Mur.%2027.

behavior. Even if Paul shared the same view of women, women's inherent weakness and foolishness would not have disqualified them from God's election, call, and service, according to his own theology. The position of women as lowly and despised was not problematic in filling the role of a slave, a servant (deacon), or a shepherd (pastor). If a woman was problematic in the role of a messenger/ambassador (apostle), then Jesus himself overrode that prejudice by having his resurrection first announced by women.

On the other hand, both the book of Acts and the Pauline corpus provide ample evidence that women exercised various kinds of power and influence on behalf of Paul. Therefore, the record of the spread of Christianity contradicts any assumption that women did not exercise various kinds of authority, or that such authority would necessarily violate the first-century Greco-Roman practices. As argued above, even within marriage in which women were legally subordinated, women functioned in multiple roles in which they were expected to "rule." Heiresses (particularly those who were married *sine manu*),[33] widows, businesswomen, military wives, and women in a number of other roles and situations—all these exercised authority that is inconsistent with the rhetoric of the ideal function of women. Riet van Bremen, drawing from the Roman, Greek, Hellenistic, and Greco-Roman periods, observes,

> [There is] ambiguity between what seems to me a remarkable continuity in the way women were perceived—the ideology and mentality regarding women—and the prominent public role [that] wealthy women could be seen playing in their cities. . . . We have seen that in the Hellenistic and Roman periods a male guardian was still required to assist in legal transactions entered by women. His presence or absence does not appear to have been of great consequence as far as the actual transaction was concerned; he appears as a mere token figure most of the time, but ideologically the persistence of the idea that a woman needed a male guardian is significant. . . . I believe that there is, in the different sources, a strong suggestion that traditional ideas on women had changed little in the course of the Hellenistic and Roman periods.[34]

Women who had three or more children were allowed to waive the requirement of a guardian in Claudius's reign. This is a brief description of phenomena that have been researched and documented across the Roman

---

33. Marriage "without the hand" (*sine manu*) meant that the daughter and her property/inheritance remained under the authority of her father rather than being transferred to her husband's family. This led to cases where the wives were more independent or the husband was forced to comply with her wishes. See chap. 1., n. 51.

34. Van Bremen, "Women and Wealth," in *Images of Women in Antiquity*, ed. Averil Cameron and Amélie Kuhrt (London: Routledge, 1993), 234.

Empire, through inscriptions, papyri, and other evidence: traditional ideas regarding women remained unchanged, while the actual public role of women changed. The rhetoric about women and power must be differentiated from women's actual exercise of authority in the first-century Greco-Roman world.

Until the second half of the twentieth century, however, the New Testament has been distorted by a tradition of interpretation and translation that has adopted the Greco-Roman ideology of gender and the inferiority of women. It includes the presupposition that it is unbiblical for women to exercise any sort of authority. Therefore the indications of women's authority, status, or offices in the Pauline corpus are sometimes not recognized, or they are overlooked, mistranslated, and/or disputed as examples of authority. It will be assumed (all things being equal) that if a word or function has been understood as the exercise of authority in the culture or when applied to a male, then it should be so understood and translated as the exercise of authority when applied to a female.[35]

8.4.1 Women Exercising Authority in the New Testament

Some scholars explicitly or implicitly assume that, according to Paul's teaching, women are uniformly subordinate to the leadership of all men in the Christian community and do not exercise authority. This is thought to be fully consistent with women's status in the culture. However, although the Greco-Roman rhetoric about women seems to indicate subordination, semi-segregation to the domestic sphere, and inferiority, women were expected to wield significant authority (rule) in the domestic sphere, even in the classical period in Greece. Furthermore, women in the first century were actually functioning in public in various roles and exercised authority and influence in various ways as patrons or benefactors. The accounts of Paul's mission in Acts and the Pauline corpus indicate that women were wielding authority and influence in the household and in public. However, the language in the Pauline corpus that refers to women has sometimes been translated so that the authority is either ambiguous or indicates subordination. Women's authority in the domestic and public spheres was part of the social pyramid in the world in which Paul and the Christian community operated. Sometimes prominent women used their influence against Paul's mission, but more often the Christian movement spread within the domestic sphere, in which women played a key role.

35. For instance, the Greek word for "patron," προστάτης, means "leader" or "chief," as in the patron-client relationship, but when this word occurs in its feminine form (προστάτις) in Rom. 16:2, it has often been translated as "helper" or "great help," which creates ambiguity, often being understood in English as a subordinate role.

8.4.1.1 Female Imagery for Leadership

As mentioned in chapter 2, maternal nurture was the primary metaphor for Paul's apostolic ministry and exemplary pastoral care in the church plant in Thessalonica: "We did not ask for special treatment from people—not from you or from others, although we could have thrown our weight around as Christ's apostles. Instead, we were gentle with you like a nursing mother caring for her own children" (1 Thess. 2:6–7). Maternal care is directly contrasted with the expected behavior of a leader or someone in authority in the Greco-Roman culture. Sometimes women's tendency to nurture is given as a reason why women should not teach or exercise authority.[36] However, according to the Myers-Briggs analysis of personality types, the majority of clergy (68 percent) prefer to make decisions by feeling rather than thinking.[37] Nurture in leadership positions may serve as a corrective to unnecessary doctrinal controversies and factions, and it is optimal to work toward diversity and balance. Paul's description of the manner of his preaching as maternal care is significant in indicating what he believed about women's fitness for ministry.

8.4.1.2 Women and Authority in the Domestic Sphere

The Pauline corpus demonstrates that women displayed various forms of "status inconsistency": "their lives reflected elements of higher and lower social status" that entailed some exercise of authority in the household and society.[38] A woman could have authority as a mother, a slave owner, the ruler of the household, and the master of the house. Women filled slots of authority as a parent and slave owner, so women must be included in the role of authority in Paul's household codes. In addition, the house churches functioned completely in the domestic sphere, which was primarily the domain of women's authority, influence, and function, and led to women having a primary role in the spread of early Christianity.

Women as Parents. The contemporary discussions of male authority in the Greco-Roman household (Eph. 5:21–6:9; Col. 3:18–24) have contributed to misunderstanding. The household codes reflect the societal hierarchical

---

36. See Thomas R. Schreiner, "An Interpretation of 1 Timothy 2:9–15: A Dialogue with Scholarship," in *Women in the Church: A Fresh Analysis of 1 Timothy 2:9–15*, ed. Andreas J. Köstenberger, Thomas R. Schreiner, and H. Scott Baldwin (Grand Rapids: Baker, 1995), 145.

37. Otto Kroeger and Roy M. Oswald, *Personality Type and Religious Leadership* (Washington, DC: Alban Institute, 1988).

38. Margaret Y. MacDonald, "Reading Real Women through the Undisputed Letters of Paul," in *Women & Christian Origins*, ed. Ross Shepard Kraemer and Mary Rose D'Angelo (New York: Oxford University Press, 1999), 201.

pairings of husband-wife, parents-children, and masters-slaves.[39] Women are
the subordinates in the first pairing (wives). The other two subordinate roles
were filled by both males and females. However, they are often translated
and interpreted as being filled exclusively by men: husbands, fathers, and the
masters. The failure to use gender-accurate language in the translations of
the household codes has led to a misunderstanding that has had theological
consequences in the construction of gender. In Ephesians 6:1–2, "parents"
(γονεῦσιν) may refer to both male and female,[40] and the ensuing quotation
from Deuteronomy 5:16 interprets it as referring to obedience to both fathers
and mothers. Therefore mothers are also addressed as holding the role of
authority in a hierarchical relationship over sons as well as daughters. The
mother continued to hold authority over her adult sons as they formed an
extended household. A son could become the "guardian" of his widowed
mother, but that is comparable to having the power of attorney. It would not
remove his obligation of obedience to her. Children had a sacred obligation
of honor and obedience to their mother as well as their father.

Women as Slave Owners. The fact that women were slave owners and had
authority over the household slaves in the Greco-Roman culture is well documented. A wife was expected to run the household for her husband, which
involved the management of any household slaves. Women who had their
own households owned the slaves in the household. Paul included women
slave owners in his instructions to masters (Eph. 6:9; Col. 4:1).[41] In the social
pyramid, women slave owners occupied a legitimate and recognized position
of authority and superiority over their male slaves or other "inferiors" in the
household or society. This was one of the realities that Paul addressed.

However, many follow John Piper in suggesting that a wife's subordination
is really the subordination of women to men in the church and society. Piper
fails to recognize that some women in the church at Ephesus, for example,
would have been responsible and required to exercise legitimate authority over
their male slaves and servants. Piper argues that a mature woman "will affirm

39. See Marlis Gielen, *Tradition und Theologie neutestamentlicher Haustafelethik: Ein Beitrag
zur Frage einer christlichen Auseinandersetzung mit gesellschaftlichen Normen*, 2nd ed., BBB
75 (Frankfurt: Anton Hain, 1990), 3–4. For a summary of Gielen's proposed elements of the
New Testament household codes, see James Hering, *The Colossian and Ephesian* Haustafeln
in Theological Context: An Analysis of Their Origins, Relationship, and Message, TR 260
(New York: Peter Lang, 2007), 10.
40. The plural of both γονεύς and πατήρ is used to refer to both the male and the female
parent. For γονεύς, see BDAG, 205, and for the information that it can also be used for "father,"
see LSJ; for πατήρ, see BDAG, 786, 1a.
41. The masculine plural κύριοι ("masters") is used to refer to males and females, and would
include any women slave owners in the church.

and receive and nurture the strength and leadership of men *in some form* in all relationships with men."[42] He further argues, "To the degree that a woman's influence over man is personal and directive, it will generally offend a man's good, God-given sense of responsibility and leadership, and thus controvert God's created order."[43] Yet Piper's understanding of male leadership in the case of male slaves would be inapplicable nonsense to a female slave owner and dangerously subversive to imperial ideology. Never did Paul teach that women slave owners should nurture Piper's sort of leadership with their male slaves. Paul instructed women masters to exercise the same kind of authority as male masters, and slaves were to render them the same obedience.

The relationship between a female owner and a male slave must constrain our understanding of the prohibitions in 1 Timothy 2:12 that a woman should not teach or dominate a man. Those prohibitions could not erase the legal societal relationship if both attended a house church, so that the woman would continue to be in authority over the slave. Male slaves may well have helped in meal preparation and serving at the fellowship meals. Male slaves may have accompanied a woman to the meeting. These complications would not be an issue if we understand 1 Timothy 2:12 to apply to a husband and wife, as the context of the marriage passage in Genesis and the reference to childbirth suggest.

Women Ruling the Household. As mentioned above, the cultural ideal held that it was a wife's responsibility to rule in the domestic sphere, while it was the husband's responsibility to rule in the public sphere, and the domestic sphere included male and female slaves as well as children. Margaret MacDonald suggests, "This link between leadership and household probably had a special significance for the roles of women. . . . The household base of the movement may have enabled women to turn community leadership into an extension of their roles as household managers."[44] The wife's title was the feminine form (οἰκοδέσποινα) of "the master of the house" (οἰκοδεσπότης). Paul uses the verb form of the word in 1 Timothy 5:14: "So I would have younger widows marry, bear children, and rule their households [οἰκοδεσποτέω], so as to give the adversary no occasion to revile us" (NRSV). Most translations demote the authoritative meaning of the word to refer to "management," which conveys a sense of delegation rather than the authority that the term and the culture attributed to the woman who was in charge of the extended household.

42. Piper, "A Vision of Biblical Complementarity," in *Recovering Biblical Manhood and Womanhood: A Response to Evangelical Feminism*, ed. John Piper and Wayne Grudem (Wheaton: Crossway, 1991), 50.
43. Ibid., 51.
44. MacDonald, "Reading Real Women," in Kraemer and D'Angelo, *Women & Christian Origins*, 204.

The domestic authority of women who ran households is an important key to the spread of early Christianity in house churches and the dynamics in the early church. One of Carolyn Osiek and Margaret MacDonald's assumptions is that "the house church was the center for worship, hospitality, patronage, education, communication, social services, evangelism, and mission."[45] This is an inference that matches the evidence of the Pauline corpus and is widely accepted in scholarship. Since the women ruled the domestic sphere, their support and participation were essential for the success of the church in all these areas. Because the activities in the domestic sphere were under the direction of women, including the rituals of domestic worship, any suggestion of exclusion is unlikely. Therefore, Osiek and MacDonald's assumption that "women participated in all the activities of the house church in the first generations of the Christian era" is a well-based inference, given the traditional Greco-Roman role of women in the home.[46] Rodney Stark also argues that a primary reason why Christianity spread was the participation of women.[47] Women's central role in the domestic sphere particularly explains the unusual number of women whom Paul commends for service in Romans 16. It also makes it likely that they would hold various church offices if they were providing the bulk of the service in the house church. There is nothing that is inconsistent with the Greco-Roman culture in a woman holding an authoritative title for domestic responsibilities. Nearly all early Christian offices carried low-status labels that a woman could bear without scandal (servant, shepherd/pastor, elder).[48] The women not only played the central role in the domestic sphere, but also generally formed the communication network in every city and maintained the social ties among their acquaintances. The fact that the rhetoric about gender as well as the practice of veiling rendered women invisible led to their effectiveness in the spread of the gospel without detection in high-risk situations.

Women as Masters of the House. As mentioned above, the household was indisputably the meeting place of the house church and served as a model for the early Christian community. The homeowners who allowed the church to

45. Osiek and MacDonald, *A Woman's Place: House Churches in Earliest Christianity* (Minneapolis: Fortress, 2006), 9.

46. Ibid.

47. Stark, *The Rise of Christianity: How the Obscure, Marginal Jesus Movement Became the Dominant Religious Force in the Western World in a Few Centuries* (San Francisco: HarperSanFrancisco, 1997), 95–108.

48. The only label that may not seem to reflect low status and could be unusual to apply to a woman is "apostle." A woman's testimony was not accepted in a court, but there were extremely strong precedents for women as "sent ones" or divine messengers in the Jewish and Greek cultures. For instance, see the Oracle at Delphi and the Sibylline Oracles.

gather in their homes appropriately presided over the fellowship meal and worship, and often Paul referred to the house church in their name.[49] Widows were sometimes the masters of their own household. In 1 Corinthians 1:11, there is a reference to "members from Chloe's household" who reported to Paul about divisions in the Corinthian Christian community. The wording suggests that Chloe was in authority over Paul's informants, probably indicating that she was the head of the household; she may have been a wealthy widow who exercised control over her property and affairs.[50] However, the best example is Lydia, the first convert in Philippi (Acts 16:14–15). She insisted on being the benefactor of the mission team by housing all of them and the house church that they planted (Acts 16:40). In the culture, Chloe and Lydia would have been given the honor and the responsibility of presiding over their own tables at a fellowship meal. Women sponsored and presided over such meals in pagan worship, and it would have been a violation of the culture to refuse appropriate honor.

8.4.1.3 Women in Authority in Public

Women were in business, they were public benefactors, they could lead organizations, and they could function as priests. In Acts 16:14, Lydia is introduced as a dealer in purple cloth, which indicates that she is a well-to-do businesswoman who buys and sells a cloth worn by royalty. Such women, as well as wealthy matrons and widows, functioned as patrons and public benefactors. Osiek and MacDonald point out that women were the patrons of guilds, clubs, synagogues, and other associations.[51] Women did not appear to technically fill the formal role of patron in the formalized social network that was the backbone of the social system for men. For men, patronage was the standard means for political, social, and economic advancement and benefits. However, the social system was based on the principle of reciprocity: every act of patronage or benefaction formed an obligation on the part of the recipients that was the same as in any patron-client relationship. Women's acts of benefaction sometimes resulted in their occupying public offices, presiding

49. Robert Jewett states, "The host or hostess of house churches was usually a person of high social standing and means, with a residence large enough for the church to gather, who presided over the Eucharist celebrations and was responsible for the ordering of the congregation" (*Romans: A Commentary*, ed. Eldon J. Epp, Hermeneia [Minneapolis: Fortress, 2007], 947).

50. See the discussion on Chloe in MacDonald, "Reading Real Women," in Kraemer and D'Angelo, *Women & Christian Origins*, 200–202. However, Wayne Meeks warns, "Whether she was a Christian is not stated and cannot be inferred with any confidence" (*The First Urban Christians: The Social World of the Apostle Paul* [New Haven: Yale University Press, 1983], 59).

51. Osiek and MacDonald, *Woman's Place*, 11.

over a synagogue, or functioning as priests in local cults. Luke reports that both the opposition and support of prominent women played a role in the spread of the gentile mission (Acts 13:50; 17:12, 34). The fact that Paul first approached a group of women in Philippi gathered for prayer in a public place by the river when there was no synagogue (16:13–16) substantiates the central role of women in the success and spread of his mission.

8.4.1.4 SUMMARY

The Greco-Roman culture let women exercise authority in the area in which they were able to impact the church the most: the domestic sphere. However, women in the first-century Roman world were entering the public sphere in business and as patrons, and they impacted the early church in those roles as well. However, assumptions that women had no authority have affected interpretation and translation, which has obscured their roles and the contexts in which they made contributions and served the church. It is a false dichotomy to say that men served in the public worship service and women served in the home, because worship took place in homes, under the patronage, auspices, and hospitality of women who were expected to rule their households. On the other hand, Paul does not describe service in his churches primarily in terms of ruling or patronage. For the most part, he uses low-status labels that also suited the domestic context.

8.4.2 Women Serving in the Christian Community

Both Paul and Jesus defined leadership in the Christian community as slavery. The best place to look for Paul's understanding of the nature of service as slavery is the household code:

> Slaves, obey your earthly masters with fear and trembling, in singleness of heart, as you obey Christ; not only while being watched, and in order to please them, but as slaves of Christ, doing the will of God from the heart. Render service with enthusiasm, as to the Lord and not to men and women, knowing that whatever good we do, we will receive the same again from the Lord, whether we are slaves or free. (Eph. 6:5–8 NRSV)

As the gentile mission spread, leadership in the Pauline mission was more risky than glamorous. The church was not a road to status, power, and financial gain. Paul described his apostolic ministry as working hard at menial labor with his hands, suffering imprisonments and beatings, and being exposed to death, in danger in the city, in the country, and at sea. He was constantly in danger from bandits, Jews, gentiles, and false believers. Paul went without sleep, food, clothing, and shelter (2 Cor. 11:23–27). The Corinthian church was not at all impressed with his interpretation of apostolic ministry. The church spread through small cells of house churches. Paul and his ministry team set up people responsible for the house church, using leadership labels that he related to household functions:[52] He defined elders as caregivers in the household (Titus 1:7)[53] and as servants (deacons), both of whose functions he correlated with household management (1 Tim. 3:4–5, 12; cf. 3:15).[54] The content of the worship service would have come through the exercise of spiritual gifts; all the members came ready to participate.

In order to understand what Paul really means by the terms that he uses for those who labor hard in the house churches, we need to strip away the associations that these words developed as technical terms for positions of power and status in church history and traditions. When Christianity was legalized in 313 CE and moved into public space, the terms "elder" and "deacon" quickly became titles of power, authority, and prestige in the gentile world. The fellowship meal became a stylized ritual (Eucharist) that was controlled by men in public space. The positions of leadership became public offices instead of household roles, reflecting masculine concepts of hierarchy in the public sphere. When the context of worship changed, "elder," "deacon," and "bishop" soon became titles that were far different from Paul's use of the terms. The rhetoric of gender would lead to the exclusion of women from public leadership when it would not have excluded them from household leadership.

Therefore, apart from the assumption that the prohibitions of a woman teaching and dominating a man in 1 Timothy 2:12 apply to "public worship," there is no cultural, grammatical, or textual reason to exclude women from

52. The offices were appointed positions, mentioned throughout Acts and in Phil. 1:1; 1 Tim. 3:1–13; Titus 1:5–9.

53. The meaning of the word ἐπίσκοπος is constrained as one who "watches" in the household, which would be a tutor, caregiver, or even a babysitter rather than an ecclesial office of bishop or an overseer/supervisor.

54. The Greek word προΐστημι, which is often translated as "management," occurs 8× in the New Testament. It occurs in the middle voice in Rom. 12:8; 1 Thess. 5:12; 1 Tim. 3:4, 12; Titus 3:8, 14, and it occurs in the active voice in 1 Tim. 3:5 and 5:17. According to LSJ, the verb προΐστημι in the middle voice has a range of meaning that runs from to "put before oneself," to "prefer or value one above another," which has the action of the group or community in view. However, BDAG understands προΐστημι as an individual who possesses authority as in "to exercise a position of leadership, rule, direct, be at the head of" in Rom. 5:8; 1 Thess. 5:12; 1 Tim. 5:17. Or, BDAG understands the word as "to have an interest in, show concern for, care for, give aid" in Rom. 12:8 and 1 Thess. 5:12, both of which correspond to the passive sense in the LSJ. Contra BDAG, we can assume that Paul's alternation of middle and active voice in 1 Timothy is motivated by meaning better reflected in the LSJ. This could be an area of further research.

Pauline leadership in the house churches as far as the positions themselves are concerned or the responsibilities associated with them.[55] According to the patterns of grammatical gender in the Greek language, words for leadership would occur in the masculine singular or masculine plural unless for some exclusively female referent(s). Masculine is the default gender, and it cannot be assumed that women are excluded as referents from masculine nouns, pronouns, and so forth, particularly in catchphrases, unless they are excluded by the context. If we do not approach the text with the presupposition that women are excluded from leadership in the church, we find many references to them participating fully and effectively in so many ways that we may assume that they are included in general descriptions and instructions to church leaders that use the masculine plural and singular.

8.4.2.1 APOSTLE

In Romans 16:7, Paul directs the Roman church, "Greet Andronicus and Junia, my relatives who were in prison with me; they are prominent among the apostles, and they were in Christ before I was" (NRSV). Junia is a woman who receives a powerful commendation from Paul. Not only does he call her an apostle, but also she was a believer longer than Paul was; possibly she was part of the dispersion of the Hellenistic Jewish believers after the stoning of Stephen and may have spread the gospel to Rome.[56] She had even been imprisoned for her faith, which alone indicates that her ministry extended beyond the boundaries of her household.

Junia was recognized as a woman apostle in the virtually unanimous understanding of the church until the late Middle Ages.[57] That consensus began to shift with Aegidius (or Giles) of Rome (ca. 1316), who preferred to identify Junia as male (Junius) because she was called an apostle. In the twentieth

---

55. The prohibitions in 1 Tim. 2:12 against a woman teaching or dominating a man are constrained by the use of the singular "woman" and "man," as well as by the context, to refer to the relationship between a husband and wife. The word "dominate" (αὐθεντέω) is never used by Paul for any form of leadership, nor is it ever used in the Greek language for pastoral care for an individual (when the individual is the recipient of the action). For the exegetical analysis of the prohibitions, see chap. 9.

56. Douglas Moo states, "We might infer that Andronicus and Junia were among those early 'Hellenistic' Jews in Jerusalem and that, like Peter and his wife (cf. 1 Cor. 9:5), they moved about in the eastern Mediterranean (where they encountered and perhaps were imprisoned with Paul), seeking to bring men and women to faith in Christ" (*The Epistle to the Romans*, NICNT [Grand Rapids: Eerdmans, 1996], 924).

57. See Joseph Fitzmyer's list of commentators for the first Christian millennium who understood Junia to be a woman (*Romans: A New Translation with Introduction and Commentary*, AB 33 [New York: Doubleday, 1993], 737–38). See also Jewett, *Romans*, 961–62, where he concludes that "'Junias' is a figment of chauvinistic imagination" (962).

century, the critical Greek texts shifted to identifying Junia as a man. The consensus of recent scholarship has reversed that shift, but Michael Burer and Daniel Wallace now argue that the Greek indicates that Andronicus and Junia merely had a good reputation with the apostles.[58] Yet after examining the database and analyzing the vocabulary and grammar, Linda Belleville, Eldon Epp, and Richard Bauckham demonstrate that it is far more convincing to take the verse as meaning that Junia was a woman apostle, which was the overwhelming understanding of the early church.[59]

Of course, this passage has stirred up a storm of controversy because it is understood as a clear challenge to the view that Paul excluded women from positions and titles of leadership. "Apostle" (ἀπόστολος) would not have the sense of being one of the twelve disciples chosen by Jesus; rather, Andronicus and Junia would be apostles in the same sense as were Barnabas (Acts 14:14; 1 Cor. 9:5–6), James (Gal. 1:19), Epaphroditus (Phil. 2:25), and Titus along with "the brothers" who were sent to administrate the offering (2 Cor. 8:23). "Apostle" is one of the foundational spiritual gifts in Paul's lists that are determined by the Spirit (1 Cor. 12:28–29; Eph. 4:11).[60] Apostles are "sent ones" who minister as representatives between multiple local churches and probably include church planters. The nature of an apostle's authority would be directly related to the nature of the apostle's mission, but Junia was "outstanding" compared to the rest of the group.

8.4.2.2 Deacon

In Romans 16:1, Paul identifies Phoebe as a deacon: "I commend to you our sister Phoebe, a deacon of the church at Cenchreae" (NRSV). In the domestic

58. Burer and Wallace, "Was Junia Really an Apostle? A Re-examination of Romans 16:7," *NTS* 47 (2001): 76–91.

59. Belleville, "Ἰουνιᾶν . . . ἐπίσημοι ἐν τοῖς ἀποστόλοις: A Re-examination of Romans 16:7 in Light of Primary Source Materials," *NTS* 51 (2005): 231–49; Epp, *Junia: The First Woman Apostle* (Minneapolis: Fortress, 2005); Bauckham, *Gospel Women: Studies of the Named Women in the Gospels* (Grand Rapids: Eerdmans, 2002), 109–202, esp. 165–85. As Jewett argues, "The adjective ἐπίσημος lifts up a person or thing as distinguished or marked in comparison with other representatives of the same class, in this instance with other apostles (*Romans*, 963). Burer and Wallace ("Was Junia Really an Apostle?") start by treating one of the (well-known) English glosses as if it were the Greek, rather than recognizing that the word is a metaphoric extension, not the equivalent of a verb of perception.

60. Moo cautions that this title does not mean that they have an authoritative leadership position comparable to the Twelve and Paul, but in Paul's writings the title is "looser." He concludes that Junia was a "traveling missionary" (*Romans*, 924). However, notice that Paul calls James an apostle, and James has a central authoritative leadership position as a pillar of the Jerusalem church (Gal. 1:19). Furthermore, the fact that Andronicus and Junia were "outstanding among the apostles" probably indicates that they held some comparable level of authority.

context of a household, "deacon" (διάκονος) refers to a servile, menial servant;[61] but in a public context of a temple or religious guild, it means an "attendant" or an "official"; and in the context of government service or the service of a god, it refers to an agent, authority, or courier.[62] In other words, deacons drew their status from the person or organization that they served. The title "deacon" came to refer to a prestigious office of power in the history of the Western church, reserved for respected men.[63] However, in the New Testament, since the context of the title and the function was a house church, it would be a title directly associated with the low position of a servant of the believers, in keeping with Jesus's and Paul's teachings—a high status in God's kingdom, but a low status in the eyes of the world.

Servile and menial work in the household, such as serving food, was a low-status function in the Greco-Roman period, reserved for women, servants, and slaves in serving those with higher status. Therefore, the meaning of the term in the first-century household related more closely to the woman's low-status role than the ideal role for a man. When Paul gives instructions on the qualifications for deacons in 1 Timothy 3:8–10, he adds in verse 11, "likewise, the women," and gives specific qualifications for women who serve. Therefore, the structure indicates that these are gender-specific instructions to men, next also to women who are serving as deacons (cf. 1 Tim. 2:9–10), and then general instructions for both in verses 12–13. It is therefore most natural to understand that "deacon" is a service to the house church that is filled by men and women. The expression "one-woman man" (μιᾶς γυναικὸς ἄνδρες) in 1 Timothy 3:12 is a catchphrase or idiom for the requirement of marital faithfulness (if married), not a requirement that a deacon be male and married.[64]

61. It is often associated with the selection of the seven Hellenists in Acts 6:1–7 who were appointed to distribute food to the needy (6:2: "wait on tables," διακονεῖν τραπέζαις).

62. See LSJ, "διάκονος," which emphasizes the servile menial meaning of the noun, in contrast with BDAG, 230–31, which stresses the status of assistance to a superior.

63. Functions associated with the office of deacon are collecting the offering and giving assistance in Communion and baptism. Assistance in Communion and baptism is an obvious example of a metaphor that has been turned on its head. Serving food and bathing others were low-status functions in the Greco-Roman period, reserved for women and slaves in serving those with higher status. This low-status title of servant that is associated with low-status service in the church has become a title of honor, and the tasks have assumed the aura of privilege. If it were a case of honoring servants in view of their high position in Christ and valuing work that is regarded as low status in the eyes of the culture, that would be appropriate. However, the entire configuration has morphed.

64. Wayne Grudem says that μιᾶς γυναικὸς ἄνδρες excludes women (*Evangelical Feminism and Biblical Truth: An Analysis of More Than One Hundred Disputed Questions* [Sisters, OR: Multnomah, 2004], 80). However, it is an idiom that must be understood as the sum of its parts. Similarly, we have had titles in English with "man" in them, such as "mailman" and "chairman,"

There is considerable controversy about whether the offices of elder and deacon had developed into technical titles for church officials in the first century. However, perhaps the confusion is cleared up if one recognizes that the function of a servant in the house church would be very close to what Jesus and Paul taught about being a slave to all in function, and similar to "waiting on tables" in Acts 6:2. One should not assume that it had the same sense of the deacon office in a fourth-century public place of worship. This title reflected low-status work on behalf of the church that Paul was honoring as a countercultural value.

8.4.2.3 PROPHET

Paul's understanding of the role of the prophet has been a subject of interest and study that directly relates to gender roles, because multiple and incontestable evidence exists that women were prophets in the history of Israel and in the Pauline churches (1 Cor. 11:5), as well as in churches in the Jewish mission (Acts 21:8–9). Paul associates prophecy and the prophet with spiritual gifts that are given by the Spirit "as he wills" (1 Cor. 12:11). Even more important, Paul describes the gift in detail in contrast with tongues as the spiritual gift that should be held in highest esteem (14:1). In 1 Corinthians 14:1–25, Paul specifically contrasts prophecy with tongues, and the contrasts with his description of tongues should inform us of what is involved in the nature of prophecy. Of all the gifts, prophecy edifies the church the most (v. 4). It strengthens, encourages, and comforts (vv. 3, 31). Prophecy utilizes the understanding and instructs others in an intelligible way, so it is consistent with teaching (vv. 14, 19, 31). Prophecy confronts, convicts, and judges; it lays bare the secrets of the heart and can drive a hearer to the knees in worshiping God, so it is very useful in the evaluation of others' prophecy and revelation (vv. 24–25). Therefore, Paul values prophecy higher than any other gift for the purpose of building up the church, higher than even revelation, knowledge, or instruction (v. 6). Paul's description of prophecy should be a starting point for our understanding of how gifted women functioned in worship in the Pauline churches. This passage must define what is meant by women being silent in church, not the other way around.[65]

---

that did not indicate that the referent was male, but rather that male was the default gender. However, the ambiguity in English led to a movement to remove "man" from generic titles. See the discussion in Philip Payne, *Man and Woman, One in Christ: An Exegetical and Theological Study of Paul's Letters* (Grand Rapids: Zondervan, 2009), 446–49.

65. This clear and well-defined description must inform our understanding of how at least some women who had the gift of prophecy were functioning in the house church. Because it is assumed, on the basis of 1 Tim. 2:12, that women were not allowed to teach in "public

8.4.2.4 FELLOW WORKER

Paul recognized several women as "fellow workers" or "coworkers" (συνεργός): Priscilla, Euodia, and Syntyche. Other individuals who are called "fellow workers" include Aquila, Urbanus, Timothy, Epaphroditus, and Philemon. While we do not have information on Urbanus, we see the term repeatedly applied to Paul's own ministry, Paul's ministry team, and his closest associates.[66] Paul's extensive description of Priscilla and Aquila in Romans 16:3–4 leads Douglas Moo to say, "This is probably because the couple was in the best position to mediate Paul's ministry to the church in Rome."[67] The fact that Paul places Priscilla's name first gives her greater prominence.[68] Paul states that Euodia and Syntyche "struggled beside me in the work of the gospel, together with Clement and the rest of my co-workers,

worship," Wayne Grudem has claimed that prophecy is not teaching, but instead is extemporaneous. Paul claims that prophecy instructs and people learn. The claim that all prophecy is extemporaneous exceeds the evidence. Some claim that women were not allowed to "weigh carefully what is said" because of the command in 1 Cor. 14:34 for women not to talk during church (D. A. Carson, "'Silent in the Churches': On the Role of Women in 1 Corinthians 14:33b–36," in Piper and Grudem, *Recovering Biblical Manhood and Womanhood*, 151–53; Wayne Grudem, *The Gift of Prophecy in 1 Corinthians* [Washington, DC: University Press of America, 1982], 245–55). However, if women were involved in confrontational evaluation such as is described in 1 Cor. 14:24–25, they would hardly be excluded from evaluating another prophet. Some claim that women can confront non-Christians, but not believers. However, that contradicts the whole history of the primary use of prophecy. Attempts to redefine the nature of prophecy in order to be consistent with preconceived theological assumptions about women's role in teaching, leading, and silence collapse when confronted by sound exegesis of Paul's own description of prophecy.

66. However, Moo states, "The term always denotes work in ministry, but the kind of ministry undertaken is not specified" (*Romans*, 920). He states that his view is in contradiction to Elisabeth Schüssler Fiorenza, who argues that the term always refers to leaders in the community (Schüssler Fiorenza, "Missionaries, Apostles, Coworkers: Romans 16 and the Reconstruction of Women's Early History," WW 6 [1986]: 425–26). Perhaps Moo is trying to indicate that this term would not prove that a woman was an elder/bishop or a deacon. However, there are different forms of leadership that the culture recognizes, and Paul's use of this term to honor others connotes a form of leadership, regardless of whether they are elders or deacons.

67. Moo, *Romans*, 919.

68. Many argue that Priscilla had higher status, though her precedence indicates her more active role in serving the church through her gift of hospitality. Priscilla served God and the church by utilizing her business and household to create opportunities for frontline ministry. Jewett argues that Priscilla came from noble background; there is a Santa Prisca parish in the Aventine district of Rome, built over the ruins of two private homes; the Titilus Priscae address suggests extensive property. The Catacomb of Priscilla was located in the country estate of the Acilian family, which had an early association with Christianity (Tacitus, *Ann.* 67.14; Dio Cassius, *Hist. rom.* 67.14). See Jewett, *Romans*, 955–56. Meeks suggests that their wealth was relatively high because they were able to move from place to place and establish sizeable households, host churches, and act as patrons. On the other hand, their occupation is "low, but not at the bottom. They are artisans, but independent, and by ancient standards, they operate on a fairly large scale" (*First Urban Christians*, 59).

whose names are in the book of life" (Phil. 4:3 NRSV). All three of these women may be described as "local church leaders with a recognized position of prominence in the community."[69] Adolphus Chinedu Amadi-Azuogu offers the following chart of the distribution of συνεργός and its cognates in the New Testament:[70]

συνεργός (synergos)		Rom.	1 Cor.	2 Cor.	Phil.	Philem.	1 Thess.	Col.	3 John
		16:3	3:9	1:24	2:25	24	3:2	4:11	8
		16:9		8:23	4:3				
		16:21							
συνεργέω (synergeō)	Mark 16:20	Rom. 8:28	1 Cor. 16:16	2 Cor. 6:1					James 2:22

He demonstrates that "fellow worker" is one of Paul's preferred titles for ministers and leaders in the Pauline corpus.

8.4.2.5 Those Who Work Hard and Lead

The verb "to work hard" (κοπιάω) is a word that Paul characteristically uses to describe his own missionary labors (1 Cor. 4:12, 15:10; Gal. 4:11; Phil. 2:16; Col. 1:29; 1 Tim. 4:10). In Rome, Paul commends only women for working hard (Rom. 16:6, 12): Mary, Tryphaena, and Tryphosa.[71] He also commends Euodia and Syntyche for "fighting" or "contending" for the gospel, and calls them coworkers (Phil. 4:3). As noted above (see §8.2.3), Paul states in 1 Corinthians 16:15–16 that he expects the churches to "submit" to those who work hard: "Now, brothers and sisters, you know that members of the household of Stephanas were the first converts in Achaia, and they have devoted themselves to the service of the saints; I urge you to put yourselves at the service [ὑποτάσσησθε: be subject, subordinate yourselves] of such people, and of everyone who works and toils [τῷ συνεργοῦντι καὶ κοπιῶντι] with them" (NRSV).

In 1 Thessalonians 5:12–13, Paul directs the church to recognize and honor its leaders, who are described as "those who labor [work hard] among you, and have charge of you in the Lord and admonish you" (NRSV). These three activities represent a "status" (in Pauline terms) and spiritual authority among the people of God. In first-century Christianity, these terms closely correlate

69. Adolphus Chinedu Amadi-Azuogu, *Gender and Ministry in Early Christianity and the Church Today* (Lanham, MD: University Press of America, 2007), 2.

70. Ibid., 2.

71. Moo suggests that the sample is not large enough to establish a technical sense such as Christian missionary ministry (*Romans*, 921). However, it is used in the context of honor and recognition so consistently that one may conclude that it applies to leadership.

with what would later become ordained clergy.[72] Paul appears to use the terms consistently when honoring leaders.[73]

8.4.2.6 Missing Titles?

Paul refers to Junia as an apostle (Rom. 16:7) and Phoebe as a deacon (16:1), but there are no instances where he gives specific women the title "pastor," "elder," or "teacher." However, Paul does not give specific men these titles either, except for two cases when he calls himself a teacher (1 Tim. 2:7; 2 Tim. 1:11). The fact that Paul commends so many women so strongly with terms that he uses for his ministry team indicates that women were in various positions of leadership and service in the church, women to whom Paul gave honor, recognition, and in some cases submission, including apostle, deacon, prophet, fellow worker, and one who works hard. In two cases (Priscilla and Phoebe) he gives women honor as patrons (Rom. 16:1–3).[74] According to Pauline practice and Greek grammar, outside of 1 Timothy there is no compelling reason to suggest that women would be excluded from being pastors, elders, or teachers in a house church that is modeled on the household, since Paul has honored them for filling these other roles. Paul's teaching on spiritual gifts indicates that the Spirit distributes the spiritual gifts of pastor and teacher as he wills, so that only the Spirit is qualified to restrict any group from serving those functions. Yet the position of elder/bishop was appointed by Paul and his mission team. The only evidence for any restriction on women comes from the way the church has traditionally interpreted the prohibitions in 1 Timothy 2:12. However, the passage in which it occurs is riddled with interpretive problems and a lack of coherence. In chapter 9 (below) I will argue that the passage has been misunderstood and misapplied.

72. Amadi-Azuogu says that they "had authority" and calls them "ecclesiastical officials," but that language may be more suitable to a later power structure (*Gender and Ministry*, 9).

73. Adolf von Harnack argues that the 23 New Testament instances of the verb "to labor" indicate that it was a technical term for missionary and congregational work ("Κόπος [κοπιᾶν, οἱ κοπιῶντες] im frühchristlichen Sprachgebrauch," *ZNW* 27 [1928]: 1–10). The verb occurs in the Pauline corpus in Rom. 16:6, 12 (2×); 1 Cor. 4:12; 15:10; 16:16; Gal. 4:11; Eph. 4:28; Phil. 2:16; Col. 1:29; 1 Thess. 5:12; 1 Tim. 4:10; 5:17; 2 Tim. 2:6.

74. Jewett says that Priscilla "provided resources in concrete acts of patronage, implying the employment of substantial resources. The term προστάτις means 'protectress, patroness, helper' and its masculine counterpart took on the technical sense of a legal patron" (*Romans*, 946). It was formerly assumed that women could not be legal patrons, but the weight of evidence since 1981 has shown that they were, and Ramsay MacMullen has stated that women made up "a fifth of all rescript-addresses," and that "perhaps a tenth of the protectors and donors that *collegia* sought out were women" ("Women in Public in the Roman Empire," *Hist* 29 [1980]: 211).

In Western Christianity, in areas where the Pauline theology of power and authority has influenced political theory, it has contributed to equality and shared power for men, and the absolute authority of rulers has been rejected. The depravity of humanity together with the application of the dignity of humanity in God's image contributed to developing ideals of liberty and freedom, democracy (and the rejection of social and political hierarchy), systems of checks and balances, civil rights, and even the separation between church and state within the Western world. These concepts and practices are antithetical to the imperial theology of the first century. Today few men suggest that all Christians are obligated to create or submit to an imperial power because Paul commanded submission to an absolute tyrannical imperial power. However, when it comes to women, Paul has generally been read and interpreted through the traditional Greco-Roman assumptions about gender, power, and hierarchy that were foundational for Greco-Roman philosophy and most of the conventional human wisdom of the first century. This study suggests that we must revisit not only our restrictions on women, but also the inappropriate assumption of authority and power of men in ministry in the church. The function of women in the Pauline corpus has been misrepresented. The subordination and silencing of women in the practice of spiritual gifts in the congregation is far from what Paul taught or modeled.

nine

1 Timothy 2:11–15

Any attempt to deal with Paul and gender in a comprehensive way must address 1 Timothy 2:11–15 and how it should be read in terms of the rest of the Pauline corpus and the context of the letter. Historically, 1 Timothy 2:12 is the primary text that has been used up to the present to ban women from certain activities and functions within the church, regardless of a woman's training, skills, or spiritual gifts. It has provided a lens or exegetical grid through which all other Scripture is applied to women. In traditional interpretation, in fact, obedience to this passage, together with submission, seems to constitute the entire scope of a woman's call. Therefore, it is imperative to offer a more comprehensive exegesis of this passage and to explore the interpretive options as well as the implications of certain interpretive choices that have been made. I will conclude with a coherent reading of the passage that is faithful to the text within the context of the culture of Ephesus and the context of 1 Timothy, including its stated purpose and intent, the relevant information given in the Letters to Timothy, and the flow of the discourse.

Every interpretation of 1 Timothy 2:11–15 comes to conclusions about the text through an interpretive process. There are several major exegetical crossroads or turning points where scholars make crucial choices before they directly approach the passage in question, choices that affect the outcome. Some of these choices even appear to be relatively unexamined assumptions. I will highlight these tipping points and discuss the implications of the exegetical choices. Then, after identifying the letter's purpose to be the prevention of false teaching, as stated in the body opening in 1 Timothy 1:3–4, I will compile the letter's information about false teaching and practices that are related to gender. The information about false teaching among the men and women will provide the context or lens in which the instructions to men and women are given in 2:8–10, as well as the specific instruction for a woman to learn and the accompanying prohibitions. This will provide a fresh reading of the passage that is faithful to the context, the text, and Pauline theology.

9.1 Broad Exegetical Choices

Even before the passage is analyzed, several exegetical choices have already been made that directly impact its interpretation. The first divide is over whether the text is authoritative for the church and Christian living. The second divide occurs over the authorship of Paul. The third divide occurs over whether the intended recipient is an individual or a group. The fourth divide concerns the role that context plays in determining the meaning of the text. The fifth divide occurs concerning the identification of the setting or scenario of 1 Timothy 2:1–15. The choice that is made at each tipping point tends to guide the other choices.

9.1.1 First Timothy as Authoritative

I suggest that a primary exegetical choice is whether the text is considered to be authoritative in the church. This represents the broadest divide between interpreters and is a clear indicator of one's approach to the text. As discussed below, the majority of scholars contest the Pauline authorship of the Pastoral Epistles.[1] Consequently, those who contest authorship may either ignore the letter (which is common), or, as in feminist approaches, they may present the author as controlled by a first- or second-century worldview about women in terms that are unpalatable and unacceptable.[2] Some interpret the text in blatant contradiction to other Pauline letters rather than interpreting

1. However, the Pastoral Epistles usually are treated as a discrete group. As Howard Marshall says, "The letters can be considered together as a group of writings. They represent a common outlook with the kind of variations that one would expect to find in any group of writings by one author whose thought was liable to change and development" (*The Pastoral Epistles*, ICC [Edinburgh: T&T Clark, 1999], 1).

2. For example, Ulrike Wagener identifies the purpose of the letter as the assertion of the patriarchal system, which must be rejected by a feminist hermeneutic (*Die Ordnung des "Hauses Gottes": Der Ort von Frauen in der Ekklesiologie und Ethik der Pastoralbriefe*, WUNT 65 [Tübingen: Mohr Siebeck, 1994], 67–113).

it within the context of other Pauline texts.[3] However, there are those who accept the epistle as authoritative and do so because it is part of the canon or on the basis of Pauline authorship. Those who question Pauline authorship but accept it as an authoritative book of the canon may still move the book to the edge of the canon in terms of its authority. Those who accept the text as Pauline are more likely to be motivated to engage in close exegetical work as well, to have a stake in interpreting it in conjunction with other Pauline passages, and to utilize it while constructing a coherent Pauline theology.

9.1.2 First Timothy as Pauline

In 1 Timothy 1:1, the letter says that it is written by "Paul, an apostle of Christ Jesus," which identifies it as Pauline. The majority of those who consider 1 Timothy to be Pauline nevertheless see it as written by a Pauline circle after Paul's death and composed in the late first or early second century.[4] As such, it would be a late development or extension of Pauline theology, or possibly a correction. A minority see it as authored by the historical Paul within a framework of his life, including the additional biographical material from the Pastoral Epistles. The Pastoral Epistles extend the framework and add biographical information to what is found in Acts and the other Pauline Letters.[5] Those who hold this position also wish to interpret the epistle within the context of the theology of the greater Pauline corpus. While most laypeople may assume that the text was written by Paul alone, it is common among scholars to accept that Paul utilized an amanuensis (a scribe), such as Luke, to write the letter.[6]

The consensus of those who hold to Pauline authorship is that 1 Timothy was written after the events recorded in Acts, which would place the situation and circumstances that Paul was addressing in Ephesus around 63–65 CE,

---

3. Jürgen Roloff rejects the teaching of the passage on the basis of New Testament standards, claiming that Genesis 3 was interpreted incorrectly (*Der erste Brief an Timotheus*, EKKNT 15 [Zurich: Benzinger, 1988], 147). Similarly, Elisabeth Schüssler Fiorenza sees the passage as post-Pauline, with a patriarchal authority pattern, reverting from Paul's teachings on coequal discipleship (Gal. 3:28) (*In Memory of Her: A Feminist Theological Reconstruction of Christian Origins* [London: SCM, 1983], 260–66).

4. Marshall summarizes the dominant view: "They purport to be Pauline compositions (or what Paul would have written if he were still alive)" (*Pastoral Epistles*, 12).

5. For a historical reconstruction of Paul's life from the Pastoral Epistles, see William Mounce, *Pastoral Epistles*, WBC 46 (Nashville: Nelson, 2000), liv–lxiv.

6. See, e.g., George Knight III, *The Pastoral Epistles: A Commentary on the Greek Text*, NIGTC (Grand Rapids: Eerdmans, 1992), 48–52, where he entertains the idea that Luke had a supportive function in Paul's writing.

at least eight years after Paul's extended stay in Ephesus during his third missionary journey (Acts 19:10), and at least fourteen years after Timothy joined Paul's missionary team, around 49 CE, during the second missionary journey (Acts 16:1–3).[7]

9.1.3 First Timothy as a Personal Letter

The text identifies the recipient of the letter as "Timothy, my true son in the faith" (1:2) and formally indicates that it is a personal letter.[8] Nevertheless, the majority of scholars believe that 1 Timothy is a public letter that was written to the larger group of the church or the Christian churches. These scholars include those who contest the authorship of Paul, and those who accept authorship by Paul, but make an argument that it is a public letter, based solely on the use of the second-person plural in the closing, "Grace be with you all" (6:21).[9]

On the basis of the greeting (1:1), the pervasive use of the second-person singular, and the vocative or the nominative singular of direct address in reference to Timothy (1:18; 6:11, 20), the text has the formal features of a personal letter. The second-person plural greeting at the end does not signal a public or group letter, according to evidence in the personal letters in the papyri; closings that include blessings and/or health wishes to the recipient's families, communities, or other groups through personal letters are common.[10] However, identifying it as a personal letter is not to claim it as a private, confidential letter (i.e., a letter explicitly not meant to be read by others). In the ancient world, it was understood that personal letters were important news and were read and shared in these larger circles, yet they reflected the register of the relationship and concerns of the author and recipient, not the public. The recipient would be in a position to interpret and explain the letter to the

7. Mounce's view of Paul's relationship with Timothy is that Timothy was "an itinerant apostolic 'delegate'" who "knew Paul's theology and did not need to be taught" (*Pastoral Epistles*, lviii).

8. Ibid., xlvii. As Mounce states, "The texts appear to be epistolary and occasional, ad hoc letters written to deal with specific historical issues in Ephesus and Crete" (ibid.).

9. So argues Marshall: "They are all presented as personal messages from the writer to a single reader. Nevertheless, all three documents end with a benediction couched in the plural form (assuming that the text is correct). In their present form, therefore, they are implicitly overheard by the Christian believers associated with the named recipients, presumably the members of the congregations for which they are responsible" (*Pastoral Epistles*, 12). For instance, chaps. 2–3 are "meant directly for the congregation but mediated through Timothy" (ibid., 25).

10. See the discussion on 2 Timothy as a personal letter in Cynthia Long Westfall, "'This Is a Great Metaphor!': Reciprocity in the Ephesians Household Code," in *Christian Origins and Greco-Roman Culture: Social and Literary Context for the New Testament*, ed. Stanley E. Porter and Andrew Pitts, ECHC 1 (Leiden: Brill, 2013), 225–29.

larger circle of interest. Placing this in terms of epistolary theory, I propose that 1 Timothy, if it is a piece of genuine and transparent communication, is a nonfictitious and nonliterary letter, based on the grammar alone. If it is classified as a public letter, then according to epistolary theory, it would be fictitious because it signals that it is personal; and it may be literary if it is written for the larger public and is not rooted in the relationship between Paul and Timothy or influenced by the situation in Ephesus or the issues in Timothy's ministry.[11] Regardless, the author's signals indicate that it is meant to be read as a personal letter.

Paul's authorship is questioned because the language and style of the Pastoral Epistles are distinct from the rest of the Pauline corpus in vocabulary, syntax, and rhetorical style.[12] However, recent studies in corpus linguistics have shown that a person's writing style and topics will vary significantly when the genre changes or features in the register change (the recipient, the situational context, the content).[13] Variations could be even more extreme when the circumstances and age of the author change, or when letters are coauthored or entirely written by a secretary/amanuensis, as is claimed by many to be the case in the Pauline Epistles, given their internal evidence (Rom. 16:22; 1 Cor. 1:1; cf. 16:21; 2 Cor. 1:1; Gal. 1:1; cf. 6:11; Phil. 1:1; Col. 1:1; cf. 4:18; 1 Thess. 1:1; 2 Thess. 1:1; cf. 3:17; Philem. 19).[14] In fact, Ephesians

11. Marshall observes, "If the dominant view that [the Pastoral Epistles] are post-Pauline compositions is correct, then they have been written in the form of letters but in reality are meant for different audiences" (*Pastoral Epistles*, 12).

12. For the distinctive vocabulary of the Pastoral Epistles, P. N. Harrison's work was seminal, though challenged (*The Problem of the Pastoral Epistles* [Oxford: Oxford University Press, 1921]). For a summary, see Marshall, *Pastoral Epistles*, 59–66.

13. For studies on the variation of register in corpus linguistics, see Douglas Biber, *Variations across Speech and Writing* (Cambridge: Cambridge University Press, 1993); Douglas Biber and Susan Conrad, "Register Variation: A Corpus Approach," in *The Handbook of Discourse Analysis*, ed. Deborah Tannen, Heidi E. Hamilton, and Deborah Schiffrin, BHL (Malden, MA: Blackwell, 2001), 175–96. For the concept of register, see M. A. K. Halliday and Ruqaiya Hasan, *Language, Context, and Text: Aspects of Language in a Social-Semiotic Perspective*, 2nd ed., OELE (Oxford: Oxford University Press, 1989), 36–39; Cynthia Long Westfall, *A Discourse Analysis of the Letter to the Hebrews: The Relationship between Form and Meaning*, LNTS 297 (London: T&T Clark, 2005), 36; Helen Leckie-Tarry, *Language and Context: A Functional Linguistic Theory of Register*, ed. David Birch (London: Pinter, 1995).

14. See, e.g., E. Randolph Richards, *The Secretary in the Letters of Paul*, WUNT 2/42 (Tübingen: Mohr Siebeck, 1991). There is no need, however, to assume that such a position must pay "the cost of denying" that Paul himself was responsible for the contents of the Pauline Epistles, as Marshall asserts (*Pastoral Epistles*, 64), though certainly there should be some idea of shared responsibility when Paul's letters claim to be coauthored. Although the openings of the Pauline Epistles typically indicate that they are coauthored, the use of the first-person singular and Paul's practice of signing with his own hand (1 Cor. 16:21; Gal. 6:11; Col. 4:18; 2 Thess. 3:17) seem to indicate his primary responsibility for the material.

and the Pastoral Epistles are the only Pauline letters that do not explicitly identify coauthors or amanuenses, and there is considerable variation in the people who are mentioned as part of the letter-writing process in the other letters. A personal letter written to an intimate associate who is facing specific ministry issues has a far different register than the generally accepted letters in the Pauline corpus and can account for the change in language. However, if 1 Timothy is categorized as a public letter that is intended to be read by a larger audience, it places it in a register that is closer to the rest of the Pauline corpus and less easily accounts for the deviations in language and style.

A literary or fictitious letter tends to be relatively more self-interpreting within the context of the culture in which it is written, since it is composed to be understood by a more general audience. A personal letter between people who have had a long-term relationship, such as Paul and Timothy, evidences a higher degree of intimacy, and the communication will depend on information that is shared between the participants.[15] From the perspective of a later reader, this results in certain gaps in the information. Some of the logical connections between sentences and sections will not be apparent to an outside reader, and it will not be easily understood in places if the reader does not share the information needed to interpret it. All of the Pastoral Epistles have been described as incoherent and badly edited.[16] However, when we read someone else's private mail, it tends to appear incoherent and even to lack cohesion because contexts, acquaintances, and connections are shared (yet not explained) between writers and recipients who know each other well.

We might assume that the text was reasonably coherent and cohesive within its context in order to survive; that is, it was coherent and cohesive to its recipient(s) because the reader could fill in the gaps and supply the logical connections with the information.[17] However, we now lack these connections

15. In linguistic terms, personal letters tend to have a high occurrence of entities and information that is "evoked" from the known situation or may be inferred from shared experience/information (Westfall, *Hebrews*, 86).

16. See, e.g., James D. Miller, *The Pastoral Letters as Composite Documents*, SNTSMS 93 (Cambridge: Cambridge University Press, 1997). Miller concludes that the Pastoral Epistles cannot have a single author because he cannot detect a coherent argument or a clear development of thought. A. T. Hanson says, "The Pastorals are made up of a miscellaneous collection of material. They have no unifying theme; there is no development of thought" (*Studies in the Pastoral Epistles* [London: SPCK, 1968], 42). Hanson suggests that the author alternated his materials to "give the impression that he was writing letters" (ibid.). If that is the case, then the document should first be read as a personal letter to determine the purpose and message, rather than first attempting to reconstruct the history of the document.

17. This is one of the working hypotheses of relevance theory (see Dan Sperber and Deirdre Wilson, *Relevance: Communication and Cognition* [Oxford: Blackwell, 1986]). However, relevance theory adopts and develops Paul Grice's maxims, which involve a general agreement

and information, and so we must supply what we need in order to make sense out of the text, either consciously or unconsciously, "assisted" by subtitles in critical Greek texts and translations that provide a contextual frame for us that is not part of the text.

9.1.4 Role of the Context of the Letter

If 1 Timothy is taken to be a fictitious and/or literary epistle, then the role of context is considerably diminished. That is, if this is not a personal letter written by Paul to Timothy who was in Ephesus (as opposed to a letter written for general reading [literary], or a pseudonymous letter [fictitious]), then there would be less of a reason to look for specific events and circumstances that would frame or explain the content. If the letter is taken to have been written by the Pauline circle, then the context is important, but it is in the context of later church issues that probably are not local matters, and it reflects later theological development in ecclesiology. If 1 Timothy is taken to be a public letter written by Paul, then it might be assumed that it is an expression of Paul's fixed theology—a reflection of the code of behavior in the church at large. Fundamentally, the question is whether this letter is to be read according to its own terms, as addressing specific issues with intended social effects in the church at Ephesus, or to be read primarily as theology.

However, if 1 Timothy is accepted to be a genuine personal letter (or for some, a pseudo-personal letter that is clearly meant to be read in the context of the life of Paul and his personal relationships), then, by definition, context would play a high role in its correct interpretation.[18] It would be placed in the context of a long personal relationship between Paul and Timothy, and the information flow would reflect that relationship.[19] Paul met Timothy during the second missionary journey when he visited Lystra in 49 CE. Timothy was on the ministry team from that point on, and he had worked with Paul possibly fourteen to sixteen years before 1 Timothy was written. In other

---

between participants in conversation, and these are what I adopt: cooperation, quality, quantity, relevance, and manner (see Paul Grice, *Studies in the Way of Words* [Cambridge, MA: Harvard University Press, 1989], 22–40).

18. In either case (Pauline authorship or pseudonymity), attempts to reconstruct the intended historic social effect of 1 Timothy on the Christian community should start with reading the letter according to its own terms.

19. In the case of those who assume pseudonymity, it seems to be inarguable that the author intended it to be read in the context of Paul's life. What is not clear in this position is why the author would write three letters and why so many details would be included that could not be substantiated by the Lukan account (to which the author presumably would have access at a later time), unless there was a robust oral tradition about Paul's ministry and movements on which the author drew.

words, Timothy had already been fully mentored and taught by Paul, so the instruction in 1 Timothy would apply what Paul had taught Timothy to the situation and build on it. The situation would also reflect conditions in Ephesus in the mid-first century, so the sociohistorical setting may play an integral role in understanding the passage and understanding the specific situation in Ephesus. As far as the occasional context, Paul is addressing problems in the church in Ephesus that were so severe while he was there that he asked Timothy to stay behind to correct them (1:3). The correction of false teaching would then constrain the instructions in 2:1–15.

9.1.5 The Context/Scenario of 2:1–15

The next broad exegetical choice is the context or scenario that is assumed for the passage in 2:9–15. This may be the most important choice of all, but it is often not recognized as a choice that is completely based on several inferences, and the choice is assumed and rarely defended.[20] Most scholars assume that 2:1–15 is addressing church order during the weekly worship service or conduct in the church meeting.[21] For example, Howard Marshall states, "The theme is prayer in the church meeting."[22] He then outlines the chapter around the theme of prayer. According to Marshall, the need for prayer in its universal scope is stressed, then the moral requirements of prayer are given in respect to men, then in respect to women, which leads to a digression on the need for women not to teach but rather to learn in silence.[23]

The first problem with this reading is that there is no signal in 2:1 or 2:8 that the urged prayer is meant to be restricted spatially and temporally to church meetings. In fact, there is considerable evidence against that assumption in both the theology of Paul and the contexts of prayer practice in Judaism and the Greco-Roman world.[24] Paul's teaching elsewhere stresses the need for continual

20. For example, Philip Towner simply assumes a worship gathering, "He begins with the matter of prayer in the church," and asserts, "From 2:1 onward, Paul has been preoccupied with activities and behavior within the worship assembly" (*The Letters to Timothy and Titus*, NICNT [Grand Rapids: Eerdmans, 2006], 162, 190).

21. For example, Knight states that "in every place" in 2:8 "more likely is referring to the various meeting places of the church, in, perhaps, house churches and other groups" (*Pastoral Epistles*, 128).

22. Marshall, *Pastoral Epistles*, 417.

23. However, 2:9 does not explicitly mention that the issue of women's dress is related to the moral requirements of prayer. It is inferred by most interpreters because ὡσαύτως ("likewise") makes it parallel to the instruction to the men in 2:8, and telling women to dress properly after stressing the importance of men praying does not seem to be parallel in importance unless one assumes that prayer is still in focus.

24. Otto Knoch, for one, suggests that private prayers may be in mind, but the implications of this alternative have not impacted the general discussion (*1. und 2. Timotheusbrief,*

prayer and giving thanks at all times (Rom. 1:9; Eph. 1:16; 6:18; Phil. 1:4; 4:6; Col. 1:9; 1 Thess. 5:17–18; 2 Thess. 1:3, 11; Philem. 4), which would not be limited to specific times of church meetings. In 1 Timothy 2:8, Paul specifically instructs the men to pray ἐν παντὶ τόπῳ ("in every place"), which is spatial as opposed to the verbal noun ἐκκλησία ("meeting, assembly, gathering") that Paul normally uses for the church service, as in 3:5, 15; 5:16 (for other nonrestricted references to prayer in every place or at all times, see Rom. 1:9–10; Eph. 6:18; 1 Thess. 1:3; 2:13; 5:17; 2 Tim. 1:3). In addition, the Jewish, Christian, and Greco-Roman practices of prayer were not limited to sacred places (temples, shrines, synagogues) or restricted to worship services. Prayer took place outdoors, such as on the street, by a river, on the beach, on a ship, at a sickbed, or in prison (Matt. 6:5; Acts 16:13; 20:36; 21:5; 27:35; 28:8; James 5:13–14; Col. 1:3, 8). It could take place at random times during the month/week/day at any place, including in temples, synagogues, and homes (Acts 2:42–47; 3:1). It could occur in groups, in the family, or alone. There is nothing in 1 Timothy 2:1–8 that would narrow the context to a "public worship service," without even considering that worship services took place in the domestic sphere of the home, not in a public location. This does not clearly indicate that the rest of the chapter gives instructions on behavior in the worship meetings or in a public setting, and the content of the rest of the passage hardly fits the context of a "public worship service" either, particularly the reference to childbirth.

A second problem is the restriction of Paul's concern with women's dress and good works (2:9–10) to prayer in the worship meeting. The instructions to women are clearly meant to be parallel to the instructions to men, because of the correlation of "men/women" and the adverb ὡσαύτως ("in the same way") that links the instructions for women to the instructions for men (v. 8). But the concern for modesty, lack of ostentatiousness, and the practice of good works does not appear to be limited to prayer in the worship service alone. In 5:6, it is linked to a problem with the Ephesian widows that involved living a life characterized by luxury/pleasure rather than peaceful and quiet lives characterized by godliness and holiness. In fact, this reflects a general concern for the behavior of women that was often addressed in the culture: laws were even enacted on these issues.[25] Furthermore, if this was addressing women's

---

Titusbrief, NEchtB 14 [Würzburg: Echter, 1988], 24). However, there need be no distinction made between public and private in this passage. The men are to pray ἐν παντὶ τόπῳ ("in every place"). In the culture, public prayer was not restricted to official religious meetings (prayer on the street corners is still practiced today in the Near East [cf. Matt. 6:5]), and private prayer and devotion were practiced.

25. See A. J. Batten, "Neither Gold nor Braided Hair (1 Tim. 2:9; 1 Pet. 3:3): Adornment, Gender and Honour in Antiquity," *NTS* 55 (2009): 484–501. See also Knight's list of the contemporary Greco-Roman literature that illustrates and condemns "the inordinate time, expense,

apparel during prayer in the worship service, why did Paul not repeat the universal custom among all the "churches of God" of women wearing a veil (1 Cor. 11:16) while praying, rather than forbidding elaborate braiding (1 Tim. 2:9)?[26] The instruction to women is sometimes taken as a second concern Paul is addressing that shifts away from the action of prayer, but is still confined to public worship.[27] However, it may be better understood in the context of 2:1–3; ostentatious and immodest clothing and enhancements work directly against the goals of prayer in 2:2: "peaceful and quiet lives in all godliness and holiness." In 2:10, Paul is concerned that women who claim to worship God have appropriate behavior that lines up with the goals of prayer. This is, in fact, parallel to the instructions to the men. Anger and arguing also violate the goal of prayer in 2:2: peaceful and quiet lives. Prayer then would be Paul's antidote to specific ways Ephesian men and women are working against the goals that please God: peaceful and quiet lives, holiness, and godliness.

A fourth problem with the setting of a worship meeting as the background for 1 Timothy 2:9–10 is the shift from the plural groups of "men" and "women" to the singular "woman" (γυνή) in 2:11 and Paul's prohibition of two things that a "woman" might do to a "man" (ἀνδρός) in 2:12.[28] The shift to the

---

and effort that elaborately braided hair and jewels demanded, not just as ostentatious display, but also as the mode of dress of courtesans and harlots" (*Pastoral Epistles*, 135–36).

26. Whether one holds to Pauline authorship or pseudonymity, this failure to refer to veiling is an issue for those who suggest that this is instruction for women praying in a worship service, because of the intertextuality between 1 Timothy and 1 Corinthians; it is unlikely that the author was not acquainted with 1 Corinthians.

27. As Towner says,

The house code transition marker, "likewise" ("also," TNIV), shifts attention to the second member of the pair. At the same time it requires that the previous verb of command ("I wish"), or possibly the larger verbal idea including "prayer," be carried over. In the latter case, the assumption is that the unifying or thematic factor is "prayer," so that Paul is ultimately concerned with the manner and outward demeanor in which this activity is carried out in the worship meeting by both men and women. However, since the infinitive "to be adorned" completes the thought adequately, there is no real reason to assume that "prayer" is the unifying theme. . . . House code instruction frequently shifts from one member in a social pairing to another without such linkage. (*Timothy and Titus*, 204)

28. It is generally assumed that "to teach" is constrained by "a man." However, this might not be the best understanding of the grammar, since in the syntax διδάσκειν δὲ γυναικὶ οὐκ ἐπιτρέπω οὐδὲ αὐθεντεῖν ἀνδρός (1 Tim. 2:12), διδάσκειν ("to teach") is emphatically fronted in the phrase and distant from αὐθεντεῖν ἀνδρός ("to dominate a man"). Furthermore, the verb διδάσκειν usually takes the accusative or occasionally the dative (neither is here), while αὐθεντεῖν takes the genitive (ἀνδρός). This may suggest a general moratorium on women teaching in Ephesus, as in Marshall's suggestion "I am not permitting," indicating "What we have is apparently a fresh injunction rather than one that carries the weight of church tradition" (*Pastoral Epistles*, 454–55) (see also Ben Witherington III, *Women and the Genesis of Christianity* [Cambridge: Cambridge University Press, 1990], 120). Two alternatives would be either that 1 Tim. 2:12 contradicts other Pauline material (cf. Titus 2:3), or that it is a hendiadys, so that διδάσκειν and

singular is marked in the context because it breaks a pattern, and the use of the singular for "man" is not consistent with language addressing a church meeting or other group. Paul might talk of a woman teaching a group of men, or women teaching groups of men, but it is not normal to speak of a woman teaching "a man" in a group setting. Rather, the use of the singular signals some private interaction between a woman and a man. In the Greco-Roman culture, private interactions between a woman and man would most appropriately occur between family members, and there is much in the passage that indicates a household context. Most commentators treat the use of the singular as if it is not there, but it is a clear grammatical choice that has meaning, and it is in contrast with the grammar in the context and with the grammar of group participation.[29]

The fifth problem with the setting of a worship service as the background for this passage is the mention of childbirth (τεκνογονία) plus the peculiar concern with saving (σωθήσεται) a woman (2:15) and their questionable relevance to the order of worship and the prohibitions. There are several interpretive options (and alternate translations) for "yet she will be saved through childbearing" (σωθήσεται δὲ διὰ τῆς τεκνογονίας), but none of them make sense as a conclusion to a discussion of the conduct of men and women in a worship service.

Therefore, the choice or assumption of a church service as the frame for 2:1–15 contributes to incoherence and a lack of cohesion rather than providing a context that explains the difficult features of the passage. The body opening indicates that Paul's letter is concerned with false teaching, but if this is about conduct in the worship service, it is a digression, and he returns to the subject of false teaching in chapters 4–6. Some interpreters unnecessarily and inadvisably classify 2:11–15 as a further digression. Both the grammar and the expansion of this passage indicate that it is a focus because it receives more

---

αὐθεντεῖν would be understood to mutually interpret each other. But see Andreas J. Köstenberger, "A Complex Sentence: The Syntax of 1 Timothy 2:12," in *Women in the Church: An Analysis and Application of 1 Timothy 2:9–15*, 2nd ed., ed. Andreas J. Köstenberger and Thomas R. Schreiner (Grand Rapids: Baker Academic, 2005), 54, where he omits the issue of the separation/dislocation of the verbs as well as the distinction of case and claims that αὐθεντεῖν has a positive evaluation because διδάσκειν should have a positive evaluation, assuming that they are closely related, but denies that it is a hendiadys indicating one concept. Certainly the claim that αὐθεντεῖν has a positive evaluation because διδάσκειν should have a positive evaluation lacks sufficient criteria in terms of what counts for evidence in the language of evaluation/appraisal, particularly since both actions are prohibited, which is a negative evaluation, and the fact that the correction of false teaching is the theme of the letter. This issue merits further study where the evidence is sifted more carefully, weighing all factors.

29. With a stretch, this might refer to a woman singling out a man in the group as a target to teach and dominate, but then it would not be a prohibition for women to teach groups of men.

development than the instructions to men and women. Furthermore, it speaks directly to some of the problems with false teaching and women's behavior in the church, which are referred to later in the letter. The logical connection in 2:1, παρακαλῶ οὖν πρῶτον ("therefore first I urge"), links the passage to what precedes rather than creating a break and shift to a different concern. This suggests that 2:1–15 is developing the theme of the letter, which is the correction of false teaching (1:3).[30]

9.1.6 The Meaning of the Word αὐθεντέω

One of the most problematic aspects of interpreting 1 Timothy 2:11–15 in regard to the issue of gender is the meaning of the word αὐθεντέω in 2:12: "I do not permit a woman to teach or αὐθεντεῖν a man."

This word is a hapax legomenon (it occurs once in the New Testament), and it is the first known occurrence of the verb in the Greek language, though the *Thesaurus Linguae Graecae* (TLG) database locates over three hundred later occurrences.[31] In 1979, Catherine Kroeger wrote an article that challenged the translation of αὐθεντέω as "to have authority" and started a discussion of the verb that is ongoing.[32] The "meaning" of the verb and how it should be translated or glossed have revolved around some key questions:

30. According to John White, the development of subjects introduced in the letter opening is one of the major roles of the body of the letter (*The Form and Function of the Body of the Greek Letter: A Study of the Letter-Body in the Non-literary Papyri and in Paul the Apostle*, SBLDS 2 [Missoula, MT: Scholars Press, 1972], 61).

31. The findings here are based on a paper I first delivered in the Evangelicals and Gender section of the annual meeting of the Evangelical Theological Society in Atlanta, November 2010, published as "The Meaning of αὐθεντέω in 1 Timothy 2:12," *JGRChJ* 10 (2014): 138–73.

32. Kroeger's initial work was "Ancient Heresies and a Strange Greek Verb," *RefJ* 29 (1979): 12–15. A chronological overview of published studies subsequent to Kroeger's article includes Armin J. Panning, "*Authentein*—A Word Study," *WLQ* 78 (1981): 185–91; Carroll D. Osburn, "ΑΥΘΕΝΤΕΩ (1 Timothy 2:12)," *ResQ* 25 (1982): 1–12; George W. Knight III, "ΑΥΘΕΝΤΕΩ in Reference to Women in 1 Timothy 2:12," *NTS* 30 (1984): 143–57; Catherine Clark Kroeger, "1 Timothy 2:12—A Classicist's View," in *Women, Authority & the Bible*, ed. Alvera Mickelsen (Downers Grove, IL: InterVarsity, 1986), 225–44; Leland Edward Wilshire, "The TLG Computer and Further Reference to ΑΥΘΕΝΤΕΩ in 1 Timothy 2:12," *NTS* 34 (1988): 120–34; Paul W. Barnett, "Wives and Women's Ministry (1 Tim. 2:11–15)," *EvQ* 61 (1989): 225–38; Kevin Giles, "Response," in *The Bible and Women's Ministry: An Australian Dialogue*, ed. Alan Nichols (Canberra: Acorn, 1990), 65–87; Timothy J. Harris, "Why Did Paul Mention Eve's Deception? A Critique of P. W. Barnett's Interpretation of 1 Timothy 2," *EvQ* 62 (1990): 335–52; Gloria N. Redekop, "Let the Women Learn: First Timothy 2:8–15 Reconsidered," *SR* 19 (1990): 235–45; D. P. Kuske, "An Exegetical Brief on 1 Timothy 2:12 (οὐδὲ αὐθεντεῖν ἀνδρός)," *WLQ* 88 (1991): 64–67; Leland Edward Wilshire, "1 Timothy 2:12 Revisited: A Reply to Paul W. Barnett and Timothy J. Harris," *EvQ* 65 (1993): 43–55; Ronald W. Pierce, "Evangelicals and Gender Roles in the 1990s: First Timothy 2:8–15; A Test Case," *JETS* 36 (1993): 343–55; Andrew C. Perriman, "What Eve Did, What Women Shouldn't Do: The Meaning of ΑΥΘΕΝΤΕΩ," *TynBul* 44 (1993): 129–42; Paul W.

What is the relationship of the verb to the exercise of authority?
Is the verb pejorative, neutral, or positive?
What is the relationship of the verb to its cognates?[33]

The answers to these questions tend to polarize into two groups (with some exceptions). One group translates αὐθεντέω with a positive or neutral sense of "exercise authority" or "master"; the other group translates it with a negative or pejorative sense, such as "usurp," "domineer," "control," or "initiate violence."

Many outside of the debate assume that αὐθεντέω is a technical term for "being a pastor," since it is the primary justification for excluding women

---

Barnett, "*Authentein* Once More: A Response to L. E. Wilshire," *EvQ* 66, no. 2 (1994): 159–62; Steve Motyer, "Expounding 1 Timothy 2:8–15," *VE* 24 (1994): 91–102; H. Scott Baldwin, "A Difficult Word: Αὐθεντέω in 1 Timothy 2:12," in *Women in the Church: A Fresh Analysis of 1 Timothy 2:9–15*, ed. Andreas J. Köstenberger, Thomas R. Schreiner, and H. Scott Baldwin (Grand Rapids: Baker, 1995), 65–80; Richard Clark Kroeger and Catherine Clark Kroeger, *I Suffer Not a Woman: Rethinking 1 Timothy 2:11–15 in Light of Ancient Evidence* (Grand Rapids: Baker, 1998); Linda L. Belleville, "Women in Ministry: The Egalitarian Perspective," in *Two Views on Women in Ministry*, ed. James R. Beck and Craig L. Blomberg, Counterpoints (Grand Rapids: Zondervan, 2000), 75–154; Belleville, *Women Leaders and the Church: Three Crucial Questions* (Grand Rapids: Baker Books, 2000); Albert M. Wolters, "A Semantic Study of αὐθέντης and Its Derivatives," *JGRChJ* 1 (2000): 145–75; Kevin Giles, "*Women in the Church*: A Rejoinder to Andreas Köstenberger," *EvQ* 73 (2001): 225–43; David K. Huttar, "ΑΥΘΕΝΤΕΙΝ in the Aeschylus Scholium," *JETS* 44 (2001): 615–25; Linda L. Belleville, "Teaching and Usurping Authority: 1 Timothy 2:11–15," in *Discovering Biblical Equality: Complementarity without Hierarchy*, ed. Ronald W. Pierce and Rebecca Merrill Groothuis (Downers Grove, IL: InterVarsity, 2005), 205–23; Robert W. Wall, "1 Timothy 2:9–15 Reconsidered (Again)," *BBR* 14 (2004): 81–103; H. Scott Baldwin, "An Important Word: Αὐθεντέω in 1 Timothy 2:12," in *Women in the Church: An Analysis and Application of 1 Timothy 2:9–15*, 2nd ed., ed. Andreas J. Köstenberger and Thomas R. Schreiner (Grand Rapids: Baker Academic, 2005), 39–51; Philip B. Payne, "1 Timothy 2:12 and the Use of οὐδέ to Combine Two Elements to Express a Single Idea," *NTS* 54 (2008): 235–53; Payne, "1 Timothy 2:12: Part III, Does αὐθεντέω Mean 'Assume Authority'?," in *Man and Woman, One in Christ: An Exegetical and Theological Study of Paul's Letters* (Grand Rapids: Zondervan, 2009), 361–97; J. J. Davis, "First Timothy 2:12, the Ordination of Women, and Paul's Use of Creation Narratives," *PriscPap* 23 (2009): 5–10; James D. Miller, "Translating Paul's Words about Women," *SCJ* 12 (2009): 61–71; Albert M. Wolters, "ΑΥΘΕΝΤΗΣ and Its Cognates in Biblical Greek," *JETS* 52 (2009): 719–29; Wolters, "An Early Parallel of αὐθεντέω in 1 Timothy 2:12," *JETS* 54 (2011): 673–84. Commentaries are excluded from this list, and I acknowledge that papers delivered at various conferences have also played a key role in the discussion.

33. Scott Baldwin excludes the evidence of the meanings of the cognates that were given as evidence for the meaning of the word by Wilshire (Baldwin, "Important Word," in Köstenberger and Schreiner, *Women in the Church*, 45). This eliminates any evidence of meaning prior to Paul's usage! Moreover, it is not the practice of lexicographers to exclude the cognates from their study, but rather to recognize and study the relationships between the words, even though there is not always a complete semantic overlap. Johannes Louw and Eugene Nida's procedure is to first treat the word and then the cognates (*Lexical Semantics of the Greek New Testament*, RBS 25 [Atlanta: Scholars Press, 1992], 62). See also Wolters, "Semantic Study of αὐθέντης."

from the office of pastor and from other leadership over men. However, out of the over three hundred occurrences of the verb in the TLG database, no one has identified a case where it refers to any kind of benevolent pastoral care of an individual or group by a pastor or church official. Among the eighty-two occurrences of the verb that Scott Baldwin used to support the position that the word means "to have authority," there is no example of a male doing this to another person or a group of people in a ministry or church leadership context where the referent action had a positive evaluation in the context.[34] When the verb is transitive with a personal object or recipient of the action, there is a discernible pattern in the kind of action that happens to the recipients (where the recipient or goal is specified in the context).[35]

In the Greek corpus, the verb αὐθεντέω refers to a range of actions that are not restricted to murder or violence. However, the people who are the targets of these actions are harmed, forced against their will (compelled), or at least their self-interest is overridden, because the actions involve the imposition of the subject's will over against the recipient's will, ranging from dishonor to lethal force. An interesting example of the use of αὐθεντέω (translated here as "used force") occurs in a complaint by Bassianos at the Council of Chalcedon (451 CE), where he claims that he was made bishop by an illegitimate procedure:

> I was appointed as a bishop by violence! The canons are clearly the authority. The Fathers would say, "If there is a preferred procedure, it is for holding an election for office, and to not resign." . . . I urge you to listen to me! When this reckless deed was done, they *used force* and broke into my room and grabbed me. And then we looked to join the priesthood. But they looked for violence.[36]

Forcing a person against their will in a destructive way is appropriate for divine sovereignty in righteous judgment (Sodom and Gomorrah and the wicked), and it was believed to be appropriate for absolute authorities and government officials who were enforcers (e.g., an executioner); but if it is unauthorized, it is almost always inappropriate. Furthermore, the prohibition of

---

34. Baldwin, "Important Word," in Köstenberger and Schreiner, *Women in the Church*. In the positive occurrences in the register of church leadership, a church official or leader does this to a πρᾶγμα—a thing, a matter, or a case of law—or the verb is intransitive. A bishop presides over a case of law, the bishop of Rome exercises full authority in the matter of selecting capable papal representatives, and Peter takes charge of affairs.

35. It is important that we distinguish between a church official or individual taking this action in regard to a matter or a thing (e.g., πρᾶγμα) and a church official doing it to a person. We find positive examples in ministry of the former (such as taking control of a lawsuit), but not positive examples of the latter.

36. *Concilium universale Chalcedonese anno 451* (2.1.3.48.12), my translation, emphasis added.

this action by women is not an endorsement of the action by men, as is often taken to be the case. In fact, the closest parallel passage to 1 Timothy 2:12 is in Chrysostom's *Homilies on Colossians*, where he commands husbands not to αὐθεντεῖν their wives.[37] Chrysostom says that the husband's role is to love and the wife's role is to obey. He then says, "Therefore, don't αὐθεντεῖν because your wife is submissive to you" (μὴ τοίνυν, ἐπειδὴ ὑποτέτακται ἡ γυνή, αὐθέντει).[38] In the passage, Chrysostom compares the ideal husband to a loving ἄρχων ("leader/ruler"), and the action in view cannot be the husband's loving exercise of legal/cultural domestic rule, but rather exceeds loving domestic authority; today we would probably use the term "spousal abuse," which would nevertheless be well within the rights of the Roman paterfamilias in that patriarchal culture.[39] Notice that while Chrysostom uses ἄρχων to describe a husband's role, Paul never does.[40] Rather, Paul uses the word αὐθεντέω to criticize the behavior of wives toward their husbands in a case of role reversal, where the woman would assume an authority that may be comparable to a paterfamilias and behave in an abusive or controlling manner.

Forcing people against their will or overriding their self-interest is consistent with several Greco-Roman and biblical models of exercising authority. It is consistent with the gentile models of authority (particularly Caesar), which Jesus describes in Matthew 20:25: "The rulers [οἱ ἄρχοντες] of the Gentiles lord it over them, and their great ones are tyrants over them" (NRSV). Such exercise of absolute authority is consistent with the right of life and death held by the Roman paterfamilias over his wife and children, as well as the husband's rights in the Hellenistic culture. It is also consistent with the biblical authority of divine sovereignty, the rule of Christ, and his role as a judge. It came to be used for the authority of the pope during the reign of Pope Gregory. However,

37. John Chrysostom, *Hom. Col.* 27–31. This prohibition is similar to the criticism of the masters' brutal abuse of slaves in a prophecy (Pseudo-Hippolytus, *Consum.* 7.5). Abusing slaves was legal, but still criticized. However, see Baldwin, "Important Word," in Köstenberger and Schreiner, *Women in the Church*, 47, 51. He claims that this occurrence in Chrysostom is unique and hyperbolic. However, clearly hyperbolic elements cannot be located in the context, and it is not at all unique in the pattern where the recipient is a person. It appears that Baldwin assumes his conclusions in this case.

38. Note that this is not a grammatical parallel for many reasons. The verb αὐθέντει is intransitive, but it is clear that the goal is the wife. It is worth noting that Chrysostom believed that a wife's submission could provide a context in which she was in danger of abuse.

39. Baldwin suggests that "tyrannize" is the proper gloss ("Important Word," in Köstenberger and Schreiner, *Women in the Church*, 47, 51).

40. For the occurrences of ἄρχων in the Pauline corpus, see Rom. 13:3; 1 Cor. 2:6, 8; Eph. 2:2. In fact, its only other occurrence outside of the Gospels and Acts are these verses and Rev. 1:5. It is used for high-level rulers, never for the church or the family. The fact that Chrysostom uses it for the role of the husband indicates a transition toward hierarchy and patriarchy in the early church that was not present in the New Testament.

it is inconsistent with any biblical right of a husband or the Christian leader's exercise of authority over members of the Christian community in Pauline theology. It is inconsistent with and in contrast to Paul's model of leadership as well as Jesus's model.[41] Glossing this verb merely as "having authority" and then interpreting it as if it describes servant leadership or pastoral care is misleading in the extreme.

Since this verb and 1 Timothy 2:12 are the primary sources used to exclude women from various forms of leadership in the church, the decision or selection of a meaning/gloss for αὐθεντέω is crucial for understanding the nature of the prohibition. It should be the work of the church to flesh out an understanding of this word based on sound lexicography and linguistic methodology in order to proceed in this discussion with caution. There is now ample evidence that was not available to the nineteenth-century lexicons which we tended to depend on for our glosses; the database, search engines, and linguistic theories are now in place to move forward.[42] The church has reached its age of accountability; it is time to assume responsibility (or liability) for excluding women from church leadership positions based on the word αὐθεντέω.

9.1.7 The Significance of the Narrative Summary of Genesis 2–3

A crucial exegetical choice involves how to understand the narrative summary of Genesis 2–3 in 1 Timothy 2:13–14, which supports the command for a woman to learn in 2:11 and the prohibition in 2:12. The support material is signaled by the conjunction γάρ in verse 13, but the logical relationship between the prohibition and the Old Testament narrative must be inferred.

41. If the verb is transitive and an individual (subject) does this to another individual (object of the verb), the action is inconsistent with Christian office and pastoral ministry during the time the New Testament was written, and as is reflected in 1 Timothy. However, the power of Christian offices gradually increased. Bishops sometimes used physical and political force and anathematized another bishop, and the papal authority developed to be absolute. The verb is consistent with this later development in power.

42. Understandably, the discussion of the meaning of the word has not been informed by the theory of collocation: words tend to occur in patterns. For a definition and description of the pervasiveness of collocation, see Michael Hoey, *Lexical Priming: A New Theory of Words and Language* (London: Routledge, 2005), 1–15. Nor has the discussion been informed by the appraisal theory, with which we can more precisely determine pejorative and nonpejorative usage. The best source for the appraisal framework, "the language of attitude, arguability, and interpersonal positioning," is the Appraisal website (http://www.grammatics.com/appraisal /index.html). The website has this description: "The Appraisal framework is an extension of the linguistic theories of M. A. K. Halliday and his colleagues (Systemic Functional Linguistics) and has emerged over a period of almost two decades as a result of work conducted by a group of researchers primarily based in Australia."

Discussion on how the New Testament uses the Old Testament has flourished recently, and it should inform our understanding of the options of how a motif, an allusion, or a citation might function in the Pauline corpus or the New Testament in general.[43] There is a building consensus that the New Testament writers utilize the Old Testament in diverse and sometimes creative ways that do not necessarily interpret the passage in context or maintain the original intent of the author. However, this is a narrative summary, so we may safely assume that Paul intends the Genesis narrative to interpret his own cryptic summary.

Some are convinced that the prohibition or "ban on women teaching and exercising authority over men" in 1 Timothy 2:12 is normative for the church on the basis of the narrative alone. For example, Thomas Schreiner claims, "The appeal to creation in 1 Timothy 2:13 indicates that Paul located his prohibition in a transcendent norm."[44] However, Paul's description of creation is not a transcendent norm but rather a restrained summary of the narrative: "Adam was formed first, then Eve." Schreiner's inference that the narrative indicates "the priority of Adam" might have been considered to be a norm by some, but it was not a norm for Paul in other temporal relationships, and he did not make that inference from the Genesis account in the text.[45] The reader is left to make an inference (as is typical in interpreting narrative), and presumably the intended reader knew the relevance of that narrative to the issues at hand. In addition, the assumption that "transcendent norms" will only be used by Paul to support normative applications simply does not hold true in the patterns of Paul's use of the Old Testament and other sources. Paul generalizes from particulars, and particularizes from generalities. He generalized from a particular when he applied Deuteronomy 25:4, about muzzling oxen, to wages for elders (1 Tim. 5:18; cf. 1 Cor. 9:7–9). On the other hand, he used "transcendent norms" in the creation account to support the cultural practice of women wearing veils while prophesying and praying in the church (1 Cor. 11:3–16). He encouraged some members of the Corinthian church to pass judgment on a specific "trivial" law case because in

---

43. For discussion of the Old Testament in the New Testament, see G. K. Beale and D. A. Carson, eds., *Commentary on the New Testament Use of the Old Testament* (Grand Rapids: Baker Academic, 2007); James M. Court, ed., *New Testament Writers and the Old Testament: An Introduction* (London: SPCK, 2002); Steve Moyise, ed., *The Old Testament in the New*, 2nd ed., ABS (London: Bloomsbury T&T Clark, 2015); Stanley E. Porter, ed., *Hearing the Old Testament in the New Testament* (Grand Rapids: Eerdmans, 2006).

44. Schreiner, *Paul, Apostle of God's Glory in Christ: A Pauline Theology* (Downers Grove, IL: InterVarsity, 2001), 408.

45. Ibid. Moving from a simple statement of the order of creation to the priority of men is a logical leap that has seemed transparent to male scholars historically.

the future "the Lord's people will judge the world" (1 Cor. 6:1–3).[46] It is odd
to assert that Paul or anyone else would not support occasional or culturally
specific applications with material from the creation account or from other
generalities, and it runs counter to our current practices of hermeneutics and
homiletics by which we habitually look for relevant and timely applications
of timeless principles in Scripture.[47]

Paul's summary of certain parts of the creation narrative in support of
the command for "a woman" to learn and the prohibition on how a woman
behaves toward a man could be understood in ways other than indicating a
normative ban on women teaching or leading in the church meeting (1 Tim.
2:11–14). Instead, Paul could be directly addressing issues concerning the
false teaching among the women at Ephesus. This could be a correction of a
virulent popular myth with the proper narrative that sets the record straight;
it could involve typology; and/or it could be corrective instruction or an explanation for wives and husbands. If the text is read on its own terms, several
points indicate that the creation summary is used to correct the issues that
Timothy faced.

First, there is the context of false teaching that involved myths being told
by the older women (1 Tim. 4:7; cf. 1:4). Paul may be briefly correcting the
content of a popular myth.

Second, there were other specific issues in Ephesus with the women that
needed to be corrected. These issues include incorrect behavior in dress and
lifestyle (1 Tim. 2:9–10; 5:6, 15), spreading gossip as well as stories or myths
among other women (4:7; 5:13), and accepting false doctrine, including incorrect teaching about sex, marriage, and children (4:3, cf. 5:14; 2 Tim. 3:6–7).

Third, the prohibitions read as if they are emphasized as new information, and they do not repeat commands or prohibitions from earlier letters.
According to the majority of convincing reconstructions of where 1 Timothy
was located in Paul's life based on the information given in the text, Timothy
had been Paul's closest companion and a trusted teacher of Paul's practices
and traditions for more than a decade. Whether this letter is fictitious, literary,
or personal, the placement of these prohibitions in this letter is a conundrum

46. See F. F. Bruce, *Paul, Apostle of the Heart Set Free* (Grand Rapids: Eerdmans, 1977),
109, where he argues that Paul generalizes Jesus's statement in Mark 12:17, about rendering
to Caesar, to "Pay to all what is due them—taxes to whom taxes are due, revenue to whom
revenue is due" in Rom. 13:7 (NRSV).
47. It is a logical fallacy to assume that only transcendent applications must be drawn from
transcendent norms. This fallacy consists of an incorrect understanding of how syllogisms may
involve universal propositions and specific applications. Thus the assumption that the creation
account would support only "omnitemporal norms" is what D. A. Carson calls an "improperly
handled syllogism" (*Exegetical Fallacies*, 2nd ed. [Grand Rapids: Baker, 1996], 94–101).

for anyone who claims that the purpose of this passage is meant to reflect Paul's practices in all the churches of the gentile mission.

Fourth, since the text indicates that it is a personal letter, it is the least likely context for making transcendent statements that override the general application of Paul's teachings on spiritual gifts and leadership in the rest of the Pauline corpus. A document like Paul's Epistle to the Romans would have been a more logical place to make a clear prohibition on women teaching and in ministry. Romans was a later document and written to a church that Paul had not planted nor yet visited; in it he focuses on teaching and ministry in Romans 12:3–8. A Roman woman would take Romans 12:7–8 as containing mandates to teach or lead if she thought she had the gift, and according to Romans 16, women were prominent in their work for the church in Rome. If the directives given in 1 Timothy 2:11–12 were an essential practice in the Pauline churches, Romans 12 would have been the place to communicate such gender qualifications.

In conclusion, there is no compelling reason to suppose that a summary of the creation account would not be used by Paul to teach or correct occasional problems in the church, since he uses the creation account to teach a cultural practice (1 Cor. 11:3–16) and makes specific applications of other transcendent norms as well.

9.1.8 Summary

Exegetical choices concerning the nature of 1 Timothy and Pauline authorship play a direct role in the interpretation of 1 Timothy 2:11–15. The way forward is to trust the text and read it on its own terms. The text indicates that it is a personal letter written by Paul to Timothy. The letter as a whole and its parts should be understood, analyzed, and interpreted in a manner consistent with the text's claims, similarities in the papyri, epistolary theory, and linguistic theory—all of which inform us of how language works in a personal advisory letter between two associates who know each other well. We should expect the letter to be highly occasional, where the context plays an important role. Although we are working at a disadvantage because we do not have direct access to all of Paul and Timothy's shared information, we may learn a great deal about the context and other shared information from a close study of the text. We must be ready to discard settings or interpretive frames or scenarios that are not directly drawn from the text or Pauline practice/theology, particularly if they do not contribute to coherence or cohesion. In the case of 1 Timothy 2:1–15, we should set aside the common assumption that the practice of prayer signals a church service or meeting, then read 1 Timothy 2:1–15 in the light of the letter's stated purpose. Other crucial choices include the disputed meaning of αὐθεντέω and the way the allusions to the creation and fall support the command for a woman to learn and the prohibition concerning a woman's behavior toward "a man" in 1 Timothy 2:11–12. One choice that interpreters worry less about is the logical relationship of being "saved through childbirth" to 1 Timothy 2:15, but it must be considered with these other choices to reach a coherent reading of the passage within its context.

Regardless of views of authorship, most interpret the text as a whole and 1 Timothy 2:9–15 in particular as if they were fictitious, ignoring the relevance of the personal and occasional information that provides the context and purpose. However, if our interest in the letter is in the meaning of the message rather than recovering the probable history or supporting and reinforcing one's theology, then the text should be read on its own terms in order to determine the intended impact or outcome when it was written.

9.2 The Purpose of the Letter

If we treat 1 Timothy as a real letter, we will look for its purpose in the beginning of the body of the letter. According to John White, "The body-opening is the point at which the principal occasions for the letter are usually indicated. . . . The body-opening lays the foundation . . . from which the superstructure may grow."[48]

9.2.1 The Stated Purpose of the Letter (1:3–20)

The body opening is located in 1:3–20, where Paul's former command to Timothy to instruct certain people not to circulate wrong teachings (strange doctrines) is repeated in 1:3–4 and expanded in the rest of the chapter:[49] "When

---

48. White, Body of the Greek Letter, 3.
49. Knight comments:

    The remainder of this chapter is enveloped in Paul's command to Timothy to instruct "certain persons" not to teach strange doctrines (1:3; cf. 1:18ff.). Vv. 3–7 contain that command and a description of the false teachers. A reminder of the positive goal of the gospel, love, is set in the midst of this section. Paul then sets forth the lawful use of the law over against the false teachers' erroneous view and ends this section by correlating the law with the gospel (vv. 8–11). This reference to the gospel provides the transition to vv. 12–17, where Paul presents his own case as an example of God's saving mercy and thus as an encouragement over against the teaching of the false teachers. In vv. 18–20 Paul reiterates his general command to Timothy, this time reminding him of the need for personal struggle ("fight the good fight") and warning him by means of the bad example

I left for Macedonia, I asked you to stay behind in Ephesus so that you could instruct certain individuals not to spread wrong teaching. They shouldn't pay attention to myths and endless genealogies. Their teaching only causes useless guessing games instead of faithfulness to God's way of doing things." These instructions are reinforced in 1:18, where, based on these instructions, Timothy is charged to "wage a good war."

9.2.2 The Nature of False Teaching in Ephesus

If this were a literary letter, the author probably would have placed a precise description of the false teaching and its teachers in the body opening. However, the author merely warns and makes appeals to truth that is already known and given. Fortunately, there are some references to the nature of the wrong teachings in Ephesus located in chapters 4–6 and they may be collected and organized, though Paul focuses more on the effects of the teachings rather than the theology. If the description of the nature of the wrong teachings were placed in the body opening, it would clarify the logical relationship between the purpose of the letter and the following development in the letter. If this were a personal letter, there would be no need to give Timothy the kind of detail that would be necessary in a group or literary letter,[50] because he would already know the content of the false teaching, the identity of the false teachers, and the problems caused by the teachers and the content of the teaching that was spreading.

Although some may compile the wrong teachings into one heresy, it appears that at least two different forms or expressions of heresy can be detected.[51] Some problems can be identified as specific to the men, and other problems as specific to the women.

9.2.2.1 FALSE TEACHINGS AMONG THE MEN

The wrong teachings and practice among the men appear to be characterized by opposition to Paul, anger, arguments, and exploiting the church for money, as portrayed in 1 Timothy 6:3–5:

---

of Hymenaeus and Alexander of the danger of not holding faith and a good conscience. (*Pastoral Epistles*, 70)

50. Marshall suggests, "It seems that the writer is more concerned with the practical effects of foolish teaching on Christian living rather than with attacking the teaching on a doctrinal and theoretical level" (*Pastoral Epistles*, 31). However, Timothy presumably knew not only the content of the heresy, but also the correct teaching. So the concern would have been on the dangers posed.

51. Mounce claims, "While we are told a few of its specific doctrines, for the most part it does not appear to have been a well-thought-out, cohesive system of belief" (*Pastoral Epistles*, lxix).

Whoever teaches otherwise and does not agree with the sound words of our Lord Jesus Christ and the teaching that is in accordance with godliness, is conceited, understanding nothing, and has a morbid craving for controversy and for disputes about words. From these come envy, dissension, slander, base suspicions, and wrangling among those who are depraved in mind and bereft of the truth, imagining that godliness is a means of gain. (NRSV)

The instructions to men concerning prayer are embedded in general instructions for prayer in 2:1–7. The concern of the prayer is that it supports Paul's mission to the gentiles.[52] Marshall observes that the emphasis on God's will to save everyone is "almost polemical in character—[it] suggests that there was some opposition to the idea."[53] The opposition to Paul's mission most likely is connected with the Jewish teaching about the law that Paul corrects briefly in 1:7–11. Then in 2:8, the men are specifically instructed to "lift holy hands in prayer, without anger or argument." Therefore, the major aspects that characterize those who teach anything different in 6:3–5 occur in the close context of the instructions to men, with the exception of the obsession with making money. However, the same kinds of violence, arguing, and being free from the love of money are prohibited in the qualifications for overseers in 3:3, and the greed for money is also addressed in the qualification of male deacons.

9.2.2.2 FALSE TEACHINGS AMONG THE WOMEN

False teachings among the women include specific problematic practices that result from being deceived by false teachers, and the spread of myths, genealogies, and destructive speech passed along from house to house. Paul's warnings about false teachings in the last days in 4:1–5 must be taken as relevant to the problems in Ephesus, because Timothy is instructed to correct people in this area, and because they are directly related to problems among the women, and particularly among widows:

Now the Spirit expressly says that in later times some will renounce the faith by paying attention to deceitful spirits and teachings of demons, through the hypocrisy of liars whose consciences are seared with a hot iron. They forbid marriage and demand abstinence from foods, which God created to be received with thanksgiving by those who believe and know the truth. For everything created by God is good, and nothing is to be rejected, provided it is received with thanksgiving; for it is sanctified by God's word and by prayer. (NRSV)

52. Towner, *Timothy and Titus*, 163.
53. Marshall, *Pastoral Epistles*, 417.

Key elements in the false teaching being repeated in the Ephesian context are the deliberate deception of women, the reference to demonic activity in the deception, and the prohibition of marriage, which may have involved the promotion of celibacy among married women. In 2 Timothy 3:6–7, in a criticism of false teachers so similar that we may assume he is addressing the same problems, Paul focuses on the fact that they target women in the home and deceive them: "Some of these are false teachers who sneak into homes and capture weak women, who are overwhelmed with sins and driven by all kinds of cravings. Such women are always seeking instruction, yet never able to arrive at a knowledge of the truth."

In addition, Paul's description of younger widows in 1 Timothy 5:13–15 criticizes some of them because they have "already turned away to follow Satan." The teaching on celibacy could have influenced their view of the institution of marriage and the value and risk of childbearing. It may be connected with some widows' commitment not to remarry.[54] The doctrines of the false teachers may have had an attraction to women who, already terrified by the horrendous risks of childbirth, sought to reverse the effects of the fall by refusing to have children by abstaining from sex. This could be done by avoiding marriage or staying celibate within marriage.

The promotion of celibacy may well have encouraged "emancipatory tendencies," which may have been what we see expressed in dress and lifestyle.[55] In contrast with the other problems, the issue of immodest dress is addressed more in 2:9–10. Paul contrasts the desired modest and sensible dress for women with the immodest style to be avoided, which involved elaborate braiding, gold, pearls, and expensive clothes. In 5:6, Paul highlights a problem among the widows in Ephesus that can be characterized as this kind of immodest behavior: "But a widow who tries to live a life of luxury [σπαταλῶσα ζῶσα] is dead even while she is alive." As Philip Towner says, this "clearly recalls the women caricatured in 2:9."[56] He summarizes: "The whole of the parenesis in vv. 9–10 thus forms a challenge to a group of well-to-do Christian wives for whom the emerging trend of the new Roman woman, with its emphasis

54. Marshall suggests that there is a combination of Jewish-Christian and ascetic elements in the heresy (ibid., 51), but it is uncertain that the law played a major role in the women's avoidance of marriage.

55. So entertains Towner, drawing upon scholars such as Bruce Winter in his discussion of the "new woman" in Corinth (Towner, *Timothy and Titus*, 197–98); see Bruce W. Winter, *Roman Wives, Roman Widows: The Appearance of New Women and the Pauline Communities* (Grand Rapids: Eerdmans, 2003).

56. Towner writes, "This widow's glamorous outward appearance paradoxically conceals a profound state of inward spiritual death . . . in contrast to the real widow" (*Timothy and Titus*, 342).

on outer show and rejection of cultural norms of modesty, was becoming a potent attraction."[57]

This kind of immodest behavior of women was of great concern in the Greco-Roman culture, and the prohibition of immodest or ostentatious clothing was sometimes enacted in law. We see similar criticisms that reflect Greco-Roman values in 1 Peter 3:1–7; thus the concern for immodest dress reflects a problem apart from the issue of prayer. The fact that widows in Ephesus could possibly engage in such a display of luxury may indicate independence, wealth, and control (not only over themselves but also over any children) that they were unwilling to relinquish.[58]

Although the women are not singled out for abuse in public teaching, they are criticized directly and indirectly for repeating influential narratives (myths and genealogies) and spreading gossip and slander from house to house. This reflects a very real social pattern among women in a semi-segregated culture, where women communicate, educate, and socialize with women.[59] The women's network was a primary way that news spread and communication occurred in the community.[60] The spread of myths and genealogies gets pride of place among the problems that Timothy must solve: it is placed on a par with false teaching in the letter opening in 1:4. Paul apparently is afraid that even Timothy will become influenced by these stories, because in 4:7 he urges him to "stay away from the godless myths that are passed down from the older women [γραώδεις]" (CEB).[61] Historically, older women are often the

---

57. Ibid., 210.

58. A Roman matron's respectability and status could be enhanced if she became a widowed mother and was able to assume the control of her children's affairs (Suzanne Dixon, *The Roman Mother* [London: Croom Helm, 1988], 44).

59. Carolyn Osiek and Margaret MacDonald write, "We must keep in mind the existence of a world of women about which the texts remain silent—a world of sisterhood, conversation, and exchange among women on issues of hospitality, child care, service, and allegiance to Christ under the authority of a (sometimes pagan) paterfamilias as a wife, daughter, or slave, a world where distinctions among various categories of women possibly broke down" (*A Woman's Place: House Churches in Earliest Christianity* [Minneapolis: Fortress, 2006], 19).

60. "Women's social networks were especially valuable for their ability to spread information through already organized structures" (ibid., 14).

61. Mounce states, "It refers to the stereotyped kind of stories bandied back and forth between gossipy women who have nothing better to do" (*Pastoral Epistles*, 251). Gordon Fee calls it "a sarcastic expression often used in philosophical polemic comparing an opponent's position to the tales perpetuated by the older women of those cultures as they would sit around weaving and the like" (*1 and 2 Timothy, Titus*, NIBC 13 [Peabody, MA: Hendrickson, 1988], 103). This exactly reflects the behavior that Paul describes among the widows in 1 Tim. 5:13. But then Mounce abstracts it to mean "silly," and he quotes Knight to say that "it does not carry 'any negative overtones about either age or sex'" (Knight, *Pastoral Epistles*, 195). Yet it was a derogatory term in philosophical circles, and that supports the existence and threatening influence of women's stories. As Towner describes it, "The teaching under discussion was, not

story bearers of the culture, and they transmit the culture from generation to generation through myths, fairy tales, and lore that are repeated in front of the hearth and at bedtime. Carolyn Osiek and Margaret MacDonald state, "It has been suggested that since much teaching in oral cultures is done by storytelling, instructional stories told in these circles eventually emerged into the 'malestream' as the apocryphal Gospels and Acts."[62] Some scholars, such as Richard and Catherine Kroeger, have made convincing arguments that these stories refer to specifically Jewish myths (cf. 1:7–11) that retell and distort the story of the creation and fall.[63] Given the fact that there is a Nag Hammadi gnostic document (possibly second century) that does exactly that,[64] there possibly was an antecedent myth in the women's oral culture, and the reference to genealogies certainly sounds like Jewish influence. However, godless stories and lore could well refer to the perpetuation of traditional local myths and lore that were embedded in the pagan culture of Ephesus and involved syncretism. In addition, the spread of gossip or slander from house to house is highlighted by Paul as a problem with the widows (5:13), and slander was the one behavior uniquely prohibited for female deacons (3:11). Interestingly, the word for "slanderer" in 3:11 is διάβολος—another thinly veiled association of a problematic behavior among the women with the devil.

9.2.2.3 Summary

The purpose of 1 Timothy is to "instruct certain individuals not to spread wrong teaching and not to pay attention to myths and endless genealogies" (1:3b–4). Certain men were spreading false teaching, and the results of the false teaching were violence and arguments among the men, with a priority of making money, possibly through ministry. Some of these false teachers are

to put too fine a point on it, 'characteristic of elderly women.' In the philosophers, the adjective (e.g., 'old wives' tales' TNIV/NIV, NRSV) was derogatory, typical of the male-dominant cultural stereotype of women, and applied to trivialize a competing view. This is the most likely application in this polemical context (cf. 2 Tim. 3:6: 'silly women'). Together the two terms portray the heresy as pagan in its thrust" (*Timothy and Titus*, 305). It also indicates the power of the competition, and the source of stories from older women suggests the influence of the Aphrodite cult on the community narratives, probably in gender issues such as marriage and particularly childbirth.

62. Osiek and MacDonald, *Woman's Place*, 13–14. They are summarizing Dennis R. MacDonald, *The Legend and the Apostle: The Battle for Paul in Story and Canon* (Philadelphia: Westminster, 1983); and Stevan L. Davies, *Revolt of the Widows: The Social World of the Apocryphal Acts* (Carbondale: Southern Illinois University Press, 1999).

63. See Kroeger and Kroeger, *I Suffer Not a Woman*, 215–22. They include four accounts.

64. See "On the Origin of the World," in *The Nag Hammadi Library*, ed. James M. Robinson, rev. ed. (San Francisco: HarperSanFrancisco, 1988), 170–89, available at http://gnosis.org/naghamm/origin.html. See also Kroeger and Kroeger, *I Suffer Not a Woman*, 217–21.

characterized as demonic or satanic, as they targeted and deceived women. They taught them to avoid marriage and having children, and encouraged them in immodest and ostentatious behavior in dress and lifestyle, which is the counterpart to the men's drive for money—sounding much like a health, wealth, and prosperity gospel. Women were also the source of problematic narratives that included myths and genealogies as well as gossip and slander, all of which were perpetuated in the household and spread from house to house, becoming like devils themselves.

9.3 Antidotes to False Teaching (2:1–15)

Given the nature of the false teaching and spreading of myths and genealogies, it can be seen that the three units in 2:1–15 provide antidotes to the problems that Timothy is combating. Men are instructed to pray, women are instructed to dress modestly and sensibly, and women are to engage in spiritual formation in the home.

9.3.1 The Antidote to the False Teaching among the Men (2:1–8)

When Paul urged believers to pray for everyone, including rulers and authorities, the goal, according to 2:3–7, was for all people to be saved and come to a knowledge of the truth, which is God's will and Paul's gospel. In essence, everyone is being asked to pray for the Pauline mission, so the prayer provides an antidote to the opposition to Paul. In 2:2b, Paul writes that the outcome of the prayer for everyone was "so that we can live a quiet and peaceful life in complete godliness and dignity."[65] This outcome is the opposite of what Timothy was encountering in the behavior of the men and women in Ephesus. Then in 2:8, as Towner observes, "Paul engages the congregation according to gender groups. In this adaption of a household code, he takes the men [husbands] first, and speaks to them authoritatively."[66] The men are to lift holy hands free of anger and argument. Therefore, prayer is Paul's first antidote for wrong teaching and addresses the men's issues with anger and argument.[67]

65. Marshall misses the connection of peaceable conditions caused by prayer and the correction of strife and friction in Ephesus: "Read on their own, vv. 1–2 might suggest that prayer was being offered not for the salvation of mankind but simply for peaceable conditions for Christians!" (*Pastoral Epistles*, 417).

66. Towner, *Timothy and Titus*, 210.

67. Marshall is puzzled by the prominent ("'first of all'!") placement of prayer (*Pastoral Epistles*, 417). But this is explained by Paul's concern about the combative nature of the wrong teaching.

9.3.2 The Antidote of Appropriate Attire for the Women (2:9–10)

In order to achieve the goal of "a quiet and peaceable life in all godliness and dignity" (1 Tim. 2:2 NRSV), the women are instructed to wear modest and sensible attire as an antidote to trying to live a life of luxury. The "likewise" (ὡσαύτως) in 2:9 signals that the instructions to women are parallel to the instructions to the men, and 2:9 also shares the finite verb "I want" (βούλομαι) with the instructions to men in 2:8. But rather than treating the set of instructions on dress as giving requirements for women's prayer, they provide a parallel antidote to some of the women's behavior. They stand on their own as addressing a concern about the women in the church at Ephesus, a concern that reflects a cultural value of the Greco-Roman world in the first century. Here the life of luxury is characterized as wearing elaborate hairstyles of braiding, gold and silver jewelry, and expensive clothes. The instructions begin with describing appropriate dress (2:9) and then shift to a complementary antidote: encouraging women to make themselves attractive by doing good (2:10).

9.3.3 Directions for Correcting False Teaching among the Women (2:11–15)

The focus of the passage, supported by the greatest emphasis and the most explanation, is the antidote against women being deceived by false teaching in their homes, and the spreading of myths and genealogies from house to house among the women. Paul directs that women engage in spiritual formation in the home: "A wife should learn [sound teaching at home] quietly with complete submission" (2:11 CEB). The location in the household is signaled by the shift from the plural (wives/women) to the singular (wife/woman); each woman is to receive personal instruction. The reference to her spiritual formation or education also indicates a household context, which is confirmed by the reference to the foundation of marriage in Genesis 2 and the reference to childbirth.

Timothy most likely recognizes Paul's expectation for each man to take responsibility for his wife's spiritual formation. This passage has some relationship to Pauline tradition because of its clear parallels with instructions found in 1 Corinthians 14:[68]

> The women should be quiet during the meeting. They are not allowed to talk. Instead, they need to get under control, just as the Law says. If they want to

---

68. See the discussion in Towner, *Timothy and Titus*, 193–94.

learn something, they should ask their husbands at home. It is disgraceful for
a woman to talk during the meeting. (1 Cor. 14:34–35 CEB)

A wife should learn [sound teaching at home] quietly with complete submission.
I don't allow a wife to teach or to control her husband. Instead, she should be
a quiet listener. (1 Tim. 2:11–12 CEB)

The parallels are (1) instruction for silence/quietness (σιγάτωσαν, ἡσυχίᾳ);
(2) a prohibition to talk/teach (λαλεῖν, διδάσκειν); (3) language of submission or self-control (ὑποτασσέσθωσαν, ἐν πάσῃ ὑποταγῇ); and (4) learning in
the home as an antidote to the problem at hand (μαθεῖν, μανθανέτω).[69] The
repetition of the verb μανθάνω ("to learn") is the clearest parallel and the key
to the other similarities between the passages. Both passages include an element of expected cultural behavior between husbands and wives. A woman's
education typically took place in the home, in the domestic sphere in which
she functioned.[70] Both passages suggest that Pauline practice encouraged the
spiritual formation of the wife in the home by the husband, especially in cases
where remedial instruction or correction was needed.[71] In Corinth, women were
talking disruptively in the church meeting. Paul entertains the possibility that
they are talking because they have questions or cannot understand the teaching. His solution to the problem is that each husband take the responsibility
to answer his wife's questions at home. Thus 1 Timothy 2 and 1 Corinthians
14 indicate that generally there was a significant gap between husbands' and
wives' theological and biblical understanding, and 1 Corinthians 14 also shows
that at least some women lack the understanding of proper social behavior

69. It is often assumed that 1 Tim. 2:11–12 is a narrower application of a more general command; yet, in 1 Cor. 14:35, the prohibition against talking is not a general one against all forms
of speech (prayer and prophecy are explicitly exempt from the prohibition [cf. 1 Cor. 11:5])
but rather refers to a specific kind of disruptive talking during the meeting; the contexts of the
problem are different (home and church); and 1 Timothy teaches a quiet learning demeanor
while 1 Corinthians commands a silence in which the women might not be learning. There is
a question as to which passage is the basis for the other, given the textual problems of 1 Cor.
14:34–35. These verses are treated as an interpolation by Gordon D. Fee, *God's Empowering
Presence: The Holy Spirit in the Letters of Paul* (Peabody, MA: Hendrickson, 1994), 93–94.
70. Contra Towner, the shift to singular ("woman") signals household concerns in the domestic sphere, not "the appropriate behavior for wives in the church meeting" (*Timothy and
Titus*, 213). Towner recognizes that the language and focus of the passage "locate this passage
within the household code tradition" (ibid., 192) but then fails to drive that observation to the
simpler conclusion.
71. This is an adaptation or enhancement of E. Earle Ellis's suggestion that both passages
draw on a common household code tradition ("The Silenced Wives of Corinth [1 Cor. 14:34–
35]," in *New Testament Textual Criticism: Its Significance for Exegesis; Essays in Honour of
Bruce M. Metzger*, ed. Eldon J. Epp and Gordon D. Fee [Oxford: Clarendon, 1981], 214–15).

during public/religious education and exhortation. This reflects the differences in the literacy levels and in the practice of education of men and women; women were homeschooled, and therefore not socialized for the classroom. It is also consistent with the traditional gender roles promoted by household codes in the first-century Greco-Roman world.

Therefore, the language of submission and learning fits within the larger context of the household code and the situation within the Pauline churches: women who are demonstrably in need of teaching should assume the "posture and attitude of learners" at home, consistent in attitude and demeanor with the education of boys, and consistent in location with the domestic education of girls and women that took place in the first century.[72]

According to 1 Timothy 2:12, Paul does not permit (or is not currently permitting) any exception of a wife reversing the roles and becoming the designated spiritual guide and mentor of her husband's spiritual formation in the home: "I don't allow a wife to teach or to control her husband. Instead, she should be a quiet listener" (CEB). The domestic sphere and teacher-student relationship is understood in 2:11, so in 2:12, the prohibition to teach is in the same household context.[73] Grammatically, this could either be taken as a general practice whereby Paul did not allow a role reversal of the teaching responsibility in the home, or it could be taken as a continuation of the antidote to the issues with the women in Ephesus. The prohibition of teaching is in the prime position of emphasis, then Paul adds the prohibition of a wife "controlling" or "dominating" her husband, or "forcing him against his will."[74] Perhaps the concern about role reversal in teaching is attached to a more general concern about a complete role reversal in which the wife holds her husband under her control. This could have been a problem resulting from the false teaching and the emancipated women, or it may be a problem directly related to wealthy women, which is clearly an issue in the congregation and among the widows. If widows and wives were wealthy through inheritance,

---

72. The full quotation of Towner is "The wives/women in view were to assume the posture and attitude of learners in the worship assembly" (*Titus and Timothy*, 216). However, there is no signal that an assembly is in view at any point. Like prayer, teaching is a function in the household for women and is clearly the sphere in which they are being taught by false teachers.

73. The Greek structure of 1 Tim. 2:12 would be theologically problematic if it were not constrained by 2:11: διδάσκειν δὲ γυναικὶ οὐκ ἐπιτρέπω οὐδὲ αὐθεντεῖν ἀνδρός, ἀλλ' εἶναι ἐν ἡσυχίᾳ. The prohibition to teach would be absolute and would contradict other positive examples of women teaching and Paul's own command in Titus for the older women to teach the younger women. Of course, it could be that, given the problem of women spreading error from house to house, he was temporarily prohibiting women from engaging in any teaching in order to deal with the spread of heresy.

74. See the rendering of αὐθεντεῖν according to the discussion above.

role reversal could be a real and present experience; in fact, Aristotle described such an exception where the wife would rule the household because of her inheritance, which gave her power: "Sometimes, however, women rule, because they are heiresses. Their rule is thus not in accordance with virtue, but due to wealth and power, as in oligarchies."[75] However, this was definitely not the cultural ideal, and it had the potential of embarrassing/shaming the husbands and the church in the society.

Paul's prohibition of role reversals in the home probably reflects three concerns. First, the women are the source of myths and genealogies, which Paul is specifically trying to combat by asking the men to teach their wives at home. The myths and genealogies must have had a general attraction and given the women a certain amount of credibility in the church; indeed, Paul even needs to warn Timothy to stay away from them. Second, Paul wants to avoid the stigma and negative cultural appraisal that would occur if women in the church were taking over the role and behavior of men; it was common to attack a religion through the perceived insubordinate behavior of the women. Third, Paul's model of marriage, church leadership, and authority was countercultural. His model was not characterized by one person dominating or exercising abusive power and control over the other; in other words, he would not want the husbands to αὐθεντεῖν their wives either. However, an additional consideration may be in view. If a group of women was unilaterally determining to withhold sex from their husbands, that would be one of the worst offenses that a wife could commit in the eyes of the culture. That alone would be consistent with the semantic range of αὐθεντέω, and it would be particularly heinous in the context of the Christian community, where the man was forbidden to have sex outside of marriage. Paul would not tolerate any justification of that practice.

The references to Genesis 2–3 in 1 Timothy 2:13–14 are reframed by the need for the spiritual formation of the wives and the deception of the women by the false teachers, where the teachers are characterized as Satan (5:15). In 2:13–14, Paul writes, "Adam was formed first, and then Eve. Adam wasn't deceived, but rather his wife became the one who stepped over the line because she was completely deceived."[76] In light of the context, it is possible that Paul brings out typological parallels with the creation and fall. Positively,

75. Aristotle, *Eth. nic.* 8.1161a.10 (Roger Crisp, trans., *Nicomachean Ethics* [New York: Cambridge University Press, 2000], 157). In the culture, one of the reasons why a woman was not to be ostentatious was that she not shame her husband by appearing to be an heiress who brought more money into the relationship than he did.

76. This typology is parallel to 2 Cor. 11:3, where Paul expresses fear that the Corinthian church might be deceived just as the serpent deceived Eve.

the antidote via spiritual formation of a wife by her husband corresponds to the formation of Adam and Eve in creation, at least in terms of the order. Negatively, the deception of the women by demonic/satanic false teachers parallels the deception of Eve by the serpent. On the other hand, it could be argued that this is a brief correction of the content of the myths. A third possibility is that Paul is giving the relevant biblical background to the major controversy causing problems among the women: the consequences of the fall on childbearing.

Whatever the function of 1 Timothy 2:13–14, we are to read the reference to childbirth in 1 Timothy 2:15 in light of the narrative framework that Paul's summary of Genesis 2–3 brings to the text.[77] The results of the fall for women are given in Genesis 3:16: "To the woman [God] said, 'I will greatly increase your pangs in childbearing; in pain you shall bring forth children, yet your desire shall be for your husband, and he shall rule over you'" (NRSV). The original reader would understand Paul's reference to "childbirth" as an extension of the narrative of the creation and fall, rather than the unrelated topics about how women are saved or women's God-ordained role. The issues surrounding childbirth have a particular relevance for the problems in Ephesus. They include an increase in childbirths, an increase in pain in childbirth for women, and the rule of the wife by her husband. The false teaching of prohibiting marriage and not having children appears to be an attempt at a reversal of the fall. This would have an attraction for the women in the church because in the ancient world each pregnancy was life-threatening; complications from pregnancy and childbirth were the leading cause of death for women. One thing that ancient women's religion had in common was the use of magic, sacrifices, and prayer for help and protection in time of childbirth; perhaps women felt that they found the needed protection through the false teaching.[78] The widespread practice of magic and worship of Artemis are recognized in studies on the book of Acts as important background for the early church in Ephesus, particularly because of the Lukan accounts of the Ephesian believers

77. According to Steve Moyise, "A narrative approach . . . suggests that what a text brings with it is . . . the narrative framework to which it belongs. For example, the quotation of Genesis 15:6—'Abraham believed God and it was reckoned to him as righteousness'—might well evoke Abraham's life story, but not necessarily the particulars of the surrounding verses" (*Paul and Scripture: Studying the New Testament Use of the Old Testament* [Grand Rapids: Baker Academic, 2010], 111). In the case of 1 Tim. 2:15, Paul specifies the particular of childbirth and expands on it—this is the part of the narrative that he actually interprets.

78. Concerning the general practice of magic in Ephesus, Ben Witherington writes, "Luke, who does not give a great deal of attention to the demonic world, does so in Acts 19, for Ephesus and its environs had the reputation of being a center or haven of demonic activity" (*The Acts of the Apostles: A Social-Rhetorical Commentary* [Grand Rapids: Eerdmans, 1998], 583).

burning their magic scrolls (Acts 19:18–19) and of the riot of the silversmiths (19:24–41). Rather than conclude that the burning of the scrolls conclusively dealt with all syncretism of local magic with early Christianity, we should see it instead as evidence of how pervasive magic was among common people and that some believers continued to practice it even after their conversion to Christianity. We certainly may assume that it continued to be an issue among the women who would tend to continue to use the local tried-and-true "home remedies" in childbirth and midwifery, what was an indivisible mix of natural medicine and magic in pagan practice.

Even more germane is the fact that Artemis, the patron goddess of Ephesus, was the goddess of childbirth and thought to be a significant source of general health.[79] There was a special bond between the people of Ephesus and the cult of Artemis, and according to Paul Trebilco, its continued vitality is witnessed to by the Salutaris Inscription, written in 104 CE, which describes an elaborate procession carrying thirty-one images, nine of which were Artemis—a significant city event that occurred every two weeks.[80] Guy MacLean Rogers observes that the birth of the goddess contributed to the Ephesian people's "sense of social and historical identity in the complex and changing Roman world."[81] He asserts that the biweekly processions taught the people "to look to . . . the birth of the goddess Artemis at Ephesos, for a theological sense of how Ephesian social and historical identity was grounded in a 'sacred' reality, which was impervious to all humanly wrought challenges."[82]

Strabo wrote, "Artemis has her name from the fact that she makes people ἀρτεμέας," which means "safe and sound"; or as Artemidorus says, ὑγιές ("healthy").[83] Even more to the point, one of Artemis's titles was Σώτειρα ("savior"); and Achilles Tatius writes, "But the great goddess Artemis has saved them both,"[84] which unambiguously demonstrates that σώζω was a natural way in the common Greek to describe Artemis's help, healing, and protection in areas of life that would encompass childbirth. Little wonder that Acts 19:23–27 portrays Paul as competing directly with Artemis, targeting the cult, and deliberately persuading and drawing people away from worshiping her.

---

79. See Paul Trebilco, "Asia," in *The Book of Acts in Its Graeco-Roman Setting*, ed. David W. J. Gill and Conrad Gempf (Grand Rapids: Eerdmans, 1994), 291–362, esp. 313–50 for his study of Artemis.

80. Ibid., 328.

81. Rogers, *The Sacred Identity of Ephesos: Foundation Myths of a Roman City* (London: Routledge, 1991), 41.

82. Ibid., 69.

83. Strabo, *Geogr.* 14.1.6, my translation; Artemidorus Daldianus, *Onir.* 2.35. This is not to argue for the etymology of the name "Artemis," but rather to indicate what people thought about her.

84. Achilles Tatius, *Leuc. Clit.* 8.9.13, my translation.

One way of reading the final statement in the passage (1 Tim. 2:15) is this: Paul recognizes the legitimate risk that childbirth poses for women (maternal mortality) and encourages the husband and wife to trust God for the wife's protection as she goes through childbirth. He also offers pragmatic help in the command for both of them to treat each other with love, holiness, and self-control: "But a wife will be brought safely through childbirth, if they both continue in faith, love and holiness, together with self-control" (1 Tim. 2:15 CEB). As stated in chapter 4, if 1 Timothy 2:11–15 has a domestic context, then the closest referents to "if they continue" are the husband and wife.[85] Both are activated in 1 Timothy 2:11 with the instruction of the wife in the home, made explicit in 2:12, and typologically represented by Adam and Eve in 2:13–14. According to studies on maternal mortality, the husband has a crucial role in redressing the consequence of the fall. The failure of husbands to consider their wives in their decisions about the size of the family and about the care that their wives receive during childbirth directly contributes to the death rate. The exercise of self-control, of course, is crucial to prevent multiple pregnancies that become life-threatening as well.

When we approach the interpretation of 1 Timothy 2, all of us make exegetical choices that determine the outcome. Because of the nature of the personal letter, the reader must make inferences from the text to supply information that is not provided.

The best indicator of the context of the letter is drawn from the text itself. The correction of false teaching is arguably the purpose of the entire letter (1 Tim. 1:3–4). The problems with false teaching and related issues that are delineated in chapters 4–6 have direct ties with the instructions given to men and women in 2:1–15, so that the passage can be understood as "antidotes to false teaching." Paul is primarily concerned about anger and arguing among men, which he addresses in detail in the second half of the letter; these concerns with controversies and disputes cannot be confined to a weekly worship service. The controversial passage that addresses women in 2:9–15 does not fit the setting of a church service either. It is better understood as a type of household code, whereby the heresies involving women that had invaded the household were to be corrected in each household by the husband, who was in the best position to take responsibility for the spiritual formation of his wife. Rather than prohibiting women from participating as leaders in the church, Paul addresses the lacuna in discipleship that is holding the Ephesian women

85. For a fuller discussion of maternal mortality in the context of the fall, see §4.2.2.3.

believers back from maturity and sound teaching. Paul's references to the creation and fall are directly relevant to marriage, sex, and childbirth—issues that Paul identifies as problem areas among the women later in the letter. Paul concludes his instructions by addressing women's very real concerns about the results of the fall on the ordeal of childbirth, and he offers both a spiritual promise of healing and a pragmatic solution.

Conclusion

The conclusion of this study is to call for a thorough rereading of the Pauline passages on gender. The traditional interpretations of Scripture, theology, and practices concerning gender have come into question on a number of grounds. The traditional readings of the Pauline passages on gender fail to adequately account for the formal and semantic features of the Pauline Epistles, nor do they adequately interact with the sociohistorical, literary, and situational contexts. Such readings do not adequately account for the interpretive problems in the text, and they actually create dissonance and incoherence both within the discourses and in Pauline theology. Furthermore, the practice of a rigid hierarchy based on gender in the church and home is not consistent with the cultural move to a democratic worldview and its privileges.

In addition, this study calls for the construction of an adequate and relevant theology of gender based on a rereading of the biblical texts. The consensus of the Western worldview concerning male and female has changed so that it in many ways reflects a more biblical belief about gender: male and female are ontologically equal. The paradigm shift to the position that women are not ontologically inferior to men calls for a rereading of the biblical texts in the same way that the inclusion of gentiles into the people of God called for Paul's own rereading of the Hebrew texts. The same seriousness and attention that were given to the relationships between the persons of the Trinity and the relationship of the human and divine in the person of Christ should be applied to a coherent understanding of humanity as male and female.

Certain controls should be placed on our understanding of the gender passages in the Bible. There should be a consistent hermeneutic for passages that are applied to men and passages that are applied to women. For those who hold the Pauline texts to be authoritative, there should be a coherence between passages that are addressed to all Christians and passages that are applied to male or female. Our understanding of cultural icons, symbols, and contexts must be informed by the social and cultural contexts in which these texts had meaning. The formal features of the texts should be taken seriously. I exhort the evangelical community to make a crucial distinction between what a text is and what has been assumed about the text in the process of interpretation. I encourage evangelicals to then "trust the text." Place the actual biblical text above the interpretations of the text and the theological constructions that have gained a dogmatic foothold among so many.

The traditional interpretations and understandings of the Pauline theology of gender should not be guarded as a citadel and treated as a privileged reading of the texts that must be incontrovertibly proved wrong with hard evidence before considering other options. Rather, they should be placed on equal ground with other viable interpretive options and treated with comparable suspicion *because* of the history of interpretation, not in spite of it. I invite serious scholars and students of the text to go through the discipline of carefully identifying the information, assumptions, and inferences that have been imported into the texts, extract them from the reading, and then read the texts again with hermeneutics that are consistent with the best practices for interpreting biblical texts and language in general. Seek to weigh the contexts in which the text is placed and consider how they affect interpretation. Utilize sophisticated tools to determine the meaning of words in a linguistically informed way, because that is a major arena in the argument.

A Pauline theology of gender should be placed in relationship to other topics in Pauline theology, particularly the doctrine of salvation by grace, so crucial for the gentile mission. However, one of the complementary topics that must be constructed, or at least reexamined, is the Pauline theology of authority and power. Claims to authority and power based on gender run counter to both Paul's teaching and his model for leadership.

Gender is a topic about which people of outstanding character disagree. However, interpreters with integrity need to take responsibility for the theological trajectories of their conclusions and those of the networks with which they associate. For the Christian population, there must be a determined evaluation of the behavioral outcomes of any belief system: Jesus said that we will know people by their fruit. The mandate to subordinate women and bar them from positions of authority has been applied in the congregation and the academy, in some cases with various forms and degrees of disrespect, marginalization, suspicion, mistreatment, and rejection of women, usually in an effort to either maintain control, enforce a standard, or deflect responsibility.

The prerogative of male leaders and husbands is felt to be such a scriptural priority that there is a lack of accountability and confrontation in cases of abuse, sexual harassment, and incest in the churches. Not surprisingly, there is not enough interest in addressing the global oppression of women. The exercise of power among male leaders is also problematic as influential leaders use their public or institutional influence to inappropriately dominate and enforce doctrinal uniformity over their colleagues. Identifiable propaganda techniques and the employment of blatant power plays have been used to ruin careers. There is a transparent connection between these behaviors and the theology of power in which this behavior is systemic.

A number of issues that face Christianity and the church in contemporary society are embedded in the issue of gender. Issues that concern the body and sexuality are probably the most crucial area in which Christianity is in conflict with the culture and can address the culture. As has often been the case, the focus of the debate about gender misses the mark. The sexualization of Western culture, the general confusion about identity, and the impact of developments such as industrialization and technology on gendered behavior—all these require our careful attention.

This study is an attempt to move in the suggested direction and present viable alternative readings of gender passages, readings faithful to the text, and that attempt to be coherent. I have suggested several options that are new perspectives, and because they are innovative, they may fail to convince simply because they seem strange. However, they account for the material and take the language and the culture seriously and ultimately "connect the dots." This study was forged in the fires of over forty-five years of experience in evangelical churches and Christian colleges and universities and seminaries that drove my research and my quest for coherence. It was important to me during this time that I not facilely or prematurely adopt any given explanation or rereading. Consequently, I offer this study for your consideration grounded in my convictions but with the hope that it will advance both the conversation and the kingdom of God.

Select Bibliography

Abusch, Ra'anan. "Circumcision and Castration under Roman Law in the Early Empire." In *The Covenant of Circumcision: New Perspectives on an Ancient Rite*, edited by Elizabeth Wyner Mark, 75–86. Hanover, NH: Brandeis University Press, 2003.

Ahmed, Leila. *Women and Gender in Islam: Historical Roots of a Modern Debate.* New Haven: Yale University Press, 1992.

Allen, Ronald, and Beverly Allen. *Liberated Traditionalism: Men and Women in Balance.* Portland, OR: Multnomah, 1985.

Amadi-Azuogu, Adolphus Chinedu. *Gender and Ministry in Early Christianity and the Church Today.* Lanham, MD: University Press of America, 2007.

Auerback, Michelle. "Drawing the Line at Modesty: My Place in the Order of Things." In *The Veil: Women Writers on Its History, Lore, and Politics*, edited by Jennifer Heath, 202–12. Berkeley: University of California Press, 2008.

Bailey, Kenneth E. "Informal Controlled Oral Tradition and the Synoptic Gospels." *Them* 20, no. 2 (1995): 4–11.

———. *Jesus through Middle Eastern Eyes: Cultural Studies in the Gospels.* Downers Grove, IL: InterVarsity, 2008.

———. *Paul through Mediterranean Eyes: Cultural Studies in 1 Corinthians.* Downers Grove, IL: InterVarsity, 2011.

Balch, David L. *Let Wives Be Submissive: The Domestic Code in 1 Peter.* SBLMS 26. Chico, CA: Scholars Press, 1981.

———. "Paul, Families, and Households." In *Paul in the Greco-Roman World: A Handbook*, edited by J. Paul Sampley, 258–92. Harrisburg, PA: Trinity Press International, 2003.

Balch, David L., and Carolyn Osiek. *Families in the New Testament World: Households and House Churches.* Louisville: Westminster John Knox, 1997.

Baldwin, H. Scott. "A Difficult Word: Αὐθεντέω in 1 Timothy 2:12." In *Women in the Church: A Fresh Analysis of 1 Timothy 2:9–15*, edited by Andreas J. Köstenberger, Thomas R. Schreiner, and H. Scott Baldwin, 65–80. Grand Rapids: Baker, 1995.

———. "An Important Word: Αὐθεντέω in 1 Timothy 2:12." In *Women in the Church: An Analysis and Application of 1 Timothy 2:9–15*, 2nd ed., edited by Andreas J. Köstenberger and Thomas R. Schreiner, 39–51. Grand Rapids: Baker Academic, 2005.

Banks, Robert. *Paul's Idea of Community: The Early House Churches in Their Historical Setting.* Grand Rapids: Eerdmans, 1980.

Barger, Lilian Calles. *Eve's Revenge: Women and a Spirituality of the Body.* Grand Rapids: Brazos, 2003.

Barnett, Paul. "*Authentein* Once More: A Response to L. E. Wilshire." *EvQ* 66 (1994): 159–62.

———. *The Second Epistle to the Corinthians.* NICNT. Grand Rapids: Eerdmans, 1997.

———. "Wives and Women's Ministry (1 Tim. 2:11–15)." *EvQ* 61, no. 3 (1989): 225–38.

Bartchy, S. Scott. "Who Should Be Called Father? Paul of Tarsus between the Jesus Tradition and Patria Potestas." *BTB* 33 (2003): 135–47.

Batten, A. J. "Neither Gold nor Braided Hair (1 Tim. 2.9; 1 Pet. 3.3): Adornment, Gender and Honour in Antiquity." *NTS* 55 (2009): 484–501.

Bauckham, Richard. *Gospel Women: Studies of the Named Women in the Gospels.* Grand Rapids: Eerdmans, 2002.

Baudzej, Julia. "Re-telling the Story of Jesus: The Concept of Embodiment and Recent Feminist Reflections on the Maleness of Christ." *FT* 17 (2008): 72–91.

Baugh, S. M. "A Foreign World: Ephesus in the First Century." In *Women in the Church: An Analysis and Application of 1 Timothy 2:9–15*, 2nd ed., edited by Andreas J. Köstenberger and Thomas R. Schreiner, 13–38. Grand Rapids: Baker Academic, 2005.

Bauman-Martin, Betsy J. "Feminist Theologies of Suffering and Current Interpretations of 1 Peter 2:18–3:9." In *A Feminist Companion to the Catholic Epistles and Hebrews*, edited by Amy-Jill Levine and Maria Mayo Robbins, 63–81. FCNTECW 8. New York: T&T Clark International, 2004.

Beattie, Gillian. *Women and Marriage in Paul and His Early Interpreters.* JSNTSup 296. London: T&T Clark, 2005.

Bedale, Stephen. "The Meaning of κεφαλή in the Pauline Epistles." *JTS* 5 (1954): 211–15.

Belleville, Linda L. "'Ἰουνιᾶν . . . ἐπίσημοι ἐν τοῖς ἀποστόλοις: A Re-examination of Romans 16:7 in Light of Primary Source Materials." *NTS* 51 (2005): 231–49.

———. "Teaching and Usurping Authority: 1 Timothy 2:11–15." In *Discovering Biblical Equality: Complementarity without Hierarchy*, edited by Ronald W. Pierce and Rebecca Merrill Groothuis, 205–23. Downers Grove, IL: InterVarsity, 2005.

———. "Women in Ministry: The Egalitarian Perspective." In *Two Views on Women in Ministry*, edited by James R. Beck and Craig L. Blomberg, 75–154. Counterpoints. Grand Rapids: Zondervan, 2000.

———. *Women Leaders and the Church: Three Crucial Questions*. Grand Rapids: Baker Books, 2000.

Best, Ernest. *Ephesians*. NTG. Sheffield: JSOT Press, 1993.

Brinks, C. L. "'Great Is Artemis of the Ephesians': Acts 19:23–41 in Light of Goddess Worship in Ephesus." *CBQ* 71 (2009): 776–94.

Bruce, F. F. *Paul, Apostle of the Heart Set Free*. Grand Rapids: Eerdmans, 1977.

Burer, Michael H., and Daniel B. Wallace. "Was Junia Really an Apostle? A Re-examination of Romans 16:7." *NTS* 47 (2001): 76–91.

Bynum, Jo Ann. Foreword to *Gender and Ministry in Early Christianity and the Church Today*, by Adolphus Chinedu Amadi-Azuogu. Lanham, MD: University Press of America, 2007.

Calef, Susan A. "*Kephalē*, Coverings, and Cosmology: The Impenetrable 'Logic' of 1 Corinthians 11:2–16." *JRS* 5 (2009): 21–44.

Campbell, Douglas A., ed. *Gospel and Gender: A Trinitarian Engagement with Being Male and Female in Christ*. STS 7. London: T&T Clark, 2003.

Campbell, William S. *Paul and the Creation of Christian Identity*. LNTS 322. London: T&T Clark, 2006.

Canavan, Rosemary. "First-Century Inclusive Language." *Colloq* 39 (2007): 3–15.

Carson, Anne. "Putting Her in Her Place: Woman, Dirt, and Desire." In *Before Sexuality: The Construction of the Erotic Experience in the Ancient Greek World*, edited by David M. Halperin, John J. Winkler, and Froma I. Zeitlin, 135–69. Princeton: Princeton University Press, 1990.

Carson, D. A. "'Silent in the Churches': On the Role of Women in 1 Corinthians 14:33b–36." In *Recovering Biblical Manhood and Womanhood: A Response to Evangelical Feminism*, edited by John Piper and Wayne Grudem, 133–47. Wheaton: Crossway, 1991.

Castelli, Elizabeth. *Imitating Paul: A Discourse of Power*. Louisville: Westminster John Knox, 1991.

Cervin, Richard S. "Does κεφαλή Mean 'Source' or 'Authority Over' in Greek Literature? A Rebuttal." *TJ* 10 (1989): 85–112.

Clanton, Jann Aldredge. *In Whose Image? God and Gender*. New York: Crossroad, 1990.

Clarke, Andrew D. "Jew and Greek, Slave and Free, Male and Female: Paul's Theology of Ethnic, Social and Gender Inclusiveness in Romans 16." In *Rome in the Bible and the Early Church*, edited by Peter Oakes, 103–25. Grand Rapids: Baker Academic, 2002.

Clines, D. J. A. "*Ecce Vir*; or, Gendering the Son of Man." In *Biblical Studies/Cultural Studies: The Third Sheffield Colloquium*, edited by J. Cheryl Exum and Stephen D. Moore, 352–75. JSOTSup 266. Sheffield: Sheffield Academic, 1998.

———. "Image of God." In *Dictionary of Paul and His Letters*, edited by Gerald F. Hawthorne, Ralph P. Martin, and Daniel G. Reid, 426–28. Downers Grove, IL: InterVarsity, 1993.

———. "Paul, the Invisible Man." In *New Testament Masculinities*, edited by Stephen D. Moore and Janice Capel Anderson, 181–92. SemeiaSt 45. Atlanta: Society of Biblical Literature, 2003.

Cobb, L. Stephanie. *Dying to Be Men: Gender and Language in Early Christian Martyr Texts*. New York: Columbia University Press, 2008.

Cohick, Lynn H. *Women in the World of the Earliest Christians: Illuminating Ancient Ways of Life*. Grand Rapids: Baker Academic, 2009.

Conzelmann, Hans. *1 Corinthians: A Commentary on the First Epistle to the Corinthians*. Translated by James W. Leitch. Edited by George W. MacRae. Hermeneia. Philadelphia: Fortress, 1975.

Corbett, Greville G. *Gender*. CTL. Cambridge: Cambridge University Press, 1991.

Countryman, L. William. *Dirt, Greed & Sex: Sexual Ethics in the New Testament and Their Implications for Today*. Minneapolis: Fortress, 2007.

Crook, Zeba. "Honor, Shame, and Social Status Revisited." *JBL* 128 (2009): 591–611.

D'Angelo, Mary Rose. "Gender and Geopolitics in the Work of Philo of Alexandria: Jewish Piety and Imperial Family Values." In *Mapping Gender in Ancient Religious Discourses*, edited by Todd Penner and Carolyn Vander Stichele, 63–88. BIS 84. Leiden: Brill, 2007.

Davies, Stevan L. *Revolt of the Widows: The Social World of the Apocryphal Acts*. Carbondale: Southern Illinois University Press, 1999.

Davis, J. J. "First Timothy 2:12, the Ordination of Women, and Paul's Use of Creation Narratives." *PriscPap* 23 (2009): 5–10.

Deming, Will. *Paul on Marriage and Celibacy: The Hellenistic Background of 1 Corinthians 7*. SNTSMS 83. Cambridge: Cambridge University Press, 1995.

deSilva, David A. *Honor, Patronage, Kinship & Purity: Unlocking New Testament Culture*. Downers Grove, IL: InterVarsity, 2000.

———. "Patronage and Reciprocity: The Context of Grace in the New Testament." *ATJ* 31 (1999): 32–84.

Dibelius, Martin, and Hans Conzelmann. *The Pastoral Epistles: A Commentary on the Pastoral Epistles*. Translated by Philip Buttolph and Adela Yarbro. Edited by Helmut Koester. Hermeneia. Philadelphia: Fortress, 1972.

Dixon, Suzanne. *The Roman Mother*. London: Croom Helm, 1988.

Donaldson, James. *Woman: Her Position and Influence in Ancient Greece and Rome, and among the Early Christians*. New York: Gordon, 1973.

Doriani, Daniel. "History of Interpretation of 1 Timothy 2." In *Women in the Church: A Fresh Analysis of 1 Timothy 2:9–15*, edited by Andreas J. Köstenberger, Thomas R. Schreiner, and H. Scott Baldwin, 213–67. Grand Rapids: Baker, 1995.

Dudrey, Russ. "'Submit Yourselves to One Another': A Socio-historical Look at the Household Code of Ephesians 5:15–6:9." *ResQ* 41 (1999): 27–44.

Dunn, James D. G. *Romans 1–8*. WBC 38A. Nashville: Nelson, 1988.

———. *Romans 9–16*. WBC 38B. Nashville: Nelson, 1988.

———. *The Theology of Paul the Apostle*. Grand Rapids: Eerdmans, 1998.

Eastman, Susan Grove. *Recovering Paul's Mother Tongue: Language and Theology in Galatians*. Grand Rapids: Eerdmans, 2007.

Ehrensperger, Kathy. *That We May Be Mutually Encouraged: Feminism and the New Perspective in Pauline Studies*. New York: T&T Clark, 2004.

El Guindi, Fadwa. *Veil: Modesty, Privacy, and Resistance*. Oxford: Berg, 1999.

Elliot, Elisabeth. "The Essence of Femininity: A Personal Perspective." In *Recovering Biblical Manhood and Womanhood: A Response to Evangelical Feminism*, edited by John Piper and Wayne Grudem, 394–99, 532. Wheaton: Crossway, 1991.

Ellis, E. Earle. "The Silenced Wives of Corinth (1 Cor. 14:34–35)." In *New Testament Textual Criticism: Its Significance for Exegesis; Essays in Honour of Bruce M. Metzger*, edited by Eldon J. Epp and Gordon D. Fee, 213–20. Oxford: Clarendon, 1981.

Ellis, J. Edward. *Paul and Ancient Views of Sexual Desire: Paul's Sexual Ethics in 1 Thessalonians 4, 1 Corinthians 7 and Romans 1*. LNTS 354. London: T&T Clark, 2007.

Engberg-Pedersen, Troels, ed. *Paul in His Hellenistic Context*. Minneapolis: Fortress, 1995.

Epp, Eldon Jay. *Junia: The First Woman Apostle*. Minneapolis: Fortress, 2005.

Fee, Gordon D. *1 and 2 Timothy, Titus*. NIBC 13. Peabody, MA: Hendrickson, 1988.

———. *The First Epistle to the Corinthians*. NICNT. Grand Rapids: Eerdmans, 1987.

———. *Paul's Letter to the Philippians*. NICNT. Grand Rapids: Eerdmans, 1995.

Finney, Mark. "Honour, Head-Coverings and Headship: 1 Corinthians 11:2–16 in Its Social Context." *JSNT* 33 (2010): 31–58.

Fitzmyer, Joseph A. "Another Look at ΚΕΦΑΛΗ in 1 Corinthians 11:3." *NTS* 35 (1989): 503–11.

———. "A Feature of Qumran Angelology and the Angels of 1 Corinthians 11:10." *NTS* 4 (1957): 48–58.

———. "*Kephalē* in 1 Corinthians 11:3." *Int* 47 (1993): 32–59.

———. *Romans: A New Translation with Introduction and Commentary*. AB 33. New York: Doubleday, 1993.

Foley, Helen P., ed. *Reflections of Women in Antiquity*. New York: Gordon and Breach Science Publishers, 1981.

Fuhrmann, Sebastian. "Saved by Childbirth: Struggling Ideologies, the Female Body and a Placing of 1 Timothy 2:15a." *Neot* 44 (2010): 30–46.

Gager, John G., and E. Leigh Gibson. "Violent Acts and Violent Language in the Apostle Paul." In *Violence in the New Testament*, edited by Shelly Matthews and E. Leigh Gibson, 13–21. London: T&T Clark, 2005.

Gagnon, Robert A. J. *The Bible and Homosexual Practice: Texts and Hermeneutics.* Nashville: Abingdon, 2001.

Garland, David E. *1 Corinthians.* BECNT. Grand Rapids: Baker Academic, 2003.

Gaventa, Beverly Roberts. *Our Mother Saint Paul.* Louisville: Westminster John Knox, 2007.

Gielen, Marlis. *Tradition und Theologie neutestamentlicher Haustafelethik: Ein Beitrag zur Frage einer christlichen Auseinandersetzung mit gesellschaftlichen Normen.* 2nd ed. BBB 75. Frankfurt: Anton Hain, 1990.

Giles, Kevin. "Response." In *The Bible and Women's Ministry: An Australian Dialogue*, edited by Alan Nichols, 65–87. Canberra: Acorn, 1990.

———. "*Women in the Church*: A Rejoinder to Andreas Köstenberger." *EvQ* 73 (2001): 225–43.

Glad, Clarence E. "Paul and Adaptability." In *Paul in the Greco-Roman World: A Handbook*, edited by J. Paul Sampley, 17–41. Harrisburg, PA: Trinity Press International, 2003.

Glancy, Jennifer A. "Obstacles to Slaves' Participation in the Corinthian Church." *JBL* 117 (1998): 481–501.

———. *Slavery in Early Christianity.* Oxford: Oxford University Press, 2002.

Goodacre, Mark S. "Does περιβόλαιον Mean 'Testicle' in 1 Corinthians 11:15?" *JBL* 130 (2011): 391–96.

Gordon, T. David. "A Certain Kind of Letter: The Genre of 1 Timothy." In *Women in the Church: A Fresh Analysis of 1 Timothy 2:9–15*, edited by Andreas J. Köstenberger, Thomas R. Schreiner, and H. Scott Baldwin, 53–63. Grand Rapids: Baker, 1995.

Grenholm, Cristina, and Daniel Patte, eds. *Gender, Tradition and Romans: Shared Ground, Uncertain Borders.* RHC. New York: T&T Clark, 2005.

Gritz, Sharon Hodgin. *Paul, Women Teachers, and the Mother Goddess at Ephesus: A Study of 1 Timothy 2:9–15 in Light of the Religious and Cultural Milieu of the First Century.* Lanham, MD: University Press of America, 1991.

Grudem, Wayne. "Appendix 1: The Meaning of *Kephalē* ('Head'): A Response to Recent Studies." In *Recovering Biblical Manhood and Womanhood: A Response to Evangelical Feminism*, edited by John Piper and Wayne Grudem, 425–68. Wheaton: Crossway, 1991.

———. "Does *Kephalē* ('Head') Mean 'Source' or 'Authority Over' in Greek Literature? A Survey of 2,336 Examples." *TJ* 6 (1985): 38–59.

———. *Evangelical Feminism and Biblical Truth: An Analysis of More Than One Hundred Disputed Questions.* Sisters, OR: Multnomah, 2004.

———. *The Gift of Prophecy in 1 Corinthians*. Washington, DC: University Press of America, 1982.

———. "The Meaning of κεφαλή ('Head'): An Evaluation of New Evidence, Real and Alleged." *JETS* 44 (2001): 25–65.

———. "Prophecy—Yes, but Teaching—No." *JETS* 30 (1987): 11–23.

Gundry-Volf, Judith M. "Beyond Difference? Paul's Vision of a New Humanity in Galatians 3:28." In *Gospel and Gender: A Trinitarian Engagement with Being Male and Female in Christ*, edited by Douglas A. Campbell, 8–36. STS 7. London: T&T Clark, 2003.

———. "Christ and Gender: A Study of Difference and Equality in Galatians 3:28." In *Jesus Christus als die Mitte der Schrift: Studien zur Hermeneutik des Evangeliums*, edited by Christof Landmesser, Hans-Joachim Eckstein, and Hermann Lichtenberger, 439–77. BZNW 86. Berlin: de Gruyter, 1997.

———. "Paul on Women and Gender: A Comparison with Early Jewish Views." In *The Road from Damascus: The Impact of Paul's Conversion on His Life, Thought, and Ministry*, edited by Richard N. Longenecker, 184–212. Grand Rapids: Eerdmans, 1997.

———. "Putting the Moral Vision of the New Testament into Focus: A Review." *BBR* 9 (1999): 277–87.

Hafemann, S. J. "Letters to the Corinthians." In *Dictionary of Paul and His Letters*, edited by Gerald F. Hawthorne, Ralph P. Martin, and Daniel G. Reid, 164–79. Downers Grove, IL: InterVarsity, 1993.

Hallett, Judith P. "Women's Lives in the Ancient Mediterranean." In *Women and Christian Origins*, edited by Ross Shepard Kraemer and Mary Rose D'Angelo, 13–34. Oxford: Oxford University Press, 1999.

Hanson, A. T. *The Pastoral Letters: Commentary on the First and Second Letters to Timothy and the Letter to Titus*. CamBC. Cambridge: Cambridge University Press, 1966.

———. *Studies in the Pastoral Epistles*. London: SPCK, 1968.

Harris, Murray J. *The Second Epistle to the Corinthians: A Commentary on the Greek Text*. NIGTC. Grand Rapids: Eerdmans, 2005.

Harris, Timothy J. "Why Did Paul Mention Eve's Deception? A Critique of P. W. Barnett's Interpretation of 1 Timothy 2." *EvQ* 62 (1990): 335–52.

Harrison, P. N. *The Problem of the Pastoral Epistles*. Oxford: Oxford University Press, 1921.

Hay, David M., ed. *1 & 2 Corinthians*. PTh 2. Minneapolis: Fortress, 1995.

Hay, David M., and E. Elizabeth Johnson, eds. *Romans*. PTh 3. Minneapolis: Fortress, 1995.

Hays, Richard B. *First Corinthians*. IBC. Louisville: John Knox, 1997.

Heath, Jennifer. Introduction to *The Veil: Women Writers on Its History, Lore, and Politics*, edited by Jennifer Heath, 1–26. Berkeley: University of California Press, 2008.

Hering, James P. *The Colossian and Ephesian* Haustafeln *in Theological Context: An Analysis of Their Origins, Relationship, and Message*. TR 260. New York: Peter Lang, 2007.

Herzer, Jens. "Rearranging the 'House of God': A New Perspective on the Pastoral Epistles." In *Empsychoi Logoi: Religious Innovations in Antiquity; Studies in Honor of Pieter Willem van der Horst*, edited by Alberdina Houtman, Albert de Jong, and Magda Misset-van de Weg, 547–66. AGJU 73. Leiden: Brill, 2008.

Hess, Richard R. "Equality with and without Innocence: Genesis 1–3." In *Discovering Biblical Equality: Complementarity without Hierarchy*, edited by Ronald W. Pierce and Rebecca Merrill Groothuis, 79–95. Downers Grove, IL: InterVarsity, 2005.

Hodge, Charles. *A Commentary on the First Epistle to the Corinthians*. Grand Rapids: Eerdmans, 1994.

Hoehner, Harold W. *Ephesians: An Exegetical Commentary*. Grand Rapids: Baker Academic, 2002.

Holmes, J. M. *Text in a Whirlwind: A Critique of Four Exegetical Devices at 1 Timothy 2:9–15*. JSNTSup 196. Sheffield: Sheffield Academic, 2000.

Hooker, Morna D. "Authority on Her Head: An Examination of 1 Corinthians 11:10." *NTS* 10 (1964): 410–16.

Horrell, David G. "Disciplining Performance and 'Placing' the Church: Widows, Elders and Slaves in the Household of God (1 Tim. 5:1–6:2)." In *1 Timothy Reconsidered*, edited by Karl Paul Donfried, 109–34. MSBBES 18. Leuven: Peeters, 2008.

———. *Solidarity and Difference: A Contemporary Reading of Paul's Ethics*. London: T&T Clark, 2005.

Houlden, J. L. *The Pastoral Epistles: I and II Timothy, Titus*. London: SCM, 1976.

Hubbard, Moyer. "Kept Safe through Childbearing: Maternal Mortality, Justification by Faith, and the Social Setting of 1 Timothy 2:15." *JETS* 55 (2012): 743–62.

Hurd, J. C. "Pauline Chronology and Pauline Theology." In *Christian History and Interpretation: Studies Presented to John Knox*, edited by W. R. Farmer, C. F. D. Moule, and R. R. Niebuhr, 225–48. Cambridge: Cambridge University Press, 1967.

Hurley, James B. *Man and Woman in Biblical Perspective*. Grand Rapids: Zondervan, 1981.

Husbands, Mark, and Timothy Larsen, eds. *Women, Ministry and the Gospel: Exploring New Paradigms*. Downers Grove, IL: IVP Academic, 2007.

Huttar, David K. "AYΘENTEIN in the Aeschylus Scholium." *JETS* 44 (2001): 615–25.

Instone-Brewer, David. *Divorce and Remarriage in the Bible: The Social and Literary Context*. Grand Rapids: Eerdmans, 2002.

Jacobs, Mignon R. *Gender, Power, and Persuasion: The Genesis Narratives and Contemporary Portraits*. Grand Rapids: Baker Academic, 2007.

Jensen, Anne. "The Representation of Christ, Ecclesiastical Office, and Presiding at the Eucharist." *FZPhTh* 40 (1993): 282–97.

Jewett, Paul K. *Man as Male and Female: A Study in Sexual Relationships from a Theological Point of View*. Grand Rapids: Eerdmans, 1975.

Jewett, Robert. *Romans: A Commentary*. Edited by Eldon J. Epp. Hermeneia. Minneapolis: Fortress, 2007.

Johnson, S. Lewis, Jr. "Role Distinctions in the Church: Galatians 3:28." In *Recovering Biblical Manhood and Womanhood: A Response to Evangelical Feminism*, edited by John Piper and Wayne Grudem, 154–64. Wheaton: Crossway, 1991.

Jowers, Dennis W., and H. Wayne House, eds. *The New Evangelical Subordinationism? Perspectives on the Equality of God the Father and God the Son*. Eugene, OR: Pickwick, 2012.

Kahf, Mohja. "From Her Royal Body the Robe Was Removed: The Blessing of the Veil and the Trauma of Forced Unveilings in the Middle East." In *The Veil: Women Writers on Its History, Lore, and Politics*, edited by Jennifer Heath, 27–43. Berkeley: University of California Press, 2008.

Karras, Ruth Mazo. "Active/Passive, Acts/Passions: Greek and Roman Sexualities." *AHR* 105 (2000): 1250–65.

Keddie, Nikki R., and Beth Baron. Introduction to *Women in Middle Eastern History: Shifting Boundaries in Sex and Gender*, edited by Nikki R. Keddie and Beth Baron, 1–22. New Haven: Yale University Press, 1991.

Keener, Craig S. *The IVP Bible Background Commentary: New Testament*. Downers Grove, IL: InterVarsity, 1993.

———. "Learning in the Assemblies: 1 Corinthians 14:34–35." In *Discovering Biblical Equality: Complementarity without Hierarchy*, edited by Ronald W. Pierce and Rebecca Merrill Groothuis, 161–71. Downers Grove, IL: IVP Academic, 2005.

———. "'Let the Wife Have Authority over Her Husband' (1 Corinthians 11:10)." *JGRChJ* 2 (2001–5): 146–52.

———. "Man and Woman." In *Dictionary of Paul and His Letters*, edited by Gerald F. Hawthorne, Ralph P. Martin, and Daniel G. Reid, 583–92. Downers Grove, IL: InterVarsity, 1993.

———. "Marriage." In *Dictionary of New Testament Background*, edited by Craig A. Evans and Stanley E. Porter, 680–93. Downers Grove, IL: InterVarsity, 2000.

———. *Paul, Women & Wives: Marriage and Women's Ministry in the Letters of Paul*. Peabody, MA: Hendrickson, 1992.

———. *Romans*. NCCS 6. Eugene, OR: Cascade, 2009.

Khalili, Mohammed I. "A Comment on Heat-of-Passion Crimes, Honor Killings, and Islam." *Politics and the Life Sciences* 21, no. 2 (2002): 38–40.

Knapp, Robert C. *Invisible Romans: Prostitutes, Outlaws, Slaves, Gladiators, Ordinary Men and Women—The Romans That History Forgot*. London: Profile Books, 2011.

Knight, George W., III. "ΑΥΘΕΝΤΕΩ in Reference to Women in 1 Timothy 2:12." *NTS* 30 (1984): 143–57.

———. *The Pastoral Epistles: A Commentary on the Greek Text*. NIGTC. Grand Rapids: Eerdmans, 1992.

———. *The Role Relationship of Men and Women: New Testament Teaching*. Rev. ed. Grand Rapids: Baker, 1985.

Knoch, Otto. *1. und 2. Timotheusbrief, Titusbrief*. NEchtB 14. Würzburg: Echter, 1988.

Köstenberger, Andreas J. "A Complex Sentence: The Syntax of 1 Timothy 2:12." In *Women in the Church: An Analysis and Application of 1 Timothy 2:9–15*, 2nd ed., edited by Andreas J. Köstenberger and Thomas R. Schreiner, 53–84. Grand Rapids: Baker Academic, 2005.

Köstenberger, Andreas J., and Thomas R. Schreiner, eds. *Women in the Church: An Analysis and Application of 1 Timothy 2:9–15*. 2nd ed. Grand Rapids: Baker Academic, 2005.

Köstenberger, Andreas J., Thomas R. Schreiner, and H. Scott Baldwin, eds. *Women in the Church: A Fresh Analysis of 1 Timothy 2:9–15*. Grand Rapids: Baker Books, 1995.

Kraemer, Ross Shepard, and Mary Rose D'Angelo, eds. *Women and Christian Origins*. Oxford: Oxford University Press, 1999.

Kroeger, Catherine Clark. "Ancient Heresies and a Strange Greek Verb." *RefJ* 29 (1979): 12–15.

———. "1 Timothy 2:12—A Classicist's View." In *Women, Authority & and the Bible*, edited by Alvera Mickelsen, 225–44. Downers Grove, IL: InterVarsity, 1986.

Kroeger, Richard Clark, and Catherine Clark Kroeger. *I Suffer Not a Woman: Rethinking 1 Timothy 2:11–15 in Light of Ancient Evidence*. Grand Rapids: Baker, 1998.

Kümmel, Werner Georg. *Introduction to the New Testament*. Translated by Howard Clark Kee. Nashville: Abingdon, 1975.

Kuske, D. P. "An Exegetical Brief on 1 Timothy 2:12 (οὐδὲ αὐθεντεῖν ἀνδρός)." *WLQ* 88 (1991): 64–67.

Larson, Knute. *I & II Thessalonians, I & II Timothy, Titus, Philemon*. Nashville: Holman Reference, 2000.

Lattimore, Richmond. *Themes in Greek and Latin Epitaphs*. Urbana: University of Illinois Press, 1942.

Lee, John A. L. *A History of New Testament Lexicography*. SBG 8. New York: Peter Lang, 2003.

Lee-Barnewall, Michelle. "Turning κεφαλή on Its Head: The Rhetoric of Reversal in Ephesians 5:21–23." In *Christian Origins and Greco-Roman Culture: Social and Literary Context for the New Testament*, edited by Stanley E. Porter and Andrew Pitts, 599–614. ECHC 1. Leiden: Brill, 2013.

Lefkowitz, Mary R., and Maureen B. Fant. *Women's Life in Greece and Rome*. Baltimore: Johns Hopkins University Press, 1982.

Lehtipuu, Outi. "The Example of Thecla and the Example(s) of Paul: Disputing Women's Roles in Early Christianity." In *Women and Gender in Ancient Religions: Interdisciplinary Approaches*, edited by Stephen P. Ahearne-Kroll, Paul A. Holloway, and James A. Kelhoffer, 349–78. WUNT 263. Tübingen: Mohr Siebeck, 2010.

Levine, Amy-Jill, and Maria Mayo Robbins, eds. *A Feminist Companion to the Catholic Epistles and Hebrews*. FCNTECW 8. London: T&T Clark, 2004.

LiDonnici, Lynn R. "The Images of Artemis Ephesia and Greco-Roman Worship: A Reconsideration." *HTR* 85 (1992): 389–415.

Lincoln, Andrew T. *Ephesians*. WBC 42. Nashville: Nelson, 1990.

Llewellyn-Jones, Lloyd. *Aphrodite's Tortoise: The Veiled Woman of Ancient Greece*. Swansea: Classical Press of Wales, 2003.

Loader, William. *The New Testament on Sexuality*. Grand Rapids: Eerdmans, 2012.

Longenecker, Richard N. *Galatians*. WBC 41. Nashville: Nelson, 1990.

MacDonald, Dennis R. *The Legend and the Apostle: The Battle for Paul in Story and Canon*. Philadelphia: Westminster, 1983.

MacDonald, Margaret Y. *Early Christian Women and Pagan Opinion: The Power of the Hysterical Woman*. Cambridge: Cambridge University Press, 1996.

———. "Reading Real Women through the Undisputed Letters of Paul." In *Women & Christian Origins*, edited by Ross Shepard Kraemer and Mary Rose D'Angelo, 199–220. Oxford: Oxford University Press, 1999.

MacMullen, Ramsay. "Women in Public in the Roman Empire." *Hist* 29 (1980): 208–18.

Malherbe, Abraham J. *Social Aspects of Early Christianity*. 2nd ed. Philadelphia: Fortress, 1983.

Mark, Elizabeth Wyner, ed. *The Covenant of Circumcision: New Perspectives on an Ancient Rite*. Hanover, NH: Brandeis University Press, 2003.

Marshall, I. Howard. *The Pastoral Epistles*. ICC. Edinburgh: T&T Clark, 1999.

Martin, Troy W. "Paul's Argument from Nature for the Veil in 1 Corinthians 11:13–15: A Testicle instead of a Head Covering." *JBL* 123 (2004): 75–84.

Massey, Preston T. "Long Hair as a Glory and as a Covering: Removing an Ambiguity from 1 Corinthians 11:15." *NovT* 53 (2011): 52–72.

———. "The Meaning of καταλύπτω and κατὰ κεφαλῆς ἔχων in 1 Corinthians 11:2–16." *NTS* 53 (2007): 502–23.

Meeks, Wayne A. *The First Urban Christians: The Social World of the Apostle Paul*. New Haven: Yale University Press, 1983.

Mernissi, Fatima. *The Veil and the Male Elite: A Feminist Interpretation of Women's Rights in Islam*. Translated by Mary Jo Lakeland. New York: Basic Books, 1987.

Mickelsen, Berkeley, and Alvera Mickelsen. "Does Male Dominance Tarnish Our Translations?" *ChrTo* 5 (October 1979): 23–29.

———. "The 'Head' of the Epistles." *ChrTo* 20 (February 1981): 20–23.

————. "What Does *Kephalē* Mean in the New Testament?" In *Women, Authority & the Bible*, edited by Alvera Mickelsen, 97–110. Downers Grove, IL: InterVarsity, 1986.

Middleton, J. Richard. *A New Heaven and a New Earth: Reclaiming Biblical Eschatology*. Grand Rapids: Baker Academic, 2014.

Miller, James D. *The Pastoral Letters as Composite Documents*. SNTSMS 93. Cambridge: Cambridge University Press, 1997.

————. "Translating Paul's Words about Women." *SCJ* 12 (2009): 61–71.

Mitchell, Margaret M. "Corrective Composition, Corrective Exegesis: The Teaching on Prayer in 1 Timothy 2:1–15." In *1 Timothy Reconsidered*, edited by Karl Paul Donfried, 41–62. MSBBES 18. Leuven: Peeters, 2008.

Moffatt, James. *Epistle to the Romans*. Grand Rapids: Eerdmans, 1996.

————. *The First Epistle of Paul to the Corinthians*. MNTC. New York: Harper, 1938.

Motyer, Steve. "Expounding 1 Timothy 2:8–15." *VE* 24 (1994): 91–102.

Mounce, William D. *Pastoral Epistles*. WBC 46. Nashville: Nelson, 2000.

Moyise, Steve. *Paul and Scripture: Studying the New Testament Use of the Old Testament*. Grand Rapids: Baker Academic, 2010.

Murphy-O'Connor, Jerome. "The Divorced Woman in 1 Corinthians 7:10–11." *JBL* 100 (1981): 601–6.

————. "1 Corinthians 11:2–16 Once Again." *CBQ* 50 (1988): 265–74.

————. "Sex and Logic in I Corinthians 11:2–16." *CBQ* 42 (1980): 482–500.

————. *St. Paul's Corinth: Texts and Archaeology*. GNS 6. Wilmington, DE: Michael Glazier, 1983.

Neal, Diana. "Out of the Uterus of the Father: A Study in Patriarchy and the Symbolism of Christian Theology." *FT* 13 (1996): 8–30.

Nelson, James B. *Body Theology*. Louisville: Westminster John Knox, 1992.

Neyrey, Jerome H., and Eric C. Stewart, eds. *The Social World of the New Testament: Insights and Models*. Peabody, MA: Hendrickson, 2008.

O'Brien, Peter T. *Colossians, Philemon*. WBC 44. Waco: Word, 1982.

Økland, Jorunn. *Women in Their Place: Paul and the Corinthian Discourse of Gender and Sanctuary Space*. JSNTSup 269. London: T&T Clark, 2004.

Olson, Kelly. *Dress and the Roman Woman: Self-Presentation and Society*. New York: Routledge, 2008.

Orr, David G. "Roman Domestic Religion: The Evidence of the Household Shrines." *ANRW* 16.2:1557–91. Part 2, *Principat*, 16.2. Edited by H. Temporini and W. Haase. New York: de Gruyter, 1978.

Ortlund, Raymond C., Jr. "Male-Female Equality and Male Headship: Genesis 1–3." In *Recovering Biblical Manhood and Womanhood: A Response to Evangelical Feminism*, edited by John Piper and Wayne Grudem, 95–112. Wheaton: Crossway, 1991.

Osborne, Grant R. *Romans*. IVPNTC 6. Downers Grove, IL: InterVarsity, 2004.

Osburn, Carroll D. "ΑΥΘΕΝΤΕΩ (1 Tim. 2:12)." *ResQ* 25 (1982): 1–12.

Osiek, Carolyn, and Margaret Y. MacDonald. "Philippians." In *Searching the Scriptures*, vol. 2, *A Feminist Commentary*, edited by Elisabeth Schüssler Fiorenza, Ann Brock, and Shelly Matthews, 237–49. New York: Crossroad, 1994.

———. *A Woman's Place: House Churches in Earliest Christianity*. Minneapolis: Fortress, 2006.

Padgett, Alan G. *As Christ Submits to the Church: A Biblical Understanding of Leadership and Mutual Submission*. Grand Rapids: Baker Academic, 2011.

———. "Paul on Women in the Church: The Contradictions of Coiffure in 1 Corinthians 11:2–16." *JSNT* 20 (1984): 69–86.

———. "The Significance of ἀντί in 1 Corinthians 11:15." *TynBul* 45 (1994): 181–87.

———. "Wealthy Women at Ephesus: 1 Timothy 2:8–15 in Social Context." *Int* 41 (1987): 19–31.

Panning, Armin J. "*Authentein*—A Word Study." *WLQ* 78 (1981): 185–91.

Parker, Holt. "Loyal Slaves and Loyal Wives: The Crisis of the Outsider-Within and Roman *Exemplum* Literature." In *Women and Slaves in Greco-Roman Culture: Differential Equations*, edited by Sandra R. Joshel and Sheila Murnaghan, 152–73. New York: Routledge, 1998.

Patterson, Dorothy. "The High Calling of Wife and Mother in Biblical Perspective." In *Recovering Biblical Manhood and Womanhood: A Response to Evangelical Feminism*, edited by John Piper and Wayne Grudem, 364–77. Wheaton: Crossway, 1991.

Payne, Philip B. "1 Timothy 2:12 and the Use of οὐδέ to Combine Two Elements to Express a Single Idea." *NTS* 54 (2008): 235–53.

———. "Fuldensis, Sigla for Variants in Vaticanus, and 1 Cor. 14:34–35." *NTS* 41 (1995): 240–62.

———. *Man and Woman, One in Christ: An Exegetical and Theological Study of Paul's Letters*. Grand Rapids: Zondervan, 2009.

———. "What Does *Kephalē* Mean in the New Testament? Response." In *Women, Authority & the Bible*, edited by Alvera Mickelsen, 118–32. Downers Grove, IL: InterVarsity, 1986.

Perriman, Andrew C. "What Eve Did, What Women Shouldn't Do: The Meaning of ΑΥΘΕΝΤΕΩ." *TynBul* 44 (1993): 129–42.

Petersen, Norman R. *Rediscovering Paul: Philemon and the Sociology of Paul's Narrative World*. Philadelphia: Fortress, 1985.

Pierce, Ronald W. "Evangelicals and Gender Roles in the 1990s: First Timothy 2:8–15; A Test Case." *JETS* 36 (1993): 343–55.

Pierce, Ronald W., and Rebecca Merrill Groothuis, eds. *Discovering Biblical Equality: Complementarity without Hierarchy*. Downers Grove, IL: InterVarsity, 2004.

Piper, John. "A Vision of Biblical Complementarity: Manhood and Womanhood Defined according to the Bible." In *Recovering Biblical Manhood and Womanhood: A Response to Evangelical Feminism*, edited by John Piper and Wayne Grudem, 31–59. Wheaton: Crossway, 1991.

Polaski, Sandra Hack. *A Feminist Introduction to Paul*. St. Louis: Chalice, 2005.

Pomeroy, Sarah B. *Goddesses, Whores, Wives, and Slaves: Women in Classical Antiquity*. New York: Schocken, 1975.

———. "Women in Roman Egypt: A Preliminary Study Based on Papyri." In *Reflections of Women in Antiquity*, edited by Helene P. Foley, 303–22. New York: Gordon and Breach Science Publishers, 1981.

Porter, Stanley E. *Idioms of the Greek New Testament*. 2nd ed. BLG 2. Sheffield: Sheffield Academic, 1999.

———. "What Does It Mean to Be 'Saved by Childbirth' (1 Tim. 2:15)?" *JSNT* 49 (1993): 87–102.

Poythress, Vern S., and Wayne A. Grudem. *The Gender-Neutral Bible Controversy: Muting the Masculinity of God's Words*. Nashville: Broadman & Holman, 2000.

Redekop, Gloria N. "Let the Women Learn: 1 Timothy 2.8–15 Reconsidered." *SR* 19 (1990): 235–45.

Reuther, Rosemary Radford. *To Change the World: Christology and Cultural Criticism*. New York: Crossroad, 1981.

Rogers, Guy MacLean. *The Sacred Identity of Ephesos: Foundation Myths of a Roman City*. New York: Routledge, 1991.

Rubin, Nissan. "*Brit Milah*: A Study of Change in Custom." In *The Covenant of Circumcision: New Perspectives on an Ancient Jewish Rite*, edited by Elizabeth Wyner Mark, 87–97. Hanover, NH: Brandeis University Press, 2003.

Save the Mothers. "How Are Mothers Dying?" http://www.savethemothers.org/learn-the-issues/how-are-mothers-dying.

Scholer, David M. "'And I Was a Man': The Power and Problem of Perpetua." *DSar* 15 (1989): 10–14.

Schreiner, Thomas R. "Head Coverings, Prophecies, and the Trinity: 1 Corinthians 11:2–16." In *Recovering Biblical Manhood and Womanhood: A Response to Evangelical Feminism*, edited by John Piper and Wayne Grudem, 124–39. Wheaton: Crossway, 1991.

———. "An Interpretation of 1 Timothy 2:9–15: A Dialogue with Scholarship." In *Women in the Church: An Analysis and Application of 1 Timothy 2:9–15*, 2nd ed., edited by Andreas J. Köstenberger and Thomas R. Schreiner, 85–120, 207–29. Grand Rapids: Baker Academic, 2005.

———. "An Interpretation of 1 Timothy 2:9–15: A Dialogue with Scholarship." In *Women in the Church: A Fresh Analysis of 1 Timothy 2:9–15*, edited by Andreas J. Köstenberger, Thomas R. Schreiner, and H. Scott Baldwin, 105–54. Grand Rapids: Baker, 1995.

———. *Paul, Apostle of God's Glory in Christ: A Pauline Theology*. Downers Grove, IL: InterVarsity, 2001.

———. *Romans*. BECNT. Grand Rapids: Baker, 1998.

———. "William J. Webb's *Slaves, Women & Homosexuals*: A Review Article." *SBJT* 6 (2002): 46–64.

Schüssler Fiorenza, Elisabeth. *In Memory of Her: A Feminist Theological Reconstruction of Christian Origins*. London: SCM, 1983.

———. *Jesus: Miriam's Child, Sophia's Prophet; Critical Issues in Feminist Christology*. New York: Continuum, 1994.

———. "Missionaries, Apostles, Coworkers: Romans 16 and the Reconstruction of Women's Early History." *WW* 6 (1986): 420–33.

———. *Rhetoric and Ethic: The Politics of Biblical Studies*. Minneapolis: Fortress, 1999.

Scroggs, Robin. "Paul and the Eschatological Woman." *JAAR* 40 (1972): 283–303.

Seesengood, Robert. *Competing Identities: The Athlete and the Gladiator in Early Christian Literature*. LNTS 346. London: T&T Clark, 2006.

Shaw, Brent. "The Passion of Perpetua." *PastPres* 139 (1993): 3–45.

Stark, Rodney. "Physiology and Faith: Addressing the 'Universal' Gender Difference in Religious Commitment." *JSSR* 41 (2002): 495–507.

———. *The Rise of Christianity: How the Obscure, Marginal Jesus Movement Became the Dominant Religious Force in the Western World in a Few Centuries*. San Francisco: HarperSanFrancisco, 1997.

Strauss, Mark. *Distorting Scripture? The Challenge of Bible Translation and Gender Accuracy*. Eugene, OR: Wipf & Stock, 2010.

Strom, Mark. *Reframing Paul: Conversations in Grace & Community*. Downers Grove, IL: InterVarsity, 2000.

Theissen, Gerd. *The Social Setting of Pauline Christianity: Essays on Corinth*. Edited and translated by John H. Schütz. Philadelphia: Fortress, 1982.

Thiselton, Anthony. *The First Epistle to the Corinthians: A Commentary on the Greek Text*. NIGTC. Grand Rapids: Eerdmans, 2000.

Tidball, Derek. *The Social Context of the New Testament: A Sociological Analysis*. Grand Rapids: Zondervan, 1984.

Towner, Philip H. *The Letters to Timothy and Titus*. NICNT. Grand Rapids: Eerdmans, 2006.

Van Bremen, Riet. "Women and Wealth." In *Images of Women in Antiquity*, edited by Averil Cameron and Amélie Kuhrt, 223–42. London: Routledge, 1993.

Vander Stichele, Caroline, and Todd C. Penner. "Paul and the Rhetoric of Gender." In *Her Master's Tools? Feminist and Postcolonial Engagements of Historical-Critical Discourse*, edited by Caroline Vander Stichele and Todd Penner, 287–310. GPBS 9. Atlanta: Society of Biblical Literature, 2005.

Van Leeuwen, Mary Stewart. *My Brother's Keeper: What the Social Sciences Do (and Don't) Tell Us about Masculinity*. Downers Grove, IL: InterVarsity, 2002.

Virgili, Fabrice. *Shorn Women: Gender and Punishment in Liberation France*. Translated by John Flower. London: Berg, 2002.

Wagener, Ulrike. *Die Ordnung des "Hauses Gottes": Der Ort von Frauen in der Ekklesiologie und Ethik der Pastoralbriefe*. WUNT 65. Tübingen: Mohr Siebeck, 1994.

Wall, Robert W. "1 Timothy 2:9–15 Reconsidered (Again)." *BBR* 14 (2004): 81–103.

Walton, John H., Victor H. Matthews, and Mark W. Chavalas. *The IVP Bible Background Commentary: Old Testament*. Downers Grove, IL: InterVarsity, 2000.

Ward, Roy Bowen. "Musonius and Paul on Marriage." *NTS* 36 (1990): 281–89.

Waters, Kenneth L. "Saved through Childbearing: Virtues as Children in 1 Timothy 2:11–15." *JBL* 123 (2004): 703–35.

Webb, Robert. *Slaves, Women & Homosexuals: Exploring the Hermeneutics of Cultural Analysis*. Downers Grove, IL: InterVarsity, 2001.

Westfall, Cynthia Long. "A Discourse Analysis of Romans 7:7–25: The Pauline Autobiography?" In *The Linguist as Pedagogue: Trends in the Teaching and Linguistic Analysis of the Greek New Testament*, edited by Stanley E. Porter and Matthew Brook O'Donnell, 146–58. NTM 11. Sheffield: Sheffield Phoenix, 2009.

———. "The Meaning of αὐθεντέω in 1 Timothy 2:12." *JGRChJ* 10 (2014): 138–73.

———. "A Moral Dilemma? The Epistolary Body of 2 Timothy." In *Paul and the Ancient Letter Form*, edited by Stanley E. Porter and Sean A. Adams, 213–52. PSt 6. Leiden: Brill, 2010.

———. "On Developing a Consistent Hermeneutical Approach to the Application of General Scriptures." *PriscPap* 24 (2010): 9–13.

———. "Paul's Experience and a Pauline Theology of the Spirit." In *Defining Issues in Pentecostalism: Classical and Emergent*, edited by Steven M. Studebaker, 123–43. MTSS 1. Hamilton, ON: McMaster Divinity Press, 2008.

———. "'This Is a Great Metaphor!': Reciprocity in the Ephesians Household Code." In *Christian Origins and Greco-Roman Culture: Social and Literary Context for the New Testament*, edited by Stanley E. Porter and Andrew Pitts, 561–98. ECHC 1. Leiden: Brill, 2013.

White, John L. *The Form and Function of the Body of the Greek Letter: A Study of the Letter-Body in the Non-literary Papyri and in Paul the Apostle*. SBLDS 2. Missoula, MT: Scholars Press, 1972.

White, L. Michael. "Paul and *Pater Familias*." In *Paul in the Greco-Roman World: A Handbook*, edited by J. Paul Sampley, 470–72. Harrisburg, PA: Trinity Press International, 2003.

White, L. Michael, and O. Larry Yarbrough, eds. *The Social World of the First Christians: Essays in Honor of Wayne A. Meeks.* Minneapolis: Fortress, 1995.

Wilcox, Amanda. "Exemplary Grief: Gender and Virtue in Seneca's Consolations to Women." *Helios* 33 (2006): 73–100.

Wiley, Tatha. *Paul and the Gentile Women: Reframing Galatians.* New York: Continuum, 2005.

Wilshire, Leland Edward. "1 Timothy 2:12 Revisited: A Reply to Paul W. Barnett and Timothy J. Harris." *EvQ* 65 (1993): 43–55.

———. "The TLG Computer and Further Reference to ΑΥΘΕΝΤΕΩ in 1 Timothy 2:12." *NTS* 34 (1988): 120–34.

Wilson, Douglas. *Fidelity: What It Means to Be a One-Woman Man.* Moscow, ID: Canon Press, 1999.

Wimbush, Vincent L. "The Ascetic Impulse in Ancient Christianity." *ThTo* 50 (1993): 417–28.

———. *Paul the Worldly Ascetic: Response to the World and Self-Understanding according to 1 Corinthians 7.* Macon, GA: Mercer University Press, 1987.

Winter, Bruce W. *Roman Wives, Roman Widows: The Appearance of New Women and the Pauline Communities.* Grand Rapids: Eerdmans, 2003.

Wire, Antoinette Clark. *The Corinthian Women Prophets: A Reconstruction through Paul's Rhetoric.* Minneapolis: Fortress, 1990.

Witherington, Ben, III. *Women and the Genesis of Christianity.* Cambridge: Cambridge University Press, 1990.

———. *Women in the Earliest Churches.* SNTSMS 59. Cambridge: Cambridge University Press, 1988.

Wolters, Albert M. "ΑΥΘΕΝΤΗΣ and Its Cognates in Biblical Greek." *JETS* 52 (2009): 719–29.

———. "An Early Parallel of αὐθεντεῖν in 1 Timothy 2:12." *JETS* 54 (2011): 673–84.

———. "A Semantic Study of αὐθέντης and Its Derivatives." *JGRChJ* 1 (2000): 145–75.

Woodhead, Linda. "God, Gender and Identity." In *Gospel and Gender: A Trinitarian Engagement with Being Male and Female in Christ,* edited by Douglas A. Campbell, 84–104. STS 7. London: T&T Clark, 2003.

Yarbrough, O. Larry. *Not Like the Gentiles: Marriage Rules in the Letters of Paul.* SBLDS 80. Atlanta: Scholars Press, 1985.

———. "Parents and Children in the Letters of Paul." In *The Social World of the First Christians: Essays in Honor of Wayne A. Meeks,* edited by L. Michael White and O. Larry Yarbrough, 126–41. Minneapolis: Fortress, 1991.

Zamfir, Korinna, and Jozef Verheyden. "Text-Critical and Intertextual Remarks on 1 Timothy 2:8–10." *NovT* 50 (2008): 376–406.

Zehr, Paul M. *1 & 2 Timothy, Titus.* BCBC. Scottdale, PA: Herald Press, 2010.

Index of Greek Terms

Index of Modern Authors

Index of Ancient Sources

Index of Subjects